The PSALMS
NEW INTERNATIONAL VERSION
St. Joseph CATHOLIC Edition

The PSALMS

NEW INTERNATIONAL VERSION

St. Joseph CATHOLIC Edition

WITH HELPFUL APPENDIX
An Index of Sunday Responsorial Psalms
and a Table of the Four-Week Psalter
for Morning and Evening Prayer

CATHOLIC BOOK PUBLISHING CO.
New Jersey

IMPRIMATUR:

✠ Most Reverend Joseph A. Fiorenza

President, National Conference of Catholic Bishops

August 14, 2000

RESCRIPT

In accord with canon 825, §1 of the Code of Canon Law, the National Conference of Catholic Bishops hereby approves for publication *The Psalms, New International Version,* St. Joseph Edition, a translation of the Psalms published by the Catholic Book Publishing Company.

(T-660)

CONTENTS

ABBREVIATIONS OF BOOKS OF THE BIBLE

Ac—Acts of the Apostles
Am—Amos
Bar—Baruch
1 Ch—1 Chronicles
2 Ch—2 Chronicles
1 Co—1 Corinthians
2 Co—2 Corinthians
Col—Colossians
Da—Daniel
Dt—Deuteronomy
Ecc—Ecclesiastes
Eph—Ephesians
Est—Esther
Ex—Exodus
Eze—Ezekiel
Ezr—Ezra
Gal—Galatians
Ge—Genesis
Hab—Habakkuk
Heb—Hebrews
Hag—Haggai
Hos—Hosea
Isa—Isaiah
Jas—James
Job—Job

Jdg—Judges
Jer—Jeremiah
Joel—Joel
Jn—John
1 Jn—1 John
2 Jn—2 John
3 Jn—3 John
Jnh—Jonah
Jos—Joshua
Jud—Judith
Jude—Jude
1 Ki—1 Kings
2 Ki—2 Kings
La—Lamentations
Lev—Leviticus
Lk—Luke
1 Mac—1 Maccabees
2 Mac—2 Maccabees
Mal—Malachi
Mic—Micah
Mk—Mark
Mt—Matthew
Na—Nahum
Neh—Nehemiah
Nu—Numbers

Ob—Obadiah
1 Pe—1 Peter
2 Pe—2 Peter
Phm—Philemon
Php—Philippians
Pr—Proverbs
Ps—Psalms
Rev—Revelation
Ro—Romans
Ru—Ruth
1 Sa—1 Samuel
2 Sa—2 Samuel
Sir—Sirach
SS—Song of Songs
1 Th—1 Thessalonians
2 Th—2 Thessalonians
1 Ti—1 Timothy
2 Ti—2 Timothy
Tit—Titus
Tob—Tobit
Wis—Wisdom
Zec—Zechariah
Zep—Zephaniah

NOTE: For greater clarity and convenience, the footnotes and cross-references are printed at the bottom of each page and cross-indexed in the text itself. An *asterisk* (*) in the text indicates that there is a *footnote* to the text in question. Each footnote is in turn clearly marked with the number of the chapter and verse to which it pertains. Similarly, a lightface *superior letter* (ᵃ) in the text indicates that there is a *cross-reference* to a particular verse. The reference itself is also clearly marked with the same letter. A **boldface** *superior letter* (•) in the text indicates that there is a *textual note* to a particular passage. The note itself is also clearly marked with the same letter. Hence, the reader is always aware of a footnote, cross-reference or textual note simply by *reading the text.*

[ ] Indicates a gloss
/ = Divides verse
a,b,c,d,e,f   Identify the lines of any verse in successive order.

Par = Parallel passages

PREFACE

In the life of Christians, there can never be too many translations of the Psalter. For the Psalms are the prayer of God's assembly, the public prayer par excellence of the People of God. No prayer of Israel is comparable to the Psalter because of its universal character. The idea of the unity of the chosen people's prayer guided its elaboration as well as its adoption by the Church.

The Psalms may be looked upon as the prayer-book of the Holy Spirit. Over the long centuries of Israel's existence, the Spirit of God inspired the psalmists (typified by King David) to compose magnificent prayers and hymns for every religious desire and need, mood and feeling. Thus, the Psalms have great power to raise minds to God, to inspire devotion, to evoke gratitude in favorable times, and to bring consolation and strength in times of trial.

Furthermore, in giving us the Psalter, which sums up the major aspects of our relationship to our Creator and Redeemer, God puts into our mouths the words he wishes to hear, and indicates to us the dimensions of prayer:

"The Psalms call to mind the truths revealed by God to the chosen people, which were at one time frightening and at another filled with wonderful tenderness; they keep repeating and fostering the hope of the promised Redeemer, which in ancient times was kept alive with song, either around the hearth or in the stately temple; they show forth in splendid light the prophesied glory of Jesus Christ: first, his supreme and eternal power, then his lowly coming to this earthly exile, his kingly dignity and priestly power, and finally his beneficent labors, and the shedding of his blood for our redemption.

"In a similar way they express the joy, the bitterness, the hope and fear of our hearts and our desire of loving God and hoping in him alone, and our mystic ascent to divine tabernacles" (Pope Pius XII, *Mediator Dei*, no. 148).

In short, the Psalms constitute an inexhaustible treasury of prayers for every occasion and mood in a format that is true to the whole tradition of the history of salvation.

Jesus and the Psalms

Jesus often prayed the Psalms. At the age of twelve, as a pilgrim on the way to the temple in Jerusalem, he sang the Psalms meant for this journey: "I rejoiced with those who said to me, 'Let us go to the house of the Lord.' Our feet are standing in your gates, O Jerusalem" (Ps 122:1f).

The Gospels tell us that Jesus frequented the synagogue of Nazareth on the sabbath and that consequently he took part in the reading of the Scriptures and the recitation of the Psalms.

Again, Jesus took part in the singing of the great Alleluia Psalm with its refrain, "His love endures forever" (Ps 136).

If we read carefully the account of the Passion of Jesus we glimpse citations from many Psalms; finally, his last words on the Cross were supplied by the Psalms: "My God, my God, why have you forsaken me?" (Ps 22:1) and "Into your hands I commit my spirit" (Ps 31:5).

Under the guidance of the Holy Spirit, the first Christian community made the Psalms its own, applying to the Lord and to itself what was said in the Psalms about the People of God, Jerusalem, the king, the temple, the promised land, the kingdom, and the covenant.

Jewish prayers become the prayers of the Church; the dead and risen Lord is the new

Passover; the Eucharist is the everlasting covenant.

Thus, Christians who pray the Psalms should be aware of their total meaning, especially their Messianic meaning, which was the reason for the Church's introduction of the Psalter into her prayer. This Messianic meaning was fully revealed in the New Testament and indeed was publicly acknowledged by Christ the Lord in person when he said to his apostles: "Everything must be fulfilled that is written about me in the Law of Moses, the Prophets and the Psalms" (Lk 24:44). The best known example of this Messianic meaning is the dialogue in Matthew's Gospel on the Messiah as Son of David and David's Lord (22:44ff): there Psalm 110 is interpreted as Messianic.

Following this line of thought, the Fathers of the Church saw the whole Psalter as a prophecy of Christ and the Church and explained it in this sense; for the same reason the Psalms have been chosen for use in the sacred Liturgy.

Benefits of Different Translations

It is a well known fact that different translations of the Psalms (like different translations of any subject) bring out nuances of meaning peculiar to each one. The Bible and especially the Psalms are so chock full of meaning that we can rightly say no single edition will do full justice to them.

Hence, it has become customary for Christians to make use of many translations of the sacred books in order to strive to get to know the Bible and pray with its text.

Therefore, we have thought it worthwhile to make available a Catholic Edition of the Psalms of one of the very highly regarded and indeed most popular Bible texts in the world: the *New Interna-*

tional Version (commonly known as the NIV). The following are extracts from the Preface to the NIV that outline some of the main points that deal with the Psalter.

Nature and Qualities of the Translation

"The *New International Version* is a completely new translation of the Holy Bible made by over a hundred scholars working directly from the best available Hebrew, Aramaic, and Greek texts. . . .

"From the beginning of the project, the Committee on Bible Translation held to certain goals for the *New International Version:* that it would be an accurate translation and one that would have clarity and literary quality and so prove suitable for public and private reading, teaching, preaching, memorizing, and liturgical use. The Committee also sought to preserve some measure of continuity with the long tradition of translating the Scriptures into English.

"In working toward these goals, the translators were united in their commitment to the authority and infallibility of the Bible as God's Word in written form. They believe that it contains the divine answer to the deepest needs of humanity, that it sheds unique light on our path in a dark world, and that it sets forth the way to our eternal well-being.

"The first concern of the translators has been the accuracy of the translation and its fidelity to the thought of the biblical writers. They have weighed the significance of the lexical and grammatical details of the Hebrew, Aramaic, and Greek texts. At the same time, they have striven for more than a word-for-word translation. Because thought patterns and syntax differ from language to language, faithful communication of the meaning of the writers of the Bible demands frequent modifications in sentence structure and constant regard for the contextual meanings of words. . . .

"Concern for clear and natural English—that the *New International Version* should be idiomatic but not idiosyncratic, contemporary but not dated—motivated the translators and consultants. At the same time, they tried to reflect the differing styles of the biblical writers. . . .

The Text Used for the Translation

"For the Old Testament the standard Hebrew text, the Masoretic Text as published in the latest editions of the *Biblia Hebraica,* was used throughout. The Dead Sea Scrolls contain material bearing on an earlier stage of the Hebrew text. They were consulted, as were the Samaritan Pentateuch and the ancient scribal traditions relating to textual changes. Sometimes a variant Hebrew reading in the margin of the Masoretic Text was followed instead of the text itself. Such instances, being variants within the Masoretic tradition, are not specified by the [textual notes]. In rare cases, words in the consonantal text were divided differently from the way they appear in the Masoretic Text. [Textual notes] indicate this.

"The translators also consulted the more important early versions—the Septuagint; Aquila, Symmachus, and Theodotion; the Vulgate; the Syriac Peshitta; the targums; and for the Psalms the *Juxta Hebraica* of Jerome. Readings from these versions were occasionally followed where the Masoretic Text seemed doubtful and where accepted principles of textual criticism showed that one or more of these textual witnesses appeared to provide the correct reading. Such instances are [textually noted]. Sometimes vowel letters and vowel signs did not, in the judgment of the translators, represent the correct vowels for the original consonantal text. Accordingly, some words were read with a different set of vowels. These instances are usually indicated by [textual notes]. . . .

"As in other ancient documents, the precise meaning of the biblical texts is sometimes uncertain. This is more often the case with the Hebrew and Aramaic texts than with the Greek text. Although archaeological and linguistic discoveries in this century aid in understanding difficult passages, some uncertainties remain. The more significant of these have been called to the reader's attention in the [textual notes].

The Divine Name

"In regard to the divine name YHWH, commonly referred to as the Tetragrammaton, the translators adopted the device used in most English editions of rendering that name as 'LORD' in capital letters to distinguish it from *Adonai,* another Hebrew word rendered 'Lord,' for which small letters are used. Wherever the two names stand together in the Old Testament as a compound name of God, they are rendered 'Sovereign LORD.'

"Because for most readers today the phrases 'the LORD of hosts' and 'God of hosts' have little meaning, this version renders them 'the LORD Almighty' and 'God Almighty.' These renderings convey the sense of the Hebrew, namely, 'he who is sovereign over all the "hosts" (powers) in heaven and on earth, especially over the "hosts" (armies) of Israel.' For readers unacquainted with Hebrew this does not make clear the distinction between *Sabaoth* ('hosts' or 'Almighty') and *Shaddai* (which can also be translated 'Almighty'), but the latter occurs infrequently and is always [textually noted]. When Adonai and YHWH Sabaoth occur together, they are rendered 'the Lord, the LORD Almighty.'. . .

Textual Notes

"To achieve clarity the translators sometimes supplied words not in the original texts but required by the context. If there was uncertainty about such material it is enclosed in brackets. Also for the sake of clarity or style, nouns, including some proper nouns, are sometimes substituted for pronouns and vice versa. And though the Hebrew writers often shifted back and forth between first, second, and third personal pronouns without change of antecedent, this translation often makes them uniform, in accordance with English style and without the use of [textual notes].

"Poetical passages are printed as poetry, that is, with indentation of lines and with separate stanzas. These are generally designed to reflect the structure of Hebrew poetry. This poetry is normally characterized by parallelism in balanced lines. Most of the poetry in the Bible is in the Old Testament, and scholars differ regarding the scansion of Hebrew lines. The translators determined the stanza divisions for the most part by analysis of the subject matter. The stanzas therefore serve as poetic paragraphs. . . .

"The [textual notes] in this version are of several kinds, most of which need no explanation. Those giving alternative translations begin with 'Or' and generally introduce the alternative with the last word preceding it in the text, except when it is a single-word alternative; in poetry quoted in a [textual note] a slant mark indicates a line division. [Textual notes] introduced by 'Or' do not have uniform significance. In some cases, two possible translations were considered to have about equal validity. In other cases, though the translators were convinced that the translation of the text was correct, they judged that another translation was

possible and of sufficient importance to be represented in a [textual note]."

A St. Joseph Edition

The Psalms of the *New International Version* appear here in the renowned and exclusive format of
our St. Joseph Editions of Bibles and Missals. The
St. Joseph Edition is an editorial system developed
over a span of fifty years. It consists in a series of
features intended to ensure that a text (particularly
a biblical or liturgical text) is user friendly, leading
to greater readability and easier understanding.

The textual features or format in the present
case are a large readable typeface, additional
headings or titles (not the superscriptions), and a
full measure extension for long lines of poetry that
clearly indicates when a line has a runover. It also
includes a general introduction to the Psalter,
Psalm introductions, copious cross-references, and
pastoral notes (in addition to the NIV textual
notes). For greater clarity and convenience, the
footnotes and cross-references are printed at the
bottom of each page and cross-indexed in the text
itself.

An asterisk (*) in the text indicates that there is a
footnote to the text in question. Each footnote is in
turn clearly marked with the number of the Psalm
and the verse to which it pertains. Similarly, a
lightface superior letter (*a*) in the text indicates that
there is a cross-reference to a particular verse. The
reference itself is also clearly marked with the
same letter. A **boldface** superior letter (*a*) in the
text indicates that there is an NIV textual note to a
particular text. The textual note is also clearly
marked with the same letter. Hence, the reader is
always aware of a footnote, cross-reference, or textual note simply by reading the text.

Variations in Numbering

The Psalter contains 150 Psalms in the Hebrew and the Latin Vulgate. Their numbering, however, is slightly different since the Vulgate joins Ps 9 and 10 of the Hebrew into a single psalm, and again 114 and 115 of the Hebrew into a single psalm, while dividing 116 and 147 of the Hebrew into two psalms. The numbering is as follows:

Hebrew		Vulgate
1-8	=	1-8
9	=	9:1-21
10	=	9:22-39
11-113	=	10-112
114	=	113:1-8
115	=	113:9-26
116:1-9	=	114
116:10-19	=	115
117-146	=	116-145
147:1-11	=	146
147:12-20	=	147
148-150	=	148-150

Most Catholic translations after 1943 (in accord with the recommendation of Pope Pius XII in his ground-breaking encyclical *Divino Afflante Spiritu* to translate from the original languages—Hebrew, Aramaic, and Greek—instead of the Latin Vulgate) make use of the Hebrew numbering of the Psalms. Those completed before 1943 usually have the Vulgate numbering. This fact is important especially when Catholics desire to locate the Psalms used in the Liturgy.

Liturgical English texts sometimes follow the Latin Vulgate since they are a translation from the Latin liturgical books. Hence, to find the text of the Responsorial Psalm for any Sunday Mass, one must be guided by the above chart to get the number correct.

However, there is also a second difference in numbering—the enumeration of the verses. All but 35 of the Psalms begin with "superscriptions" (sometimes called "titles"). These contain the name of the supposed author of the psalm, the circumstances of its composition, a note about its liturgical use, and obscure phrases about its melody or its musical accompaniment. Catholic Bibles have traditionally assigned a verse number to these superscriptions. In the present text, these superscriptions are not assigned a number.

This means that, in most cases, the numbers that give the references for psalm verses used in the Liturgy are at least one digit higher than the corresponding verses in the *New International Version*. For the convenience of our readers, one part of the Appendix lists the correct NIV verse numbers for the Responsorial Psalm for every Sunday celebration.

We trust this new edition of the Psalms will—in the words of the translators of the *New International Version*—"lead many into a better understanding of the Holy Scriptures and a fuller knowledge of Jesus Christ the incarnate Word, of whom the Scriptures so faithfully testify."

INTRODUCTION

A Liturgical Anthology

Many prayers and liturgical chants are scattered throughout the Bible, but the most substantial part of Israel's praise and petition is to be found in the one hundred and fifty poetical compositions called "Psalms" after their Greek name, with "Psalter" designating the entire collection (*psaltêrion,* the stringed instrument that accompanied the singing of the psalms). In Hebrew, on the other hand, the hymns, which form the most considerable part, have given the entire collection the name *Sefer Tehillim* (Books of Praises). The Psalter, in more or less its present form, was already available to the liturgical authorities in Jerusalem during the period of the second temple (third century B.C.).

By analogy with the five Books of the Pentateuch (the Torah), the Psalter was divided, quite arbitrarily, into five books; this division seems to go back to the third century B.C. On the other hand, three main sections can be distinguished according to the name used for God ("the Lord," Yahweh, in the first and third sections; "God," Elohim, in the second); the three sections are Psalms 1-41, 42-89, and 90-150.

There are also psalms that are part of less important pre-existing collections belonging to groups of cantors, such as those of Asaph (73-83) or Korah (42-50; 84-88), who had been charged with organizing the liturgical functions. In addition, the Psalter includes other distinguishable collections: the pilgrim psalms (120-134), songs of the kingdom (93-100), the canticles of Zion and the Alleluia hymns (113-119, 135-136, and 146-150).

More than one psalm already had a history and life of its own before being given its definitive text and definitive place in the Psalter as we now have it. In fact, some very ancient psalms were used and reread from century to century, adapted to new circumstances, and often revised. It would be of interest were we able to discover the meaning and function that such psalms as 2 and 110 had in various periods.

At the beginning of each psalm the Hebrew text provides some introductory notes that are still rather mysterious to us. These are the "superscriptions" or "titles." They indicate the presumed author of the psalm, the historical occasion that supposedly inspired it, some instructions on the musical instruments to be used, and so on. Some critics think that these superscriptions are ancient, perhaps composed before the Exile; others think that they are much later additions, inserted when the collection had already been completed. In any case, rather than giving the objective meaning of the psalm, the superscription shows how it was understood and sung at a time far removed from its origin.

Many superscriptions attribute a given psalm to David (all those of the first book, except for 32; and others). There is no doubt that the royal musician and poet who danced before the ark and organized Israel's worship gave a decisive impulse to the liturgy and sacred songs, and that some of his compositions have been preserved (see 2 Sa 1:19-27; 23:1-7).

Moreover, as head of Israel, he represented the entire people. Furthermore, once the monarchy disappeared, he became, after the Exile, the model for believers and the type of the future Messiah, of the Jesus who would speak in the name of all the people and even of all humankind. For this reason, even if David did not himself compose any of the hundred and fifty psalms, at least in their present form (as modern exegetes prefer to think), the memory of him certainly inspired the cantors, who therefore legitimately put his name over their own liturgical compositions.

Various Attitudes toward God

It is difficult to discern any particular order in the present sequence of the Psalter. Prayers of entreaty stand side by side with the most enthusiastic thanksgivings, just as in real life. The most that can be observed is that the burden of misfortune weighs more heavily in the first half of the Book, while praise becomes more sustained toward the end of it. In the commentary that follows we try unobtrusively to suggest this rhythm.

Each psalm will therefore be viewed in itself without trying to establish any relationship of continuity. This does not mean that the Psalms cannot be grouped into some typical categories, depending on the ideas and emotions they express, on the liturgical needs they meet, and even on their rhythm and structure. Identification of the category to which a psalm belongs can contribute greatly to the understanding of it.

The Hebrew name for the Psalter is "Book of Praises," and in fact there are many hymns of praise. The Alleluia psalms belong for the most part in this category. Another homogeneous group of psalms acclaim the Lord as King of the people and of the universe; these are the psalms of the kingdom, the Messianic hymns (47; 93; 96; 97; 98; 99; 145). Still another group voices the love of the people for Jerusalem, the mountain on which God dwells and on which the dynasty of its Messianic King is perpetuated; we shall call these the canticles of Zion (24; 46; 48; 78; 84; 87; 122).

The songs of thanksgiving expressed wonder and gratitude in lengthy modulations. Petitions, complaints, and prayers of repentance and sorrow are perhaps the most frequent subjects of the Psalms. Some songs by unhappy singers become psalms of trust and gratitude (e.g., 13; 16; 22; 23; 31; 32; etc.).

The sapiential psalms are somewhat didactic in tone. The wise men in question endeavor to penetrate the riddle of life and unveil its meaning.

Finally, there are the royal psalms: songs and prayers that focus on the king and were perhaps used, at least initially, for the festival of consecration or the anniversary of enthronement. Like the psalms of the kingdom, in the course of time these were reread in a Messianic perspective.

We should also note that some psalms turn the history of Israel into a prophecy in which the lesson of the past is solemnly proposed on the occasion of some great feast (78; 105; 106).

Hebrew Poetry

Verses in Hebrew poetry are composed of two (sometimes three or more) parts, which are called "stichs," the second of them being in some way symmetrical with the first. This is the characteristic element in all Hebrew poetry and is called "parallelism." The parallelism can take any of three forms. One is *synonymy*, which is the most common form; here the same idea is repeated in different words (e.g., Ps 114:4: "The mountains skipped like rams,/the hills like lambs"; Ps 49:1: "Hear this, all you peoples;/listen, all who live in this world").

A second is *antithesis*, with the contrast putting the same idea into relief (e.g., "A wise son brings joy to his father,/but a foolish son grief to his mother"—Pr 10:1); this is, consequently, the form most used in sententious sayings.

A third form, which lends itself to great variety, is a *parallelism in a broad sense,* when the second stich simply completes the first (e.g., Ps 3:4: "To the LORD I cry aloud,/and he answers me from his holy hill"). In this third form, then, each of the two stichs often presents part of the idea, so that the entire thought is given by the two together. Thus in the example given from Proverbs the point is not that the good son gives joy to the father alone, while the bad son gives pain to the mother alone, but rather that each of the two sons obviously brings joy or sorrow to the "parents." So too, in Psalm 92:2, "to proclaim your love in the morning/and your faithfulness at night" means to extol the divine goodness all day long, or "night and day."

Although verses composed of two stichs are by far the most common, there are, as was said above, verses containing three or more stichs. In fact, the Psalter begins with a three-membered verse: "Blessed is the man who does not walk in the counsel of the wicked/or stand in the way of sinners/or sit in the seat of mockers." If we look closely, it seems clear that since "mockers" is parallel to "wicked" and "sinners," it is a synonym for these, "mocking" being a form of wickedness and sin.

Generally speaking, attention to parallelism is a great help for grasping the precise meaning of a passage. When we read: "Endow the king with your justice, O God,/the royal son with your righteousness" (Ps 72:1), we will not think of two different persons for whom two different favors are being asked, but, at most, that the king in question belongs to a royal dynasty.

As can be readily inferred from what has been said, there is no question of having a set number of syllables, as in our own classical meters. Meter is indeed not lacking, but it is meter after the fashion of modern poetry, which is concerned with rhythm alone. That is, a verse must have a certain number of accented syllables, but there is no other requirement. The number of such syllables can vary from two to five; in this last case, the rhythm is usually 3 + 2, that is, the second half is shorter (elegiac rhythm). Between two accented syllables there are ordinarily one, two, or three unaccented syllables.

The conclusions reached on this subject by modern scholars do not permit us to restore the original rhythmic beauty of biblical poetic compositions by accurately dividing the stichs or even the verses, which not infrequently have been wrongly divided in the traditional Masoretic Text.

Scholars have not yet reached unanimity in regard to strophes or stanzas; it is generally admitted that they exist, but in practice it is not easy to distinguish them.

The External Form

Some psalms are acrostic or alphabetical; that is, their verses (or strophes) start with a word that begins with one of the twenty-two letters of the Hebrew alphabet (in alphabetical order). This device, like others common in poetry (rhyme, strophes, etc.), has for its purpose to heighten merit, but it can also result in embarrassment from the viewpoint of artistic inspiration and literary perfection.

Hope Stimulated by Remembrance of the Past

The history of the Psalms is ongoing. It is true, of course, that the Psalter reflects the spiritual adventure of the ancient People of God, with its lights and shadows. But the Jewish tradition began at a quite early date to regard this Book as the herald of a unique religious experience that looked to the Messiah as witness and privileged beneficiary of the divine work of salvation. Thus the entire Psalter, which is a synthesis of the Old Testament in the form of poetry and prayer, becomes a Messianic prayer. The Christian tradition has therefore legitimately regarded it as also a prophecy and prefiguration of Jesus, who suffers before entering into his glory (Ps 22:19 and Jn 19:24; Ps 2:1-2 and Ac 4:25-27; etc.).

Because they had been used by Jesus and were fervently recited with new understanding by the first Christian community, which had emerged from Judaism, the Psalms automatically became the prayer of the Church, as they had been that of Israel; from that time on, they have been continually prayed by the Church. The new and spiritual Jerusalem sees partially realized in itself the glory of Zion, which the chosen people saw as still in the future.

There is no feast or celebration or reading of the Word of God for which the Liturgy cannot find appropriate expressions or at least allusions in the Psalms. In praying the Psalms, the children of the Church express through these imperfect but irreplaceable songs from another age the human and supernatural experience of sorrow and joy that they, the new People of God, also have as they travel toward the radiant goal of the history of the Church and humanity: "Zion, perfect in beauty," where "God shines forth" (Ps 50:2 and Rev 21:2).

Calls for Vengeance?

At the same time, however, many of these songs are filled with curses and calls for vengeance, sometimes expressing a cruelty that is truly disconcerting (5:10; 31:17; 54:5; 83:13; 109:6f; 139:19f). We are dismayed to read: "Happy is . . . he who seizes your infants and dashes them against the rocks" (137:8f). But we ought not be astonished by such language. The Psalms date from a time when the Gospel was not yet known; when placed on the lips of those being persecuted, they voice an urgent appeal for divine justice. (See note on Ps 5:10 and introduction to Ps 35.)

On the other hand, these vengeance psalms have a deeper meaning: at one time, they struck out against the enemies of the chosen people, the "heathen," that is, the enemies of God; today they give voice to a different hatred, that which Christians ought to have for the evil that Jesus intended to destroy by his death and against which Paul the apostle exhorts us to fight (Eph 6:11-13).

PROLOGUE — PSALMS 1–2*

PSALM 1*

True Happiness

¹ Blessed is the man
    who does not walk in the counsel of the
      wicked
    or stand in the way of sinners
    or sit in the seat of mockers.*ᵃ

---

a Ps 26:4-5; 40:4; Pr 1:22; 4:18-19; Isa 28:14; Jer 15:17; Hos 7:5; Mt 7:13-14.

1—2 These first two psalms are regarded as a preface to the entire Psalter. Collections of psalms that were originally different were gradually regrouped to comprise the Psalter as we have it; the psalms attributed to David (3—41 and 51—72), the songs of Ascents (120—134), and the chants of the Hallel (105—107, 111—118, 135—150) constitute the most remarkable of these primary collections. But as presently arranged in our Bible, the Book of Psalms is divided like the Pentateuch (the first five Books of the Bible that are called the Law) into five unequal parts, each of which ends with a formula of acclamation.

Ps 1 At the entrance to the collection of the Psalms, we are immediately placed before a life-choice: God or nothingness. This option imposes itself on us throughout all the pages of the Bible. In the historical accounts, law codes, prophecies, prayers, and meditative texts, a line of division is set forth. It distinguishes between righteousness and impiety, self-reliance and faith, good and evil, wickedness and love. The words are varied and the experiences are numerous in order to bear witness to this rupture.

They mark a division between peoples, between individuals, and between the acts and projects of our lives. Appearances may produce change and daily contradict the faithful's overly naive dreams about prosperity; however, one fact remains: a life of righteousness and truth is a path of happiness, a path of God, whereas those who deaden their conscience for their own ends have no other future but ruin.

Every time a reader prays a psalm, he or she is forced to choose between the "two ways" (see Dt 30:15; Pr 4:18f; Jer 21:8), the difference between which is underscored by Jesus (see Mt 7:13; 25). The righteous are blessed for they are separated from sin, Bible-centered, and prosperous. Unlike them are the wicked who are doomed to judgment.

1:1 The Psalter begins by declaring the blessedness of the righteous (v. 1) and concludes by summoning all creation to praise God in heaven and on earth (Ps 150). Human beings are made for happiness, and the revealed moral law is oriented toward that happiness. *Blessed:* the happy state of life in fellowship with God, revering him and obeying his laws (see Ps 94:12; 112:1; 119:1f; 128:1; Pr 29:18). *Mockers:* those who reject God and his law (see Pr 1:10-19).

2 But his delight is in the law of the LORD,*
    and on his law he meditates day and
       night.[b]
3 He is like a tree planted by streams of water,[c]
    which yields its fruit in season
    and whose leaf does not wither.*
  Whatever he does prospers.

4 Not so the wicked!
    They are like chaff
    that the wind blows away.*[d]
5 Therefore the wicked will not stand in the
      judgment,*
    nor sinners in the assembly of the righ-
      teous.[e]

6 For the LORD watches over* the way of the
      righteous,
    but the way of the wicked will perish.[f]

---

b Ps 112:1; 119:16, 35; Jos 1:8; Sir 39:1; Eze 11:20; Ro 7:22.—c Ps 52:8; 92:13-15; Jer 17:8; Eze 47:12.—d Ps 35:5; 83:14-16; Job 21:18; Isa 40:24; Jer 13:24.—e Ps 5:5; 35:18; 82:1; 111:1.—f Ps 37:18; 112:10; 121:5; Na 1:7.

1:2 *The law of the LORD:* either the first five Books of the Bible, known as the Torah (law), or divine instruction. *Meditates:* literally, "murmurs," i.e., assimilates the law of life that incarnates the presence of God and teaches the believer how to attain joyous intimacy with the Lord. Indeed, there is a law and a judgment of God and a happiness for human beings.

1:3 *Like a tree . . . does not wither:* the righteous are able to withstand the rigors of life. Like a tree planted on fertile ground, they are able to enhance their spiritual life.

1:4 *Like chaff . . . blows away:* the wicked are completely powerless spiritually, for they are like chaff that is easily borne away, even by the slightest breeze.

1:5 At the time of the judgment—either God's judgment of the wicked during life (see Ps 76:7f; 130:3; Ezr 9:15) or his judgment of them at the end of time (see Mal 3:2; Mt 25:31-46; Rev 6:17)—the wicked will bear the brunt of their misdeeds. *Righteous:* a name for the faithful People of God, i.e., those who reverence God and diligently strive to carry out his laws in every phase of their lives.

1:6 *Watches over:* the Lord takes an avid interest in their conduct (see Ps 31:7; 37:18; Ge 18:19; Am 3:2; Na 1:7). *The way of the wicked will perish:* a similar fate is set forth for the wicked in Ps 112:10: "the longings of the wicked will come to nothing." The theme of the two ways has already been found in Dt 30:15f and Jer 21:8; it will be taken up again in Pr 4:18f and Mt 7:13.

PSALM 2*

Universal Reign of the Messiah

1 Why do the nations conspire[a]
   and the peoples plot in vain?[g]
2 The kings of the earth take their stand[h]
   and the rulers gather together
against the LORD
   and against his Anointed One.*[b]
3 "Let us break their chains," they say,
   "and throw off their fetters."[i]

4 The One enthroned in heaven laughs;
   the LORD scoffs at them.[j]
5 Then he rebukes them in his anger
   and terrifies them in his wrath, saying,[k]

---

a Hebrew; Septuagint *rage.*—b Or *anointed one.*

g Ps 21:11; Pr 24:2; Ac 4:25-28; Rev 11:18.—h Ps 48:4; 83:5; Ac 4:25-26; Rev 19:19.—i Ps 149:8; 2 Sa 3:34; Job 36:8.—j Ps 37:13; 59:8; Pr 1:26; Wis 4:18; Isa 37:16; 40:15-17.—k Ps 6:1; 21:9; 110:5.

Ps 2 Although the surrounding peoples are rising up, the People of God are enthroning a new king: empowered by God's assistance, he shatters the coalition of their foes. This is the drama evoked in the present psalm, and it recurs more than once in the history of Israel. Thus, this poem found its place in a liturgy for royal consecration, for each king was a "messiah," that is, a man anointed with the sacred unction in the name of God. But the Prophets and the New Testament enlarged these perspectives. Hence this ancient text evokes in our eyes the whole drama of the world. It proclaims the sovereignty of God in the midst of the tumult of peoples and our human rebellions.

Behind the king of v. 6 can be glimpsed the Messiah (the Christ), a descendant of David and the Son of God, who will save his people (see Isa 9:5-6; Ac 4:25; 13:33; Heb 1:5). There is a premonition of the struggle that will take place at the end of time (see Eze 38—39; Da 12), a struggle already begun in the Passion of Jesus and in the persecutions of the Church (see Ac 4:25-28). But the psalm also expresses the hope of a final conversion of all the nations as they at last acknowledge the Lord (see Isa 45; Rev 19:15). God's plan will be achieved in the glory of the Messianic Kingdom.

2:2 *Anointed One:* in Hebrew, *Mashiah* (whence the word "Messiah"), which in the Greek translation is *Christos;* it referred originally to the Davidic King but ultimately to Jesus Christ. This phrase has given rise to two titles of Jesus: "Messiah" from the Hebrew and "Christ" from the Greek. In Israel the power of office was bestowed by anointing both on kings (see Jdg 9:8; 1 Sa 9:16; 16:12f) and on high priests (see Lev 8:12; Nu 3:3).

⁶ "I have installed my King[c][l]
   on Zion, my holy hill."*

⁷ I will proclaim the decree* of the LORD:

He said to me, "You are my Son;[d]
   today I have become your Father.[e][m]
⁸ Ask of me,
   and I will make the nations your inheri-
     tance,[n]
   the ends of the earth your possession.*
⁹ You will rule them with an iron scepter;[f]
   you will dash them to pieces like pot-
     tery."*[o]

¹⁰ Therefore, you kings, be wise;
   be warned, you rulers of the earth.[p]
¹¹ Serve the LORD with fear
   and rejoice with trembling.[q]
¹² Kiss* the Son, lest he be angry
   and you be destroyed in your way,
  for his wrath can flare up in a moment.
   Blessed are all who take refuge in him.[r]

---

c Or *king.*—d Or *son;* also in verse 12.—e Or *have begotten you.*—f Or *will break them with a rod of iron.*

---

l Ps 10:16; 24:10; 110:2.—m Ps 89:26f; 110:2-3; Isa 49:1; Lk 3:22; Heb 1:5; 6:5.—n Ps 22:27; Mt 21:38; Rev 2:26.—o Ps 110:5-6; Job 34:24; Jer 19:10; Rev 2:27; 12:5; 19:15.—p Ps 141:6; Pr 27:11; Wis 6:1.—q Ps 9:2; 34:9; 103:11.—r Ps 84:12; 146:5; Pr 16:20; Rev 6:16.

2:6 *Holy hill:* reference to the site of the temple (see 2 Ch 3:4; 15:1; 33:15). Ps 43:3 and 46:4 have "holy mountain" and "holy place" respectively.
2:7 *Decree:* this is nothing less than the prophecy of Nathan (see 2 Sa 7:14) applied to the Messiah by 1 Ch 17:13 (see Ps 89:26). Here the Messiah speaks after the rebels (v. 3) and after God who in an oracle (v. 6) has just enthroned him as King of Israel. He has also declared him his Son according to a formula familiar to the ancient Orient.
2:8 The Messiah's reign will be coextensive with that of God (see Isa 49:6; Da 7:14). This verse is applied by Heb 1:5 (see Heb 5:5), then by tradition and the Liturgy, to the eternal generation of the Word.
2:9 The Book of Revelation applies this verse to Christ's triumphant reign (see Rev 12:5; 19:15).
2:12 *Kiss:* a sign of submission (see 1 Sa 10:1; 1 Ki 19:18; Hos 13:2). *Blessed:* see note on Ps 1:1.

BOOK I—PSALMS 3–41*

PSALM 3*

Trust in God in Time of Danger

A psalm of David. When he fled from his son Absalom.[s]

[1] O LORD, how many are my foes!
  How many rise up against me!
[2] Many are saying of me,
  "God will not deliver him."[t]   *Selah*[g]

[3] But you are a shield around me, O LORD;[u]
    you bestow glory on me and lift[h] up my
    head.*
[4] To the LORD I cry aloud,
    and he answers me from his holy hill.[v]
                                                    Selah

[5] I lie down and sleep;[w]
    I wake again, because the LORD sustains
    me.*

---

g A word of uncertain meaning, occurring frequently in the Psalms; possibly a musical term.—h Or LORD, / my Glorious One, who lifts.

---

s 2 Sa 15:13ff.—t Ps 71:11; Isa 36:15.—u Ps 7:10; 18:2; 62:6-7; Dt 33:29; Isa 60:19.—v Ps 2:6.—w Ps 4:8; 17:15; Pr 3:24.

Ps 3—41 At the beginning of the Book we find a collection of psalms attributed to David. His life, replete with difficulties and brimming with confidence, was erected into an example: it inspired in Israelite cantors poems that David did not himself compose. One theme dominates the diversity of psalms that make up this first part: the innocent find themselves in the grip of the wicked, whose assaults reveal all its visages; hope is ceaselessly renewed as is torment: "My God, my God, why have you forsaken me?" (Ps 22:1). It is the trial of darkness; still one certitude remains: "You will fill me with joy in your presence" (Ps 16:11). Is not this the dialogue that takes place in the life of believers!

Ps 3 In time of great danger and anguish, the psalmist finds refuge in God as his shield (protector) and encourager. God answers his prayer and bestows peace and deliverance.

3:2 *Selah:* see NIV textual note.

3:3 God will preserve the psalmist from dishonor and humiliation by means of his grace (see Ps 18:2; 27:5; 62:7; 110:5; Dt 33:29; Sir 11:12f).

3:5 This passage (see Pr 3:24) is applied by the Fathers of the Church to the dead and risen Christ.

⁶ I will not fear the tens of thousands
    drawn up against me on every side.ˣ

⁷ Arise, O LORD!
    Deliver me, O my God!
Strike all my enemies on the jaw;*
    break the teeth of the wicked.ʸ

⁸ From the LORD comes deliverance.
    May your blessing be on your people.ᶻ
                           Selah

PSALM 4*

Joyful Confidence in God

For the director of music. With stringed instruments.
A psalm of David.

¹ Answer me when I call to you,
    O my righteous God.
Give me relief from my distress;
    be merciful to me and hear my prayer.ᵃ

² How long,* O men, will you turn my glory
    into shame?ⁱ
How long will you love delusions and seek
    false gods?ʲ ᵇ   *Selah*

---

i Or *you dishonor my Glorious One.*—j Or *seek lies.*

---

x Ps 23:4; 118:11; Job 11:15.—y Ps 6:4; 7:1; 58:6; Isa 25:9; Jer 42:11.—
z Ps 27:1; 28:9; Isa 43:3; Jnh 2:9; Rev 7:10.—a Ps 13:3; 27:7; 30:10;
118:5.—b Ps 62:3; Ex 16:7; 2 Ki 19:26; Jer 13:25.

3:7 God treats the wicked like ferocious beasts whose jaws are shattered
(see Ps 22:13f; 35:16; 58:6; Job 29:17; Eze 22:25). The initial appeal reminds one
of Jer 2:27. See note on Ps 5:10 and introduction to Ps 35.

Ps 4 Those who are well established in life delude themselves by seeking happiness in riches and worldly vanities. The psalmist, rich in divine trust and joy,
invites them to discover the price of God's friendship: "the light of [God's] face."
This is an evening prayer (see vv. 4 and 8), filled with desire for God; Christians
move beyond its earthly perspectives. Prayer brings openness of heart, assurance
of God's help, faith, divine approval, joy, and peace.

The words *For the director of music* in the superscription are thought to be a
musical or liturgical notation.

4:2 *How long . . . ?:* see note on Ps 6:3.

³ Know that the LORD has set apart the godly*
    for himself;
  the LORD will hear when I call to him.ᶜ

⁴ In your anger do not sin;
    when you are on your beds,ᵈ
    search your hearts and be silent.*   *Selah*

⁵ Offer right sacrifices
    and trust in the LORD.ᵉ

⁶ Many are asking, "Who can show us any
    good?"
  Let the light of your face shine upon* us, O
    LORD.ᶠ
⁷ You have filled my heart* with greater joy
    than when their grain and new wine
    abound.ᵍ
⁸ I will lie down and sleep in peace,
    for you alone, O LORD,
    make me dwell in safety.ʰ

---

c Ps 12:1; 1 Ti 4:7; 2 Pe 3:11.—d Ps 63:6; Da 2:28; Eph 4:26.—e Ps
31:6; 51:19; Isa 26:4; Jn 14:1.—f Ps 31:16; 44:3; 67:1; 80:3; Nu 6:25; Job
13:24; Da 9:17.—g Isa 9:3; Ac 14:17.—h Ps 3:5; Lev 26:6.

4:3 *Godly:* one of several words (sometimes translated as "saints") for the
People of God, who should be faithful to him (see Ps 12:1; 31:23; 32:6; 34:9).
4:4-5 One must fear to offend God but rather pray to him in the calm and silence of adoration. *In your anger do not sin:* these words are cited by Paul in Eph
4:26 with the sense that if anger takes hold of you, let it not lead you to act
evilly—for there is such a thing as righteous anger (see Mk 3:5). *Beds:* can refer
to the spot where one prostrated oneself to pray (see Ps 95:6; Sir 50:17), which is
also suggested by the presence of the term *Selah* or pause.
4:6 *Face shine upon:* this image of benevolence and contentment (see Nu
6:25; Pr 16:15; Da 9:17) occurs frequently in the Psalter (see Ps 31:16; 67:1;
119:135; and especially note on Ps 13:1). The reading in the Septuagint and Vulgate is: "The light of your countenance, O Lord, is signed [or: imprinted] on us." It
was interpreted as referring to the soul created in the image of God and regener-
ated by the baptismal character that makes a Christian a child of light (see Lk
16:8; Jn 12:36; 1 Th 5:5; Eph 5:8).
4:7 *Heart:* the biblical center of the human spirit, which harbors a person's
thoughts and emotions and gives rise to action.

PSALM 5*

Morning Prayer for Divine Help

For the director of music. For flutes. A psalm of David.

¹ Give ear to my words, O LORD,
   consider my sighing.*i*
² Listen to my cry for help,
   my King and my God,
   for to you I pray.*j*
³ In the morning,* O LORD, you hear my voice;
   in the morning I lay my requests before you
   and wait in expectation.*k*

⁴ You are not a God who takes pleasure in evil;
   with you the wicked cannot dwell.*l*
⁵ The arrogant cannot stand in your presence;
   you hate all who do wrong.*m*
⁶ You destroy those who tell lies;
   bloodthirsty and deceitful men
   the LORD abhors.*n*

⁷ But I, by your great mercy,*
   will come into your house;

---

i Ps 17:1; 40:1; 86:6; 130:1-2; Isa 35:10. — j Ps 44:4; 84:3. — k Wis 16:28; Isa 28:19; Eze 46:13; Ro 8:19. — l Ps 1:5; Pr 2:22. — m Ps 73:3; 2 Ki 19:32; Pr 8:13. — n Ps 101:7; Pr 6:17-19; Wis 14:9; Hab 1:13; Ac 5:3; Rev 21:8.

Ps 5 This is a morning prayer (see v. 3) in which the psalmist prays for the Lord to hear his prayer and grant a sense of God's goodness and justice, bestow guidance, punish enemies, and bless the righteous. Broken by tribulation, the persecuted man appeals to the justice of God against his own enemies. Christians will not make their own the calls for vengeance uttered here but will ask for the courage to avoid all complicity with evil. To love God is to choose the cause of justice and bear the witness of a purified joy.

The words *For the director of music* in the superscription are thought to be a musical or liturgical notation.

5:3 The morning is the privileged moment for divine favors (see Ps 17:14f; 30:5; 46:5; 59:16). *I lay my requests*: other possible translations are: "I offer my vows" and "I prepare my offering."

5:7 *Mercy:* Hebrew *hesed*; this word denotes firstly the sentiments that flow from a natural community, family, clan, or society (benevolence, favor), then from the covenant between the Lord and the community of Israel, regarded as his spouse and child, and finally the sentiments that are found in each of its members (grace and love on the part of the Lord, and piety on the part of the faithful).

in reverence will I bow down
    toward your holy temple.[o]
8 Lead me, O LORD, in your righteousness[p]
    because of my enemies—
    make straight your way before me.*

9 Not a word from their mouth can be trusted;[q]
    their heart is filled with destruction.
Their throat is an open grave;
    with their tongue they speak deceit.*
10 Declare them guilty, O God!
    Let their intrigues be their downfall.[r]
Banish them for their many sins,
    for they have rebelled against you.*

11 But let all who take refuge in you be glad;
    let them ever sing for joy.[s]
Spread your protection over them,
    that those who love your name* may re-
        joice in you.
12 For surely, O LORD, you bless the righteous;
    you surround them with your favor as with
        a shield.[t]

---

o Ps 138:2; 1 Ki 8:44; Da 6:10; Jnh 2:4.—p Ps 23:3; Pr 4:11; Isa 26:7; Jn
1:23.—q Ps 12:2; Pr 15:4; Jer 5:16; Ro 3:13.—r Ps 78:40; 141:10; La
1:5.—s Ps 33:1; 64:10; Rev 7:15-16.—t Ps 32:7; 69:36; 112:2; 119:132.

5:8 *Make straight your way before me:* the Greek reads: "Make straight my way
before you."
5:9 With mouth, heart, throat, and tongue they spread harm around. *Their
throat is an open grave:* their words bring death to their hearers (see Jer 5:16)—
a theme cited in Ro 3:13.
5:10 This verse reminds us that the so-called imprecatory (or cursing) psalms
(see introduction to Ps 35) have been a problem for Christians from the beginning of the use of the Psalter. Christ instructed Christians to pray for enemies
(see Mt 5:44) and gave an example of this on the cross (see Lk 23:34). Yet the
psalmists at times call for punishment (even of the most drastic kind) on enemies. Christians may look upon these statements as appeals for strict redress of
evil in accord with the divine justice or direct them toward the enemies of their
souls, the devil and his minions who are implacable foes of God.
5:11 *Your name:* name usually designates the person, hence the Lord himself.

PSALM 6*

Evening Prayer for God's Mercy

For the director of music. With stringed instruments.
According to *sheminith*.ᵏ A psalm of David.

¹ O LORD, do not rebuke me in your anger
   or discipline me in your wrath.ᵘ
² Be merciful to me, LORD, for I am faint;
   O LORD, heal me, for my bones are in agony.ᵛ
³ My soul* is in anguish.
   How long, O LORD, how long?ʷ

⁴ Turn, O LORD, and deliver me;
   save me because of your unfailing love.*
⁵ No one remembers you when he is dead.ˣ
   Who praises you from the grave?*ˡ

⁶ I am worn out from groaning;
   all night long I flood my bed with weeping
   and drench my couch with tears.

---

k Probably a musical term.—l Hebrew *Sheol*.

---

u Ps 38:2; Jer 10:24.—v Ps 61:2; Jer 17:14-15.—w Ps 13:2-3; 31:7; 74:10; 89:47.—x Ps 30:9; 88:10-12; 115:17; Ecc 9:10; Isa 38:18.

Ps 6 This is the first of the so-called Penitential Psalms (6; 32; 38; 51; 102; 130; 143), a designation for psalms suitable for expressing repentance that goes back to the sixth century A.D. In affliction, the psalmist invokes the divine mercy, begs to be saved from death, confesses his wretchedness, and expresses faith in his own deliverance and his enemies' total abasement.

The words *For the director of music* in the superscription are thought to be a musical or liturgical notation; *according to sheminith* was probably a musical term referring to an eight-stringed instrument.

6:3 *Soul:* the Hebrew word *nephesh* usually means a person's life-giving breath, which disappears at death. It is thus applied to a person's very self as a living, conscious being ("my soul" equals "myself"). *How long?:* elliptical formula used in psalms of lamentation both in Babylonia and in Israel (see Ps 74:10; 80:4; 90:13; 94:3) to express anxiety over the divine aid that is late in coming.

6:4 *Unfailing love:* Hebrew *hesed*, which may also be translated as "mercy" and refers to all that God promised to give to his people (see Dt 7:9, 12) through the Davidic dynasty (see Ps 89:24, 28, 33; 2 Sa 7:15; Isa 55:3).

6:5 The psalmist offers a motive for God to save him from death: it is the living who praise him. The netherworld was viewed as the place where the souls of the dead had a kind of shadowy existence, with no activity or lofty emotion. Just what that existence entailed at any given Old Testament period is difficult to gauge until the second century B.C. It is then that the sacred Books begin to speak more clearly about life after death (see Wis 3; Da 12:1-3).

7 My eyes grow weak with sorrow;
   they fail* because of all my foes.*y*

8 Away from me, all you who do evil,*
   for the LORD has heard my weeping.*z*

9 The LORD has heard my cry for mercy;
   the LORD accepts my prayer.

10 All my enemies will be ashamed and dis-
    mayed;
      they will turn back in sudden disgrace.*a*

PSALM 7*

Appeal to the Divine Judge

A *shiggaion*m of David, which he sang to the LORD
concerning Cush, a Benjamite.

1 O LORD my God, I take refuge in you;
   save and deliver me from all who pursue
   me,*b*

2 or they will tear me like a lion
   and rip me to pieces with no one to rescue
   me.

---

m Probably a literary or musical term.

y Ps 31:9; 38:10; 40:12; Isa 38:14.—z Ps 119:115; 139:19; Mt 7:23; Lk 13:27.—a Ps 35:4, 26; 40:14; 71:13; 2 Ki 19:26.—b Ps 2:12; 6:4; 22:20.

6:7 *Eyes grow weak . . . fail:* a sign of failing strength (see Ps 38:10; 1 Sa 14:27, 29; Jer 14:6) or sorrow in affliction (see Ps 31:9; 88:9; Job 17:7; La 2:11) or dashed hopes (see Ps 69:3; 119:82, 123; Dt 28:32; Isa 38:14).

6:8 This apostrophe (taken up in Mt 7:23) has been prepared for by the end of v. 8. The enemies of the sick person, like the friends of Job, see in his trials a heavenly chastisement for hidden faults; they insult him and accuse him unjustly—a theme that is more developed elsewhere (see Ps 31; 35; 38; 69).

6:10 See note on Ps 5:10 and introduction to Ps 35.

Ps 7 Falsely accused, the psalmist implores the divine assistance, affirms his innocence, invokes God's just judgment, and expresses limitless confidence in the punishment of his enemy as well as his own salvation, concluding with praise for God's righteousness.

For *shiggaion* in the superscription, see NIV textual note; *Cush* is not otherwise known, but as a Benjamite he was probably a supporter of Saul. Hence the psalm is associated with Saul's determined attempts on David's life.

³ O L<small>ORD</small> my God, if I have done this
  and there is guilt on my hands—
⁴ if I have done evil to him who is at peace with
      me
  or without cause have robbed my foe—
⁵ then let my enemy pursue and overtake me;
  let him trample my life to the ground
  and make me sleep in the dust.*c*   *Selah*

⁶ Arise, O L<small>ORD</small>, in your anger;
  rise up against the rage of my enemies.
  Awake, my God; decree justice.*d*
⁷ Let the assembled peoples gather around you.
  Rule over them from on high;
⁸   let the L<small>ORD</small> judge the peoples.
  Judge me, O L<small>ORD</small>, according to my righ-
      teousness,
  according to my integrity, O Most High.
⁹ O righteous God,
  who searches minds and hearts,*
  bring to an end the violence of the wicked
  and make the righteous secure.*e*

¹⁰ My shieldⁿ is God Most High,
  who saves the upright in heart.*f*
¹¹ God is a righteous judge,
  a God who expresses his wrath every day.
¹² If heᵒ does not relent,
  he will sharpen his sword;
  he will bend and string his bow.*g*
¹³ He has prepared his deadly weapons;
  he makes ready his flaming arrows.*h*

---

n Or *sovereign.*—o Or *If a man does not repent. / God.*

c Ps 143:3; Isa 10:6.—d Ps 9:4; 138:7.—e Ps 17:3; 26:2; 35:24; 43:1; 139:23; Wis 1:6; Jer 11:20; 17:10; 20:12; Rev 2:23.—f Ps 3:3; Job 33:3.—g Ps 11:2; Eze 3:19.—h Ps 18:14; Isa 50:11.

7:9 *Minds and hearts:* literally, "hearts and kidneys." The Israelites used the words as virtual synonyms (but "heart" most often) to refer to the innermost center of human life. To "search mind and heart" was a conventional expression for God's examination of a person's hidden character and motives (see Jer 11:20; 17:10; 20:12).

14 He who is pregnant with evil*
     and conceives trouble gives birth to disillu-
     sionment.*i*

15 He who digs a hole and scoops it out
     falls into the pit he has made.*j*

16 The trouble he causes recoils on himself;
     his violence comes down on his own head.

17 I will give thanks to the Lord because of his
     righteousness
     and will sing praise* to the name of the
     Lord Most High.*k*

PSALM 8*

The Majesty of God and the Dignity of Human Beings

For the director of music. According to *gittith*.*p*
A psalm of David.

1 O Lord, our Lord,
     how majestic is your name* in all the earth!

You have set your glory
     above the heavens.

---

p Probably a musical term.

---

i Job 15:35; Isa 59:4; Jas 1:15.—j Ps 9:15; 35:8; 57:6; 94:13; Pr 26:27; Ecc 10:8; Sir 27:26.—k Ps 18:49; 30:4; 135:3; 146:2; Ro 15:11.

7:14-16 See note on Ps 5:10 and introduction to Ps 35.

7:17 *I will give thanks . . . and will sing praise:* a vow to praise the Lord in keeping with the Israelite belief that praise must follow deliverance. The praise involved thank offerings and celebrating God's saving deed in the presence of others in the temple (see Ps 50:14f, 23).

Ps 8 In the midst of disconsolate supplications, here is a hymn that chants the splendor of God. But is not the best reflection of the divine majesty the grandeur of the human being? For the Lord has made this tiny being lost in the immensity of the world the crown of all creation. In the man "crowned with glory" Paul and the author of the Letter to the Hebrews see the glorified and risen Christ, who, while on earth, was for a time made lower than the heavenly creatures, the angels (see 1 Co 15:25-27; Eph 1:22; Heb 2:5-9).

The words *For the director of music* in the superscription are thought to be a musical or liturgical notation; the *gittith* may have been a musical instrument from the Philistine city of Gath, or else a song for the harvest and the winepress.

8:1 *Name:* according to Semitic usage, this word designates the person with all its essential qualities.

² From the lips of children and infants*
    you have ordained praise[q]
  because of your enemies,
    to silence the foe and the avenger.[l]

³ When I consider your heavens,
    the work of your fingers,
  the moon and the stars,
    which you have set in place,
⁴ what is man that you are mindful of him,[m]
    the son of man* that you care for him?[n]
⁵ You made him a little lower than the heav-
    enly beings*[r]
  and crowned him with glory and honor.

⁶ You made him ruler over the works of your
    hands;[o]
  you put everything under his feet:
⁷ all flocks and herds,
    and the beasts of the field,
⁸ the birds of the air,
    and the fish of the sea,
  all that swim the paths of the seas.

⁹ O LORD, our LORD,
    how majestic is your name in all the earth!

---

q Or *strength.*—r Or *than God.*

l Ps 143:12; Wis 10:21; Mt 21:16.—m Ps 144:3; Job 7:17.—n 1 Ch 29:14;
Heb 2:6ff.—o Ps 19:1; Ge 1:26, 28; Wis 9:2; 1 Co 15:27; Eph 1:22.

8:2 *From the lips of children and infants:* Jesus cites this passage with reference to the children who acclaim him on the day of his triumphal entry into Jerusalem (see Mt 21:16).

8:4 *Son of man:* a phrase used here and elsewhere as a synonym for man (see
Ps 80:17; Eze 2) and a sign of humility. Later it became a Messianic title in Daniel
(7:13f) and Jewish apocryphal tradition (see 1 Enoch, 2 Esdras, and 2 Baruch).
Eventually, Jesus made use of it to express his twofold destiny of suffering (see Mk
8:31; 9:13, 31; 10:33; 14:21) and of glory (see Mk 8:38; 12:36; 14:62).

8:5 *A little lower than the heavenly beings:* that is, a little lower than the beings
who comprise the heavenly court. The text for heavenly beings is *elohim,* that is,
"God"; in effect, God created human beings in his own image and likeness. Some
translate: "a little less than godlike"; and in Heb 2:9 this passage is said to be eminently fulfilled in Jesus Christ, the God-man. See also 1 Co 15:27 and Eph 1:22,
where Paul applies to Christ the words "you put everything under his feet" (v. 6).

PSALM 9—10*

PSALM 9*ˢ

Thanksgiving for the Triumph of Justice

For the director of music. To [the tune of] "The Death of
the Son." A psalm of David.

¹ I will praise you, O LORD,
　　with all my heart;
　　I will tell of all your wonders.*
² I will be glad and rejoice in you;
　　I will sing praise to your name, O Most
　　　High.

³ My enemies turn back;
　　they stumble and perish before you.
⁴ For you have upheld my right and my cause;
　　you have sat on your throne, judging righ-
　　teously.
⁵ You have rebuked the nations and destroyed
　　the wicked;
　　you have blotted out their name for ever
　　and ever.ᵖ

---

s Psalms 9 and 10 may have been originally a single acrostic poem, the
stanzas of which begin with the successive letters of the Hebrew alphabet.
In the Septuagint they constitute one psalm.

---

p Ge 20:17; Job 18:17.

Ps 9—10 In this psalm we are perhaps in the period of the return from the
Exile, toward the end of the sixth century; the foreign occupiers and the people
who had remained in Palestine regarded returning deportees as intruders and
they mistreated them. This is the first alphabetical psalm; in the Masoretic Text it
is divided into two psalms, while in the Greek Septuagint and Latin Vulgate
Psalms 9 and 10 constitute one psalm. This accounts for the difference in the
numbering of the psalms in these versions.

Ps 9 is predominantly praise of God for his royal blessings and glories, including deliverance from hostile nations, concluding with a short prayer for God's
continuing righteous judgments (see v. 4) on the nations.

The words *For the director of music* in the superscription are thought to be a
musical or liturgical notation; nothing is known about the words *To [the tune of]*.

9:1 The praise rendered to the Lord by the psalmists in the Psalter is customarily public praise for his goodness and glory as well as the saving acts he has
performed on behalf of his people. Some have described such praise as the fore-
runner of the Gospel preaching in the New Testament.

6 Endless ruin has overtaken the enemy,
you have uprooted their cities;
even the memory of them has perished.

7 The LORD reigns forever;
he has established his throne for judgment.
8 He will judge the world in righteousness;
he will govern the peoples with justice.[q]
9 The LORD is a refuge for the oppressed,
a stronghold in times of trouble.[r]
10 Those who know your name will trust in you,
for you, LORD, have never forsaken those who seek you.

11 Sing praises to the LORD, enthroned in Zion;*
proclaim among the nations what he has done.
12 For he who avenges blood remembers;
he does not ignore the cry of the afflicted.[s]

13 O LORD, see how my enemies persecute me!
Have mercy and lift me up from the gates of death,[t]
14 that I may declare your praises
in the gates of the Daughter of Zion*
and there rejoice in your salvation.
15 The nations have fallen into the pit they have dug;
their feet are caught in the net they have hidden.*

q Ps 7:11; 96:10; 98:9.—r Ps 10:18; 37:39; Isa 25:4.—s Ps 10:17; Job 16:18.—t Nu 10:9; Wis 16:13.

9:11 *Enthroned in Zion:* the Lord is enthroned not only in heaven (see Ps 2:4; 113:5) but also on earth—in the temple of Jerusalem from which he rules the world (see note on Ps 2:6; see also Ps 132:13).

9:14 *Daughter of Zion:* a personification of Jerusalem and its inhabitants in accord with ancient Near Eastern practice.

9:15-18 Under the Lord's just rule and in accord with the law of talion (see Ex 21:23-25; Lev 24:19f; Dt 19:21), the wicked who attack others are punished by the very actions they perform (see Ps 7:16). But the "needy" (v. 18), those who are attacked, will be saved by their trust in the Lord. Thus, God's honor and glory are vindicated when he judges and punishes the wicked.

16 The LORD is known by his justice;
>   the wicked are ensnared by the work of
>   their hands.ᵘ   *Higgaion*ᵗ
>   *Selah*

17 The wicked return to the grave,ᵘ
>   all the nations that forget God.
18 But the needy will not always be forgotten,
>   nor the hope of the afflicted ever perish.ᵛ

19 Arise, O LORD, let not man triumph;
>   let the nations be judged in your presence.
20 Strike them with terror, O LORD;
>   let the nations know they are but men.
>   *Selah*

PSALM 10*ᵛ

Prayer for Help against Oppressors

1 Why, O LORD, do you stand far off?
>   Why do you hide yourself in times of trou-
>   ble?

2 In his arrogance the wicked man hunts down
>   the weak,
>   who are caught in the schemes he devises.ʷ
3 He boasts of the cravings of his heart;
>   he blesses the greedy and reviles the LORD.ˣ
4 In his pride the wicked does not seek him;
>   in all his thoughts there is no room for
>   God.*ʸ

---

t Or *Meditation*; possibly a musical notation.—u Hebrew *Sheol*.—v Psalms 9 and 10 may have been originally a single acrostic poem, the stanzas of which begin with the successive letters of the Hebrew alphabet. In the Septuagint they constitute one psalm.

u Pr 5:22; Sir 27:26.—v Ps 25:3; Ps 23:18.—w Job 20:19; Isa 32:7.—x Ps 36:1; 49:6.—y Ps 14:1; 36:1; Job 22:13; Isa 29:15; Jer 5:12; Zep 1:12.

Ps 10 A prayer of one in trouble and seeking to be rescued, it explores the ways and motives of the wicked and calls on God the King to arise and defend the oppressed.

10:4 In denying the action of Providence the wicked in practice denies God (see Ps 10:13; 14:1; 36:1f; Zep 1:12), who is some far-off personage (v. 5).

5 His ways are always prosperous;
  > he is haughty and your laws are far from
  > him;
  > he sneers at all his enemies.
6 He says to himself, "Nothing will shake me;
  > I'll always be happy and never have trou-
  > ble."
7 His mouth is full of curses and lies and
  > threats;*
  > trouble and evil are under his tongue.z
8 He lies in wait near the villages;
  > from ambush he murders the innocent,
  > watching in secret for his victims.a
9 He lies in wait like a lion in cover;
  > he lies in wait to catch the helpless;
  > he catches the helpless and drags them off
  > in his net.b
10 His victims are crushed, they collapse;
  > they fall under his strength.
11 He says to himself, "God has forgotten;
  > he covers his face and never sees."c

12 Arise, LORD! Lift up your hand, O God.
  > Do not forget the helpless.
13 Why does the wicked man revile God?
  > Why does he say to himself,
  > "He won't call me to account"?
14 But you, O God, do see trouble and grief;
  > you consider it to take it in hand.d
  The victim commits himself to you;
  > you are the helper of the fatherless.e

---

z Ps 73:8; Isa 32:7; Ro 3:14.—a Ps 11:2; 17:12; Job 24:14; Jer 5:26; Hos
6:9; Hab 3:14.—b Ps 17:12; Job 18:8; Pr 1:11; Jer 5:26.—c Ps 44:24; 64:5;
73:11; 94:7; Job 22:13; Eze 9:9.—d Ps 22:11; 31:7; 56:8; 2 Ki 20:5; Isa
25:8; Rev 7:17.—e Ex 22:21-22; Dt 33:29.

10:7 *Curses and lies and threats:* this text, which contains the three most
common weapons of the tongue in Israel's experience, is cited in Ro 3:14. *Curses*
were believed to have real power over those upon whom they were leveled; *lies* referred to slander and false testimony for evil purposes (see 1 Ki 21:8-15).

¹⁵ Break the arm of the wicked and evil man;
      call him to account for his wickedness
      that would not be found out.*

¹⁶ The LORD is King for ever and ever;
      the nations will perish from his land.ᶠ

¹⁷ You hear, O LORD, the desire of the afflicted;
      you encourage them, and you listen to
      their cry,

¹⁸ defending the fatherless and the oppressed,
      in order that man, who is of the earth, may
      terrify no more.ᵍ

PSALM 11*

Unshakable Confidence in God

For the director of music. Of David.

¹ In the LORD I take refuge.*
      How then can you say to me:
      "Flee like a bird to your mountain.ʰ

² For look, the wicked bend their bows;*
      they set their arrows against the strings
   to shoot from the shadows
      at the upright in heart.ⁱ

---

f Ps 145:13; Ex 15:18; Jer 10:10.—g Ps 146:9; Dt 10:18.—h Ps 7:1;
55:6; 91:3.—i Ps 7:13; 10:8; 37:14; 64:4.

10:15 See note on Ps 5:10 and introduction to Ps 35.

Ps 11 This is a confession of confident trust in the Lord's righteous rule at a
time when the wicked adversaries seem to have the upper hand. To escape trouble, friends counsel flight to a mountain refuge, but the innocent psalmist stands
fast, for the Lord protects those who seek asylum in his temple.

In praying this psalm, we should be mindful that although we can rely on God,
we are never sure of ourselves. The Spirit of God is quick to help, but the "flesh,"
human nature, is weak—so much so that we must ask not to be put to the test
(see Mt 26:41) and must flee from it if this is possible and permitted (see Mt
10:23).

The words *For the director of music* in the superscription are thought to be a
musical or liturgical notation.

11:1-3 The psalmist remains confident in the Lord even though he is under attack by the wicked and receives counsel from his advisers to flee.

11:2 The wicked are likened to archers setting traps; they are treacherous,
furtive, and bent on maligning the upright and making them fall (see Ps 10:7-10;
37:14). *The upright:* i.e., the righteous who know and love the Lord (see Ps 7:10;
36:10; 73:1).

³ When the foundations are being destroyed,
    what can the righteous do?"*ʷ

⁴ The LORD is in his holy temple;*
    the LORD is on his heavenly throne.
  He observes the sons of men;
    his eyes examine them.ʲ
⁵ The LORD examines the righteous,
    but the wickedˣ and those who love vio-
    lence
    his soul hates.
⁶ On the wicked he will rain
    fiery coals and burning sulfur;* ᵏ
    a scorching wind will be their lot.

⁷ For the LORD is righteous,
    he loves justice;
    upright men will see his face.*

---

w Or *what is the Righteous One doing?*—x Or *The Lord, the Righteous One, examines the wicked.*

---

j Ps 14:2; 18:6; 27:4; 102:19; Dt 26:15; Isa 66:1; Hab 2:20; Mt 5:34.—k Ps 120:4; 140:10; Ge 19:24; Pr 16:27; Eze 10:2; 38:22; Rev 8:5; 20:10.

11:3 The psalmist's advisers are concerned about the collapse of the "foundations" (i.e., the order of society; see Ps 75:3; 82:5; Eze 30:4). This order has been established by the Lord at creation and is being maintained by him.
11:4-7 The psalmist relies on God, who is seated on his heavenly throne—a symbol of his royal rule and authority to judge (see Ps 9:7; 47:8)—and totally against those who love violence. At the right time, he will mete out to the wicked the judgment they deserve, and he will deliver the upright and grant them access to himself.
11:6 *Fiery coals and burning sulfur:* an image of judgment taken from the destruction of Sodom and Gomorrah (see Ge 19:24; Dt 29:23; Eze 38:22). *Scorching wind:* another image of judgment taken from the hot desert winds that blow over the Middle East and devastate the vegetation (see Isa 21:1; 40:7f; Jer 4:11). *Their lot:* literally, "the portion of their cup." The cup that God gives people to drink is a symbol for their destiny (see Ps 16:5; Mt 20:22; 26:39; Rev 14:10).
11:7 *See his face:* an expression usually denoting access, especially to the king. Here the expression indicates access to the heavenly King, with reference to his presence at the temple (God's royal house on earth). It is legitimate for us to see in this text an allusion to ultimate access to the heavenly temple (see Ps 16:11; 17:15; 23:6; 140:13).

PSALM 12*

Prayer against the Arrogance of Sinners

For the director of music. According to *sheminith.*y
A psalm of David.

1 Help, LORD, for the godly are no more;
  the faithful have vanished from among
  men.*l*
2 Everyone lies to his neighbor;
  their flattering lips speak with deception.*m*

3 May the LORD cut off all flattering lips
  and every boastful tongue
4 that says, "We will triumph with our tongues;
  we own our lips*z* —who is our master?"*n*

5 "Because of the oppression of the weak
  and the groaning of the needy,
 I will now arise," says the LORD.
  "I will protect them from those who malign
  them."*o*
6 And the words of the LORD are flawless,*p*
  like silver refined in a furnace of clay,
  purified seven times.*

---

y Probably a musical term.—z Or / *our lips are our plowshares.*

l Ps 14:3; 116:11; Isa 57:1; 59:15; Mac 7:2.—m Ps 28:3; 55:21; Isa 59:3-4; Jer 9:8.—n Ps 31:18; Sir 5:3.—o Ps 44:24; Isa 33:10.—p Ps 18:30; 19:7; Pr 30:5.

Ps 12 The psalmist, surrounded by the treachery and arrogance of sinners (see Mic 7:1-7), calls for help and is certain that God will judge them as their iniquity reaches its zenith. The words of the Lord can be fully relied on, whereas the boastful words of the adversaries are completely futile.

We Christians can make this supplication our own, for we feel deeply every disorder in the social realm. Eager for justice, we are outraged by every injustice, every disloyalty and fraud in social relations.

The words *For the director of music* in the superscription are thought to be a musical or liturgical notation; for *according to sheminith,* see introduction to Ps 6.

12:6 *Purified seven times:* the number seven signified fullness or completeness; hence the phrase means "refined through and through." The words of the Lord are absolutely pure and true (see Ps 18:30; 19:8; Pr 30:5).

7 O LORD, you will keep us safe*
   and protect us from such people forever.
8 The wicked freely strut about
   when what is vile is honored among men.

PSALM 13*

Prayer of One in Sorrow

For the director of music. A psalm of David.

1 How long,* O LORD? Will you forget me forever?
   How long will you hide your face from me?q
2 How long must I wrestle with my thoughts
   and every day have sorrow in my heart?
   How long will my enemy triumph over me?

3 Look on me and answer, O LORD my God.
   Give light to my eyes, or I will sleep in death;
4 my enemy will say, "I have overcome him,"
   and my foes will rejoice when I fall.r

5 But I trust in your unfailing love;
   my heart rejoices in your salvation.
6 I will sing to the LORD,s
   for he has been good to me.*

q Ps 6:3; 42:9; 44:24; 77:7; 79:5; 89:46; 94:3; Dt 31:17; La 5:20. —r Ps
25:2; 38:16.—s Ps 7:17; 116:7.

12:7-8 The psalmist voices his confidence that, although the wicked are at
present lording it over the righteous, God will take care of the latter.

Ps 13 The suffering psalmist cries out to God in despair over his impending
death and the triumph of his enemies. Suddenly (perhaps after a religious experience of some kind), his tone changes; he speaks from a heart brimming with
complete trust in God and voices his joy and gratitude.

In praying this psalm, we can think of Christ in his abandonment on the cross
and provisional defeat by death, in the face of his enemies' ephemeral success.
We too experience the critical trial of God's silence and apparent absence. Far
from weakening our confidence in God, this eventuality should strengthen it.

The words *For the director of music* in the superscription are thought to be a
musical or liturgical notation.

13:1 *How long:* see note on Ps 6:3. *Hide your face:* when God hides his face, the
righteous become concerned (see Ps 30:7; 104:29), for when God's face shines on
people it brings deliverance and blessings (see Ps 31:16; 67:1; 80:3; 119:135).

13:6 The Septuagint and Vulgate add another line: "I will sing to the name of
the LORD most high."

PSALM 14*

Corruption and Punishment of the Godless

For the director of music. Of David.

¹ The fool[a] says in his heart,
"There is no God."
They are corrupt, their deeds are vile;[t]
there is no one who does good.*

² The LORD* looks down from heaven
on the sons of men[u]
to see if there are any who understand,[v]
any who seek God.
³ All have turned aside,
they have together become corrupt;
there is no one who does good,[w]
not even one.*

⁴ Will evildoers never learn—
those who devour my people as men eat
bread[x]
and who do not call on the LORD?*[y]

a The Hebrew words rendered *fool* in Psalms denote one who is morally deficient.

t Ps 10:4; 36:1; Isa 32:6; Jer 5:12; Mic 7:2; Zep 1:12.—u Ps 11:4; 102:19; Job 41:34.—v 2b-3: Ro 3:11-12.—w Ps 12:1; 1 Sa 8:3.—x Ps 27:2; Isa 9:11.—y Ps 79:6; 82:5.

Ps 14 The psalmist envisions the world divided into "the fools" (also termed "evildoers") and "the company of the righteous" (also termed "the poor" and "my people"). Although the fools act as though there is no God and persecute the righteous, the psalmist is confident that God will eventually punish evildoers and reward the righteous. Ps 53 is a somewhat revised duplicate of this psalm.

When Paul rereads this psalm, he will see in it a description of our sinful condition. No one is just in God's sight; we all need to be saved by Jesus Christ (Ro 3:10-25).

The words *For the director of music* in the superscription are thought to be a musical or liturgical notation.

14:1 Elsewhere the psalmists included themselves among those who are not righteous in God's eyes (see Ps 130:3; 143:2; see also 1 Ki 8:39; Job 9:2; Ecc 7:20).

14:2 *The LORD:* in contrast with what "the fool" (v. 1) thinks, the Lord is very much in evidence and has his eyes on the whole earth. *Who seek God:* see Ps 15 for a description of those who truly seek God.

14:3 After this verse, many Greek and Latin manuscripts add the Old Testament citations that were first combined in Ro 3:13-18.

14:4 Evildoers live by the violence of their own doing rather than by reliance on the Lord (see Ps 10:2-4).

5 There they are, overwhelmed with dread,
for God is present in the company of the
righteous.*
6 You evildoers frustrate the plans of the poor,*
but the LORD is their refuge.

7 Oh, that salvation for Israel would come out
of Zion!z
When the LORD restores the fortunes of his
people,
let Jacob rejoice and Israel be glad!*

PSALM 15*

The Righteous: Guests of God

A psalm of David.

1 LORD, who may dwell in your sanctuary?a
Who may live on your holy hill?*

2 He whose walk is blameless*
and who does what is righteous,
who speaks the truth from his heartb
3 and has no slander on his tongue,

---

z Ps 85:1; 126:1.—a Ps 24:3-6; Isa 56:7; Mic 6:6-8.—b Ps 119:1; Eph 1:4.

14:5 God is present in the company of the righteous and, anytime he wishes, strikes sudden terror in the hearts of the wicked (see Dt 28:67; 1 Sa 14:15; 2 Ch 14:13; Job 3:25). *Righteous:* see note on Ps 1:5.

14:6 *Poor:* see note on Ps 22:26.

14:7 The righteous poor are identified with God's people.

Ps 15 The psalmist presents a summary of moral conduct in the form of an instruction to those who have access to God at his temple (see Ps 24:3-6; Isa 33:14-16; Mic 6:6-8). He indicates that sanctity of life is necessary for those who wish to approach God and emphasizes the social virtues of justice and charity.

In praying this psalm, Christians keep in mind that by becoming man the Word has pitched his tent among us (see Jn 1:14), and in his body dwells the fullness of the divinity. In close contact and in profound communion with the Body of Jesus, of whom she is the visible extension on earth, the Church constitutes the dwelling of God in the world (see 1 Co 3:16f).

15:1 *Holy hill:* an ancient designation for the temple, the place where God dwells (see Ps 2:6; 3:4; 43:3; 48:1).

15:2-5 It is not sacrifices or ritual purity but moral righteousness that gives access to the Lord (see the basic covenantal law: Ex 20:1-17; see also Isa 1:10-17; 33:14-16; 58:6-10; Jer 7:2-7; Eze 18:5-9; Hos 6:6; Am 5:14f, 21-24; Mic 6:6-8; Zec 7:9f; 8:16f). *Those who fear the LORD:* a frequent expression in the Psalter

who does his neighbor no wrong
and casts no slur on his fellowman,
⁴ who despises a vile man
but honors those who fear the LORD,
who keeps his oath
even when it hurts,
⁵ who lends his money without usury
and does not accept a bribe against the in-
nocent.ᶜ

He who does these things
will never be shaken.

PSALM 16*

God the Supreme Good

A *miktam*ᵇ of David.

¹ Keep me safe, O God,
for in you I take refuge.ᵈ

² I said to the LORD, "You are my Lord;
apart from you I have no good thing."

---

b—Probably a literary or musical term.

c Ex 22:25; 23:8.—d Ps 2:12; 25:20.

(see, e.g., Ps 115:11), it refers to those who fear God and live in accordance with his will because of their reverence for him. Later it will take on a technical sense and refer to proselytes to Judaism not yet circumcised (see Ac 2:11; 10:2). *Usury:* laws dealing with interest on loans are found in Ex 22:25-27; Lev 25:35-37; Dt 15:7-11; 23:19f). In general, interest for profit was not to be charged to Israelites. Jesus went even further (see Lk 6:34f).

Ps 16 A prayer for safekeeping, pleading for the Lord's protection against the threat of death. It could also be called a psalm of trust. This psalm prepares the way for belief in an everlasting life with God. And it is easy to see how early Christian preachers could understand the final verses as a detailed prophecy of the Resurrection of Christ (Ac 2:24-28; 13:25).

This psalm is in a special way the prayer of those who have "chosen God" in one or other form of consecrated life. Rarely has the joy of a life lived in the presence of God been expressed with such enthusiasm. The wonder felt penetrates to the innermost being of the believer (that is, the "heart," which for the ancients was the seat of one's thoughts as well as desires and affections).

The meaning of *miktam* in the superscription is unknown. Some translate it as "song" or "poem"; others suggest that it means "in a low voice."

3 As for the saints who are in the land,
>they are the glorious ones in whom is all
>my delight.^{c}
4 The sorrows of those will increase
>who run after other gods.
>I will not pour out their libations of blood
>or take up their names* on my lips.

5 LORD, you have assigned me my portion and
>my cup;*
>you have made my lot secure.^{e}
6 The boundary lines have fallen for me in
>pleasant places;
>surely I have a delightful inheritance.

7 I will praise the LORD, who counsels me;
>even at night my heart instructs me.
8 I have set the LORD always before me.
>Because he is at my right hand,
>I will not be shaken.^{f}

9 Therefore my heart is glad and my tongue re-
>joices;*
>my body also will rest secure,
10 because you will not abandon me to the grave,^{d}
>nor will you let your Holy One*^{e} see decay.^{g}

---

c Or *As for the pagan priests who are in the land / and the nobles in whom all delight I said.*—d Hebrew *Sheol.*—e Or *your faithful one.*

e Ps 23:5; 73:26; Nu 18:20; Dt 10:9; Sir 45:20-22; La 3:24.—f Ps 15:5; 73:23; 121:5; Ac 2:25-28.—g Ps 28:1; 30:3; 49:15; 86:13; Nu 16:30; Hos 13:14; Jnh 2:6; Ac 13:35.

16:4 *Take up their names:* that is, appeal to or worship them (see Jos 23:7).

16:5 *Cup:* a metaphor referring to what the host offers his guests to drink. To the righteous the Lord offers a cup of blessings (see Ps 23:5) or salvation (see Ps 116:13), but he makes the wicked drink from a cup of wrath (see Jer 25:15; Rev 14:10; 16:19).

16:9-11 The Lord, in whom the psalmist takes refuge, wills life for him (hence he has made known to him the path of life, v. 11) and will not abandon him to the grave, even though "flesh and . . . heart . . . fail" (Ps 73:26). But implicit in these words of assurance (if not actually explicit) is the confidence that, with the Lord as his refuge, even the grave cannot rob him of life (see Ps 17:15; 73:24). If this could be said of David, how much more of David's promised Son! So Peter quotes vv. 8-11 and declares that with these words David prophesied of Christ and his Resurrection (Ac 2:25-28; see Paul's similar use of v. 10b in Ac 13:35).

16:10 *Holy One:* the reference is first of all to David, but the psalm is ultimately fulfilled in Christ.

[11] You have made[f] known to me the path of life;
    you will fill me with joy in your presence,
    with eternal pleasures at your right hand.

PSALM 17*

Prayer in Time of Persecution

A prayer of David.

[1] Hear, O LORD, my righteous plea;
    listen to my cry.
  Give ear to my prayer—
    it does not rise from deceitful lips.
[2] May my vindication come from you;
    may your eyes see what is right.

[3] Though you probe my heart* and examine
    me at night,
  though you test me, you will find nothing;
  I have resolved that my mouth will not sin.[h]
[4] As for the deeds of men—
    by the word of your lips*
  I have kept myself
    from the ways of the violent.
[5] My steps have held to your paths;
    my feet have not slipped.[i]

[6] I call on you, O God, for you will answer me;
    give ear to me and hear my prayer.

---

f Or *You will make.*

h Ps 26:2; 139:23; Job 7:18; 23:10.—i Ps 18:36; 44:18; Job 23:11-12.

Ps 17 Here again we have a picture of smug and pitiless people whose heart is closed to the word of God as well as to the cry of the poor. The psalmist who endures their unjust accusations begs God to show forth his innocence and to punish his evil accusers. He is willing to leave earthly goods to them (v. 14) as long as he can rejoice in God's presence. Perhaps we can see in this desire for awakening enlightened by God's face (v. 15) the burgeoning hope of the resurrection.

In praying this psalm, we should recall that in the Church (his Mystical Body) and in each Christian (as in a part of that Body), Jesus relives the mystery of his undeserved Passion and glorious Resurrection (see Ac 9:4f).

17:3 *Heart:* see note on Ps 4:7.

17:4 *Word of your lips:* God's revelation by which he made known the "paths" his faithful are to follow.

7 Show the wonder of your great love,
    you who save by your right hand
       those who take refuge in you from their foes.
8 Keep me as the apple of your eye;*j*
    hide me in the shadow of your wings*
9 from the wicked who assail me,*k*
    from my mortal enemies who surround me.

10 They close up their callous hearts,
    and their mouths* speak with arrogance.
11 They have tracked me down, they now sur-
    round me,
    with eyes alert, to throw me to the ground.
12 They are like a lion hungry for prey,
    like a great lion crouching in cover.

13 Rise up, O LORD, confront them, bring them
    down;*
    rescue me from the wicked by your sword.
14 O LORD, by your hand save me from such
    men,
    from men of this world whose reward is in
    this life.*

You still the hunger of those you cherish;
    their sons have plenty,
    and they store up wealth for their children.
15 And I—in righteousness I will see your face;*
    when I awake, I will be satisfied with see-
    ing your likeness.*l*

---

j 8-9: Ps 36:7; 57:1; 61:4; 63:7; 91:4; Dt 32:10; Ru 2:12; Pr 7:2; Zec 2:12; Mt 23:37.—k 9b-12: Ps 10:9; 22:13, 21; 35:17; 57:4; 58:6; Job 4:10-11.—l Ps 4:6; 31:16; 67:1; 73:25-26; 80:13; Nu 6:25; Da 9:17; Rev 22:4.

17:8 *Apple of your eye . . . shadow of your wings:* conventional Hebrew metaphors for protection (see Dt 32:10; Pr 7:2; Isa 49:2).
17:10 *Mouths:* see note on Ps 5:9. *Speak with arrogance:* see note on Ps 10:7.
17:13 *Bring them down:* see note on Ps 5:10 and introduction to Ps 35.
17:14 *From men . . . life:* or: "from mortals whose part in life is transitory." *You still . . . children:* or: "With your treasures you fill their bellies; / their sons are enriched / and bequeath their abundance to their little ones."
17:15 *See your face:* see note on Ps 11:7. *When I awake:* from the night of death; however, inasmuch as death is often compared to sleep (see Ps 76:5; Da 12:1f), it may refer to a new awakening after death.

PSALM 18*

Thanksgiving for God's Help

For the director of music. Of David the servant of the
LORD. He sang to the LORD the words of this song
when the LORD delivered him from the hand of all
his enemies and from the hand of Saul. He said:

1 I love you, O LORD, my strength.[m]

2 The LORD is my rock,* my fortress and my
   deliverer;
   my God is my rock, in whom I take refuge.
   He is my shield and the horn[g] of my salvation, my stronghold.[n]

3 I call to the LORD, who is worthy of praise,
   and I am saved from my enemies.

4 The cords of death entangled me;
   the torrents of destruction overwhelmed me.

5 The cords of the grave[h] coiled around me;
   the snares of death* confronted me.[o]

---

g *Horn* here symbolizes strength.—h Hebrew *Sheol.*

---

m 1-50: 2 Sa 22:1-51.—n Ps 3:3; 28:8; 31:2-3; 42:9; Ge 49:24; Dt
32:4.—o Ps 88:8; 93:3-4; 116:3-4; Nu 16:33f; Pr 13:14.

Ps 18 This song of David occurs also in 2 Sa 22 with minor variations. It is
composed of an introduction (vv. 1-3), a conclusion (vv. 46-50), and three major
divisions: (1) the Lord's deliverance from mortal enemies (vv. 4-19); (2) the
moral grounds for the Lord's help (vv. 20-29); and (3) the Lord's help recounted
(vv. 30-45).

Already emerging in this splendid psalm, which is both a song of thanksgiving
and a song of victory, is the image of the King-Messiah, Jesus, born of the house
of David and beloved Son of the Father; he will conquer the forces of evil. This
poem is a festal song expressing wonder and thanksgiving and glorifying God.

To the extent that we can allow ourselves to be identified with Christ and become
kings in him (see Ps 2), we can use this psalm to praise God the Father for the wonders that Paul celebrates in the hymn of the Letter to the Ephesians (1:3-15).

The words *For the director of music* in the superscription are thought to be a
musical or liturgical notation.

18:2 *Rock:* a common symbol for God indicating his strength as a refuge or as
a deliverer (see Ps 19:14; 31:2f; 42:9; 62:2, 7; 71:3; 78:35; 89:26; 94:22; 95:1; Dt
32:15; Isa 17:10). See Jesus' use of the word in Mt 16:18. *Horn:* see NIV textual
note and Dt 33:17; Jer 48:25; it often had Messianic overtones (see Ps 132:17;
Eze 29:21).

18:5 *Cords of the grave . . . snares of death:* the psalmist had been in the grip
of death and a prisoner of the grave (see Ps 116:3; Job 36:8).

6 In my distress I called to the LORD;
I cried to my God for help.
From his temple* he heard my voice;
my cry came before him, into his ears.[p]

7 The earth trembled and quaked,*
and the foundations of the mountains shook;[q]
they trembled because he was angry.
8 Smoke rose from his nostrils;
consuming fire came from his mouth,
burning coals blazed out of it.
9 He parted the heavens and came down;
dark clouds were under his feet.[r]
10 He mounted the cherubim* and flew;
he soared on the wings of the wind.
11 He made darkness his covering, his canopy around him—
the dark rain clouds of the sky.
12 Out of the brightness of his presence clouds advanced,
with hailstones and bolts of lightning.[s]
13 The LORD thundered from heaven;[t]
the voice of the Most High resounded.[i]
14 He shot his arrows* and scattered [the enemies],
great bolts of lightning and routed them.[u]

i Some Hebrew manuscripts and Septuagint (see also 2 Samuel 22:14); most Hebrew manuscripts *resounded, / amid hailstones and bolts of lightning.*

p Ps 30:2; Jnh 2:2.—q Ps 97:3-4; 99:1; Jdg 5:4-5; Isa 64:1; Jer 10:10; Hab 3:9-11.—r Ps 50:3; 104:3; 144:5; Isa 64:1.—s Ps 104:2; Ex 13:21; 19:16; Dt 4:11.—t Ps 29; 77:18; Ex 19:19; Job 36:29-30; 37:3-4.—u Ps 144:6; Wis 5:21; Rev 4:5.

18:6 *Temple:* God's heavenly dwelling where he is enthroned (see Ps 11:4; 113:5; Isa 6:1; 40:22).

18:7-15 In these powerful images the ancients sang of the presence and glory of God in creation and in events (see Ps 67:8f; 97:2-5; Ex 19:15-18; Jdg 5:4f; Job 36:29f; Isa 30:27f; Hab 3:3-15). The description gives a presentiment of the struggle at the end of time in which God triumphs.

18:10 *Cherubim:* winged beings, represented at the entrance of Mesopotamian temples. Two stood on the ark of the covenant (see Ex 25:18; 1 Ki 6:23-28). God was regarded as enthroned on them (see Ps 80:1; 99:1) and riding upon the storm clouds (see Ps 104:3) or upon the cherubim.

18:14 *Arrows:* shafts of lightning (see Ps 77:17; 144:6; Hab 3:11).

15 The valleys of the sea were exposed
    and the foundations of the earth laid bare
at your rebuke, O LORD,*
    at the blast of breath from your nostrils.ᵛ

16 He reached down from on high and took hold
        of me;ʷ
    he drew me out of deep waters.*
17 He rescued me from my powerful enemy,
    from my foes, who were too strong for me.
18 They confronted me in the day of my disaster,
    but the LORD was my support.
19 He brought me out into a spacious place;
    he rescued me because he delighted in me.

20 The LORD has dealt with me according to my
        righteousness;*
    according to the cleanness of my hands he
        has rewarded me.ˣ
21 For I have kept the ways of the LORD;*
    I have not done evil by turning from my God.
22 All his laws are before me;
    I have not turned away from his decrees.
23 I have been blameless before him
    and have kept myself from sin.
24 The LORD has rewarded me according to my
        righteousness,
    according to the cleanness of my hands in
        his sight.

25 To the faithful you show yourself faithful,
    to the blameless you show yourself blame-
        less,ʸ

---

v Ps 77:16; Ex 15:8; Zec 9:14.—w Ps 144:7; Ex 15:5.—x Ps 26:1; 1 Sa
26:23; Job 22:30.—y Ps 31:23; 125:4.

18:15 The psalmist may be referring to the wondrous deed God accomplished
at the Red Sea during the Exodus (see Ex 14:15-22).
  18:16 *Deep waters:* symbols of great danger (see Ps 32:6; 40:2; 42:7; 66:12;
69:2, 14; 88:17; 130:1; Job 22:11; Isa 30:28; Jnh 2:5f).
  18:20 *Righteousness:* see note on Ps 1:5.
  18:21 *Ways of the LORD:* see note on Ps 25:10.

²⁶ to the pure you show yourself pure,
> but to the crooked you show yourself
> shrewd.*
²⁷ You save the humble
> but bring low those whose eyes are
> haughty.ᶻ
²⁸ You, O LORD, keep my lamp burning;*
> my God turns my darkness into light.ᵃ
²⁹ With your help I can advance against a troop;ʲ
> with my God I can scale a wall.

³⁰ As for God, his way is perfect;
> the word of the LORD is flawless.
> He is a shield
> for all who take refuge in him.ᵇ
³¹ For who is God besides the LORD?
> And who is the Rock except our God?ᶜ
³² It is God who arms me with strength
> and makes my way perfect.
³³ He makes my feet like the feet of a deer;
> he enables me to stand on the heights.ᵈ
³⁴ He trains my hands for battle;ᵉ
> my arms can bend a bow of bronze.*
³⁵ You give me your shield of victory,
> and your right hand sustains me;
> you stoop down to make me great.
³⁶ You broaden the path beneath me,
> so that my ankles do not turn.ᶠ

---

j Or *can run through a barricade.*

z Job 22:29; Pr 3:34; Mt 23:12.—a Ps 27:1; 36:9; 43:3; 119:105; 132:17; Job 29:3; Mic 7:8.—b Ps 12:6; 77:13; Dt 32:4; Pr 30:5.—c Ps 35:10; Isa 44:8; 45:21.—d Dt 32:13; Isa 58:14; Hab 3:19.—e Ps 144:1.—f Ps 17:5; 31:8.

18:26 God treats people the way they treat him and others. *The crooked:* those who stray from the straight way of the Lord. *Show yourself shrewd:* the LORD counters the evil acts of the wicked one after the other.
18:28 *Keep my lamp burning:* a figure of life and happiness (see 1 Ki 11:36). *Light:* see note on Ps 27:1.
18:34 *Bow of bronze:* a bow difficult to bend that would shoot arrows with greater force.

37 I pursued my enemies and overtook them;
  I did not turn back till they were destroyed.
38 I crushed them so that they could not rise;
  they fell beneath my feet.
39 You armed me with strength for battle;
  you made my adversaries bow at my feet.
40 You made my enemies turn their backs in
    flight,
  and I destroyed my foes.
41 They cried for help, but there was no one to
    save them—
  to the LORD, but he did not answer.
42 I beat them as fine as dust borne on the
    wind;
  I poured them out like mud in the streets.

43 You have delivered me from the attacks of
    the people;
  you have made me the head of nations;
  people I did not know are subject to me.
44 As soon as they hear me, they obey me;
  foreigners cringe before me.
45 They all lose heart;
  they come trembling from their strong-
    holds.*g*

46 The LORD lives! Praise be to my Rock!
  Exalted be God my Savior!*h*
47 He is the God who avenges me,
  who subdues nations under me,*i*
48   who saves me from my enemies.
  You exalted me above my foes;
  from violent men you rescued me.
49 Therefore I will praise you among the na-
    tions, O LORD;*j*
  I will sing praises to your name.*

---

g Mic 7:17; Heb 12:3.—h Ps 21:13; 144:1.—i Ps 20:6; 144:2.—j Ps 7:17;
9:11; 30:4; 57:9; 135:3; 146:2; Ro 15:9.

18:49 This text is cited by Paul (Ro 15:9) as a prediction of the conversion of
the Gentiles.

⁵⁰ He gives his king great victories;
     he shows unfailing kindness to his
        anointed,*
     to David and his descendants forever.ᵏ

PSALM 19*

God's Glory in Creation

For the director of music. A psalm of David.

¹ The heavens declare the glory of God;*
     the skies proclaim the work of his hands.ˡ
² Day after day they pour forth speech;
     night after night they display knowledge.
³ There is no speech or language
     where their voice is not heard.ᵏ
⁴ Their voiceˡ goes out into all the earth,
     their words to the ends of the world.*

---

k Or *They have no speech, there are no words; / no sound is heard from them.*—l Septuagint, Jerome and Syriac; Hebrew *line.*

k Ps 89:4, 28-37; 144:10; 1 Sa 2:10.—l Ps 8:1; 50:6; 89:5; 97:6; 147:4-5; Ge 1:1-8.

18:50 *He shows unfailing kindness to his anointed:* the Lord is mindful of his covenant with his anointed king and never ceases bestowing blessings upon him. This is even more true of the King and Anointed par excellence, Jesus Christ.

Ps 19 The universe is a hymn to the glory of the Lord, but this is even more true of the Mosaic Law. The silent revelation of creation is offered to all human beings, but the Law, privilege of Israel, reveals to the hearts of believers God's perfection, justice, truth, and goodness and engages them to imitate the divine life.

The ode to the sun in this psalm (vv. 4-6) seems to be an imitation of a fragmentary Assyrian text in which the sun-god rises from the ocean and passes through the gates of the east to meet the goddess. The Christmas liturgy uses this image to recall, in poetic language, the coming to earth of the Son of God.

By its splendor and vastness, the star-studded heavens teach us the glory, the splendor and infinite power, the prodigious artistry of the Father, the Son, and the Holy Spirit who work together in its continuous creation. The Law, perfect as far as its epoch and its place in the divine economy of salvation are concerned, was brought to its absolute perfection by Christ (see Mt 5:17).

The words *For the director of music* in the superscription are thought to be a musical or liturgical notation.

19:1-4a The heavens show forth the glory of their Creator to all peoples (see Ps 148:3).

19:4a Paul interprets this proclamation of the heavens as referring also to the proclamation of the Gospel (see Ro 10:18).

In the heavens he has pitched a tent for the
sun,*
5   which is like a bridegroom coming forth
from his pavilion,
like a champion rejoicing to run his course.
6 It rises at one end of the heavens
and makes its circuit to the other;
nothing is hidden from its heat.

7 The law of the LORD is perfect,
reviving the soul.
The statutes of the LORD are trustworthy,
making wise the simple.*m
8 The precepts of the LORD are right,
giving joy to the heart.*
The commands of the LORD are radiant,
giving light to the eyes.
9 The fear of the LORD* is pure,
enduring forever.
The ordinances of the LORD are sure
and altogether righteous.
10 They are more precious than gold,
than much pure gold;
they are sweeter than honey,n
than honey from the comb.*

---

m Ps 12:6; 119:142; Jer 1:25.—n Ps 119:103, 127; Sir 24:19.

19:4b-6 The heavens are the divinely pitched tent for the lordly sun—widely worshiped in the ancient Near East (see Dt 4:19; 17:3; 2 Ki 23:5, 11; Jer 8:2; Eze 8:16), but here a mere creature of God (as in Ge 1:16; Ps 136:7f). Of the created realm, the sun is the supreme metaphor of the glory of God (see Ps 84:11; Isa 60:19f), as it makes its daily triumphant sweep across the whole extent of the heavens and pours out its heat (felt presence) on every creature. The literature of the time applied to the sun the six synonyms for God's revelation in vv. 8-11.

19:7 *The simple:* those who are inexperienced and hence childlike (see Ps 119:98-100; Pr 1:4); the New Testament shows that heavenly wisdom is a gift to "little children," hidden from the worldly wise (see Lk 10:21; 1 Co 1:18ff; 2:8-10; 2 Ti 3:15).

19:8 *Heart:* see note on Ps 4:7.

19:9 *Fear of the LORD:* see note on Ps 15:2-5.

19:10 See Ps 119:103, 127. This entire hymn to the Law is closely connected to the long Psalm 119.

¹¹ By them is your servant warned;
    in keeping them there is great reward.

¹² Who can discern his errors?
    Forgive my hidden faults.
¹³ Keep your servant also from willful sins;
    may they not rule over me.
  Then will I be blameless,
    innocent of great transgression.

¹⁴ May the words of my mouth and the medita-
        tion of my heart
    be pleasing in your sight,
  O LORD, my Rock and my Redeemer.*

PSALM 20*

Prayer in Praise of the Messiah King

For the director of music. A psalm of David.

¹ May the LORD answer you when you are in
        distress;
    may the name* of the God of Jacob protect
        you.

19:14 This meditation is presented to the Lord as a praise offering (see Ps 50:14; 104:33).

Ps 20 During a liturgy of prayer for the king just before he engages in battle with a powerful foe (2 Ch 20:6), the people (perhaps the assembled soldiers) pray for their king: is he not a "messiah," that is, an "anointed one" of the Lord (v. 6) and the head of the chosen people of the God of Jacob (v. 2)? A choir chants the petition (vv. 2-5) and a soloist (perhaps a Levite: see 2 Ch 20:14) responds (vv. 6-8); he announces assurance that the prayer will be heard, for Israel does not rely on the force of arms as its pagan neighbors do but on its God and Savior. Thus, the people already celebrate the coming triumph of the Lord.

In praying this psalm, we can ask the Father to grant the integral victory of Christ in his mystical members, just as he gained it in and for himself (see 1 Co 15:22f). For the Father is the accomplisher of all things (see Ro 11:36).

The words *For the director of music* in the superscription are thought to be a musical or liturgical notation.

20:1 *Name:* see note on Ps 8:1. *Protect you:* literally, "raise you to a high, safe place."

2 May he send you help from the sanctuary
and grant you support from Zion.*[o]
3 May he remember* all your sacrifices
and accept your burnt offerings. *Selah*
4 May he give you the desire of your heart*
and make all your plans succeed.
5 We will shout for joy when you are victorious
and will lift up our banners in the name of our God.*
May the Lord grant all your requests.

6 Now I know that the LORD saves his anointed;*
he answers him from his holy heaven
with the saving power of his right hand.[p]
7 Some trust in chariots and some in horses,[q]
but we trust in the name of the LORD our God.*
8 They are brought to their knees and fall,
but we rise up and stand firm.[r]

9 O LORD, save the king!
Answer[m] us when we call!

---

m Or *save! / O King, answer.*

---

o Ps 30:10; 128:5; 134:3.—p Ps 18:50; 28:8; 144:10; 1 Sa 2:10.—q Ps 147:10-11; 1 Sa 17:45; 2 Ch 14:10; Pr 21:31; Isa 31:1; 36:9; 40:30-31; Hos 1:7.—r Ps 27:2; Isa 40:30.

20:2 *Zion:* see note on Ps 9:11.

20:3 *Remember:* with God remembering and acting go together (see Ge 8:1; Ex 2:24).

20:4 *Heart:* see note on Ps 4:7.

20:5 *We will shout . . . name of our God:* see note on Ps 7:17. The Hebrew word "victorious" could also be translated as "saved."

20:6 *His anointed:* i.e., the king of Israel (see Ps 2:2; 132:10); the divine help is his as intrinsic to his kingship (see Ps 18:50).

20:7 The force of arms is nil in the face of the divine power. The Prophets were always against the use of horses and chariots in Israel, in imitation of the neighboring pagans (see Dt 17:16; Isa 31:1; Hos 1:7; Mic 5:10; Zec 12:4). The same affirmation occurs in Ps 33:16f; 147:10; Pr 21:31.

PSALM 21*

Thanksgiving for Messianic Blessings

For the director of music. A psalm of David.

¹ O LORD, the king rejoices in your strength.
   How great is his joy in the victories you
       give!ˢ
² You have granted him the desire of his heart*
   and have not withheld the request of his
       lips.   *Selah*
³ You welcomed him with rich blessings*
   and placed a crown of pure gold on his
       head.
⁴ He asked you for life, and you gave it to
       him—
   length of days, for ever and ever.ᵗ
⁵ Through the victories you gave, his glory is
       great;
   you have bestowed on him splendor and
       majesty.*

---

s Ps 63:11; 2 Sa 22:51.—t 1 Ki 3:14; 2 Ki 20:1-7; Isa 38:1-20.

Ps 21 One would have a poor understanding of feasts if one did not allow chants to intermingle desires and reality. On a feast, the king appears to share the privileges of God: authority, long rule, and majesty, for the Lord has blessed and established him to save his people from their foes. The history of Israel will more than once give the lie to this ideal figure of the monarch. The Church sees therein the traits of Jesus Christ, King and Savior of the People of God; upon him resides the blessing for the whole world. The psalm continued to be sung in Israel even when the kingship ended after the sixth century A.D.—but this time concerning a future Messianic King.

By a very simple spiritual transposition, this psalm enables us to sing of the divine blessings granted to Christ, especially his Resurrection, and to hope for his complete and decisive triumph over his enemies (the devil, sin, and death).

The words *For the director of music* in the superscription are thought to be a musical or liturgical notation.

21:2 *Heart:* see note on Ps 4:7.

21:3 *You welcomed him with rich blessings:* as you once welcomed Abraham (see Ge 12:2) and Joseph (see Ge 48:20). *Placed a crown . . . on his head:* alludes either to his own crown reinforcing his kingship after his victory or to the crown of the king that he had defeated (see 2 Sa 12:30). This verse is eminently applied to the Messiah (see Ps 45:4; 72:17; 2 Sa 7:29; 1 Ch 17:27).

21:5 *Glory . . . splendor and majesty:* like those of the heavenly King (see Ps 96:3).

⁶ Surely you have granted him eternal blessings*
   and made him glad with the joy of your
   presence.
⁷ For the king trusts in the LORD;
   through the unfailing love* of the Most
   High
   he will not be shaken.

⁸ Your hand will lay hold on all your enemies;*
   your right hand will seize your foes.
⁹ At the time of your appearing*
   you will make them like a fiery furnace.
   In his wrath the LORD will swallow them up,
   and his fire will consume them.
¹⁰ You will destroy their descendants from the
   earth,
   their posterity from mankind.*
¹¹ Though they plot evil against you
   and devise wicked schemes, they cannot
   succeed;
¹² for you will make them turn their backs
   when you aim at them with drawn bow.

¹³ Be exalted, O LORD, in your strength;*
   we will sing and praise your might.ᵘ

---

u Ps 18:1; Nu 10:35.

21:6 *Eternal blessings:* this phrase may refer to blessings of enduring value or
an unending number of blessings. *Your presence:* God's favor, which is the greatest cause of joy inasmuch as it is the supreme blessing, which leads to all
others.
   21:7 *Unfailing love:* see note on Ps 6:4.
   21:8-12 The king's future victories are described as certain because of the
Lord's action.
   21:9 The expression *at the time of your appearing,* literally, "on the day of your
face [judgment]" (see Ps 34:16; La 4:16) and the mention of the fire are eschatological themes (see Ps 2:12; 2 Sa 23:7; Isa 30:33; Hos 7:7; Mal 4:1).
   21:10 The foes of the king will have no descendants to make war on him.
   21:13 The word "strength" in the concluding verse connects the theme with
the opening verse: O LORD, assert your strength in which "the king rejoices" (v. 1),
and we will offer you our praise.

PSALM 22*

Suffering and Triumph of the Messiah

For the director of music. To [the tune of] "The Doe of the
Morning." A psalm of David.

1 My God, my God, why have you forsaken
me?*
   Why are you so far from saving me,
      so far from the words of my groaning?ᵛ
2 O my God, I cry out by day, but you do not
answer,
   by night, and am not silent.*ʷ

3 Yet you are enthroned as the Holy One;ˣ
   you are the praise of Israel.ⁿ
4 In you our fathers put their trust;
   they trusted and you delivered them.
5 They cried to you and were saved;
   in you they trusted and were not disap-
pointed.ʸ

---

n Or *Yet you are holy, / enthroned on the praises of Israel.*

v Ps 10:1; Job 3:24; Isa 49:14; 54:7; Mt 27:46; Mk 15:34.—w Ps 42:3;
Sir 2:10.—x Ps 71:22; Isa 6:3.—y Ps 25:3; Isa 49:23; Da 3:28; Ro 9:33.

Ps 22 This psalm draws its inspiration from the "Songs of the Suffering Righteous Man" (Isa 52:13—53:12) and from the "Confessions of Jeremiah" (Jer
15:15; 17:15; 20:7); it ends, as they do, with the proclamation that the sufferings
of the righteous man will restore life to humanity. Such a text seems planned, as
it were, to become the prayer of Christ (Mk 15:34), and the Gospels have also sin-
gled out details from it that describe in advance the Passion of Jesus (e.g., Mt
27:35, 39, 43; Jn 19:23f, 28). The author of Hebrews even placed the words of v.
22 on the lips of Jesus (Heb 2:12). Indeed, no other psalm is so often quoted in
the New Testament.

In praying this psalm, we can keep in mind that Christ continues to pray it
through the Church and Christians, since he continues the mystery of his abandonment in his Mystical Body.

The words *For the director of music* in the superscription are thought to be a
musical or liturgical notation; about *To[the tune of]*, nothing is known.

22:1-11 Why? The question erupts from the heart of a righteous man. Yesterday he was still enjoying God's favor as a son, but now he feels abandoned for no
reason and afflicted with atrocious sufferings and made the laughingstock of
free-thinkers. Has God changed?

22:2 *And am not silent:* the Hebrew text is obscure here. Some translate: "You
do not heed me" or "No relief is forthcoming."

⁶ But I am a worm and not a man,*
  scorned by men and despised by the peo-
    ple.ᶻ
⁷ All who see me mock me;ᵃ
  they hurl insults, shaking their heads:*
⁸ "He trusts in the Lord;ᵇ
  let the Lord rescue him.
 Let him deliver him,
  since he delights in him."*

⁹ Yet you brought me out of the womb;
  you made me trust in you
   even at my mother's breast.
¹⁰ From birth I was cast upon you;*
  from my mother's womb you have been
    my God.ᶜ
¹¹ Do not be far from me,
  for trouble is near
   and there is no one to help.ᵈ

¹² * Many bulls* surround me;
  strong bulls of Bashan encircle me.
¹³ Roaring lions tearing their prey
  open their mouths wide against me.ᵉ

---

z Ps 31:11; Isa 53:3.—a Ps 35:16; 109:25; Mt 27:39; Mk 15:29; Lk
23:36.—b Ps 71:11; 91:14; Wis 2:18-20; Mt 27:43.—c Ps 71:6; Ge 50:23;
Isa 44:2; 46:3.—d Ps 35:22; 38:21; 40:13; 71:12.—e Ps 17:12; Job 4:10;
Eze 22:25; 1 Pe 5:8.

22:6 *I am a worm and not a man:* this passage clearly depicts the psalmist's
sense of isolation (see Job 25:6; Isa 41:14).

22:7 *Hurl insults, shaking their heads:* words and gestures of scorn, also in-
dulged in by Christ's foes on Calvary (see Mt 27:39; Mk 15:29). See also note on
Ps 5:9.

22:8 Cited in Mt 27:43. *Since he delights in him:* may be taken as "since God
delights in the sufferer" or "since the sufferer delights in God."

22:10 *From birth I was cast upon you:* the father customarily acknowledged
the newborn by taking it upon his knees (see Ge 50:23; Job 3:12).

22:12-21 Around the beleaguered man there arises a wave of hostility; he experiences in his flesh the whole of human sorrow. The images are delusive, and
the cries become pathetic. Here is a man whose life is being taken away.

22:12f, 16 *Bulls . . . lions. . . . Dogs:* these are metaphors for the enemies.
Bashan: a land east of the Jordan that was noted for its good pasturage and the
size and quality of its animals (see Dt 32:14; Eze 39:18; Am 4:1).

14 I am poured out like water,
    and all my bones are out of joint.
My heart has turned to wax;
    it has melted away within me.
15 My strength is dried up like a potsherd,
    and my tongue sticks to the roof of my
       mouth;
    you lay me*o* in the dust of death.*
16 Dogs have surrounded me;
    a band of evil men has encircled me,
    they have pierced*p* my hands and my feet.*
17 I can count all my bones;*
    people stare and gloat over me.*f*
18 They divide my garments among them*g*
    and cast lots for my clothing.*

19 But you, O LORD, be not far off;
    O my Strength, come quickly to help me.
20 Deliver my life from the sword,
    my precious life from the power of the
       dogs.
21 Rescue me from the mouth of the lions;
    save*q* me* from the horns of the wild
       oxen.*h*

o Or / *I am laid.*—p Some Hebrew manuscripts, Septuagint and Syriac; most Hebrew manuscripts / *like the lion.*—q Or / *you have heard.*

f Ps 109:24; Mic 7:8.—g Lev 16:8; Mt 27:35; Mk 15:24; Lk 23:34; Jn 19:24.—h Ps 7:1-2; 17:12; 35:17; 57:4; 58:6; Job 4:10; 2 Ti 4:17.

22:15 *The dust of death:* the netherworld, domain of the dead; the author is using the language of his day, as in Mesopotamian descriptions of the netherworld (see Job 7:9, 21).
22:16 *Pierced my hands and my feet:* his limbs are wounded by the dogs as he seeks to fend off their attacks (see also Isa 53:5; Zec 12:10; Jn 19:34). Although the phrase finds its complete fulfillment in Christ's crucifixion, it is not expressly used by the Evangelists in the Passion account.
22:17 *I can count all my bones:* this could also be translated as "I must display all my bones." The meaning is that one is attacked and stripped of his garments (see v. 18).
22:18 Explicitly cited in Jn 19:24 as a prophecy fulfilled in the action of the soldiers who divided Christ's garments among them on Calvary.
22:21 *Save me:* see NIV textual note for alternative translation: "you have heard me." The psalmist knows he has been heard and will be delivered from death.

²² I will declare your name to my brothers;*
   in the congregation I will praise you.*ⁱ*
²³ You who fear the LORD, praise him!
   All you descendants of Jacob, honor him!
   Revere him, all you descendants of Israel!
²⁴ For he has not despised or disdained
   the suffering of the afflicted one;
   he has not hidden his face* from him
   but has listened to his cry for help.

²⁵ From you comes the theme of my praise in
   the great assembly;
   before those who fear you*ʳ* will I fulfill my
   vows.
²⁶ * The poor* will eat and be satisfied;
   they who seek the LORD will praise him—
   may your hearts live forever!*ʲ*
²⁷ All the ends of the earth
   will remember and turn to the LORD,
   and all the families of the nations
   will bow down before him,*ᵏ*
²⁸ for dominion belongs to the LORD
   and he rules over the nations.*ˡ*

---

r Hebrew *him*.

i Ps 26:12; 35:18; 40:10; 68:26; 109:30; 149:1; 2 Sa 22:50; Heb 2:12.—j
Ps 23:5; 69:33; 107:9.—k Ps 86:9; 102:22; Job 13:11; Isa 45:22; 52:10;
Zec 14:16.—l Ps 47:7; 103:19; Ob 21; Zec 14:9.

22:22-31 God reverses the righteous man's condition; his hope returns. In the
temple, he celebrates his deliverance and offers a sacrifice of communion amidst
the poor who love God. Then the perspective is enlarged even more. The whole
earth gives thanks to God who rules the world and dispenses justice. The poor are
called to the table of God, and the line of the righteous shall never be extinguished from the midst of human beings. Indeed, the passion of the righteous
man has changed something in the human world.

22:24 *Hidden his face:* a metaphor for God withdrawing from someone (see Ps
13:1; 27:9; 69:17; 88:14; 102:2; 143:7; Isa 8:17; Mic 3:4).

22:26-31 In an allusion to the Messianic Banquet (see Ps 23:5; Pr 9:1f; Isa
25:6; 55:1; 65:13), the psalmist describes a worldwide company of people from
every state in life who will ultimately take up God's praise from age to age. It
constitutes one of the grandest visions of the scope of the worshipers who will
come to praise the saving acts of the Lord.

22:26 *The poor:* the *anawim,* originally the poor who depended on God for their
livelihood; later, the humble, pious, and devout—those who hoped in God alone.

[29] All the rich of the earth will feast and worship;

all who go down to the dust will kneel before him—

those who cannot keep themselves alive.

[30] Posterity will serve him;

future generations will be told about the
LORD.

[31] They will proclaim his righteousness

to a people yet unborn—

for he has done it.*[m]

PSALM 23*

Prayer to the Good Shepherd

A psalm of David.

[1] The LORD is my shepherd, I shall not be in
want.[n]

[2] He makes me lie down in green pastures,*

he leads me beside quiet waters,

[3] he restores my soul.*

---

m Ps 48:13-14; 71:18; 78:6; 102:18; Isa 53:10; Eph 2:7.—n Ps 80:1;
95:7; 100:3; Dt 2:7; Eze 34:2; Jn 10:11.

22:29-31 *Those who cannot keep themselves alive . . . for he has done it:* the
more common translation (and the one found in the new Vulgate) is: "and I will
live for the LORD. . . . This is the LORD's doing."

Ps 23 This psalm is a profession of joyful trust in the Lord as the good Shepherd-King that has become one of the world's greatest prayers. The image of God
in shepherd's garb has parallels in the Prophets (see Isa 40:11; Eze 34:11-16)
and will be the best known of the allegories in which Jesus speaks of himself (see
Jn 10:11-18), so much so that the New Testament writers love to give him this
title (see Heb 13:20; 1 Pe 2:25; Rev 7:17). The water, oil, and cup of wine of
which the text speaks made Christians think of the Sacraments of initiation:
Baptism, Confirmation, and Eucharist. As a result, the psalm used to be sung
during the Easter Vigil by the newly baptized, who were filled with the joy of God.

In praying this psalm, we can dwell on the fact that the heavenly Father's love
embraces us from eternity, preparing for us in Christ all kinds of spiritual blessings: election, adoption, redemption, incorporation into Christ (see Eph 1:3-14).
He watches over us solicitously (see Mt 6:25-34) and follows us through the Good
Shepherd who seeks out the straying sheep until he finds it again (see Lk 15).

23:2 *Green pastures:* a symbol for everything that makes life flourish. *Quiet
waters:* literally, "waters of resting places," waters that bring refreshment and
well-being (see Isa 49:10).

He guides me in paths of righteousness
for his name's sake.[o]
4 Even though I walk
through the valley of the shadow of death,*[s]
I will fear no evil,
for you are with me;
your rod and your staff,
they comfort me.[p]

5 You prepare a table* before me
in the presence of my enemies.[q]
You anoint my head with oil;
my cup overflows.*[r]
6 Surely goodness and love* will follow me
all the days of my life,
and I will dwell in the house of the LORD
forever.[s]

---

s Or *through the darkest valley.*

---

o Ps 115:1; Pr 4:11.—p Ps 107:14; Job 10:21; Isa 50:10.—q Ps 22:26; 63:5; 92:10.—r Ps 16:5.—s Ps 27:4; Ne 9:25.

23:3 *Restores my soul:* the Lord revitalizes the psalmist's spirit (see Ps 19:7; Ru 4:15; Pr 25:13; La 1:16). *Paths of righteousness:* paths that conform to the will of the Lord, the "right way."

23:4 *Valley of the shadow of death:* another possible translation is: "through the darkest valley." It refers to any situation that is death-threatening.

23:5-6 What was only a comparison used by the psalmist to indicate the happiness of those who dwell in the house of the Lord has become a wonderful reality in the New Covenant. God sets the table for all who as members of his Church seek rest and protection in the house of God during their pilgrimage. He gives them the Bread of Heaven and the cup of his love and the riches of his grace—Christ's Precious Blood and the anointing of the Spirit with his sevenfold gifts.

23:5 In the ancient Near East, covenants were frequently made at a meal (see Ps 41:9; Ge 31:54; Ob 7). *Anoint my head with oil:* reception customarily accorded to an honored guest at a banquet (see Lk 7:46; see also 2 Sa 12:20; Ecc 9:8; Da 10:3). *Cup:* the same image is found in Ps 16:5; 75:8; 116:13. This verse indicates that the Messianic Banquet (see Ps 22:26) is reserved for the righteous; the wicked are excluded from it (see Isa 65:13f).

23:6 *Goodness and love:* the terms often refer to blessings of God's covenant with Israel; here they are personified (see Ps 25:21; 43:3; 79:8; 89:14). *Days of my life:* see Ps 25:10; 27:4. *Forever:* this word could mean "throughout the years." However, since even the pagan people surrounding Israel believed that human life continued after death in some kind of shadowy existence in the netherworld (see notes on Ps 11:7; 16:9-11), the word "forever" legitimately can be taken in its true sense.

PSALM 24*

The Lord's Solemn Entry into Jerusalem

Of David. A psalm.

1 The earth is the LORD's, and everything in it,[t]
    the world, and all who live in it;*
2 for he founded it upon the seas
    and established* it upon the waters.[u]

3 Who may ascend the hill of the LORD?
    Who may stand in his holy place?[v]
4 He who has clean hands and a pure heart,*
    who does not lift up his soul to an idol
    or swear by what is false.[t]
5 He will receive blessing from the LORD
    and vindication from God his Savior.
6 Such is the generation of those who seek him,
    who seek your face, O God of Jacob.[u] *Selah*

---

t Or *swear falsely.*—u Two Hebrew manuscripts and Syriac (see also Septuagint); most Hebrew manuscripts *face. Jacob.*

t Ps 50:12; 89:11; Dt 10:14; Isa 66:1-2; 1 Co 10:26.—u Ps 75:3; 136:6; Isa 42:5.—v Ps 15:1; 65:4.

Ps 24 A procession wends its way toward the temple; perhaps it bears the ark of the covenant to the holy place. Chants are expressed. They acclaim the Creator and thus recall the conditions for a true participation in worship: "clean hands and a pure heart" (vv. 3-6). At the entrance to the sanctuary, the cortege comes to a halt as the participants take time to meditate wonderingly about the presence of God. They must needs celebrate God the Vanquisher who takes possession of his holy dwelling; the titles given him (vv. 8-10) evoke the time when, represented by the ark, the Lord would take his place at the head of the armies of Israel and lead them to victory (Nu 10:35; Jos 6).

This psalm is well adapted to celebrating feasts of the Lord and to calling for the coming of his kingdom. It is also a psalm that makes demands, since it tells us of the conditions required for receiving the kingdom of God. The Church has always used this psalm in celebrating Christ's Ascension into the heavenly Jerusalem and into the sanctuary on high.

24:1 See Ps 89:12; Dt 10:14. This text is cited in 1 Co 10:26.

24:2 *Founded . . . established:* a metaphor taken from the founding of a city. Extra-Biblical records indicate that temples were regarded as microcosms of the created world; hence language applicable to temples was also applicable to the earth.

24:4 *Clean hands . . . pure heart:* those who do no evil and think no evil. Jesus said that the "pure in heart . . . will see God" (Mt 5:8).

7 * Lift up your heads, O you gates;*
   be lifted up, you ancient doors,
   that the King of glory may come in.*w*

8 Who is this King of glory?
   The LORD strong and mighty,
   the LORD mighty in battle.

9 Lift up your heads, O you gates;
   lift them up, you ancient doors,
   that the King of glory may come in.

10 Who is he, this King of glory?
   The LORD Almighty*—
   he is the King of glory.   *Selah*

PSALM 25*v

Prayer for Guidance and Help

Of David.

1 To you, O LORD, I lift up my soul;*x
2   in you I trust, O my God.*y

---

v This psalm is an acrostic poem, the verses of which begin with the successive letters of the Hebrew alphabet.

w Ps 118:19-20; Eze 44:2; Mal 3:1.—x Ps 86:4; 143:8.—y Ps 71:1.

24:7-10 These verses speak of the arrival of the Lord, the King of glory, at his sanctuary in Zion after his victorious journey from Egypt. "The LORD Almighty" (v. 10), "the LORD mighty in battle" (v. 8; see Ex 15:1-18), has routed his enemies and now comes in triumph to his own city (see Ps 46; 48; 76; 87).

24:7, 9 *Lift up your heads, O you gates . . . you ancient doors:* the gates and doors are personified in accord with extra-Biblical parallels.

24:10 *The LORD Almighty:* in Hebrew, "the Lord of hosts" or "armies" *(Yahweh Sabaoth).* The expression suggests, first of all, the God who leads the Israelite army, therefore the Almighty who is surrounded by angels and stars and who controls the cosmic forces; then the expression becomes simply a way of emphasizing the greatness and power of God.

Ps 25 One admires the inner quality of the righteous man who addresses himself to God in this alphabetical psalm. He does not believe that he is free of taking false steps and is convinced that he deserves his wretchedness and his isolation, because of his sins. His confession testifies to much uprightness and honesty. It is the attitude of a humble person who knows he is loved by God and remains trusting in him; he hopes to receive pardon, counsel, and assistance from the Lord. The theme of this beautiful prayer is given in the cry of hope in vv. 1-2, which the Liturgy puts on the lips of Christians at the beginning of Advent.

In praying this psalm, we can dwell on the fact that in his unfailing love God is pleased to lead us back to the right path when we go astray and to keep us on it. Christ gives us salvation through the remission of sins (see Lk 1:77-79).

25:1-3 Prayer for relief from distress and the ensuing slander from one's foes.

Do not let me be put to shame,
nor let my enemies triumph over me.
³ No one whose hope is in you
will ever be put to shame,
but they will be put to shame
who are treacherous without excuse.ᶻ

⁴ Show me your ways, O LORD,*
teach me your paths;ᵃ
⁵ guide me in your truth and teach me,
for you are God my Savior,
and my hope is in you all day long.
⁶ Remember, O LORD, your great mercy and
love,
for they are from of old.ᵇ
⁷ Remember not the sins of my youth
and my rebellious ways;
according to your love remember me,
for you are good, O LORD.ᶜ

⁸ Good and upright is the LORD;*
therefore he instructs sinners in his ways.
⁹ He guides the humble in what is right
and teaches them his way.
¹⁰ All the ways of the LORD* are loving and
faithful
for those who keep the demands of his
covenant.
¹¹ For the sake of your name,* O LORD,
forgive my iniquity, though it is great.

---

z Ps 22:5; Isa 24:16; 49:23; Da 3:40.—a Ps 27:11; 86:11; 119:12, 35;
143:8, 10; Ex 33:13; Jn 14:6.—b Ps 98:3; Sir 51:8.—c Ps 106:4; Job 13:26;
Isa 64:8.

25:4-7 Prayer for guidance and pardon. *Your ways:* that is, "your commandments" (see Ps 27:11; 86:11; 143:8).
25:8-15 Trust in the Lord's covenant blessings.
25:10 *Ways of the LORD:* God's manner of dealing kindly with those who remain faithful to the covenant (see Ps 103:7; 138:5). See also Ps 85:9; Ge 32:10; Dt 33:9; and Paul's magnificent summary in Ro 8:28: "We know that in all things God works for the good of those who love him."
25:11 *Name:* see note on Ps 8:1.

12 Who, then, is the man that fears the LORD?*d*
    He will instruct him in the way chosen for
    him.*
13 He will spend his days in prosperity,*e*
    and his descendants will inherit the land.*
14 The LORD confides in those who fear him;*
    he makes his covenant known to them.
15 My eyes are ever on the LORD,
    for only he will release my feet from the
    snare.*f*

16 Turn to me and be gracious to me,*
    for I am lonely and afflicted.*g*
17 The troubles of my heart* have multiplied;
    free me from my anguish.
18 Look upon my affliction and my distress
    and take away all my sins.
19 See how my enemies have increased
    and how fiercely they hate me!
20 Guard my life and rescue me;
    let me not be put to shame,
    for I take refuge in you.
21 May integrity and uprightness protect me,
    because my hope is in you.

22 Redeem Israel, O God,
    from all their troubles!*

---

d Job 1:8; Pr 19:23.—e Ps 37:9, 29; Isa 57:13.—f Ps 123:2; 141:8; Heb
12:2.—g Ps 6:4; 86:16; 119:132.

25:12 *The way chosen for him:* may also be translated as: "the way he should choose."
25:13 *Inherit the land:* according to the teaching of the sages, God rewards the righteous here below by bestowing on them earthly goods that he withholds from the wicked (see Ps 37:9, 29; Pr 19:23). To this is added the returned exiles' hope for the enjoyment of the land of their ancestors (see Isa 57:13; 60:21; 65:9).
25:14 *The LORD confides in those who fear him:* some translations have "The LORD confides *his secret* to those who fear him," which is to be understood as divine intimacy and friendship (see Ps 73:28; Ex 33:11; Job 29:4; Pr 3:32; Jn 15:5) united with the understanding of divine things (see Jer 16:21; 31:34; Hos 6:6).
25:16-21 Renewed prayer for relief from distress and foes.
25:17 *Heart:* see note on Ps 4:7.
25:22 Concluding prayer on behalf of all God's people. *Redeem:* i.e., "deliver."

PSALM 26*

Prayer for the Righteous

Of David.

1 Vindicate me, O LORD,
    for I have led a blameless life;
I have trusted in the LORD
    without wavering.*h*

2 Test me, O LORD, and try me,
    examine my heart and my mind;*i*

3 for your love is ever before me,
    and I walk continually in your truth.*j*

4 I do not sit with deceitful men,
    nor do I consort with hypocrites;

5 I abhor the assembly of evildoers
    and refuse to sit with the wicked.

6 I wash my hands in innocence,*
    and go about your altar, O LORD,*k*

---

h Ps 15:2; 59:3.—i Ps 7:9; 17:3; 139:23.—j Ps 86:11; 119:30.—k Ps 73:13; Dt 21:6-7; Mt 27:4.

Ps 26 This psalm is a prayer for God's discerning mercies to spare his faithful servant from the death that overtakes the wicked. In the psalms of supplication, we often hear this protestation from those accused who call upon God to bear witness to their innocence. The prayer that we now read is perhaps that of a Levite, but certainly of a man who loves the life of the temple. He is very sure of his rectitude in the face of the agitation of others. Possibly he is also quite conscious of the faults that everyone has in his life.

He teaches us a great certainty: it is better to throw ourselves upon the judgment of God than to let ourselves be crushed by the judgment of others. This believer, who is at ease in the temple to praise the Lord, loves a clear and decided fidelity. Who would fail to be attracted by such a desire for uprightness and sincerity before God!

In praying this psalm, we can recall that since we share by faith and Baptism in the mystery of Christ dead and risen, our old self has been crucified with Christ so that the sinful body might be destroyed and we might cease to be enslaved by sin. Divested of our old nature and invested with the new nature of Christ who becomes all in all (see Col 3:9-11), we share in his holiness and irreproachable innocence before God, being purified from all injustice (see Ro 8:1; 1 Jn 1:9).

26:6 *Wash my hands in innocence:* a liturgical action (see Ex 30:19, 21; 40:31f), which symbolized both inner and outer cleanliness (see Isa 1:16). Those who come to God must have "clean hands and a pure heart" (Ps 24:4). *Go about your altar:* celebrating God's saving acts beside his altar was regarded as a public act of devotion in which assembled worshipers could be invited to participate (see Ps 43:4).

⁷ proclaiming aloud your praise
and telling of all your wonderful deeds.
⁸ I love the house where you live, O LORD,ˡ
the place where your glory dwells.*

⁹ Do not take away my soul along with sinners,ᵐ
my life with bloodthirsty men,*
¹⁰ in whose hands are wicked schemes,
whose right hands are full of bribes.
¹¹ But I lead a blameless life;ⁿ
redeem me and be merciful to me.º

¹² My feet stand on level ground;*
in the great assembly I will praise the LORD.ᵖ

PSALM 27*

Trust in God, Our Light and Salvation

Of David.

¹ The LORD is my light* and my salvation—
whom shall I fear?

---

l Ps 29:9; 63:2; 96:6; Ex 24:16; 25:8.—m Ps 28:3; 139:19.—n Ps
101:6.—o Ps 25:16; 31:5.—p Ps 22:22; 35:18; 40:10; 52:9; 149:1.

26:8 *Where your glory dwells*: the presence of God's glory meant the presence
of God himself (see Ex 24:16; 33:22). His glory dwelt in the tabernacle (see Ex
40:35) and later in the temple (see 1 Ki 8:11). Jn 1:14 places that same presence
in the Word made flesh who "made his dwelling among us."
26:9 A premature death was a divine chastisement (see Ps 5:6; 28:4; 55:23).
26:12 *Level ground*: where there is safety and no danger of falling. *Assembly*:
worshiping at the sanctuary (as in Ps 1:5; 22:25; 35:18; 40:9f; 111:1; 149:1).
Ps 27 Although enemies or the difficulties of existence may be multiplied, the
believer finds a sure refuge in God—such is the cry of trust that opens this
psalm. Then the movement of the prayer deepens, becoming the search and avid
desire for God. It is at the temple that one discovers the presence of the Lord in
the sacrifice, chant, supplication, and the Law. If such a search becomes necessary for life, will not God be present to his most forsaken and pressured servant?
In praying this psalm, we can place a similar confidence in God and the Lord
Jesus, one capable of enabling us to overcome all adversity and death itself.
27:1 *The LORD is my light*: "light" often symbolizes happiness and well-being
(see Ps 18:28; 36:9; 43:3; 97:11) or life and salvation (see Isa 9:2; 49:6; 58:8; Jer
13:16; Am 5:18-20), whose source is the Lord (see Isa 10:17; Mic 7:8f).

The LORD is the stronghold of my life—
　　of whom shall I be afraid?^q

² When evil men advance against me
　　to devour my flesh,*^w
when my enemies and my foes attack me,
　　they will stumble and fall.^r

³ Though an army besiege me,
　　my heart will not fear;
though war break out against me,
　　even then will I be confident.*

⁴ One thing I ask of the LORD,
　　this is what I seek:
that I may dwell in the house of the LORD
　　all the days of my life,^s
to gaze upon the beauty of the LORD
　　and to seek him in his temple.*

⁵ For in the day of trouble
　　he will keep me safe in his dwelling;
he will hide me in the shelter of his taberna-
　　cle*^t
　　and set me high upon a rock.

⁶ Then my head will be exalted
　　above the enemies who surround me;
at his tabernacle will I sacrifice* with shouts
　　of joy;
I will sing and make music to the LORD.

---

w Or *to slander me.*

q Ps 9:9; 18:28; 36:9; 43:3; 56:4; Isa 10:17; Mic 7:8.—r Ps 14:4; Job 19:22.—s Ps 23:6; 42:2; 61:4.—t Ps 31:20; Rev 7:15-16.

27:2 *To devour my flesh:* the psalmist's enemies are like rapacious beasts (see Ps 7:2; 17:12; 22:12f, 16); in the figurative sense, this refers to calumny (see Da 3:8).

27:3 With the Lord as his stronghold and helper, the psalmist fears nothing— not even an army arrayed against him. So long as this strong union with God remains unbroken, the psalmist is secure. *Heart:* see note on Ps 4:7.

27:4 Tarrying in the house of the Lord is an expression and sign of spiritual union with God and intimacy with him. *Beauty of the LORD:* i.e., his goodness (see Ps 90:17).

27:5 *Dwelling . . . tabernacle:* references to the sanctuary of Jerusalem (see Rev 7:15f). See also Ps 31:20; 32:7; 61:4; 91:1.

27:6 *Will I sacrifice:* see note on Ps 7:17.

7 Hear my voice when I call, O LORD;*
  be merciful to me and answer me.
8 My heart says of you, "Seek his[x] face!"*
  Your face, LORD, I will seek.[u]
9 Do not hide your face from me,
  do not turn your servant away in anger;
  you have been my helper.
Do not reject me or forsake me,
  O God my Savior.
10 Though my father and mother forsake me,[v]
  the LORD will receive me.*
11 Teach me your way, O LORD;
  lead me in a straight path
  because of my oppressors.[w]
12 Do not turn me over to the desire of my foes,
  for false witnesses rise up against me,
  breathing out violence.

13 I am still confident of this:
  I will see the goodness of the LORD*
  in the land of the living.[x]
14 Wait for the LORD;
  be strong and take heart
  and wait for the LORD.

---

x Or *To you, O my heart, he has said, "Seek my.*

u Ps 24:6; 105:4; Hos 5:15. —v Isa 49:15; Jer 31:20; Hos 11:8. —w Ps 5:8; 25:4; 86:11. —x Ps 116:9; 142:5; Isa 38:11.

27:8 *Seek his face:* an idiom meaning to commune with the Lord, originating in the custom of pilgrimages to sacred places (see Ps 24:6; 105:4; 2 Sa 21:1; Hos 5:15). It then took on the general sense of seeking to know the Lord, anticipate his desires, and live in his presence. In a word, to seek the Lord is to serve him faithfully (Dt 4:29-31).

27:10 Union with God gives confidence in prayer; and prayer is something that even the most devout person must do. Sirach says: "Pray in [the LORD's] presence" (17:20) and "Let nothing hinder you from discharging your vows [i.e., your prayer]" (18:22).

27:13 *Goodness of the LORD:* the good things promised in the covenant with David (see 2 Sa 7:28). *Land of the living:* reference to this life or to the temple (see Ps 52:5; 116:9; Isa 38:11), where the God of life is present; in short, the psalmist is speaking of the world of the living as opposed to the world of the dead.

PSALM 28*

Thanksgiving for Supplications Heard

Of David.

¹ To you I call, O LORD my Rock;* ʸ
    do not turn a deaf ear to me.
For if you remain silent,
    I will be like those who have gone down to
       the pit.*ᶻ
² Hear my cry for mercy
    as I call to you for help,
as I lift up my hands*
    toward your Most Holy Place.ᵃ

³ Do not drag me away with the wicked,ᵇ
    with those who do evil,*
who speak cordially with their neighbors
    but harbor malice in their hearts.ᶜ

---

y Ps 18:2.—z Ps 30:3; 88:4; 143:7; Dt 1:45; Pr 1:12.—a Ps 5:7; 134:2; 1
Ki 8:48.—b Ps 26:9.—c Ps 12:2; 55:21; 62:4; Pr 26:24-28; Jer 9:8.

Ps 28 The psalmist calls upon God and curses his persecutors; such vehemence indicates that he is close to the end of his strength. He sends us out and
Lord finally hears his servant; after anguish here is the thanksgiving. The concluding formula transforms the psalm into a prayer for Israel, the "anointed
one," that is, the people consecrated (v. 8) to the service of God. Believers will
one day refuse the sentiments of vengeance that spring up here from the experience of the oppressed psalmist; for God could not indistinctly combine honesty
with wrongdoing.

In praying this psalm, we should keep in mind that in this life Christ does not
normally answer our desire for escape or special privilege. He sends us out and
immerses us in the world and its tribulations (see Jn 17:18; 15:18—16:4) after
his election has drawn us out of it (see Jn 15:19). Yet we already foresee victory,
for the same divine power that raised Christ from the dead will raise us also and
lead our humanity into a state of glory (see Eph 1:17-20).

28:1 *Rock:* the Lord is the Rock, who gives strength and sustenance to his
people and provides refuge for them (see Ps 18:2 and note; 19:14; 27:5; 73:26;
92:15; 144:1). *Pit:* metaphor for the grave.

28:2 *Lift up my hands:* the usual posture for prayer (see Ps 63:4; 134:2;
141:2). *Most Holy Place:* the innermost part of the temple, the Holy of Holies,
which contained the ark of the covenant and was looked upon as the place of
God's presence on earth (see 1 Ki 6:16, 19-23; 8:6-8).

28:3 The psalmist prays that the Lord will deliver him from his adversities (see
Ps 26:9-12) so that he will not be numbered with the wicked nor judged with
them.

⁴ Repay them for their deeds*
    and for their evil work;
  repay them for what their hands have done
    and bring back upon them what they de-
      serve.ᵈ
⁵ Since they show no regard for the works of
      the LORD
    and what his hands have done,
  he will tear them down
    and never build them up again.ᵉ

⁶ Praise be to the LORD,
    for he has heard my cry for mercy.*
⁷ The LORD is my strength and my shield;
    my heart trusts in him, and I am helped.
  My heart leaps for joy
    and I will give thanks to him in song.*

⁸ The LORD is the strength of his people,
    a fortress of salvation for his anointed
      one.*
⁹ Save your people and bless your inheritance;
    be their shepherd* and carry them for-
      ever.

---

d 2 Sa 3:39; Jer 50:29.—e Isa 5:12; 52:5.

28:4-5 The wicked have not learned to respond to the Lord and his wondrous deeds in redemptive history ("what his hands have done"). Therefore, they will be judged according to "what their hands have done." Justice requires that evil be removed so that its power will be completely voided. See note on Ps 5:10 and introduction to Ps 35.
28:6 The psalmist gives praise to the Lord for having heard his prayer; this will result in righteous judgment and vindication.
28:7 No longer does the psalmist feel threatened to the point of despairing. He is overjoyed and jubilant because he knows that the Lord will come to his aid as his strength (see Ex 15:2) and his shield (see Ps 3:3). *Heart:* see note on Ps 4:7. *I will give thanks:* see note on Ps 7:17.
28:8 *Anointed one:* here the reference seems to be to the entire people of God, which is consecrated to his service (see Ps 105:15; Ex 19:6; Hab 3:13).
28:9 *Be their shepherd:* a theme found also in Ps 80:1; Isa 40:11; Jer 31:10; Eze 34; Mic 5:4. The Lord answered this prayer by sending the Good Shepherd, Jesus Christ (Jn 10:11, 14), who died for his sheep.

PSALM 29*

God's Majesty in the Storm

A psalm of David.

¹ Ascribe to the LORD, O mighty ones,*
    ascribe to the LORD glory and strength.
² Ascribe to the LORD the glory due his name;
    worship the LORD in the splendor of his^y
    holiness.^{f}

³ The voice of the LORD* is over the waters;
    the God of glory thunders,
    the LORD thunders over the mighty waters.
⁴ The voice of the LORD is powerful;
    the voice of the LORD is majestic.^{g}
⁵ The voice of the LORD breaks the cedars;
    the LORD breaks in pieces the cedars of
    Lebanon.*
⁶ He makes Lebanon skip like a calf,
    Sirion*^{z} like a young wild ox.

---

y Or *LORD with the splendor of.*—z That is, Mount Hermon.

f Ps 68:34; 96:7-9; 1 Ch 16:29.—g Ps 46:6; 77:18-19; 104:7; Job 37:4; Isa 30:30; Eze 10:5.

Ps 29 The psalmist sings a hymn of praise to the Lord, the King of creation, evoking his power and glory in the storm that terrifies the foes of Israel, while sparing the chosen people. He concludes by asking the Lord to give similar power to the king and to Israel.

We can pray this psalm in the knowledge that the voice of God has acquired a body in Christ Jesus, living Word of the Father. It calls upon all who are in heaven, on earth, and in the netherworld to attribute to Christ all glory and power, and to adore him alone.

29:1 *Mighty ones:* literally, "sons of God," which in the beginning probably referred to the pagan deities but later came to be understood as referring to the angels (see Ps 82:1; 89:7; Job 1:6). To eliminate the polytheistic meaning of the expression, the Septuagint and Vulgate added immediately after "mighty ones" the line "bring to the LORD the offspring of rams." This passage is sometimes applied to Israel, the son of God (see Ex 4:22; Dt 14:1; see Ac 17:28).

29:3 *The voice of the LORD:* this phrase appears seven times in imitation of the sound of thunder and symbolizes the power of God, the Lord of history as well as the Master of the elements, whose voice no one can resist (see Job 37:4f; Eze 10:5).

29:5 *The cedars of Lebanon:* i.e., the strongest of all trees (see Isa 2:13).

29:6 *Sirion:* a Phoenician name for Mount Hermon in northern Palestine. The mountains there were originally given the general name of Lebanon.

7 The voice of the LORD strikes
    with flashes of lightning.
8 The voice of the LORD shakes the desert;
    the LORD shakes the Desert of Kadesh.*
9 The voice of the LORD twists the oaks[a]
    and strips the forests bare.
And in his temple all cry, "Glory!"*

10 The LORD sits[b] enthroned over the flood;*
    the LORD is enthroned as King forever.[h]
11 The LORD gives strength to his people;
    the LORD blesses his people with peace.[i]

PSALM 30*

Thanksgiving for Deliverance from Death

A psalm. A song. For the dedication of the temple.[c]
Of David.

1 I will exalt you, O LORD,
    for you lifted me out of the depths*
    and did not let my enemies gloat over me.

---

a Or *LORD makes the deer give birth.*—b Or *sat.*—c Or *palace.*

h Ge 6—9; Isa 54:9; Bar 3:3.—i Ps 68:5; Da 7:27.

29:8 *The Desert of Kadesh:* probably a border location in southern Palestine; some believe it is a location north of Palestine near Lebanon and Mount Hermon.

29:9 The cry of "Glory!" takes place either in heaven (v. 2) or in the temple of Jerusalem whose liturgy echoes the heavenly praises.

29:10 *Enthroned over the flood:* a reference to God's control of the unruly primordial waters (see Ge 1:2, 6-10) or to his sending of the flood (see Ge 6:17), which was the first manifestation of the divine justice. Thus, the Lord will know how to make the cause of his people triumph (see Job 20:28; 22:16; Isa 24:18; 59:9ff).

Ps 30 This is a psalm of thanksgiving arising out of the experience of someone who was at death's door because of an illness, compounded by feelings of haughtiness in time of prosperity and despair in times of humiliation. The Lord listened to his cry and healed him; hence the psalmist calls for praise. This psalm came to be applied to Israel itself, especially in its experience of the Exile, and was chanted at the Feast of the Dedication of the Temple in commemoration of the purification of the temple in 164 B.C. (see Ezr 6:16; 1 Mac 4:36ff).

This psalm reminds us that while we await life eternal and union with Christ, the present life with its adversities offers us the opportunity to receive from the divine goodness a cure, various deliverances, and even spiritual resurrection.

30:1 *Out of the depths:* a common Old Testament phrase of extreme distress (see Ps 69:2, 15; 71:20; 88:6; 130:1; La 3:55; Jnh 2:2) usually connected with the words "the grave" and "the pit."

2 O LORD my God, I called to you for help
   and you healed me.*
3 O LORD, you brought me up from the grave;*d
   you spared me from going down into the pit.j

4 Sing to the LORD, you saints of his;
   praise his holy name.
5 For his anger lasts only a moment,
   but his favor lasts a lifetime;
weeping may remain for a night,*
   but rejoicing comes in the morning.

6 When I felt secure, I said,
   "I will never be shaken."*
7 O LORD, when you favored me,
   you made my mountaine stand firm;
but when you hid your face,
   I was dismayed.k

8 To you, O LORD, I called;*
   to the LORD I cried for mercy:
9 "What gain is there in my destruction,f
   in my going down into the pit?
Will the dust praise you?
   Will it proclaim your faithfulness?
10 Hear, O LORD, and be merciful to me;
   O LORD, be my help."

---

d Hebrew *Sheol.*—e Or *hill country.*—f Or *there if I am silenced.*

j Ps 28:1; Nu 16:33; 1 Sa 2:6; Jnh 2:6.—k Ps 104:29; Dt 31:17.

30:2 *You healed me:* other passages that proclaim God as a healer are: Ps 103:3; 107:20; Hos 6:1; 7:1; 11:3; 14:5.

30:3 *Grave:* symbol for a life-threatening experience (see Ps 18:5; Jnh 2:2). *Pit:* metaphor for the grave.

30:5 *Remain for a night:* literally, "come in at evening to lodge," like a guest seeking a night's rest.

30:6 *When I felt secure . . . I will never be shaken:* security brings forgetfulness of God (see Dt 8:8-10; Hos 13:6; Pr 30:9). The secure psalmist spoke the very words of the wicked in Ps 10:6 and so lost the blessing promised to the righteous (see Ps 15:5).

30:8-10 In the stillness and inactivity of the pit, no one gives praise to God; the psalmist prays to be delivered so that he may rejoin those who worship the Lord (see Ps 6:5; 88:10-12; 115:17; Isa 38:18).

[11] You turned my wailing into dancing;
> you removed my sackcloth* and clothed
> me with joy,[l]
[12] that my heart* may sing to you and not be
silent.
> O LORD my God, I will give you thanks for-
> ever.

PSALM 31*

Prayer of Trust and Thanksgiving

For the director of music. A psalm of David.

[1] In you, O LORD, I have taken refuge;*
> let me never be put to shame;[m]
> deliver me in your righteousness.
[2] Turn your ear to me,
> come quickly to my rescue;
> be my rock* of refuge,
> a strong fortress to save me.
[3] Since you are my rock and my fortress,
> for the sake of your name lead and guide
> me.[n]

---

l Ps 126:1-2; Est 9:22; Isa 61:3; Jer 31:13.—m 1-3: Ps 18:2; 71:1-2.—n Ps 18:2; 71:3.

30:11 *Sackcloth:* a symbol of mourning (see Ps 35:13; Ge 37:34).

30:12 *Heart:* see note on Ps 4:7.

Ps 31 Faith, distress, and gratitude alternate in this prayer, evoking the "confessions" of the prophet Jeremiah, his dolorous destiny, and his intimacy with the Lord (Jer 17:14-18; 20:7-18). At the moment of death on the cross, Jesus will use this psalm to express his trusting abandonment to the Father (see Lk 23:46).

We should be mindful that God will often place us in a situation in which we can unite our voice to that of Christ in reciting this psalm, especially by letting us share his sufferings and making us become like him in death so that we may rise with him from the dead (see Php 3:10f).

The words *For the director of music* in the superscription are thought to be a musical or liturgical notation.

31:1-8 No matter what may be the conflict in which we are enmeshed, God remains the one certitude. The images of the rock and the fortress attest to a serene and unshakable trust in God.

31:2 *Rock:* see note on Ps 18:2.

4 Free me from the trap that is set for me,
   for you are my refuge.
5 Into your hands I commit my spirit;*
   redeem me, O LORD, the God of truth.o

6 I hate those who cling to worthless idols;
   I trust in the LORD.
7 I will be glad and rejoice in your love,p
   for you saw my affliction
   and knew the anguish of my soul.*
8 You have not handed me over to the enemy
   but have set my feet in a spacious place.

9 Be merciful to me, O LORD, for I am in dis-
      tress;*
   my eyes grow weak with sorrow,
   my soul and my body with grief.
10 My life is consumed by anguish
   and my years by groaning;
   my strength fails because of my affliction,g
   and my bones grow weak.q
11 Because of all my enemies,
   I am the utter contempt of my neighbors;
   I am a dread to my friends—
      those who see me on the street flee from
      me.r
12 I am forgotten by them as though I were
      dead;
   I have become like broken pottery.*

---

g Or *guilt.*

o Isa 45:19; Lk 23:46; Ac 7:59.—p Ps 10:14; Lk 22:44.—q Ps 6:2; 32:3;
38:10.—r Ps 38:11; Job 19:13-19.

31:5 *Into your hands I commit my spirit:* last word of Christ on the cross (see
Lk 23:46) and St. Stephen (see Ac 7:59). *Spirit:* life itself.
31:7 *Soul:* see note on Ps 6:3.
31:9-18 The prayer changes tone; after serenity comes a gasping cry. The
stricken person is also one who is despised and rejected, an object of utter contempt by others. This is the despairing cry at times when we seem completely
alone.
31:12 *Like broken pottery:* a customary comparison for something that has
been rendered useless (see Isa 30:14; Jer 19:11; 22:28).

13 For I hear the slander of many;
   there is terror on every side;*
they conspire against me
   and plot to take my life.

14 But I trust in you, O LORD;
   I say, "You are my God."[s]
15 My times are in your hands;*
   deliver me from my enemies
   and from those who pursue me.
16 Let your face shine* on your servant;
   save me in your unfailing love.[t]
17 Let me not be put to shame, O LORD,*
   for I have cried out to you;
but let the wicked be put to shame
   and lie silent in the grave.[h]
18 Let their lying lips be silenced,
   for with pride and contempt
they speak arrogantly against the righteous.[u]

19 How great is your goodness,*
   which you have stored up* for those who
      fear you,
which you bestow in the sight of men
   on those who take refuge in you.

---

h Hebrew *Sheol.*

---

s Ps 4:5; 140:6; Isa 25:1.—t Ps 4:6; 67:1; Nu 6:25.—u Ps 12:3; 120:2.

31:13 *There is terror on every side:* a cry used when danger lurks (see Jer 6:25; 20:10; 46:5; 49:29).

31:15 *My times are in your hands:* God is the ultimate master of every moment of everyone's life.

31:16 *Face shine:* see note on Ps 13:1.

31:17-18 See note on Ps 5:10 and introduction to Ps 35.

31:19-24 A moment arrives when the believer experiences anew the power of God's presence. This holds good despite the mockery and false accusations of enemies, that is, the war of words that constitutes one of the greatest trials of our human relationships. Certain of God, the believer does not let himself become enmeshed in conflicts.

31:19 *Stored up:* the psalmist relies on the Lord who has stored up his goodness (his covenant promises) for his faithful ones.

²⁰ In the shelter of your presence you hide them
       from the intrigues of men;
   in your dwelling you keep them safe
       from accusing tongues.ᵛ

²¹ Praise be to the LORD,
       for he showed his wonderful love to me
       when I was in a besieged city.
²² In my alarm I said,
       "I am cut off from your sight!"
   Yet you heard my cry for mercy
       when I called to you for help.ʷ

²³ Love the LORD, all his saints!*
       The LORD preserves the faithful,
       but the proud he pays back in full.
²⁴ Be strong and take heart,
       all you who hope in the LORD.

PSALM 32*

The Joy of Being Forgiven

Of David. A *maskil.*ⁱ

¹ Blessed is he*
       whose transgressions are forgiven,
       whose sins are covered.ˣ

---

i Probably a literary or musical term.

---

v Ps 27:5; 109:3; Rev 7:15.—w Ps 116:11; Jnh 2:4.—x Ps 65:3; Pr 28:13;
Isa 1:18; Hos 14:2; Ro 4:7-8.

31:23 *Saints:* see notes on Ps 4:3 and 34:9. *The proud:* often equal to the
wicked, for the proud act as if they have no need of God and are a law to themselves (see Ps 10:2-11; 73:6; 94:2-7; Dt 8:14; Isa 2:17; Eze 28:2, 5; Hos 13:6).

Ps 32 This is the second of the seven Penitential Psalms (6; 32; 38; 51; 102;
130; 143), a joyous testimony of gratitude for God's gift of forgiveness for those
who confess their sins and follow the law of God. Instead of constantly pondering
their sins, believers acknowledge their wretchedness before God and accept forgiveness and reconciliation. Their torment ceases, and a new person is born,
overwhelmed by grace, confidence, and a sense of obedience.

  In praying this psalm, we can focus not only on the happiness resulting from
the forgiveness of particular sin but the more profound happiness obtained by
the complete victory given us by God in Christ over sin under all its forms.

  The word *maskil* in the superscription cannot be given a precise translation;
perhaps it means "teaching" or "training."

32:1-2 Joyous declaration of the happiness of having one's sins forgiven by
God (see Ps 65:4; 85:1; Job 31:33). This text is cited by Paul in Ro 4:6-8.

2 Blessed* is the man
>> whose sin the LORD does not count against
>> him
>> and in whose spirit is no deceit.

3 When I kept silent,*
>> my bones wasted away
>> through my groaning all day long.*y*

4 For day and night
>> your hand was heavy upon me;*
> my strength was sapped
>> as in the heat of summer.   *Selah*

5 Then I acknowledged my sin to you
>> and did not cover up my iniquity.
> I said, "I will confess
>> my transgressions* to the LORD"—
> and you forgave
>> the guilt of my sin. *z*   *Selah*

6 Therefore let everyone who is godly pray to
>> you
>> while you may be found;
> surely when the mighty waters rise,*a*
>> they will not reach him.*

7 You are my hiding place;
>> you will protect me from trouble
>> and surround me with songs of deliver-
>> ance.*   *Selah*

---

y Ps 6:6; 31:10.—z Ps 38:18; 51:3; Job 31:33.—a Ps 18:4; 69:13.

32:2 *Blessed:* see note on Ps 1:1.

32:3 *I kept silent:* did not confess the sin before God.

32:4 According to St. Augustine, even before penitents acknowledge their sin, God hears the cry of their heart and pardons it because of their true contrition (see 2 Sa 12:13).

32:5 *Sin . . . iniquity . . . transgressions:* these are the three most common Hebrew words for evil thoughts and actions (see Ps 51:1-2; Isa 59:12).

32:6 The psalmist encourages the godly to draw near to God; even in the greatest adversities, the Lord will protect them. *Mighty waters:* symbol of great danger (see Ps 18:16).

32:7 After receiving God's help, the psalmist will be surrounded by people celebrating this latest act of deliverance while he brings thank offerings.

8 I will instruct you and teach you in the way
    you should go;
  I will counsel you and watch over you.
9 Do not be like the horse or the mule,
    which have no understanding
  but must be controlled by bit and bridle
    or they will not come to you.
10 Many are the woes of the wicked,
    but the LORD's unfailing love*
    surrounds the man who trusts in him.

11 Rejoice in the LORD and be glad, you righ-
    teous;
    sing, all you who are upright in heart!*b

PSALM 33*

Praise of God's Providence

1 Sing joyfully to the LORD, you righteous;
    it is fitting for the upright to praise him.c
2 Praise the LORD with the harp;
    make music to him on the ten-stringed
        lyre.d
3 Sing to him a new song;*
    play skillfully, and shout for joy.

---

b Pr 33:1; 64:10; 92:1.—c Ps 5:11; 32:11; 147:1.—d Ps 92:3; 144:9; Rev
5:8.

32:10 *Unfailing love:* see note on Ps 6:4.
32:11 *Heart:* see note on Ps 4:7.
Ps 33 This psalm follows a classical pattern. First, the psalmist calls for
praise to God. Then he proclaims praise for his great deeds: his word that created
the three-tiered universe (vv. 4-9), his intervention in history when he chose his
people from among the nations (vv. 10-12), and finally his powerful help for
those who fear him (vv. 13-19). Thus, he contemplates God's work in creation, in
the history of Israel, and in the lives of the righteous. The people acclaim Providence, whose wise plan is universal in its scope.
    In Ephesians (1:9; 3:4f), Paul will explain this hidden plan of God that is car-
ried to fulfillment in Christ's Passover in order that humankind may have life and
the world may attain its goal.
    33:3 *Sing to him a new song:* celebrate God's saving deed with a new song to
make known his greatness to others and to give him praise (see Ps 7:17, and
note; 40:3; 96:1; 98:1; 144:9; 149:1; Isa 42:10; Rev 5:9; 14:3).

⁴ For the word of the LORD is right and true;
    he is faithful in all he does.
⁵ The LORD loves righteousness and justice;*ᵉ*
    the earth is full of his unfailing love.*

⁶ By the word of the LORD were the heavens
        made,*ᶠ*
    their starry host by the breath of his mouth.*
⁷ He gathers the waters of the sea into jars;*ʲ
    he puts the deep into storehouses.*ᵍ*
⁸ Let all the earth fear the LORD;*
    let all the people of the world revere him.
⁹ For he spoke, and it came to be;*
    he commanded, and it stood firm.*ʰ*
¹⁰ The LORD foils the plans of the nations;
    he thwarts the purposes of the peoples.
¹¹ But the plans of the LORD stand firm forever,
    the purposes of his heart through all gener-
        ations.*ⁱ*

---

j Or *sea as into a heap.*

---

e Ps 11:7; 119:64.—f Ge 2:1; Jn 1:1; Heb 11:3.—g Ps 78:13; Ge 1:9-10; Ex 15:8; Job 38:8.—h Ps 148:5; Ge 1:3f; Jud 16:14; Isa 48:13; Jn 1:3.—i Pr 19:21; Isa 40:8; 46:10.

33:5 The psalmist celebrates especially the perfections of the Lord. His nature and his self-revelation are in complete harmony; he is faithful ("righteous and true") in everything that he does. He also loves righteousness and justice, i.e., he carries out his plans by his verdicts, rule, and covenant relationship with his people. Furthermore, his love is evident in his works on earth; he shows the same loyalty, constancy, and love toward the rest of creation that he shows to his people (v. 22). *Unfailing love:* see note on Ps 6:4.

33:6 The Fathers of the Church applied this verse to the Blessed Trinity. *Starry host:* the stars of the sky were viewed as an army (see Neh 9:6; Isa 40:26; 45:12; Jer 33:22). See also note on Ps 24:10.

33:7 *He gathers the waters . . . into jars:* God rules the dangerous waters so easily that it is like a person putting water in a jar (see Ps 104:9; Ge 1:9f; Job 38:8-11; Pr 8:29; Jer 5:22).

33:8 The nations of the world feared many gods, each of whom reigned over the various heavenly bodies and over the land, sea, and sky. But the psalmist stresses that the Lord is the Creator-Ruler of the world and everything in it. Hence, he calls upon all nations and all peoples to fear the Lord because of his greatness and his goodness.

33:9-12 Whatever God spoke came into existence (see Heb 11:3). Everything reflects his wise rule. The nations are completely under his control (see Pr 19:21; 21:30; Isa 8:10; 19:17; 46:10f; Jer 29:11; Mic 4:12). God's providence works out his purposes.

¹² Blessed is the nation whose God is the LORD,*
    the people he chose for his inheritance.*ʲ
¹³ From heaven the LORD looks down*
    and sees all mankind;ᵏ
¹⁴ from his dwelling place he watches
    all who live on earth—
¹⁵ he who forms the hearts of all,
    who considers everything they do.
¹⁶ No king is saved by the size of his army;
    no warrior escapes by his great strength.
¹⁷ A horse is a vain hope for deliverance;
    despite all its great strength it cannot save.
¹⁸ But the eyes of the LORD are on those who
    fear him,*
    on those whose hope is in his unfailing
    love,
¹⁹ to deliver them from death
    and keep them alive in famine.

²⁰ We wait in hope for the LORD;*
    he is our help and our shield.ˡ
²¹ In him our hearts rejoice,
    for we trust in his holy name.
²² May your unfailing love rest upon us, O LORD,
    even as we put our hope in you.

---

j Ps 144:15; Ex 8:22; Dt 7:6.—k Ps 53:2; Job 34:21; Sir 15:19; Jer
16:17; 32:19.—l Ps 27:14; 115:9.

33:12-22 The psalmist now meditates on the election of God's people out of all
the nations, after he has stressed the Lord's power and steadfast carrying out of
his plans.

33:12 The Lord freely chose his people as his inheritance (see Ps 28:9; 74:2;
78:62, 71; 94:5, 14; 106:5, 40; Ex 19:5; Dt 4:20; 9:26, 29).

33:13-17 The Lord sees everything that happens on earth (vv. 13-15) and controls human destinies.

33:18-19 Success in any venture does not depend on earthly means but on
God alone, who watches over his faithful and delivers them from death and every
danger. *Eyes of the LORD:* a metaphor for the Lord's loving care.

33:20-22 The people respond by expressing a renewal of their covenant commitment. The Lord is their help and shield (see Ps 3:3; 28:7), and they trust in his
holy name, with which they associate past acts of deliverance (see Ps 30:4). They
promise to be submissive and abandon themselves to him as he works out his
plans for the establishment of his kingdom and the renewal of the earth.

PSALM 34*ᵏ

Presence of God, Protector of the Righteous

Of David. When he pretended to be insane before
Abimelech, who drove him away, and he left.

¹ I will extol the LORD at all times;*
   his praise will always be on my lips.ᵐ
² My soul* will boast in the LORD;
   let the afflicted hear and rejoice.
³ Glorify the LORD with me;
   let us exalt his name together.

⁴ I sought the LORD, and he answered me;
   he delivered me from all my fears.
⁵ Those who look to him are radiant;
   their faces are never covered with shame.
⁶ This poor* man called, and the LORD heard
   him;
   he saved him out of all his troubles.

---

k This psalm is an acrostic poem, the verses of which begin with the successive letters of the Hebrew alphabet.

---

m Ps 71:6; 145:2.

Ps 34 This alphabetical psalm has two parts. The first voices thanksgiving for
the solicitude with which God surrounds the righteous and the poor to deliver
them from their anguish. Doubtless the psalmist has experienced this in life and
gives his disciples the fruit of his experience. The second part takes the tone of
an instruction (vv. 12-22): a sage invites the listeners to discover the path to
happiness in the fear of the Lord.

The poorest of the poor and the wisest of the sages is Christ, and it is upon his
lips that we can place this psalm after the example of John (19:36), numbering
ourselves—in accord with the express indication of Peter (see 1 Pe 3:10-12)—
among the children to whom he teaches the way of life and happiness. From
Christian beginnings this psalm served to teach those who were preparing for the
Christian life and for Baptism (1 Pe 2:3).

The superscription refers to 1 Sa 21:11-15, but (probably as the result of a
scribal error) erroneously substitutes Abimelech for Achish, King of Gath.

34:1-3 The praise of the Lord is continual, God-centered, and the response of
a grateful heart—an offering that the Lord will never reject (see Ps 50:14-23;
Hos 14:2; Heb 13:15). Its purpose is to acknowledge the Lord's greatness (see Ps
30:1; 69:30; 99:5; 107:32; 145:1).

34:2 *Soul:* see note on Ps 6:3.

34:6 *Poor:* this word is usually applied to one who depends completely on God
for his deliverance and his very life. See also note on Ps 22:26.

7 The angel of the LORD* encamps around
those who fear him,
and he delivers them.[n]

8 Taste and see that the LORD is good;[o]
blessed is the man who takes refuge in
him.*

9 Fear the LORD,* you his saints,
for those who fear him lack nothing.[p]

10 The lions* may grow weak and hungry,
but those who seek the LORD lack no good
thing.

11 * Come, my children,* listen to me;
I will teach you the fear of the LORD.[q]

12 Whoever of you loves life[r]
and desires to see many good days,*

13 keep your tongue* from evil
and your lips from speaking lies.

14 Turn from evil and do good;
seek peace and pursue it.[s]

---

n Ge 16:7; Ex 14:19.—o Ps 2:12; 1 Pe 2:3.—p Dt 6:13; Pr 3:7.—q Ps
66:16; Pr 1:8; 4:1.—r 12-16: 1 Pe 3:10-12.—s Ps 37:27; Mt 5:9; Heb
12:14.

34:7 *Angel of the LORD:* i.e., the Lord's protection or the presence of God. However, such protection, although promised by the Lord (see Ps 91:11; Ge 32:2; 2 Ki 6:17; Mt 4:5f), is not automatic; it depends on one's allegiance to the covenant—the "fear of the LORD"—entailing the practices mentioned in vv. 11-14.

34:8 This verse is applied to the Holy Eucharist by the Fathers of the Church and the Liturgy (see 1 Pe 2:3). *Blessed:* see note on Ps 1:1.

34:9 *Fear the LORD:* see note on Ps 15:2-5. *Saints:* that is, those consecrated to God and sharing in his holiness (see Ex 19:6; Lev 19:2; Nu 16:3; Isa 4:3; Da 8:24). See also note on Ps 4:3.

34:10 *Lions:* fierce animals were symbols of people with power.

34:11-14 To gain wisdom entails two things: fearing the Lord and doing his will. The latter calls for integrity of language rather than deception (v. 13; see Jer 4:2), practicing good rather than evil (v. 14; see Ps 37:3, 27), and working for rather than against peace (vv. 14, 17; see Ps 37:37; Mt 5:9; Ro 12:18; 14:19; Heb 12:14).

34:11 *Children:* a term (also translated as "simple" or "sons") for students in Wisdom literature (see Pr 1:22; 4:1; 8:32; Sir 3:1; 23:7).

34:12 This verse is found word for word in an Egyptian text of the 18th dynasty (tomb of Ai) (see 1 Pe 3:10f).

34:13 *Tongue:* see note on Ps 5:9.

15 The eyes of the LORD are on the righteous*
        and his ears are attentive to their cry;[t]
16 the face of the LORD is against those who do
        evil,
        to cut off the memory of them from the earth.

17 The righteous cry out, and the LORD hears
        them;*
        he delivers them from all their troubles.
18 The LORD is close to the brokenhearted
        and saves those who are crushed in spirit.

19 A righteous man may have many troubles,*
        but the LORD delivers him* from them all;
20 he protects all his bones,
        not one of them will be broken.[u]

21 Evil will slay the wicked;*
        the foes of the righteous will be con-
        demned.
22 The LORD redeems his servants;
        no one will be condemned who takes
        refuge in him.

---

t Ps 33:18; Mal 3:16. — u Jn 19:36.

34:15-16 The eyes and ears of the Lord are attuned to the righteous (see Ps 33:18), but the face of the Lord (see note on Ps 13:1) is against evildoers (see Lev 17:10; Jer 23:30; 1 Pe 3:10-12).

34:17-18 Compunction and humility are requirements for benefiting from the grace of salvation (see Ps 51:17; Mt 11:29f). The Lord hears the cry of the righteous (see Ps 145:19) and the brokenhearted (see Ps 147:3) and saves them from their afflictions.

34:19-20 No matter how many are the troubles of the righteous man, the Lord will deliver him (see Job 5:19; 2 Ti 3:11), protecting "all his bones," a phrase representative of his whole being. *Not one of them will be broken:* John applies this text to Jesus on the cross as the righteous man par excellence. Hence this text is regarded as a prophecy about Christ when he was crucified. Although it was the custom of the Romans to break the legs of a person they had crucified so that death would come more quickly, it was not carried out in this case and not one of Christ's bones was broken.

34:19 *Delivers him:* God promises to be our source of power, courage, and wisdom to help us through our troubles; at times he even chooses to take them away from us.

34:21-22 The wicked will perish in their own evil and be condemned (see Ps 9:16), but the righteous will be saved by the Lord (see Ex 6:6; Lk 1:68; Rev 14:3).

PSALM 35*

Appeal for Help against Injustice

Of David.

1 Contend, O LORD, with those who contend
    with me;
    fight against those who fight against me.
2 Take up shield and buckler;
    arise and come to my aid.
3 Brandish spear and javelin[1]
    against those who pursue me.
    Say to my soul,*
    "I am your salvation."

4 May those who seek my life
    be disgraced and put to shame;
    may those who plot my ruin
    be turned back in dismay.v
5 May they be like chaff before the wind,
    with the angel of the LORD* driving them
    away;w

---

1 Or *and block the way.*

v Ps 38:12; 40:14; 71:13.—w Ps 1:4; 34:7; 83:13; Job 21:13.

Ps 35 This is one of the so-called imprecatory (or cursing) psalms that call upon God to mete out justice to enemies (see Ps 3:7; 5:10; 6:10; 17:14-16; 10:15; 28:4f; 31:17f; 35:24-26; 37:2, 9-10, 15, 20, 35f; 40:14f; 54:5; 55:9, 15, 23; 58:7-11; 63:9-11; 64:7-9; 69:22-28; 71:13; 79:6, 12; 83:9-18; 129:5-8; 137:8-9; 139:19-22; 140:9-11; 141:10; 143:12). In their thirst for justice, the authors of these psalms use hyperbole (or overstatement) in order to move others to oppose sin and evil (see also note pn Ps 5:10). In three successive waves, the frantic and indignant cry of the persecuted righteous man rises toward God; and three successive times the suppliant rediscovers hope. He is a man overwhelmed by the underhanded wickedness, betrayal, and calumnies of friends as well as the dark designs of adversaries. It reminds us once again of the evils suffered by the prophet Jeremiah (Jer 20:10-13), and we cannot refrain from thinking of the trial of Jesus before a tribunal bent on sending him to his death (Mt 26:57ff).

Christians are aware that the world continues to pursue Christ in the person of his disciples (see Mt 5:11; 10:17f; Jn 15:18-25), unjustly directing accusations and persecutions against them. Hence, the prayer formulated in this psalm must spring forth from the lips and hearts of the disciples united with their Master.

35:3 *Soul:* see note on Ps 6:3.

35:5 *Like chaff before the wind:* i.e., easily carried away. *Angel of the LORD:* see note on Ps 34:7.

⁶ may their path be dark and slippery,
    with the angel of the LORD pursuing them.
⁷ Since they hid their net for me without cause
    and without cause dug a pit for me,
⁸ may ruin overtake them by surprise—
    may the net they hid entangle them,
    may they fall into the pit, to their ruin.ˣ
⁹ Then my soul* will rejoice in the LORD
    and delight in his salvation.
¹⁰ My whole being will exclaim,
    "Who is like you, O LORD?
You rescue the poor from those too strong for
        them,
        the poor and needy* from those who rob
        them."ʸ

¹¹ Ruthless witnesses come forward;
    they question me on things I know nothing
        about.
¹² They repay me evil for good
    and leave my soul forlorn.ᶻ
¹³ Yet when they were ill, I put on sackcloth*
    and humbled myself with fasting.
When my prayers returned to me unanswered,
¹⁴   I went about mourning
    as though for my friend or brother.
I bowed my head in grief
    as though weeping for my mother.
¹⁵ But when I stumbled, they gathered in glee;
    attackers gathered against me when I was
        unaware.
    They slandered me without ceasing.

---

x Ps 7:15; 9:15; 57:6; Pr 26:27; Ecc 10:8; Sir 27:26; Isa 47:11; 1 Jn
5:3.—y Ps 51:8; 86:8; 89:7, 9; Ex 15:11.—z Ps 27:12; 38:20-21; 109:5; Pr
17:13; Jer 18:20.

35:9 *Soul:* see note on Ps 6:3.
35:10 *Poor and needy:* see notes on Ps 22:26 and 34:6.
35:13 *Sackcloth:* a symbol of mourning. *Fasting:* an act of mourning (see Ps
69:10).

¹⁶ Like the ungodly they maliciously mocked;ᵐ
they gnashed their teeth at me.
¹⁷ O LORD, how long* will you look on?
Rescue my life from their ravages,
my precious life from these lions.ᵃ
¹⁸ I will give you thanks in the great assembly;
among throngs of people I will praise you.ᵇ

¹⁹ Let not those gloat over me
who are my enemies without cause;
let not those who hate me without reason*
maliciously wink the eye.ᶜ
²⁰ They do not speak peaceably,
but devise false accusations
against those who live quietly in the land.ᵈ
²¹ They gape at me and say, "Aha! Aha!
With our own eyes we have seen it."ᵉ

²² O LORD, you have seen this; be not silent.
Do not be far from me, O LORD.ᶠ
²³ Awake, and rise to my defense!
Contend for me, my God and LORD.
²⁴ Vindicate me in your righteousness, O LORD
my God;*
do not let them gloat over me.
²⁵ Do not let them think, "Aha, just what we
wanted!"
or say, "We have swallowed him up."

²⁶ May all who gloat over my distress
be put to shame and confusion;
may all who exalt themselves over me
be clothed with shame and disgrace.

---

m Septuagint; Hebrew may mean *ungodly circle of mockers.*

---

a Ps 6:3; 17:12; 22:21; 58:6.—b Ps 22:22; 26:12; 40:10; 42:4; 149:1.—c
Ps 38:16; 69:4; Jn 15:25.—d Ps 38:12; 120:6-7.—e Ps 40:15; La 2:16; Eze
25:3.—f Ps 22:11; 38:21; 109:1; Ex 3:7.

35:17 *How long. . .?:* see note on Ps 6:3. *Lions:* a metaphor for enemies.
35:19 *Enemies without cause . . . those who hate me without reason:* cited in
Jn 15:25, since this psalm as well as Ps 69 was regarded by the New Testament
authors as foreshadowing the Passion of Christ.
35:24-26 See introduction above and note on Ps 5:10.

[27] May those who delight in my vindication
      shout for joy and gladness;
   may they always say, "The LORD be exalted,
      who delights in the well-being of his ser-
      vant."
[28] My tongue will speak of your righteousness
      and of your praises all day long.[g]

PSALM 36*

Human Weakness and Divine Goodness

For the director of music. Of David the
servant of the LORD.

[1] An oracle* is within my heart
      concerning the sinfulness of the wicked:[n]
   There is no fear of God
      before his eyes.[h]
[2] For in his own eyes he flatters himself
      too much to detect or hate his sin.*

---

n Or *heart: / Sin proceeds from the wicked.*

g Ps 5:8; 71:15.—h Jer 2:19; Ro 3:18.

Ps 36 This psalm combines two contrasting pictures, which were perhaps separated at one time. On the one hand, there is a person destroyed by sin, whose
heart holds no sentiment that is not turned to sin (vv. 1-4). On the other, there
are creatures filled with God, that is, the righteous, who are peaceful and happy
(vv. 5ff). These same traditional images of happiness will be found among the
Prophets, suggestive of the ideal time for the installment of the future Messiah
(Isa 12:2; 25:6; Jer 31:14; Eze 47).
   Christians know better than the psalmist that pride constitutes a maleficent
force residing in all humans. In practice, it carries us inevitably along toward evil
(see Ro 6:1-11). Through Christ, the Father preserves for us, his faithful, his salvation that shines continually upon us to render us holy and to defend us against
outrages on the part of evil and the impious. The New Testament applies images
from the second part of this psalm to Christ: light of humankind and inexhaustible wellspring of life (Jn 7:37f; 8:12; Rev 21:6).
   The words *For the director of music* in the superscription are thought to be a
musical or liturgical notation.
   36:1 *Oracle:* the Hebrew word used here occurs elsewhere only with reference
to the Lord's words to his Prophets; it thus provides insight into the nature of the
wicked. *Heart:* see note on Ps 4:7. Paul cites this verse in Ro 3:18.
   36:2 *Hate his sin:* because it is an offense against God and hence punished by
him.

³ The words of his mouth are wicked and deceitful;
he has ceased to be wise and to do good.
⁴ Even on his bed* he plots evil;
he commits himself to a sinful course
and does not reject what is wrong.*ⁱ*

⁵ Your love, O LORD, reaches to the heavens,
your faithfulness to the skies.*ʲ*
⁶ Your righteousness is like the mighty mountains,
your justice like the great deep.*
O LORD, you preserve both man and beast.
⁷   How priceless is your unfailing love!*
Both high and low among men
find° refuge in the shadow of your wings.*ᵏ*
⁸ They feast on the abundance of your house;*ˡ*
you give them drink from your river of delights.**m*
⁹ For with you is the fountain of life;*
in your light we see light.*ⁿ*

---

o Or *love, O God! / Men find; or love! / Both heavenly beings and men /
find.*

---

i Pr 4:16; Mic 2:1.—j Ps 57:10; 71:19; 89:1.—k Ps 6:4; 17:8.—l Ps 63:5;
Ge 2:8, 10.—m Isa 55:1; Jn 4:14.—n Ps 80:3, 7, 19.

36:4 *On his bed:* rather than meditating on God's law both day and *night* (Ps
1:2; 119:55), the wicked plots evil even on his bed.

36:5f *Your love . . . great deep:* God's influence reaches from one end of the
world to the other and into every sphere.

36:7 *Unfailing love:* see note on Ps 6:4. *Shadow of your wings:* see note on Ps
17:8.

36:8 People rejoice together before the Lord. The image is of the abundance of
meat from the sacrifices. This is already a prefiguration of the Messianic Banquet
of which Jesus will speak, the "Supper of the Lamb" (Rev 19:9). *House:* the earth
that provides food for all living creatures (see Ps 24:2; 104:14). *River:* the means
by which God brings forth the rain out of his "storehouses" (Ps 33:7), which flow
into the water sources on earth and give life to creatures.

36:9 *Fountain of life:* an expression to be taken in the widest possible sense as
life implying prosperity, peace, and happiness (see Ps 46:4; 133:3; Isa 12:5;
55:1; Jer 2:13; 17:13; 31:12). In Proverbs this expression designates wisdom
(13:14; 16:22; 18:4) and the fear of the Lord (14:27). The passage is applied to
Christ, life and light of human beings (Jn 4:10, 14). *Light:* through God's loving
kindness (see Ps 4:6; 31:16; 89:15; 97:11; Job 29:3) we enjoy fullness of life and
well-being.

10 Continue your love to those who know you,
your righteousness to the upright in heart.
11 May the foot of the proud not come against me,
nor the hand of the wicked drive me away.
12 See how the evildoers lie fallen—
thrown down, not able to rise!

PSALM 37* [p]

Fate of the Wicked and Reward of the Righteous

Of David.

1 Do not fret because of evil men
or be envious of those who do wrong;[o]
2 for like the grass they will soon wither,[p]
like green plants they will soon die away.*

3 Trust in the LORD and do good;
dwell in the land* and enjoy safe pasture.[q]

---

p This psalm is an acrostic poem, the stanzas of which begin with the successive letters of the Hebrew alphabet.

---

o Pr 3:31; 23:17; 24:1, 19; Mal 2:17; 3:14.—p Ps 90:6; 102:11; 103:15-16; Job 14:2; Jas 1:10.—q Ps 128:2; Dt 30:20.

Ps 37 A peaceful aged psalmist strings together, in alphabetical order, sayings about the opposing lots of the righteous and the wicked. It is a fine lesson in wisdom for those who grow angry at the successes of evildoers: their triumph is ephemeral. Experience and meditation on the word of God have revealed to this sage the happy destiny that the Lord has reserved for his friends; each of the righteous is called to enjoy the promises made to the people of Israel in reward for their faithfulness: to dwell in the holy land in peace (vv. 3, 11).

The horizon remains limited to this world. Hence it is a modest happiness if it were not irradiated by the nearness of the Lord and did not contain the still hidden promise of a love that cannot be extinguished, of an eternal joy.

Christ will reveal this infinite perspective: eternal happiness in the Kingdom of God, the true promised land, belongs to the poor, those who forgive and thirst for righteousness and peace (Mt 5).

37:2 See note on Ps 5:10 and introduction to Ps 35 (this also applies to vv. 9f, 15, 20, 35f).

37:3 *The land:* the promised land (Ps 25:13; Dt 16:20), which in the New Testament became a type of heaven (see Mt 5:3-12; Lk 6:20-26; Heb 11:9, 13-16). This word is also used in vv. 9, 11, 22, 27, 29, and 34.

⁴ Delight yourself in the Lord^r
   and he will give you the desires of your
      heart.*

⁵ Commit your way to the Lord;
   trust in him and he will do this:^s
⁶ He will make your righteousness shine like
      the dawn,^t
   the justice of your cause like the noonday
      sun.*

⁷ Be still before the Lord and wait patiently for
      him;
   do not fret when men succeed in their
      ways,
   when they carry out their wicked schemes.

⁸ Refrain from anger and turn from wrath;
   do not fret—it leads only to evil.
⁹ For evil men will be cut off,
   but those who hope in the Lord will inherit
      the land.* ^u

¹⁰ A little while, and the wicked will be no
      more;
   though you look for them, they will not be
      found.
¹¹ But the meek* will inherit the land
   and enjoy great peace.^v

¹² The wicked plot against the righteous
   and gnash their teeth at them;

---

r Ps 21:2; Pr 10:24.—s Ps 4:5; 55:22; Pr 3:5; 16:3.—t Ps 18:24; Wis 5:6;
Isa 58:10.—u Ps 25:13; 101:8; Pr 2:21; Isa 57:13.—v Nu 14:24; Mt 5:5.

37:4 *Heart:* see note on Ps 4:7.
37:6 *Dawn . . . noonday sun:* light and brightness symbolize truth, well-being,
and happiness (see Job 22:28; SS 1:7; Wis 5:6).
37:9 Those who hope in the Lord for their sustenance and their well-being
(i.e., "the poor") will inherit the land, while those who bypass God and by wicked
means try to take hold of it will come to nought (see note on Ps 5:10 and introduction to Ps 35).
37:11 *The meek:* another word for the poor, those who count solely on God and
follow his law (see Mt 5:5).

¹³ but the LORD laughs at the wicked,
    for he knows their day* is coming.ʷ

¹⁴ The wicked draw the sword
    and bend the bow
  to bring down the poor and needy,
    to slay those whose ways are upright.ˣ
¹⁵ But their swords will pierce their own hearts,
    and their bows will be broken.

¹⁶ Better the little that the righteous have
    than the wealth of many wicked;ʸ
¹⁷ for the power of the wicked will be broken,
    but the LORD upholds the righteous.

¹⁸ The days of the blameless* are known to the
    LORD,
    and their inheritance will endure forever.
¹⁹ In times of disaster they will not wither;
    in days of famine they will enjoy plenty.

²⁰ But the wicked will perish:
    The LORD's enemies will be like the beauty
      of the fields,*
    they will vanish—vanish like smoke.ᶻ

²¹ The wicked borrow and do not repay,
    but the righteous give generously;
²² those the LORD blesses will inherit the land,
    but those he curses will be cut off.

²³ If the LORD delights in a man's way,ᵃ
    he makes his steps firm;*

---

w Ps 2:4; 59:8; Wis 4:18; Eze 12:23.—x Ps 11:2; 35:10; 57:4; 64:4.—y
Pr 15:16; 16:8.—z Ps 34:21; Wis 5:14.—a Ps 147:11; Pr 20:24.

37:13 *Their day:* the time for their ultimate defeat, their death (see 1 Sa 26:10,
where "his day" is translated as "his time").

37:18 *Blameless:* those who are God's faithful and obedient servants as was
Abraham (see Ge 17:1).

37:20 *Beauty of the fields:* the beauty of grass and flowers that comes and
goes year after year (see Ps 90:5f; 102:11; 103:15f; Job 14:2; Isa 40:6-8; Jas
1:10f).

37:23 See Pr 20:24.

²⁴ though he stumble, he will not fall,
>   for the LORD upholds him with his hand.*

²⁵ I was young and now I am old,
>   yet I have never seen the righteous for-
>   saken
>   or their children begging bread.ᵇ
²⁶ They are always generous and lend freely;
>   their children will be blessed.

²⁷ Turn from evil and do good;ᶜ
>   then you will dwell in the land forever.*
²⁸ For the LORD loves the just*
>   and will not forsake his faithful ones.*

> They will be protected forever,
>   but the offspring of the wicked will be cut
>   off;
²⁹ the righteous will inherit the land
>   and dwell in it forever.ᵈ

³⁰ The mouth of the righteous man utters wis-
>   dom,*
>   and his tongue speaks what is just.ᵉ
³¹ The law of his God is in his heart;ᶠ
>   his feet do not slip.*

---

b Job 4:7; Sir 2:10; Heb 13:5.—c Ps 34:14-15; Am 5:14; 3 Jn 1:11.—d Ps 25:13; Pr 2:21; Isa 34:17; 57:13.—e Ps 49:3; Pr 10:31.—f Ps 40:8; Dt 6:3; Isa 51:7; Jer 31:33.

37:24 See Pr 24:16.
37:27 See Ps 34:14.
37:28-29 The righteous will inherit the land and dwell in it forever through their descendants (see Mt 5:5).
37:28 The psalmist insists that the Lord loves the just (see Pr 2:8) who are his faithful ones, and he will never forsake them. Hence, Paul could say with complete confidence: "[Nothing] will be able to separate us from the love of God that is in Christ Jesus our Lord" (Ro 8:38f).
37:30-31 The wise man reveres the Lord and desires to do his will. The law is written on his heart (see Ps 40:8; Dt 6:6; Isa 51:7; Jer 31:33; Eze 36:27). He speaks wisely (see Ps 49:3) and establishes peace (see Ps 36:6). *Heart:* see note on Ps 4:7. *His feet do not slip:* from the way of the righteous (see Ps 1:6).

32 The wicked lie in wait for the righteous,*
    seeking their very lives;
33 but the LORD will not leave them in their
    power
    or let them be condemned when brought to
    trial.

34 Wait for the LORD
    and keep his way.
  He will exalt you to inherit the land;
    when the wicked are cut off, you will see it.g

35 I have seen a wicked and ruthless man*
    flourishing like a green tree in its native soil,h
36 but he soon passed away and was no more;
    though I looked for him, he could not be
    found.

37 Consider the blameless, observe the upright;*
    there is a futureq for the man of peace.i
38 But all sinners will be destroyed;
    the futurer of the wicked will be cut off.

39 The salvation of the righteous comes from
    the LORD;*
    he is their stronghold in time of trouble.j
40 The LORD helps them and delivers them;
    he delivers them from the wicked and
    saves them,
    because they take refuge in him.

---

q Or *there will be posterity.*—r Or *posterity.*

g Ps 27:14; 31:24.—h Ps 92:7-8; Job 20:6-7; Isa 2:13; Eze 31:10-11.—i
Ps 18:25; Pr 23:18; 24:14.—j Ps 3:8; 9:9; Isa 25:4.

37:32-33 The righteous need not fear the machinations of the wicked, for the
Lord has promised to come to their assistance. He gave Canaan to Israel and the
earth to all who love him (see Isa 65:17-25; 66:22; Rev 21:1).
37:35-36 God confounds the proud (see Job 20:6f; Isa 2:12; 14:13-15; Eze
31:10f).
37:37-38 The righteous have a bright future; the wicked have no future at all
(see Pr 23:18; 24:14).
37:39-40 The Lord is the protector of all who take refuge in him, all who call
upon him for protection, deliverance, and victory (see Ps 9:9; 12:1; 34:6f).

PSALM 38*

Prayer of a Sinner in Great Peril

A psalm of David. A petition.

1 O LORD, do not rebuke me in your anger
or discipline me in your wrath.[k]

2 For your arrows* have pierced me,
and your hand has come down upon me.[l]

3 Because of your wrath there is no health in
my body;
my bones* have no soundness because of
my sin.[m]

4 My guilt has overwhelmed me*
like a burden too heavy to bear.[n]

5 My wounds fester and are loathsome
because of my sinful folly.

---

k Ps 6:1.—l Ps 31:10; 64:7; Job 6:4; La 3:12.—m Pr 3:8; Isa 1:5-6.—n Ps
40:12; Ge 4:13; Ezr 9:6.

Ps 38 The psalmist of this third Penitential Psalm (seven in all: Ps 6; 32; 38;
51; 102; 130; 143) is a man prostrated beneath the weight of his sickness and
the vilification heaped on him by others, a man marked by the chastisement of
God. He utters a suppliant and monotone plaint that seems as interminable as
his suffering. Before God, he is pitiable, abandoned, and betrayed. This new Job
(Job 6:4; 19:13-21) does not rebel. He thinks of himself as a sinner who deserves
his lot and he suffers in silence, leveling neither recriminations nor imprecations
against his adversaries. Indeed, hope stirs secretly in him.

The complete abandonment to God that is expressed here is also found in the
third Lamentation (La 3:26-29) and in the Songs of the Servant of the Lord (see
Isa 53:7). The Christian Liturgy sees in this man of sorrows an image of the
Christ who was silent during his Passion.

In praying this psalm, we should look to ourselves, scrutinizing our lives and
our consciences with a penetrating and impartial perspicacity, the better to discern the place of sin therein and the better to realize that we are and remain sinners (see Ro 7:14-20; 1 Jn 1:8f). This will in no way prevent us from begging God
not to chastise us in his wrath but to save us as soon as possible from our afflictions and our foes.

The term *A petition* in the superscription occurs elsewhere only in Ps 70, and
an alternative translation is: "For remembrance," i.e., "For the memorial sacrifice" or "portion" (see Lev 2:2, 9, 16; 5:12; Isa 66:3).

38:2 *Arrows:* i.e., the trials God has sent him (see Dt 32:23; Job 6:4; 34:6; La
3:12; Eze 5:16).

38:3 *Bones:* see note on Ps 34:19-20.

38:4 *Guilt has overwhelmed me:* his guilt has resulted in both physical and
psychological suffering.

6 I am bowed down and brought very low;
all day long I go about mourning.[o]
7 My back is filled with searing pain;
there is no health in my body.
8 I am feeble and utterly crushed;[p]
I groan in anguish of heart.*

9 All my longings lie open before you, O LORD;
my sighing is not hidden from you.
10 My heart pounds, my strength fails me;
even the light has gone from my eyes.[q]
11 My friends and companions avoid me because of my wounds;
my neighbors stay far away.
12 Those who seek my life set their traps,
those who would harm me talk of my ruin;
all day long they plot deception.*

13 I am like a deaf man, who cannot hear,*
like a mute, who cannot open his mouth;
14 I have become like a man who does not hear,
whose mouth can offer no reply.
15 I wait for you, O LORD;
you will answer, O LORD my God.[r]
16 For I said, "Do not let them gloat
or exalt themselves over me when my foot slips."*

17 For I am about to fall,
and my pain is ever with me.
18 I confess my iniquity;
I am troubled by my sin.[s]

o Ps 35:14; 57:6.—p Ps 34:18; 102:3-5.—q Ps 6:7; 31:10; 88:9.—r Ps 13:3; 27:14.—s Ps 32:5; 51:3.

38:8 *Heart:* see note on Ps 4:7.

38:12 This passage recalls the fourth Song of the Servant (Isa 53:4, 7; see also Ps 31:11; 35:20; 37:32; 88:8; Job 12:4f; 19:13f).

38:13-16 Like a man deaf and dumb, the psalmist does not reply to those who slander him; he waits for the Lord to vindicate his cause.

38:16 Passage close to Ps 35:11; 109:3-5. Some Greek manuscripts and many versions add: "They have rejected me, the loved one, like some hideous corpse" (see Isa 14:19 Greek). This allusion to the crucified Christ is made even more explicit in the Coptic version by the words: "They have nailed my flesh."

¹⁹ Many are those who are my vigorous ene-
mies;
those who hate me without reason* are numerous.
²⁰ Those who repay my good with evil
slander me when I pursue what is good.^t

²¹ O LORD, do not forsake me;
be not far from me, O my God.^u
²² Come quickly to help me,
O LORD my Savior.^v

PSALM 39*

The Brevity and Vanity of Life

For the director of music. For Jeduthun.^w
A psalm of David.

¹ I said, "I will watch my ways
and keep my tongue from sin;

---

t Ps 35:12; 109:5.—u Ps 22:1, 11, 19; 27:9; 35:22.—v Ps 40:13, 17.—w
Ps 62:1; 77:1; 1 Ch 16:41.

38:19 *Hate me without reason:* although the psalmist acknowledges that he
sinned against the Lord, he protests his innocence of wrongdoing against his
enemies (see note on Ps 35:19).

Ps 39 The psalmist is not a sage who reflects on existence but a man grap-
pling with God. In the face of the blows that strike him, he realizes the total
frailty of existence and even of life itself. He would like to cast out from his heart
all intentions to rebel, but it is impossible for him to hold back his complaint any
longer. A real faith in the resurrection is still absent and, apart from an intervention of God providing a new breath of life, everything seems a mockery. It reminds
us of the lucid reflections of Ecclesiastes (1:2).

This psalm reminds us that while doing our utmost to acquire and develop the
eternal divine life in us, we must regard our bodily life as the highest good, the
most precious natural talent entrusted to us by God for our vigilant concern and
fruitful action. The heavenly Father himself watches over this life, assigning it
food and drink (see Mt 6:25-34) and life itself (see Ac 17:25-28). Jesus himself
watches over material life, looking after the hunger of the crowd (see Mt 15:32),
curing the sick, and raising the dead. We must thus greatly value our life and
seek to prolong it for the glory of God and our spiritual progress (see Phil 1:23-
26). Christians too have this same feeling in times of great distress: without the
Lord what value is there in life?

The words *For the director of music* in the superscription are thought to be a
musical or liturgical notation; *Jeduthun* was one of the three men appointed
choral directors by David (see 1 Ch 25:1).

I will put a muzzle on my mouth*
　　as long as the wicked are in my presence."
2 But when I was silent and still,
　　not even saying anything good,
　　my anguish increased.ˣ
3 My heart grew hot within me,
　　and as I meditated, the fire burned;
　　then I spoke with my tongue:

4 "Show me, O Lᴏʀᴅ, my life's end*
　　and the number of my days;
　　let me know how fleeting is my life.
5 You have made my days a mere handbreadth;
　　the span of my years is as nothing before
　　you.ʸ
　　Each man's life is but a breath.   *Selah*
6 Man is a mere phantom as he goes to and fro:
　　He bustles about, but only in vain;
　　he heaps up wealth, not knowing who will
　　get it.*

7 "But now, Lᴏʀᴅ, what do I look for?
　　My hope is in you.
8 Save me from all my transgressions;
　　do not make me the scorn of fools.*
9 I was silent; I would not open my mouth,
　　for you are the one who has done this.
10 Remove your scourge from me;
　　I am overcome by the blow of your hand.
11 You rebuke and discipline men for their sin;
　　you consume their wealth like a moth—
　　each man is but a breath.   *Selah*

---

x Ps 37:1; Jer 20:9.—y Ps 62:9; 89:45; 90:9-10; 144:4; Job 7:6, 16; 14:1;
Wis 2:5; Eccl 6:12.

39:1 *Muzzle on my mouth:* to repress saying anything derogatory in the presence of the wicked.

39:4-6 The psalmist begs God to help him know and accept the brevity and vanity of life, a brevity and vanity stressed in other psalms (see Ps 62:9; 73:19; 90:10) and in Isa 40:17.

39:6 This passage is reminiscent of Ecclesiastes.

39:8 *Fools:* see Ps 14 (introduction and notes on vv. 1 and 2).

12 "Hear my prayer, O LORD,
　　listen to my cry for help;
　　be not deaf to my weeping.
　For I dwell with you as an alien,*
　　a stranger, as all my fathers were.ᶻ
13 Look away from me, that I may rejoice again
　　before I depart and am no more."*

PSALM 40*

Thanksgiving and Prayer for Help

For the director of music. Of David. A psalm.

1 I waited patiently for the LORD;*
　　he turned to me and heard my cry.ᵃ

---

z Ps 119:19; Ge 23:4; Ex 12:48; Lev 25:23; Heb 11:13; 1 Pe 2:11.—a Ps 6:9; La 3:24.

39:12 *Alien:* that is, one who is only a temporary sojourner on earth (see Lev 25:23: "The land is mine and you are but aliens and my tenants"; see also Ps 119:19; 1 Pe 2:11).

39:13 *Am no more:* in the time of the psalmist there apparently was no idea of any resurrection, even a mitigated one in the netherworld (see note on Ps 6:5).

Ps 40 This psalm, one of the most engaging of the entire Psalter, is divided into two parts. The first (vv. 1-11) is a thanksgiving reminiscent of Jeremiah (7:22; 17:7; 31:33). The second (vv. 13-17) is a lament that appears also as Ps 70.

Every Christian (and the whole Church) can naturally recite this beautiful psalm in his or her own right as one really (though not yet completely) saved.

The words *For the director of music* in the superscription are thought to be a musical or liturgical notation.

40:1-11 The psalmist expresses a great hope in the Lord. No one knows God's goodness better than one who has experienced abandonment from God. Purified by trial, the psalmist welcomes God into the depths of his being, his life becomes a kind of inner offering, the only true sacrifice, and he joyfully bears witness to the Lord's righteousness, love, and truth. In reading this psalm, we get the impression of entering into the confidence of Christ himself, of divining his inner attitude toward the course of his action and above all toward his Passion. A few Greek translations have accentuated this resemblance even more; thus, the Letter to the Hebrews cites this psalm to make us understand the profound decision of Christ (Heb 10:5-10).

The best praise of God and the best sacrifice are the gift of one's heart and life. The Prophets often opposed ritual formalism and replaced it with the true religion that is internal (Isa 1:11; Jer 6:20; 31:33; Am 5:22; Hos 6:6). It is this experience to which the Songs of the Servant bear witness (Isa 50:5; 53:10), which was also the experience of Christ.

² He lifted me out of the slimy pit,
    out of the mud and mire;
  he set my feet on a rock
    and gave me a firm place to stand.*b*

³ He put a new song* in my mouth,
    a hymn of praise to our God.
  Many will see and fear
    and put their trust in the LORD.*c*

⁴ Blessed* is the man
    who makes the LORD his trust,*d*
  who does not look to the proud,
    to those who turn aside to false gods.*s*

⁵ Many, O LORD my God,
    are the wonders you have done.
  The things you planned for us
    no one can recount to you;*e*
  were I to speak and tell of them,
    they would be too many to declare.*f*

⁶ Sacrifice and offering you did not desire,*
    but my ears you have pierced;*t u*
  burnt offerings and sin offerings*g*
    you did not require.*

⁷ Then I said, "Here I am, I have come—
    it is written about me in the scroll.* v*

---

s Or *to falsehood.*—t Hebrew; Septuagint *but a body you have prepared for me* (see also Symmachus and Theodotion).—u Or *opened.*—v Or *come / with the scroll written for me.*

---

b Ps 18:4; 28:1; 30:3; 69:2, 14-15; 88:4; Pr 1:12; Jer 38:6; Jnh 2:6.—c Pr 33:3; Rev 5:9.—d Ps 1:1; 34:8; Pr 16:20; Jer 17:7.—e Ps 35:10; Dt 4:34.—f Ps 71:15; 139:17-18.—g Ps 51:16-17; Isa 1:11-15; 50:5; Jer 6:20; Hos 6:6; Am 5:21; Heb 10:5-7.

40:3 *New song:* see note on Ps 33:3. *Many will see:* see note on Ps 9:1.
40:4 *Blessed:* see note on Ps 1:1.
40:6-8 These verses are applied to Christ by Heb 10:5-10.
40:6 Obedience is better than sacrifice (see Ps 50:7-15; 51:16f; 69:31f; 1 Sa 15:22; Isa 1:10-20; Jer 7:22; Hos 6:6; Am 5:22-25; Mic 6:6-8; Ac 7:42f). *But my ears you have pierced:* a variant reading from the Greek versions (see NIV textual note) has: "but a body you have prepared for me," which was interpreted in a Messianic sense and applied to Christ (see Heb 10:5ff).
40:7 *It is written about me in the scroll:* the scroll is the Torah or the Mosaic Law, transcribed on parchment scrolls. The alternative Greek reading is "with the scroll written for me," which suggests a Messianic sense.

8 I desire to do your will, O my God;
   your law is within my heart."[h]

9 I proclaim righteousness in the great assem-
      bly;
   I do not seal my lips,
   as you know, O LORD.[i]
10 I do not hide your righteousness in my
      heart;*
   I speak of your faithfulness and salvation.
   I do not conceal your love and your truth
      from the great assembly.

11 Do not withhold your mercy from me, O
      LORD;
   may your love and your truth always pro-
      tect me.[j]
12 For troubles without number surround me;
   my sins have overtaken me, and I cannot
      see.
   They are more than the hairs of my head,[k]
   and my heart fails within me.*

13 Be pleased, O LORD, to save me;*
   O LORD, come quickly to help me.[l]
14 May all who seek to take my life*
   be put to shame and confusion;
   may all who desire my ruin
   be turned back in disgrace.[m]

---

h Ps 37:31; Jn 4:34; 8:29.—i Ps 22:22, 31; 26:12; 35:18; 149:1.—j Ps 89:33; Zec 1:12.—k Ps 6:7; 38:4; Ezr 9:6.—l 13-17: Ps 70:1-15; 71:12.—m Ps 35:4, 26; 71:13.

40:10 *Heart:* see note on Ps 4:7.

40:12 Hyberbolic statements expressing the intense nature of the sinner's suf-ferings (see Ps 6:7; 38:4, 10; 69:4), which serve as a transition to the second part of the psalm.

40:13-17 Distress can remind a person of his attachment to sin. Is there any reason why people should vilify the person who acknowledges his faults? Realiz-ing his incoercible attraction toward evil, the psalmist cries out to God, and the poor man rediscovers with astonishment the joyous assurance that God thinks about him.

40:14-15 See note on Ps 5:10 and introduction to Ps 35.

[15] May those who say to me, "Aha! Aha!"*
    be appalled at their own shame.[n]
[16] But may all who seek you
    rejoice and be glad in you;
  may those who love your salvation always
      say,
    "The LORD be exalted!"[o]

[17] Yet I am poor and needy;*
    may the LORD think of me.
  You are my help and my deliverer;
    O my God, do not delay.

PSALM 41*

Trust in God in Sickness and Misfortune

For the director of music. A psalm of David.

[1] * Blessed is he who has regard for the weak;*
    the LORD delivers him in times of trouble.[p]

---

n Ps 35:21, 25.—o Ps 35:27; 69:6, 32; 104:1.—p Job 4:7-11; Pr 14:21.

40:15 *Aha! Aha!:* the mocking words of the psalmist's adversaries.
40:17 *Poor and needy:* see note on Ps 34:6. *My help and my deliverer:* the salvation promised to the faithful (see Isa 25:9), first conceived as natural with reference to the Exodus or the return from the Exile, was later conceived as spiritual without restriction of space or time (see, e.g., Ps 18: superscription; 19:14).
Ps 41 The psalmist is well aware that mercy is rarely given by human beings. In his illness, he received no mercy from others; instead his enemies gleefully engaged in malicious gossip about him and his coming death and even his friend betrayed him. However, the psalmist does not retaliate in kind; he turns to God for mercy, asking for a rich life with all his powers restored so that he can stand once again in the presence of the Lord.
In praying this psalm, we can recall that the entire psalm is applicable to Christ personally, with the exception of v. 4, which he can assume only in place of and in the role of his sinful members. Since Christ assures his disciples of God's complete solicitude, we can recite this supplication on our account amid our earthly trials.
The words *For the director of music* in the superscription are thought to be a musical or liturgical notation.
41:1-3 The psalmist voices his confidence that the Lord will restore him to fullness of health and life because of the psalmist's regard for the weak.
41:1 *Blessed is he who has regard for the weak:* other psalms use the same designation ("Blessed") for those whom God favors (see Ps 32:1f; 34:8; 40:4; 65:4; see also note on Ps 1:1).

2 The LORD will protect him and preserve his
       life;
    he will bless him in the land
    and not surrender him to the desire of his
       foes.
3 The LORD will sustain him on his sickbed
    and restore him from his bed of illness.

4 I said, "O LORD, have mercy on me;
    heal me, for I have sinned* against you."
5 My enemies say of me in malice,
    "When will he die and his name perish?"
6 Whenever one comes to see me,
    he speaks falsely, while his heart* gathers
       slander;
    then he goes out and spreads it abroad.q

7 All my enemies whisper together against me;
    they imagine the worst for me, saying,
8 "A vile disease has beset him;
    he will never get up from the place where
       he lies."
9 Even my close friend, whom I trusted,
    he who shared my bread,r
    has lifted up his heel against me.*

10 But you, O LORD, have mercy on me;
    raise me up, that I may repay them.
11 I know that you are pleased with me,
    for my enemy does not triumph over me.
12 In my integrity you uphold me
    and set me in your presence forever.

q Ps 31:11; 38:11-12; 88:8; Job 19:13-19; Jer 20:10; Mt 5:11.—r Ps
55:13-14; Job 19:19; Jn 13:18.

41:4 *Sinned:* the psalmist acknowledges his sin and asks for forgiveness and
healing—in keeping with the idea that sickness was a divine punishment for sin
(see Job 32:3; Ps 107:17). In the cure of the man born blind, Jesus was to indicate that such was not the case (see Jn 9:2f).
41:6 *Heart:* see note on Ps 4:7.
41:9 This passage repeats a theme frequently developed (see Ps 31:12; 38:12;
55:13f; 88:9; Job 19:13; Jer 20:10; 38:22). It is cited by Jesus with reference to
Judas (Jn 13:18) according to the sense of the Septuagint.

¹³ Praise be to the LORD, the God of Israel,ˢ
from everlasting to everlasting.
Amen and Amen.*

BOOK II—PSALMS 42–72

PSALM 42* ʷ

Prayer of Longing for God

For the director of music. A *maskil*ˣ of the Sons of Korah.

¹ As the deer pants for streams of water,ᵗ
so my soul pants for you, O God.*

---

w In many Hebrew manuscripts Psalms 42 and 43 constitute one psalm.—x Probably a literary or musical term.

s Ne 9:5; Da 2:20.—t 1-2: Ps 36:9; 63:1; 84:2; 143:6; Isa 26:9; Jn 7:37.

41:13 This doxology is not part of the psalm; it concludes the first of the five books of the Psalter (see Ps 72:18f; 89:52; 106:48; 150).

Ps 42—72 The drama of the righteous confronted with the rise of evil terminated Book I of the Psalter. This conflict remains, but other themes come to the fore with greater insistence. Now the prayer often evinces a desire for God and to be far from human beings, oftentimes with a more mystical note added. At other times, crucial moments of history will appear to provoke alternatively both praise and supplication: the drama of the righteous remains—as that of the people. In short, in the psalms that follow, the collective aspect will be readily underlined.

Ps 42 This psalm, which really forms one with the next psalm, has a fascinating literary beauty but also expresses feeling of a rare kind. It is the lament of the exiled Levite combining nostalgia, distress, and fervent desire. Living in a foreign land, far from the temple of Jerusalem, the sole place where it was believed one would encounter God, the sacred ministers feel the Exile more deeply; the sanctuary is the only place where they find their happiness. They are the first to suffer the mockings of the pagans, who do not recognize the God to whom they have dedicated their lives. Three times the lament is voiced, and three times the chant that gives hope is also uttered, as the psalm vibrantly expresses the fervor for the temple, where the people flocked to celebrate the love and presence of God.

At the heart of this fervor we glimpse the deepest human yearning: the desire for God. It is this that here on earth inspires the candidates who seek to enter the Church, the "house of God," and we also place it on the lips of the dead who are waiting to be admitted into the new Jerusalem, the heavenly city of God. Consecrated men and women recognize herein also the movement of their souls. Is not this the sublime desire at the root of all human restlessness? Down the centuries Augustine has proclaimed: "Our hearts are restless until they rest in you."

The words *For the director of music* in the superscription are thought to be a musical or liturgical notation; for *maskil*, see introduction to Ps 32. *The Sons of Korah* were Levites (see 1 Ch 26:19). In Book II, seven psalms bear this inscription (Ps 42; 44—49) and four in Book III (Ps 84—85; 87—88).

42:1 *God:* from Ps 42 to Ps 84, the ineffable tetragrammaton ("Yahweh") is generally replaced by "God" ("Elohim"), marking this as the "Elohist Psalter."

² My soul* thirsts for God, for the living God.
  When can I go and meet with God?ᵘ
³ My tears have been my food
    day and night,ᵛ
  while men say to me all day long,
    "Where is your God?"ʷ
⁴ These things I remember
    as I pour out my soul:ˣ
  how I used to go with the multitude,
    leading the procession to the house of
      God,ʸ
  with shouts of joy and thanksgiving
    among the festive throng.

⁵ Why are you downcast, O my soul?
    Why so disturbed within me?
  Put your hope in God,
    for I will yet praise him,
    my Savior and ⁶ my God.*

Myʸ soul is downcast within me;
    therefore I will remember youᶻ
  from the land of the Jordan,
    the heights of Hermon—from Mount Mizar.*

---

y A few Hebrew manuscripts, Septuagint and Syriac; most Hebrew
manuscripts *praise him for his saving help. / O my God, my.*

u Ps 27:4; Jos 3:10.—v Ps 80:5; 102:9 Mic 7:3.—w Ps 79:10; Joel 2:17;
Mal 2:17.—x 1 Sa 1:15; La 3:20.—y Ps 27:4; 122:1, 4.—z Ps 43:3;
63:6.

42:2 *Soul:* see note on Ps 6:3. *Living God:* see Dt 5:26. *Meet with God:* a more
commonly used translation is: "see the face of God," taken to mean God's personal presence (see Gn 33:10; Ex 10:28f). In other places the expression "see
God" (or "see the face of God") indicates the presence of God in the temple (see
Ps 11:7; 17:15; 63:2; Ex 24:10; 33:7-11; Job 33:26).
42:5-6 *Why . . . my God:* this refrain appears three times in this double psalm
(42:5, 11; 43:5) and indicates that the two parts were originally one psalm (see
note on 42:11).
42:6 *Mount Mizar:* not identified. The translation "from the land . . ." sup-
poses a Levite exiled to the springs of the Jordan, at the foot of Mount Hermon. If
we think of him as exiled in Babylon, the translation would be: "I will remember
you more than the land of the Jordan and Hermon, than the lowly mountain
[Zion]."

7 Deep calls to deep
    in the roar of your waterfalls;*
all your waves and breakers
    have swept over me.ᵃ

8 By day the LORD directs his love,
    at night his song is with me—*
  a prayer to the God of my life.

9 I say to God my Rock,*
    "Why have you forgotten me?
  Why must I go about mourning,
    oppressed by the enemy?"ᵇ
10 My bones suffer mortal agony
    as my foes taunt me,
  saying to me all day long,
    "Where is your God?"*

11 Why are you downcast, O my soul?
    Why so disturbed within me?
  Put your hope in God,
    for I will yet praise him,
    my Savior and my God.*

---

a Ps 18:4; 32:6; 69:2; 88:7; Jnh 2:3.—b Ps 18:2, 31; 31:2-3.

42:7 *Deep calls to deep . . . your waterfalls:* the psalmist alludes to the "waterfalls" that carry God's waters from the "deep" above to the "deep" below (see note on Ps 36:8), bringing God's breakers sweeping over him (see Ps 69:1f; 88:7; Jnh 2:3, 5). And God is involved in this danger of water toward the psalmist (see note on Ps 32:6)—he lets it happen.
42:8 Nonetheless, the psalmist is confident of God's unfailing love, and this sustains him (see note on Ps 6:4). *God of my life:* some propose the translation: "my living God" and understand it as the "God who gives me life."
42:9 *Rock:* see note on Ps 18:2. *Why. . .? Why. . .?:* see note on Ps 6:3.
42:10 The psalmist has been abandoned by God to his godless enemies, who taunt him with the words "Where is your God?" He resembles a dying man, and his whole being ("bones"; see note on Ps 34:19-20) is distressed by his foes and by God's silence.
42:11 The refrain is voiced for the second time in this double-psalm (see v. 5, above) and will be repeated once more in Ps 43:5. This threefold refrain reflects the attitude of many of God's people during the Exile or any crisis situation. In such loneliness and alienation, faith is tried and leads to salvation. For hope is mindful of the Lord's glorious works of salvation and victory recounted in the Sacred Writings. See Mt 26:38 for the application of these words to Christ's agony in the Garden of Gethsemane.

PSALM 43*ᶻ

Prayer To Worship God Anew

1 Vindicate me, O God,
    and plead my cause against an ungodly na-
        tion;
    rescue me from deceitful and wicked men.ᶜ
2 You are God my stronghold.
    Why have you rejected me?
Why must I go about mourning,
    oppressed by the enemy?
3 Send forth your light and your truth,*
    let them guide me;ᵈ
let them bring me to your holy mountain,
    to the place where you dwell.ᵉ
4 Then will I go to the altar of God,
    to God, my joy and my delight.
I will praise you* with the harp,
    O God, my God.

5 Why are you downcast, O my soul?
    Why so disturbed within me?
Put your hope in God,
    for I will yet praise him,
    my Savior and my God.*

---

z In many Hebrew manuscripts Psalms 42 and 43 constitute one psalm.

c Ps 109:2; 119:154.—d Ps 18:28; 27:1; 36:9; 57:3; Mic 7:8.—e Ps 2:6; 122:1.

Ps 43 The psalmist asks God to be vindicated and to be able to return to the temple and render him praise once again.
    We can pray this psalm to augment our tranquil hope, and place our cause in God, who has sworn that he will obtain redress from our enemies (see Ro 12:19; Heb 10:30). He will enable us to journey toward the heavenly Jerusalem in the vast mobile column of his Church, the true liturgical procession and uninterrupted processional march that takes the elect to him (see Heb 10:19-22).
    43:3 *Your light and your truth:* the psalmist personifies the divine attributes of light (see note on Ps 27:1) and truth (see Ps 25:5; 26:3; 40:10) and asks that they bring him safely to the temple. *Holy mountain:* see note on Ps 2:6.
    43:4 *Altar of God . . . I will praise you:* see notes on Ps 7:17 and 26:6.
    43:5 See note on Ps 42:11.

PSALM 44*

Past Glory and Present Need of God's People

For the director of music. Of the Sons of Korah. A *maskil*.[a]

1 We have heard with our ears, O God;*
    our fathers have told us
what you did in their days,
    in days long ago.[f]
2 With your hand you drove out the nations
    and planted our fathers;
you crushed the peoples
    and made our fathers flourish.[g]
3 It was not by their sword that they won the
        land,
    nor did their arm bring them victory;[h]
it was your right hand, your arm,
    and the light of your face,* for you loved
        them.[i]

4 You are my* King and my God,
    who decrees[b] victories for Jacob.[j]

---

a Probably a literary or musical term.—b Septuagint, Aquila and Syriac;
Hebrew *King, O God; / command.*

---

f Ps 78:3; 2 Sa 7:22-23.—g Ps 78:55; 80:9f; Ac 7:45.—h Dt 8:17f; Jos
24:12.—i Ps 4:6; 31:16; 67:1; 78:54; Nu 6:25; Da 9:17; Hos 1:7.—j Ps 5:2;
145:1.

Ps 44 In the history of Israel, times of joy and defeat alternate with one another. This hymn transmits the strong feeling of the people about the triumphs of
bygone days and the defeat at hand. But they do not believe God can forget forever the people that he loves.

As the true "remnant" and the elite of God's servants, the Church very naturally uses this psalm of the remnant of Israel to beseech the Lord and Master to
take pity on her in the severe trials that assail her. This national lamentation is a
prayer for times when we feel overwhelmed by failure, uncertainty, and confusion.

The words *For the director of music* in the superscription are thought to be a
musical or liturgical notation; for *the Sons of Korah*, see introduction to Ps 42; for
maskil, see introduction to Ps 32.

44:1-8 The liturgy transmits with gratitude the memory of the great hours of
the conquest. Isn't God the one who at that time was responsible for this people's
victory? A hymn recalls these wondrous deeds.

44:3 *The light of your face*: see notes on Ps 4:6 and 13:1.

44:4 *My*: this psalm is sung in the name of all Israel.

5 Through you we push back our enemies;
　　through your name we trample our foes.
6 I do not trust in my bow,
　　my sword does not bring me victory;
7 but you give us victory over our enemies,
　　you put our adversaries to shame.
8 In God we make our boast all day long,
　　and we will praise your name forever. *Selah*

9 *k* But now you have rejected and humbled
　　us;* *l*
　　you no longer go out with our armies.*
10 You made us retreat* before the enemy,
　　and our adversaries have plundered us.*m*
11 You gave us up to be devoured like sheep
　　and have scattered us among the nations.*n*
12 You sold your people for a pittance,
　　gaining nothing from their sale.*o*

13 You have made us a reproach to our neigh-
　　bors,*p*
　　the scorn and derision of those around us.
14 You have made us a byword among the na-
　　tions;
　　the peoples shake their heads* at us.
15 My disgrace is before me all day long,
　　and my face is covered with shame

---

k 9-26: Ps 89:38-51.—l Ps 60:10; 68:7.—m Lev 26:17; Dt 28:25; Jdg 2:14.—n Lev 26:33; Dt 28:64.—o Dt 32:30; Isa 52:3; Jer 15:13.—p 13-16: Ps 79:4; 80:6; 123:3-4; 2 Ch 29:8; Job 12:4; Da 9:16.

44:9-16 Only a lament can evoke the situation of that moment; we are doubt-less at the time of the Exile, after 587 B.C. This prayer could have been utilized and adapted at other times of national calamity; thus, vv. 17-22 make us think of the Maccabean period when Israel is conscious of being the faithful commu-nity that did not deserve persecution (167-164 B.C.); the people suffer for their faith rather than for punishment of sin. For Paul, this lament (v. 22) reflects the condition of Christians (Ro 8:36).

44:9 *You no longer go out with our armies:* as commander-in-chief (see Ps 60:12; 68:7; Ex 15:3; Jdg 5:4).

44:10 *You made us retreat:* God is responsible for the defeats as well as the victories (v. 4) of Israel.

44:14 *Shake their heads:* a gesture of scorn (see Ps 64:8).

¹⁶ at the taunts of those who reproach and revile me,
because of the enemy, who is bent on revenge.

¹⁷ All this happened to us,
though we had not forgotten you
or been false to your covenant.*
¹⁸ Our hearts* had not turned back;
our feet had not strayed from your path.
¹⁹ But you crushed us and made us a haunt for
jackals*
and covered us over with deep darkness.*q*

²⁰ If we had forgotten the name of our God
or spread out our hands* to a foreign god,
²¹ would not God have discovered it,
since he knows the secrets of the heart?
²² Yet for your sake we face death all day long;*r*
we are considered as sheep to be slaugh-
tered.*

²³ Awake, O LORD! Why* do you sleep?
Rouse yourself! Do not reject us forever.*s*
²⁴ Why do you hide your face*
and forget our misery and oppression?*t*

---

q Isa 34:13; Jer 9:10.—r Isa 53:7; Ro 8:36.—s Ps 10:1; 74:1; 77:7; 79:5;
83:1; 89:46.—t Ps 10:11; 13:1; 89:46; Job 13:24.

44:17 Israel's present state is not the result of infidelity to God's covenant
(see Ex 19—24).
44:18 *Hearts:* see note on Ps 4:7. *Your path:* the path or way shown them by
the Lord (see Ps 18:30).
44:19 *You crushed us and made us a haunt for jackals:* i.e., relegated Israel to
a place unfit for human beings (see Isa 13:22; Jer 9:11; 10:22). Another translation proposed is: "you crushed us as you did the sea monster." *Deep darkness:*
they have been left without "light," which symbolizes the fruits of God's loving
kindness (see note on Ps 36:9).
44:20 *Spread out our hands:* the usual posture for prayer (see Ex 9:29), with
palms turned upward.
44:22 In truth, Israel has suffered the hostility of the peoples because she has
been the nation faithful to the Lord. Applying this verse to the Christian community (Ro 8:36), Paul is able to give it a positive slant because of Christ's victory
through his Passion and Resurrection (Ro 8:37-39).
44:23 *Why. . .?:* see note on Ps 6:3.
44:24 *Hide your face:* see note on Ps 13:1.

²⁵ We are brought down to the dust;ᵘ
    our bodies cling to the ground.*
²⁶ Rise up and help us;
    redeem us because of your unfailing love.*

PSALM 45*

Nuptial Ode for the Messianic King

For the director of music. To [the tune of] "Lilies." Of the
Sons of Korah. A *maskil*.ᶜ A wedding song.

¹ * My heart* is stirred by a noble theme
    as I recite my verses for the king;
    my tongue is the pen of a skillful writer.

---

c Probably a literary or musical term.

---

u Ps 7:5; 119:25.

44:25 *Our bodies cling to the ground:* posture of those who are defeated, those at prayer, or those in affliction (see Ps 7:6; 119:25; Nu 24:4; Dt 9:18).

44:26 *Unfailing love:* see note on Ps 6:4.

Ps 45 This unique psalm, probably composed for a royal wedding, opens with the dedication to the king, then lets the ceremony unfold before our eyes. First, it celebrates the monarchy, depicting it under the characteristics of a new David, the Anointed One already acclaimed by Isaiah (see Isa 9:5f; 11:3-5). He is a splendid war chief, a lieutenant of God who comes forth with a dazzling cortege; upon him rests the promise made to the House of David (see 2 Sa 7). Next it addresses and celebrates the queen—a foreigner (vv. 11-17)—placed at the right hand of her royal spouse, richly adorned and heaped with gifts. She is ushered into the palace followed by her bridesmaids and offered an array of good wishes.

The psalm also conjures up a different kind of marriage. The Prophets had spoken of God as espoused to his people (see Isa 62:5; Eze 16:8f; Hos 2:16), a rich, though bold image. As Jews reread this beautiful lyric text, they had a presentiment of the covenant that the future Messiah was to establish and extend to include the pagan peoples. The Christian tradition finds in it a prediction of the marriage of Christ and the Church (Mt 9:15; 22:9; Jn 3:29; 2 Co 11:5; Eph 5:22; Rev 19:9; 21:2), the new and definitive covenant that is extended to all peoples.

The Liturgy draws upon this psalm in celebrating the most impressive fulfillment of these mystical espousals: the Virgin Mary, Queen and Bride of the King; and those who, following her, have chosen Christ for their Bridegroom.

The words *For the director of music* in the superscription are thought to be a musical or liturgical notation; nothing is known about *To [the tune of] "Lilies"*; for *the Sons of Korah*, see introduction to Ps 42; for *maskil*, see introduction to Ps 32.

45:1-9 The poet addresses the King-Messiah and applies to him attributes of Yahweh (see Ps 145:4-7, 12f, etc.) and of Immanuel (see Isa 9:5f; 11:3-5). He is urged so to conduct himself that his reign will be adorned even more splendidly than the wedding vestments he has on (vv. 3-5). The best way he can do so is to make the glory of his kingdom consist in justice and righteousness (vv. 6-9).

45:1 *Heart:* see note on Ps 4:7.

² You are the most excellent of men*
and your lips have been anointed with
grace,
since God has blessed you forever.ᵛ
³ Gird your sword upon your side, O mighty
one;
clothe yourself with splendor and ma-
jesty.ʷ
⁴ In your majesty ride forth victoriously
in behalf of truth, humility and righteousness;
let your right hand display awesome
deeds.
⁵ Let your sharp arrows pierce the hearts of
the king's enemies;
let the nations fall beneath your feet.
⁶ Your throne, O God,* will last for ever and
ever;ˣ
a scepter of justice will be the scepter of
your kingdom.
⁷ You love righteousness and hate wickedness;
therefore God, your God, has set you
above your companions
by anointing you with the oil of joy.
⁸ All your robes are fragrant with myrrh and
aloes and cassia;*
from palaces adorned with ivory
the music of the strings makes you glad.

---

v SS 5:10-16; Lk 4:22.—w Ps 21:5; 149:6.—x 6-7: La 5:19; Heb 1:8-9.

45:2 *Most excellent of men:* so far above all other men was a king of that era regarded (see 1 Sa 9:2; 16:18) that he is akin to a god (see note on v. 6). Older versions translated this phrase as "fairest among the sons of men." *Lips . . . animated with grace:* see Pr 22:11; Ecc 10:12; see also Isa 50:4; Lk 4:22.
45:6 *O God:* a title of honor applied in the Bible to the Messiah (see Isa 9:6), as well as to the leaders and judges (see Ps 82:6), to Moses (see Ex 4:16; 7:1), the spirit of Samuel (see 1 Sa 28:13), and the House of David (see Zec 12:8). The fullest meaning of this description of the Davidic king is attained when it is applied to Christ (see Heb 1:8f).
45:8 *Myrrh and aloes and cassia:* Oriental perfumes (see Ge 37:25; Ex 25:6; SS 1:13; 4:14). *Adorned with ivory:* see 1 Ki 22:39; Am 3:15; 6:4.

⁹ Daughters of kings* are among your honored women;
  at your right hand is the royal bride in gold of Ophir.

¹⁰ Listen, O daughter, consider and give ear:
  Forget your people and your father's house.*
¹¹ The king is enthralled by your beauty;
  honor him, for he is your lord.
¹² The Daughter of Tyre* will come with a gift,ᵈ
  men of wealth will seek your favor.ʸ

¹³ All glorious is the princess within [her chamber];ᶻ
  her gown is interwoven with gold.
¹⁴ In embroidered garments she is led to the king;
  her virgin companions follow her
  and are brought to you.*
¹⁵ They are led in with joy and gladness;
  they enter the palace of the king.

¹⁶ Your* sons will take the place of your fathers;ᵃ
  you will make them princes throughout the land.

---

d Or *A Tyrian robe is among the gifts.*

y Ps 72:10-11; Jos 19:29; Isa 60:5f.—z 13-15: Isa 61:10; Eze 16:10-13.—
a Ge 17:6; 35:11.

45:9 *Daughters of kings:* in the allegorical sense, these are the pagan nations converted to the true God (see SS 1:3; 6:8; Isa 60:3f; 61:5) and admitted to his service (v. 15). *Gold of Ophir:* the most prized kind of gold (see 1 Ki 9:28; 10:11; Job 22:24). The location of Ophir is not known; it is sometimes identified with the southern coast of Arabia or eastern Africa.
45:10 *Forget your people and your father's house:* all her concern should be with what follows, not with what went before; she is the queen and should be concerned with her husband the king.
45:12 *Daughter of Tyre:* the city of Tyre, famous for its wealth, which was the first foreign city to recognize the Davidic dynasty (see 2 Sa 5:11) and remained close to Solomon (see 1 Ki 5; 9:10-14, 26-28).
45:14 *To you:* i.e., to the king.
45:16 *Your:* i.e., the king's. *Land:* or "earth."

[17] I will perpetuate your memory through all
    generations;[b]
therefore the nations will praise you for
    ever and ever.*

PSALM 46*

God, Refuge of His People

For the director of music. Of the Sons of Korah.
According to *alamoth*.[e] A song.

[1] God is our refuge and strength,*
    an ever-present help in trouble.[c]
[2] Therefore we will not fear, though the earth
    give way
    and the mountains fall into the heart of the
    sea,[d]

---

e Probably a musical term.

b Isa 60:15; 61:9; 62:2.—c Ps 9:9; 48:3; Isa 33:2.—d Ps 3:6; 93:3-4; Job
9:5-6; Isa 24:18-20; 54:10.

45:17 Filled with blessings (see Ge 17:6; 35:11), the new Zion will be glorious
and sovereign (see Isa 60:15, 21; 61:9; 62:2, 7), especially in Messianic times.
Ps 46 This psalm exalts the power of the God of Israel, Master of nature and
Ruler of both armies and peace. Upon a horizon of wars and cataclysms rises the
city of Zion, peaceful and unshakable. God is in her, a refuge protecting her from
all agitations, a river bringing her a richness of life. The psalm lets us relive the
explosion of joy prompted by the defeat of the Assyrian armies in 701 B.C. (see 2
Ki 18:13—19:37; 2 Ch 32).
This great moment of the past allows the Prophets to designate in advance
the drama at the end of time. Amidst the turmoil of nations, God intervenes to
save his people, and the world is turned upside down before obtaining definitive
peace. It is an image of the movement of history with its cataclysms and the
hope of universal salvation.
In praying this psalm, we should recall that the new and eternal Jerusalem,
our mother, is the Church (see Gal 4:26) to whom Christ guaranteed his perpetual protection that renders her indefectible.
The words *For the director of music* in the superscription are thought to be a
musical or liturgical notation; for *the Sons of Korah,* see introduction to Ps 42;
alamoth is probably a musical term.
46:1-3 The divine presence in the temple guarantees the security of the holy
city even though creation itself may seem to be falling apart (see Ps 104:6-9; Ge
1:9f).

³ though its waters roar and foam
    and the mountains quake with their surg-
      ing.*   *Selah*

⁴ There is a river* whose streams make glad
    the city of God,
    the holy place where the Most High
      dwells.ᵉ
⁵ God is within her, she will not fall;ᶠ
    God will help her at break of day.*
⁶ Nations are in uproar, kingdoms fall;
    he lifts his voice,* the earth melts.ᵍ

⁷ The LORD Almighty* is with us;
    the God of Jacob is our fortress.   *Selah*

⁸ Come and see the works of the LORD,
    the desolations he has brought on the
      earth.ʰ
⁹ He makes wars cease to the ends of the earth;ⁱ
    he breaks the bow and shatters the spear,
    he burns the shieldsᶠ with fire.*

---

f Or *chariots.*

e Ps 36:8; 48:1-2; 76:2.—f Dt 23:14; 2 Ki 19:35; Isa 17:14.—g Ps 2:1-5;
48:4-7; 76:6-8; Job 12:23; Isa 17:12-14.—h Ps 48:8-9; 66:5.—i Ps 76:3; Isa
2:4.

46:3 Some Catholic translations add here the refrain that obviously belongs,
as in vv. 7 and 11: "The LORD Almighty is with us;/the God of Jacob is our
fortress." The first part of this refrain is similar in structure and meaning to the
name of the royal child in Isaiah: "Immanuel"—"God is with us" (Isa 7:14; 8:8,
10).
    46:4 *River:* symbol of God's blessings; the symbolic waters (see Ps 36:8) that
spring forth (see Eze 47:1, 12; Joel 3:18; Zec 14:8), fructify the holy land, purify it
(see Zec 13:1), and turn it into a new Eden (see Ge 2:10).
    46:5 *At break of day:* the most favored time for attacks to be set in motion
against cities but also for God's blessings (see Ps 17:15; 49:14; 101:8; SS 2:17;
Isa 17:14). The psalm here most likely alludes to the retreat of Sennacherib's
armies in 701 B.C. (see 2 Ki 19:35).
    46:6 *His voice:* God's thunder (see Ps 104:7; Jer 25:30; Am 1:2). *Earth melts:*
under the heat of God's lightnings. But Israel has no need to fear any of these
calamities.
    46:7 *The LORD Almighty:* see note on Ps 24:10.
    46:9 This verse speaks of universal peace and anticipates the Messianic vic-
tory.

10 "Be still, and know that I am God;
     I will be exalted among the nations,[j]
     I will be exalted in the earth."*

11 The LORD Almighty is with us;
     the God of Jacob is our fortress.   *Selah*

PSALM 47*

The Lord, King of All Nations

For the director of music. Of the Sons of Korah. A psalm.

1 Clap your hands,* all you nations;
     shout to God with cries of joy.[k]
2 How awesome is the LORD Most High,
     the great King over all the earth![l]
3 He subdued nations under us,
     peoples under our feet.[m]
4 He chose our inheritance for us,
     the pride of Jacob,* whom he loved.[n] *Selah*

5 God has ascended amid shouts of joy,*
     the LORD amid the sounding of trumpets.[o]

---

j Ps 48:10; Dt 32:39; Eze 12:16.—k Ps 33:3; 89:15; Zep 3:14.—l Ps 95:3; Ge 14:18; Ex 15:18; Isa 24:23; 52:7.—m Ps 2:8; 18:39.—n Ps 16:6; Isa 58:14.—o Ps 24:8, 10; 68:18-19; 98:6; Nu 23:21.

46:10 *I will be exalted . . . in the earth:* because of his wondrous deeds for his people, especially the Life, Passion, and Resurrection of Jesus Christ.

Ps 47 This psalm is concerned with the feast of the New Year. The ark is transported: "God has ascended. . .," and during the procession this chant of the kingdom (see introduction to Ps 93) goes forth. Israel proclaims the kingship of God (see Ps 15:18; Isa 52:7; Zep 3:15) who has handed over to his people the land of Canaan and the city of Jerusalem while also defeating the nearby peoples. The ancient chant remains, but it appears as a prelude to the Lord's reign over the whole universe (see Jer 10:7). The pagans will be converted and join God's people in acclaiming the only true King (see Ezr 6:21; Isa 19:23-25; 25:6; 60:11).

The Roman and Byzantine liturgies see in this text a psalm for the Ascension of Christ: Christ "has ascended amid shouts of joy" and "is seated on his holy throne" as Lord at the right hand of the Father; from there salvation is offered to all peoples (see Ac 2:34; Php 2:9-11; Rev 5:7-9, 12f).

The words *For the director of music* in the superscription are thought to be a musical or liturgical notation; for *the Sons of Korah,* see introduction to Ps 42.

47:1 *Clap your hands:* a gesture used at occasions of great joy, e.g., at enthronements (see Ps 98:8; 2 Ki 11:12; Isa 55:12).

47:4 *Our inheritance . . . the pride of Jacob:* the promised land (see Ge 12:7; 17:8; Ex 3:8; Dt 1:8; Jer 3:18), which God gave Israel by a sovereign act.

47:5-6 God ascends liturgically to the temple in the ark of the covenant.

6 Sing praises to God, sing praises;
sing praises to our King, sing praises.

7 For God is the King of all the earth;[p]
sing to him a psalm[g] of praise.
8 God reigns over the nations;
God is seated on his holy throne.
9 The nobles of the nations assemble
as the people of the God of Abraham,
for the kings[h] of the earth belong to God;[q]
he is greatly exalted.*

PSALM 48*

Thanksgiving for the Deliverance of God's People

A song. A psalm of the Sons of Korah.

1 Great is the LORD, and most worthy of praise,[r]
in the city of our God, his holy mountain.*
2 It is beautiful in its loftiness,
the joy of the whole earth.[s]

---

g Or *a maskil* (probably a literary or musical term).—h Or *shields*.

---

p 7-8: Ps 72:11; 93:1; 96:10; 97:1; 99:1; Jer 10:7; Zec 14:9; Col 3:16.—q Ps 89:18; Ex 3:6; Ezr 6:21; Isa 2:2-4.—r Ps 86:10; 96:4; 145:3.—s Ps 50:2; La 2:15; Eze 16:14.

47:9 In Messianic times, the reconciled peoples will form only one people with God's chosen ones. The covenant with Abraham (see Ps 105:6; Ex 3:6; Est C:2-5 [13:9-13]) will be extended to all humankind (see Ps 72:11; Ge 9:9; Isa 2:2; 45:20f; 56:6; Zec 8:20; 14:16). *Nobles . . . kings [shields]:* some translate "Princes . . . guardians" and suggest that these terms refer to the angelic spirits who watch over the nations (see Dt 32:8f; Da 10:13).

Ps 48 With overflowing joy, this psalm sings of God and the holy city. All the glory of Jerusalem stems from the Lord who dwells, enveloped in mystery, in the temple on the hill in the heart of the city. From there he protects his people; he has even delivered this city from the assaults of the enemy. It is secure from the north (v. 2), east (v. 7), south (v. 10), and west (v. 13). There Israel encounters its God and gives him thanks. And from this dwelling of God, salvation, joy, and praise are spread to all peoples and the whole universe. It is a grandiose vision; how can one not love this land of God in the midst of human beings!

To Christians, Zion stands for the Church of Jesus, soul of the world and sign of salvation for humankind, until all are gathered together into the kingdom of God, the heavenly Jerusalem (see Heb 12:22; Rev 14:1; 21:10-26).

For *the Sons of Korah* in the superscription, see introduction to Ps 42.

48:1 *Holy mountain:* see note on Ps 2:6.

Like the utmost heights of Zaphon* [i] is Mount
Zion,[t]
the[j] city of the Great King.
3 God is in her citadels;
he has shown himself to be her fortress.*

4 When the kings joined forces,*
when they advanced together,
5 they saw [her] and were astounded;
they fled in terror.[u]
6 Trembling seized them there,
pain like that of a woman in labor.[v]
7 You destroyed them like ships of Tarshish*
shattered by an east wind.

8 As we have heard,
so have we seen*
in the city of the LORD Almighty,
in the city of our God:
God makes her secure forever. *Selah*

---

i *Zaphon* can refer to a sacred mountain or the direction north.—j Or
earth, / Mount Zion, on the northern side / of the.

t Isa 14:13.—u Ex 15:16; Jdg 5:19.—v Ex 15:14; Job 4:14; Jer 4:31.

48:2 *The utmost heights of Zaphon:* Mount Zaphon was in the far north, the
home of the Canaanite storm-god Baal. The psalmist declares that, although
Zion is only a small hill, it is higher than any other mountain because it is the
home of the only true God (see Ps 68:15f).
48:3 The psalmist shows that Zion is impregnable not because of her walls
but because of the fact that the Lord is present there as the strength of his people (see Ps 18:2; 122:7).
48:4-7 In recalling past defeats of Israel's enemies who attacked Zion, the
psalmist may have in mind the victory over the Moab-Ammon coalition at the
time of Jehoshaphat (see 2 Ch 20:22-28) or over the Assyrians at the time of
Hezekiah (see 2 Ki 19:35f).
48:7 *Ships of Tarshish:* i.e., the most powerful ships, built for long voyages—
like those that went as far as Tarshish, perhaps Tartessus in southern Spain (see
1 Ki 10:22). *East:* geographical allusion mentioned in the introduction.
48:8 *Heard . . . seen:* the psalmist may be referring to the glorious things that
new pilgrims had heard about the beauty and awesomeness of the holy city and
now saw with their own eyes. He may also be referring to the things the pilgrims
had heard from their fathers about the security of the temple at Jerusalem (see
Ps 44:1; 78:3) and now saw for themselves.*The LORD Almighty:* see note on Ps
24:10.

⁹ Within your temple, O God,
    we meditate on your unfailing love.*
¹⁰ Like your name, O God,
    your praise reaches to the ends of the
        earth;
    your right hand* is filled with righteous-
        ness.ʷ
¹¹ Mount Zion rejoices,
    the villages of Judah are glad
    because of your judgments.*ˣ

¹² Walk about Zion, go around her,*
    count her towers,
¹³ consider well her ramparts,
    view her citadels,
    that you may tell of them to the next gener-
        ation.ʸ
¹⁴ For this God is our God for ever and ever;
    he will be our guide even to the end.*

---

w Ps 113:3; Mal 1:11.—x Ps 97:8.—y Ps 22:30-31; 71:18.; 2 Sa 20:15.

48:9 The godly meditate on God's mighty acts, taking comfort in, rejoicing in, and gratefully making offerings to the revelation of the perfections of the Lord. *Unfailing love:* see note on Ps 6:4.

48:10 The reaction of praise is a positive response by the godly in contrast to the dread that befell the nations. The godly praise God from one end of the earth to another, declaring his righteousness, i.e., the Lord's victories and glorious work whose benefits his people share. That work is symbolized by his "right hand," which includes power, justice, righteousness, and love. As alluded to in the introduction to this psalm, "right hand" also has a connotation of "south" in Hebrew.

48:11 *Judgments:* God's actions in human affairs (see Ps 105:7; Isa 26:9), especially his victories over Israel's enemies (see Ps 48:11; 105:5; Dt 33:21).

48:12-13 The psalmist calls upon the people to walk around Jerusalem and see its great defenses (towers, ramparts, citadels). The physical defense system of Jerusalem may have been a symbol of a far greater strength—the protection of the Lord himself. Furthermore, inasmuch as the Lord was present in the temple at Jerusalem, defense of the city was an expression of loyalty to him.

48:14 After seeing the well-nigh impregnable fortifications of Jerusalem, the people will feel more secure and better understand the greatness of the Lord, who protects his city and his people in accord with his promises; they will then recount it to their children and grandchildren. The Lord is their God for ever, the great Shepherd-King (see note on Ps 23:1), who will continue to guide them even to their "end," literally, "death").

PSALM 49*

Deceptive Riches

For the director of music. Of the Sons of Korah. A psalm.

1 Hear this, all you peoples;*
   listen, all who live in this world,
2 both low and high,
   rich and poor alike:
3 My mouth will speak words of wisdom;ᶻ
   the utterance from my heart will give un-
      derstanding.*
4 I will turn my ear to a proverb;
   with the harp I will expound my riddle:*

5 Why should I fear when evil days come,
   when wicked deceivers surround me—
6 those who trust in their wealth
   and boast of their great riches?ᵃ

---

z Ps 37:30; 78:2; Mt 13:35.—a Job 31:24; Pr 10:15; Jer 9:23.

Ps 49 The psalmist meditates on the vanity of riches and the problem of retribution (see Ps 37 and 73), after introducing his discourse with a solemnity that is somewhat pretentious. He believes that he has the answer to the problems that torment many (though they are still far from experiencing the crisis of Job). Certainly, fortune is powerless to save the rich from the clutches of death, and no one can buy escape from death; on the contrary, the poor are "filled" because God pays for them what the rich cannot offer themselves despite all their wealth.

The author also seems convinced that death cannot take away from him the divine friendship. The lot of the righteous cannot be the same as that of the wicked, for he suspects (without knowing how to imagine it) that the former will receive some kind of liberation at God's hand (v. 16).

In praying this psalm, we should be mindful that riches cannot assure our physical life and constitute an obstacle to our spiritual life. However, if we remain united with Christ, who has conquered death, we will rise with him (1 Cor 15:45f).

The words *For the director of music* in the superscription are thought to be a musical or liturgical notation; for *the Sons of Korah,* see introduction to Ps 42.

49:1-4 Solemn introduction: the first part (vv. 1-2) recalls the Prophets (see 1 Ki 22:28; Isa 34:1; Mic 1:2) and the second (vv. 3-4) recalls Ps 78:2; Job 33:4; 34:19; Pr 8:4f.

49:3 See Mt 12:34. *Heart:* see note on Ps 4:7.

49:4 The psalmist alludes to a kind of inspiration: since all wisdom is from God (see Job 28), he lent his ear to hear it; at the same time, he makes use of the "harp," the instrument that accompanied prophesying (see 1 Sa 10:5f; 2 Ki 3:15).

7 No man can redeem the life of another[b]
    or give to God a ransom for him—*
8 the ransom for a life is costly,
    no payment is ever enough—
9 that he should live on forever
    and not see decay.

10 * For all can see that wise men die;[c]
    the foolish and the senseless alike perish[d]
    and leave their wealth to others.*
11 Their tombs will remain their houses[k] forever,
    their dwellings for endless generations,
      though they had[l] named lands after them-
        selves.

12 But man, despite his riches, does not endure;[e]
    he is[m] like the beasts that perish.*

13 This is the fate of those who trust in them-
        selves,
    and of their followers, who approve their
        sayings.*   *Selah*

---

k Septuagint and Syriac; Hebrew *In their thoughts their houses will remain.*—l Or *l for they have.*—m Hebrew; Septuagint and Syriac read verse
12 the same as verse 20.

b Job 33:24; Pr 11:4; Eze 7:19; Mt 16:26.—c Ps 92:6; Ecc 2:16—d Ps
39:6; Sir 11:18-19.—e Ecc 3:18-21; 2 Pe 2:12.

49:7-9 Wealth is useless to evade death; only God has the power to bring it
about (see v. 15 and Ps 116:15; Job 33:24-26; Pr 11:4; Eze 7:19; Mt 16:26; Ro
3:24). *Decay:* literally, "the pit," which as a synonym for "Sheol" (see Ps 16:10)
signifies death and perhaps retribution for evil done during life (see Ps 94:13).
49:10-11 Those who have amassed wealth for themselves (see Lk 12:20) or
those who have rejected the voice of wisdom (see Pr 1:17f) are "the foolish and
the senseless." These have taken pains to ensure their memory by naming prop-
erty after themselves but will be remembered only by the names engraved on
their tombs (v. 11; see Isa 22:16). For they will perish, forever bereft of their
wealth.
49:10 A passage very close to Ecc 2:16 (see Ps 39:6; 92:6f).
49:12 The psalmist states that death is an inevitable part of earthly existence.
He says nothing about life beyond death or the difference between human and
animal life.
49:13 The psalmist does not condemn riches in themselves but only the attitude of self-sufficiency so often associated with wealth, which then leads to in-
sensitivity, scheming, deception, and arrogance (see Jas 5:1-6) in both the rich
and their followers.

14 Like sheep* they are destined for the grave,[n]
and death will feed on them.
The upright will rule over them in the morning;
their forms will decay in the grave,[n]
far from their princely mansions.
15 But God will redeem my life[o] from the grave;
he will surely take me* to himself.[f]   *Selah*

16 Do not be overawed when a man grows rich,*
when the splendor of his house increases;
17 for he will take nothing with him when he
dies,[g]
his splendor will not descend with him.*
18 Though while he lived he counted himself
blessed—
and men praise you when you prosper—
19 he will join the generation of his fathers,[h]
who will never see the light [of life].*

20 A man who has riches without understanding
is like the beasts that perish.*

---

n Hebrew *Sheol;* also in verse 15.—o Or *soul.*

f Ps 16:10; 73:24; 86:13; 103:4; 116:8.—g Ps 17:14; Ecc 5:15; Sir 11:18-19; 1 Ti 6:7.—h Ge 15:15; Job 10:21-22.

49:14 *Like sheep:* death has become their shepherd, leading them to the grave. *In the morning:* the customary time for eschatological judgments and the triumph of the righteous (see Ps 17:15; 46:5; 101:8; SS 2:17; Isa 17:14).

49:15 *Take me:* this is the same Hebrew verb that is used for God "taking up" his favored servants: Enoch (see Ge 5:24), Elijah (see 2 Ki 2:11f), and the righteous person (see Ps 73:24). The psalmist thus harbors the hope that God will rescue the righteous from the grave in some way. This hope will become stronger in Israel, as later Books show (see 2 Mac 7:9f; 12:44f; 14:46; Wis 2:23; 3:9; 6:19; Da 12:2).

49:16-19 Faith enables the godly to avoid fearing anything that is transitory. Riches, splendor, and praise (garnered from self or from others) make no difference in the grave. Although wealth can protect one from the rigors of life, it is powerless against death, a place of utter darkness without even a ray of hope ("light").

49:17 In contrast, God will glorify the righteous (see Ps 62:7; 73:24; 91:15; 1 Sa 2:30; Wis 3:7; 1 Ti 6:6-8).

49:19 See note on Ps 27:1.

49:20 The psalmist indicates that the godly who are wealthy are different from the senseless rich. For such godly persons have understanding about riches as well as about their own mortality and about God, and they act accordingly.

PSALM 50*

The Worship Acceptable to God

A psalm of Asaph.

¹ * The Mighty One, God, the LORD,*
    speaks and summons the earth
        from the rising of the sun to the place
        where it sets.*ⁱ*

² From Zion, perfect in beauty,
    God shines forth.*ʲ*

³ Our God comes and will not be silent;
    a fire devours before him,*ᵏ*
    and around him a tempest rages.*

⁴ He summons the heavens above,
        and the earth, that he may judge his peo-
        ple:

---

i Ps 113:3; Dt 10:17; Jos 22:22.—j Ps 2:6; 48:2.—k Ps 97:3; Isa 42:14; Da 7:10.

Ps 50 This psalm takes the form of an indictment against God's people for formalistic practice of their religion and a request for sacrifices of praise accompanied by obedience. It is divided into three parts: (1) the announcement of the Lord's arrival and the convening of the court (vv. 1-6); (2) the Lord's words of correction (vv. 7-15); (3) his rebuke for the wicked and promise of reward or punishment (vv. 16-23). The psalm itself may have been composed for a temple liturgy for reaffirming commitment to the covenant.

In praying this psalm, we should recall that Jesus also condemned formalism. Christ does not reproach us for our external worship, our beautiful liturgical celebrations, vows, oblations, or sacrifices. However, all these must truly reflect sentiments of profound religion—"living sacrifices, holy and pleasing to God" (Ro 12:1).

The *Asaph* mentioned in the superscription was probably a choral leader in the Jerusalem temple (see introduction to Ps 73—89).

50:1-6 The author knows how to conjure up the whole apparatus of a divine manifestation. God himself solemnly appears to challenge those who dishonor worship and the Law and to recall for them the great demands of the covenant. Israel must realize that the God of Zion is the God of Sinai (see Ex 19:16-20). It is a picture of the Last Judgment.

50:1 *The Mighty One, God, the LORD:* this threefold formula for the divine name is found elsewhere only in Jos 22:22 (but see Dt 10:17). This psalm is notable for the seven names or other titles it uses for God (v. 1: "Mighty One," "God," "LORD"; v. 6: "judge"; v. 14: "Most High"; v. 21: "I AM"—see NIV textual note; v. 22: "God").

50:3 The Lord is the Ruler of the universe and his appearance is attended by phenomena calculated to create awe in his subjects: fire and a tempest. When he comes in judgment, he is like a consuming fire (see Dt 4:24; 9:3; Isa 66:16; Heb 12:29); in his anger, he may also storm like a tempest (see Isa 66:15).

⁵ "Gather to me my consecrated ones,
　　who made a covenant with me by sacri-
　　fice."*
⁶ And the heavens proclaim his righteousness,ˡ
　　for God himself is judge.*   *Selah*

⁷ "Hear, O my people, and I will speak,*
　　O Israel, and I will testify against you:
　　I am God, your God.
⁸ I do not rebuke you for your sacrifices
　　or your burnt offerings, which are ever be-
　　fore me.
⁹ I have no need of a bull from your stall
　　or of goats from your pens,ᵐ
¹⁰ for every animal of the forest is mine,
　　and the cattle on a thousand hills.
¹¹ I know every bird in the mountains,
　　and the creatures of the field are mine.
¹² If I were hungry I would not tell you,
　　for the world is mine, and all that is in
　　it.ⁿ
¹³ Do I eat the flesh of bulls
　　or drink the blood of goats?

---

l Ps 19:1; 97:6; Job 9:15.—m Ps 69:31; Lev 1:5; Am 5:21-22.—n Ps 24:1; 89:11; Ex 19:5; Dt 10:14; 1 Co 10:26.

50:5 Those consecrated to the Lord had made a covenant with him that was sealed by sacrifices (see Ex 24:4-8).

50:6 *Judge:* a title for God (see Ps 94:2; Ge 18:25; Jdg 11:27).

50:7-15 Pagans might have imagined that they owed food subsidies to their god; the Almighty has no need of our earthly goods, for everything belongs to him. This diatribe against purely external worship occurs often in the Bible, notably in the Prophets (see 1 Sa 15:22; 1 Ch 29:16-19; Isa 1:10-16; 29:13f; 58:1-8; Jer 6:20; 7:21; Hos 6:6; Joel 2:12; Mic 6:5-8; Zec 7:4-6; Mal 1:10) and is also found elsewhere in the Psalter (see Ps 40:6-8; 51:16f, etc.). The passages do not condemn sacrifices or worship in general, but only the formalism that is satisfied with performing external rites. We cannot bribe God; we can only acknowledge him by prayer and thanksgiving: this was the constant attitude of Jesus toward his Father. Truly religious persons are aware of their limitations; they await everything from God and realize that they owe him everything. The Gospel will lay a heavy emphasis on this teaching (see Mt 5:23; 12:7; Mk 12:33), and Paul will in turn repeat it in his teaching on worship in spirit (Ro 12:1; Php 2:17; 3:3).

14 Sacrifice thank offerings to God,
fulfill your vows to the Most High,[o]
15 and call upon me in the day of trouble;
I will deliver you, and you will honor me."[p]

16 But to the wicked, God says:

"What right have you to recite my laws*
or take my covenant on your lips?
17 You hate my instruction
and cast my words behind you.
18 When you see a thief, you join with him;
you throw in your lot with adulterers.
19 You use your mouth for evil
and harness your tongue to deceit.
20 You speak continually against your brother
and slander your own mother's son.
21 These things you have done and I kept silent;
you thought I was altogether*[p] like you.
But I will rebuke you
and accuse you to your face.

22 "Consider this, you who forget God,*
or I will tear you to pieces, with none to rescue:
23 He who sacrifices thank offerings honors me,
and he prepares the way
so that I may show him[q] the salvation of God."[q]

---

p Or *thought the 'I AM' was.*—q Or *and to him who considers his way / I will show.*

---

o Ps 76:11; Hos 14:2; Heb 13:15.—p Ps 4:1; 77:2.—q Ps 91:16; 98:3.

50:16-23 Another type of formalism is to have religion or the Law on one's lips more than in one's heart and life. There is no authentic faith unless it includes a moral commitment and notably that of justice and respect toward others: "Not everyone who says to me, 'Lord, Lord,' will enter the kingdom of heaven, but only he who does the will of my Father who is in heaven" (Mt 7:21).

50:21 *I was altogether:* or "the 'I AM' was" (as in NIV textual note).

50:22 *God:* here the Hebrew is a relatively rare poetic word, *Eloah,* found frequently in Job (see also Ps 18:32; 139:19; Dt 32:15, 17; Hab 3:3).

PSALM 51*

The Miserere: Repentance for Sin

For the director of music. A psalm of David. When the
prophet Nathan came to him after David had committed
adultery with Bathsheba.[r]

1 Have mercy on me, O God,
      according to your unfailing love;*
   according to your great compassion
      blot out my transgressions.
2 Wash away all my iniquity
      and cleanse me from my sin.

---

r 2 Sa 12:1.

Ps 51 This psalm, the "Miserere," the best known of the seven Penitential
Psalms (Ps 6; 32; 38; 51; 102; 130; 143), is still the most authentic expression of
our prayer as human beings. The kind of sincerity in the confession of sinfulness
that it expresses requires a limitless trust in the mercy of God. Whether it voices
the repentance of King David after his adultery (see 2 Sa 2:13) or that of the Jewish people after their return from the Exile during which they had become aware
of their infidelity, the entreaty shows the authentic visage of repentance.

Men and women become conscious of the sin that alienates them from God
(see Eze 2:3; 16:43); evil plunges its roots deep within their being (see Jer 5:23;
7:24; 17:9; Eze 36:26). A hasty forgiveness, an external purification, is not
enough; it is the heart that must be transformed. God alone can effect this new
creation and infuse a new spirit (see Eze 36:26), who allows sinners to come to
their senses and humbly commit themselves to him again. He alone can answer
the desire for complete renewal that is inscribed in a true request for forgiveness.
Our thoughts turn immediately to Paul who movingly describes the dramatic situation of sinners (Ro 7:14ff) and then contrasts it with the exalted life of Christians who let themselves be led by the Holy Spirit (Ro 8).

Especially striking in this regard is v. 5 of this psalm: the individual—or the
people—has been conceived in sin, begotten in guilt. The psalmist is surely not
thinking of a sin of the mother that might infect the child, nor does the Old Testament consider the conjugal union to be sinful; by this exceptionally violent
image the psalmist intends rather to convey the idea that the human being is
born as a prisoner of a sinful environment.

All Christians—whether under the shock of some personal failing or under the
at times searing impression of a life of mediocrity and nullity in God's eyes or in
union with the entire Church imploring the mercy of the Crucified upon the sinful
world—have recited this psalm with its bubbling lyricism to express contrition
and distress of soul, and to ask the Savior's mercy and their own inner renewal.

The words *For the director of music* in the superscription are thought to be a
musical or liturgical notation; for the event referred to, see 2 Sa 11:1—12:25.

51:1 *Unfailing love:* see note on Ps 6:4. *Blot out:* the psalmist pictures God
keeping a record of a person's deeds as earthly kings were wont to do (see Ps
56:8; 87:6; 130:3; 139:16; Ex 32:32f; Ne 13:14; Da 7:10) on a scroll and then
blotting out the evil deeds when forgiveness is given.

3 For I know my transgressions,
    and my sin is always before me.[s]
4 Against you, you only,* have I sinned
    and done what is evil in your sight,
  so that you are proved right when you speak
    and justified when you judge.[t]
5 Surely I was sinful at birth,[u]
    sinful from the time my mother conceived
      me.*
6 Surely you desire truth in the inner parts;[r]
    you teach[s] me wisdom in the inmost place.*

7 Cleanse me with hyssop,* and I will be clean;
    wash me, and I will be whiter than snow.[v]
8 Let me hear joy and gladness;
    let the bones you have crushed rejoice.
9 Hide your face from my sins
    and blot out all my iniquity.
10 Create* in me a pure heart, O God,
    and renew a steadfast spirit within me.[w]

---

r The meaning of the Hebrew for this phrase is uncertain.—s Or *you desired . . . ; / you taught.*

s Ps 32:5; 38:18; Isa 59:12; Eze 6:9.—t Lk 15:21; Ro 3:4.—u Lev 5:2; Job 14:4.—v Ex 12:22; Job 9:30; Isa 1:18; Eze 36:25; Heb 9:13-14.—w Eze 11:19; Eph 4:23-24.

51:4 *Against you . . . only:* the very essence of sin is that it constitutes an offense against God, even though it may also entail an offense against human beings. *Justified when you judge:* permitted by God, sin calls for the intervention of his judgment (see Ro 3:4).
51:5 All human beings have a congenital inclination toward evil (see Ge 8:21; 1 Ki 8:46; Job 4:17; 14:4; 15:14; 25:4; Pr 20:9). God must take account of this situation, which is a mitigating circumstance, and show mercy. Later, the doctrine of original sin will be made explicit (see Ro 5:12f; Eph 2:3).
51:6 Despite his sins against God's teaching, the psalmist craves that teaching with his whole being; he wants to be among the wise who follow God's law, not the fools who reject it (see Ps 37:30f).
51:7 *Hyssop:* a plant with many branchlets that is a convenient sprinkler, prescribed for sprinkling sacrificial blood or water for cleansing (see Ex 12:22; Lev 14:4; Nu 19:18). *Whiter than snow:* purity beyond compare (see Isa 1:18; Da 7:9; Rev 7:14; 19:14).
51:10 *Create:* verb reserved only for God (see Ge 1) and describing the act by which he brings into existence something new and wonderful (see Ex 34:10; Isa 48:7; 65:17; Jer 31:22). The justification of a sinner is the divine work par excellence (see Eze 36:25f). *Heart:* see note on Ps 4:7.

¹¹ Do not cast me from your presence
     or take your Holy Spirit* from me.ˣ
¹² Restore to me the joy of your salvation
     and grant me a willing spirit, to sustain me.

¹³ Then I will teach transgressors your ways,
     and sinners will turn back to you.
¹⁴ Save me from bloodguilt, O God,
     the God who saves me,
     and my tongue will sing of your righteous-
          ness.ʸ
¹⁵ O LORD, open my lips,
     and my mouth will declare your praise.
¹⁶ You do not delight in sacrifice, or I would
          bring it;ᶻ
     you do not take pleasure in burnt offerings.*
¹⁷ The sacrifices of God areᵗ a broken spirit;
     a broken and contrite heart,
     O God, you will not despise.*

¹⁸ In your good pleasure make Zion prosper;*
     build up the walls of Jerusalem.ᵃ

---

t Or *My sacrifice, O God, is.*

---

x Wis 1:5; 9:17; Isa 57:15; 63:10; Hag 2:5; Ro 8:9.—y Ps 30:9; 39:8.—z Ps 40:6; 50:8; 1 Sa 15:22; Isa 1:11-15; Hos 6:6; Am 5:21-22; Heb 10:5-7.—a Isa 58:12; Jer 31:4; Eze 36:33.

51:11 *Holy Spirit:* the full phrase is found in the Old Testament only here and in Isa 63:10f, but the word "Spirit" alone is found throughout. It is by his Spirit that God creates (see Ps 104:30; Ge 1:2; Job 33:4) and redeems (see Isa 32:15; 44:3; 63:11, 14; Hag 2:5), inspires the Prophets (see Nu 24:2f; 2 Sa 23:2; Ne 9:30; Isa 59:21; 61:1; Eze 11:5; Mic 3:8; Zec 7:12) and directs their ministries (see 1 Ki 18:12; 2 Ki 2:16; Isa 48:16; Eze 2:2; 3:14), prepares his servants for their given work (see Ex 31:3; Nu 11:29; Jdg 3:10; 1 Sa 10:6; 16:13; Isa 11:2; 42:1), and bestows on his people a "new heart and . . . a new spirit," enabling them to live in accord with his will (see Eze 36:26f).

51:16 See note on Ps 50:7-15.

51:17 *Broken spirit; a broken and contrite heart:* God is most pleased by a person who trusts in him despite trials of all sorts and who repents of sin and asks forgiveness.

51:18-19 Scholars believe that these verses are a postexilic addition, made perhaps before the rebuilding of the walls of Jerusalem in 445 B.C. *Righteous sacrifices:* sacrifices that are not mere empty ritual but filled with praise and thanksgiving to God for his great works.

¹⁹ Then there will be righteous sacrifices,
  whole burnt offerings to delight you;
  then bulls will be offered on your altar.

PSALM 52*

Prayer for Help against Calumniators

For the director of music. A *maskil*ᵘ of David. When Doeg
the Edomite had gone to Saul and told him: "David has
gone to the house of Ahimelech."ᵇ

¹ Why do you boast of evil, you mighty man?*
  Why do you boast all day long,
    you who are a disgrace in the eyes of
      God?ᶜ
² Your tongue plots destruction;
  it is like a sharpened razor,
    you who practice deceit.
³ You love evil rather than good,
  falsehood rather than speaking the truth.ᵈ
                                          Selah

⁴ You love every harmful word,
  O you deceitful tongue!ᵉ

---

u Probably a literary or musical term.

b 1 Sa 21:7; 22:6ff.—c Ps 10:3; 12:3; 59:7; 120:2-3; Sir 51:3.—d Jer
4:22; 9:5; Jn 3:19-20.—e Ps 5:9; Jer 9:4.

Ps 52 The psalmist indicates that a tragic end is reserved for arrogant cynicism and the perfidious tongue, while the righteous subsist, for they take refuge
in God; they will have the happiness of living in the temple, i.e., in the presence
of the Lord. This psalm constitutes one of the most violent indictments brought
against wicked tongues; it resembles the wisdom psalms (see Ps 57:4; 59:7) and
writings (Job 20).
    In praying this psalm, we can dwell on the fact that Jesus teaches us to fear
more than anything else those schemers who seek the death of our souls: the
devil and the corruptive world, the givers of scandal (see 1 Jn 2:16; 1 Pe 5:8). The
workers of evil know how to disguise themselves (see 2 Co 11:15); by the power of
Satan, they perform even lying works and use all the wicked deceptions of evil
(see 2 Th 2:9-12).
    The words *For the director of music* in the superscription are thought to be a
musical or liturgical notation; for *maskil*, see introduction to Ps 32. For the event
referred to, see 1 Sa 22:9f.
    52:1 *Mighty man:* title of scorn; he is mighty only in his own mind, and God
can easily put him in his place (see Isa 22:17).

⁵ Surely God will bring you down to everlasting ruin:*
    He will snatch you up and tear you from
        your tent;*
    he will uproot you from the land of the
        living.ᶠ   *Selah*
⁶ The righteous will see and fear;
    they will laugh at him, saying,ᵍ
⁷ "Here now is the man
    who did not make God his stronghold
  but trusted in his great wealth
    and grew strong by destroying others!"ʰ

⁸ * But I am like an olive tree*
    flourishing in the house of God;
  I trust in God's unfailing love
    for ever and ever.ⁱ
⁹ I will praise you forever for what you have
        done;*
    in your name I will hope, for your name is
        good.
    I will praise you in the presence of your
        saints.ʲ

---

f Ps 27:13; 28:5; 56:13; Job 18:14; Pr 2:22; Isa 22:19; 38:11; Eze 17:24.—g Ps 40:3; 44:13; 64:8.—h Job 31:24; Pr 11:28; Mk 10:23.—i Ps 1:3; 6:4; 92:12-14; Jer 11:16; 17:8.—j Ps 22:22; 26:12; 30:12; 35:18; 149:1.

52:5-7 The wicked will be brought down by God while the righteous will subsist and mock them (see Ps 28:5; Job 18:14; Pr 2:22; Isa 22:17). Their end will be that of the foolish rich of Ps 49.

52:5 *Tent:* the earthly dwelling (see Job 18:14).

52:8-9 The godly or righteous stands in contrast to the "mighty man" (v. 1). The mighty man relies on himself, does evil, and amasses ill-gotten riches and power; the Lord uproots him like a tree, turns him into a wanderer and destroys him like a building (v. 5). The godly relies on the Lord and is like a tree flourishing in the Lord's house. The mighty one boasts of his abilities; the godly praises the Lord for his wondrous works.

52:8 *Like an olive tree:* symbol of a long and fruitful life inasmuch as it lives hundreds of years (see Ps 92:12-14; 128:3). *Unfailing love:* see note on Ps 6:4.

52:9 *What you have done:* in punishing the wicked and saving the righteous (see Ps 13:5f; 22:31; 31:22; 57:3). *Saints:* people of God who are and should be devoted to him.

PSALM 53*

Foolishness of the Wicked

For the director of music. According to *mahalath.*[v]
A *maskil*[w] of David.

1 The fool says in his heart,*
  "There is no God."[k]
They are corrupt, and their ways are vile;
  there is no one who does good.[l]

2 God looks down from heaven
    on the sons of men[m]
  to see if there are any who understand,
    any who seek God.[n]
3 Everyone has turned away,
    they have together become corrupt;
  there is no one who does good,
    not even one.[o]

4 Will the evildoers never learn—
    those who devour my people as men eat
      bread[p]
  and who do not call on God?[q]

---

v Probably a musical term.—w Probably a literary or musical term.

k 1-5a: Ps 14:1-5a.—l Ps 10:4; 36:1; 74:22; Isa 32:6; Jer 5:12.—m Ps 11:4; 82:5; 102:19.—n 2b-3: Ro 3:11-12.—o Ps 12:1.—p Ps 27:2; Isa 9:12.—q Ps 79:6.

Ps 53 The psalmist stresses that when people banish God from their heart, they are led to renounce and exploit their neighbors. A generation turns away from God and erects injustice into a law, but the Lord of the poor and oppressed remains vigilant. The text reproduces Ps 14 with some variants: e.g., "God" is used for "the LORD" and v. 5 (which corresponds with vv. 5-6 of Ps 14) is different.

In praying this psalm, we can recall that all the attacks of spiritual or physical tyrants upon us are futile. Christ is with his faithful till the end of time, with the whole Church and with every Christian, to enable them to overcome all external and internal adversities. And without ceasing Christ offers to his Father, out of gratitude for deliverance, a sacrifice of thanksgiving—the Eucharist.

The words *For the director of music* in the superscription are thought to be a musical or liturgical notation; the word *mahalath* may signify a modulation indicating sadness; for *maskil,* see introduction to Ps 32.

53:1-4 See notes on Ps 14:1-4.

⁵ There they were, overwhelmed with dread,
   where there was nothing to dread.
God scattered the bones of those who attacked you;
     you put them to shame, for God despised
     them.*

⁶ Oh, that salvation for Israel would come out
   of Zion!
When God restores the fortunes of his people,
     let Jacob rejoice and Israel be glad!ʳ

PSALM 54*

Prayer in Time of Danger

For the director of music. With stringed instruments. A
*maskil*ˣ of David. When the Ziphites had gone to Saul and
   said, "Is not David hiding among us?"ˢ

¹ Save me, O God, by your name;
   vindicate me by your might.*
² Hear my prayer, O God;
   listen to the words of my mouth.

---

x Probably a literary or musical term.

r Ps 85:1.—s 1 Sa 23:19; 26:1.

53:5 This verse corresponds with the theme of Ps 14:5-6 that God crushes
evildoers who attack his people, but the text is quite different. *Scattered the
bones:* bodies left unburied (regarded as a horrible fate) in the wake of a devas-
tating defeat—an allusion to Israel's divine deliverance from the siege of Sennacherib in 701 B.C. as a sign of what happens to all who attack God's people
(see 2 Ki 19:35f; Isa 37:36f).

Ps 54 The "name" stands for God himself, the Almighty One. To him the
psalmist directs his supplication, from him help will come, and toward him will
thanksgiving be extended. For Christians, the "name" is that of Jesus Christ, who
saves those who invoke it (see Ac 2:21; Ro 10:9; 1 Co 1:2). "There is no other
name under heaven given to men by which we must be saved" (Ac 4:12). The
name "Jesus" means "God saves" (see Mt 1:21).

The words *For the director of music* in the superscription are thought to be a
musical or liturgical notation; for *maskil,* see introduction to Ps 32; for the event
in David's life, see 1 Sa 23:19.

54:1 The beleaguered psalmist summons God to give him justice (see Ps 17).
Name: see note on Ps 14:7.

³ Strangers* are attacking me;
  ruthless men seek my life—
  men without regard for God.ᵗ   *Selah*

⁴ Surely God is my help;
  the LORD is the one who sustains me.ᵘ

⁵ Let evil recoil on those who slander me;ᵛ
  in your faithfulness destroy them.*

⁶ I will sacrifice a freewill offering to you;*
  I will praise your name, O LORD,
  for it is good.

⁷ For he has delivered me from all my troubles,
  and my eyes have looked in triumph on my
  foes.ʷ

PSALM 55*ˣ

Prayer in Time of Betrayal by a Friend

For the director of music. With stringed instruments. A
*maskil*ʸ of David.

¹ Listen to my prayer, O God,*
  do not ignore my plea;ˣ

---

y Probably a literary or musical term.

t Ps 18:48; 86:14.—u Ps 20:2; 118:7.—v Ps 94:23; 143:12.—w Ps 58:10;
59:10; 91:8; 92:11.—x 1-2: Ps 5:1-2; 27:9; 86:6; 130:1-2; La 3:56; Jnh 2:2.

54:3 *Strangers:* probably a reference to the people of the desert of Ziph (see 1
Sa 23:19). *Men without regard for God:* the same type of sinners as in Ps 53.
54:5 See note on Ps 5:10 and introduction to Ps 35.
54:6-7 God and his faithful have the same enemies, and their defeat is a subject for joy and thanksgiving. *Praise your name:* see note on Ps 7:17.
Ps 55 The psalmist, a sensitive and pious Levite, interminably repeats his
lament. Three times he describes his torment as the victim of calumny distressed
to see the holy city corrupted, and abandoned by his best friend. If only he could
escape this misfortune that obsesses him! We are reminded of David in the wake
of Absalom's rebellion against him (see 2 Sa 15—17) as well as of Jeremiah ex-
coriated by his enemies (Jer 4:19; 5:1; 6:6; 9:1, 3, 7) and of Christ, the man of
sorrows, betrayed by his friend (see Mt 26:21-23).
  This psalm is a prayer for days when we feel exhausted by the struggles of life,
by the hostility of people and things, when we would like nothing more than to escape, to flee into some deserted spot and encounter nobody. However, the psalmist
knows that only God's presence can free the heart imprisoned by suffering.
  The words *For the director of music* in the superscription are thought to be a
musical or liturgical notation; for *maskil,* see introduction to Ps 32.
55:1-3 The psalmist begs God to listen to his plight.

²   hear me and answer me.
My thoughts trouble me and I am distraught
³   at the voice of the enemy,
       at the stares of the wicked;
   for they bring down suffering upon me
       and revile me in their anger.

⁴ * My heart* is in anguish within me;
       the terrors of death assail me.
⁵ Fear and trembling have beset me;
       horror has overwhelmed me.
⁶ I said, "Oh, that I had the wings of a dove!
       I would fly away and be at rest—^y
⁷ I would flee far away
       and stay in the desert;^z   *Selah*
⁸ I would hurry to my place of shelter,
       far from the tempest and storm."

⁹ * Confuse the wicked, O LORD, confound their
       speech,
       for I see violence and strife in the city.*
¹⁰ Day and night they prowl about on its walls;
       malice and abuse are within it.
¹¹ Destructive forces are at work in the city;
       threats and lies never leave its streets.^a

¹² If an enemy were insulting me,*
       I could endure it;
   if a foe were raising himself against me,
       I could hide from him.

---

y Ps 11:1.—z 1 Sa 23:14; Jer 9:2; Rev 12:6.—a Ps 5:9; Jer 5:1; 6:6; Eze
22:2; Hab 1:3; Zep 3:1.

55:4-8 So great is the physical danger and the mental anguish (see Ps 18:4f;
116:3) that the psalmist wishes he could run away from it all (see Jer 9:2-6).
   55:4 *Heart:* see note on Ps 4:7.
   55:9-11 The psalmist issues an urgent call for God to come to his assistance.
   55:9 See note on Ps 5:10 and introduction to Ps 35. *Confuse . . . confound
their speech:* possibly a reference to God's action at Babel (see Ge 11:5-9). Sins
of the tongue, calumnies, false witness, and insults are often denounced in
psalms of lamentation. *Violence . . . strife:* entities are personified here and in v.
10 *(malice . . . abuse),* and vv. 9b-10 recall Jer 5:1; 6:6; 9:6; Eze 22:2; Zep 3:1.
   55:12-14 Doubtless, the betrayer is a Levite; the targum identifies the false
friend as Ahithophel (see Ps 44:10; 2 Sa 15:12). See also Mt 26:21-25.

13 But it is you, a man like myself,
        my companion, my close friend,*b*
14 with whom I once enjoyed sweet fellowship
        as we walked with the throng at the house
            of God.

15 Let death take my enemies by surprise;*c*
        let them go down alive to the grave,*z*
        for evil finds lodging among them.*

16 But I call to God,
        and the LORD saves me.*
17 Evening, morning and noon*
        I cry out in distress,
        and he hears my voice.*d*
18 He ransoms me unharmed
        from the battle waged against me,*
        even though many oppose me.
19 God, who is enthroned forever,
        will hear them and afflict them—   *Selah*
    men who never change their ways
        and have no fear of God.*e*

20 My companion attacks his friends;
        he violates his covenant.
21 His speech is smooth as butter,
        yet war is in his heart;
    his words are more soothing than oil,
        yet they are drawn swords.*f*

---

z Hebrew *Sheol.*

b Ps 41:9; 2 Sa 15:12; Jer 9:4; Mt 26:21-24 par.—c Ps 49:14; 64:7; Nu 16:33; Pr 1:12; Isa 5:14.—d Ps 141:2; Da 6:10.—e Ps 29:10; 93:2; Dt 33:27; Bar 3:3.—f Ps 12:2; 28:3; 57:4; 62:4; 64:3; Pr 12:18; 26:24-28; Jer 9:8.

55:15 The psalmist calls for the sudden, premature death of his enemies (see note on v. 9 above), which was the same as the punishment wished on one's enemies (see Ps 73:19; 102:24; Job 15:32; Pr 1:12; Isa 38:10; Jer 17:11), a punishment that overtook the rebellious band of Korah (see Nu 16:32f).
55:16-19 The psalmist believes that God will hear his prayer and come to his aid.
55:17 *Evening, morning and noon:* the hours for prayer (see Da 6:10f). The legal day begins at the setting of the sun ("evening").
55:18-23 The psalmist reflects once again on his friend's treachery and then puts his full trust in the Lord.

²² Cast your cares on the LORD
   and he will sustain you;*
   he will never let the righteous fall.ᵍ
²³ But you, O God, will bring down the wicked
   into the pitʰ of corruption;*
bloodthirsty and deceitful men
   will not live out half their days.

But as for me, I trust in you.ⁱ

PSALM 56*

Boundless Trust in God

For the director of music. To [the tune of] "A Dove on Distant Oaks." Of David. A *miktam*.ᵃ When the Philistines
had seized him in Gath.ʲ

¹ Be merciful to me, O God, for men hotly pursue me;
   all day long they press their attack.
² My slanderers pursue me all day long;
   many are attacking me in their pride.

---

a Probably a literary or musical term.

g Ps 37:5; Pr 3:5; 16:3; Mt 6:25; 1 Pe 5:7.—h Ps 9:15; 28:1; 30:3; 40:2;
73:18; 88:4; 143:7; Pr 1:12; Jnh 2:6.—i Ps 25:2; 56:3; 130:5.—j 1 Sa
21:10; 24:3.

55:22 Text cited in 1 Pe 5:7 (see also Ps 121:2; Isa 50:10).
55:23 See note on v. 9 above. *Pit of corruption:* i.e., the grave.
Ps 56 A psalmist subjected to harassment appeals to the Lord to take note
of the injustice he is undergoing. He calls for the judgment of God to come upon
his persecutors; but, more importantly, a profound religious sense enables him to
divine that the prayer and tears of human beings are precious in God's eyes. The
spirit of this psalm resides in the refrain: a firm protestation of trust in the word of
the Lord (vv. 4, 10-11) despite all the plots of humans. So strong is the psalmist's
certitude on this point that it transforms his fervent prayer from a lament into a
thanksgiving.
   It is easy to place this psalm on the lips of Christ, for its themes are all found
in the Passion: a plea for the Father's mercy, assaults of pagan tyrants, calumnies, plots and snares on the part of enemies, tears, cries of confidence, and a
vow of thanksgiving. The psalm also provides Christians with a beautiful prayer
of supplication in time of adversity, whether external or internal.
   The words *For the director of music* in the superscription are thought to be a
musical or liturgical notation; nothing is known about *To [the tune of] . . .*; for
miktam, see introduction to Ps 16. For the event, see 1 Sa 21:10-15.

3 When I am afraid,
    I will trust in you.
4 In God, whose word* I praise,*k*
    in God I trust; I will not be afraid.
    What can mortal man do to me?*l*

5 All day long they twist my words;
    they are always plotting to harm me.
6 They conspire, they lurk,
    they watch my steps,
    eager to take my life.*m*

7 On no account let them escape;
    in your anger, O God, bring down the na-
        tions.
8 Record my lament;*n*
    list my tears on your scroll*b*—
    are they not in your record?*

9 Then my enemies will turn back
    when I call for help.
    By this I will know that God is for me.
10 In God, whose word I praise,
    in the LORD, whose word I praise—
11 in God I trust; I will not be afraid.
    What can man do to me?

---

b Or *I put my tears in your wineskin.*

k Ps 52:9; 84:12; 130:5.—l Ps 118:6; Heb 13:6.—m Ps 59:3; 140:4-5.—n
Ps 10:14; 2 Ki 20:5; Isa 25:8; Mal 3:16; Rev 7:17.

56:4 *Word:* as in v. 10, God's "word" is the promise by which he committed
himself to his faithful; this is a very familiar theme in the Psalter (see Ps 105:8-
11; 119:42, 65; 130:5). *Mortal man:* literally, "flesh," representative of human
frailty with respect to the divine power. People can indeed inflict pain, suffering,
and death upon us, but they cannot rob us of our souls or our eternal future (see
Ps 118:6; Heb 13:6). Jesus said: "Do not be afraid of those who kill the body but
cannot kill the soul" (Mt 10:28); thus, we are to fear no one but God alone, who is
also our helper.
56:8 God cares for his faithful and keeps a careful record of everything about
them (see note on Ps 51:1)—even the tears they shed when they are in trouble.
The theme of God's record is frequent (see, e.g., Ps 139:16; Job 19:23; Mal 3:16).
Each tear of the righteous will be compensated (see 2 Ki 20:5; Isa 25:8; Rev
7:17). Indeed, Jesus indicated that God has such concern for us that he knows
the number of hairs on our head (Mt 10:30).

¹² I am under vows* to you, O God;
     I will present my thank offerings to you.^o
¹³ For you have delivered me^c from death
     and my feet from stumbling,
  that I may walk before God*
     in the light of life.^d

PSALM 57*

Trust in God amid Suffering

For the director of music. [To the tune of] "Do Not
Destroy." Of David. A *miktam.*^e When he had
fled from Saul into the cave.^P

¹ Have mercy on me, O God, have mercy on
  me,
     for in you my soul* takes refuge.
 I will take refuge in the shadow of your
  wings
     until the disaster has passed.^q

---

c Or *my soul.*—d Or *the land of the living.*—e Probably a literary or musical term.

---

o Lev 7:11f; Nu 30:3.—p 1 Sa 22:1.—q Ps 2:12; 17:8; 36:7.

56:12 *I am under vows:* the psalmist is certain of being delivered and vows to make thanksgiving for it (see note on Ps 7:17).

56:13 *Walk before God:* see note on Ps 11:7. *Light of life:* a happy life on earth (see note on Ps 36:9).

Ps 57 The psalmist pictures evildoers like lions tearing away at him and ravaging his reputation. It is altogether natural for him, then, to call upon God to come in power to chastise the enemy and establish his kingdom on earth. A second tableau ends the psalm: the believer sings of God's deliverance, which comes like a dawn in the midst of the night of danger. Part of this psalm is duplicated in Ps 108 (57:7-11=108:1-5).

This supplication may be justly applied to Christ during his whole Public Life and Passion. Surrounded and attacked by his enemies, he seeks refuge in his Father, who cannot abandon him. It can also fittingly be applied to us who are constantly threatened by our spiritual enemies.

The words *For the director of music* in the superscription are thought to be a musical or liturgical notation; the words *Do not destroy* are probably a note by an early scribe intended to prevent his manuscript from being discarded. For *miktam,* see introduction to Ps 16; for the event, see 1 Sa 24:1-3.

57:1 *My soul:* see note on Ps 6:3. *Shadow of your wings:* conventional Hebrew metaphor for protection; it may have been inspired by the wings of the cherubim spread over the ark in the inner chamber of the temple (see 1 Ki 6:23-28).

2 I cry out to God Most High,
     to God, who fulfills [his purpose] for me.*
3 He sends from heaven and saves me,
     rebuking those who hotly pursue me; *Selah*
God sends his love and his faithfulness.

4 I am in the midst of lions;[r]
     I lie among ravenous beasts—
men whose teeth are spears and arrows,
     whose tongues are sharp swords.[s]

5 Be exalted, O God, above the heavens;[t]
     let your glory be over all the earth.*

6 They spread a net for my feet—
     I was bowed down in distress.[u]
They dug a pit in my path—
     but they have fallen into it themselves.*
                         Selah

7 My heart is steadfast, O God,*
     my heart is steadfast;*
I will sing and make music.[v]

8 Awake, my soul!
     Awake, harp and lyre![w]
I will awaken the dawn.*

---

r Ps 17:11-12; 22:21; 58:6.—s Ps 11:2; 64:3; Pr 30:14.—t Ps 72:19; 102:15; Nu 14:21.—u Ps 7:15; 10:9; 140:5-6.—v Ps 108:1; 112:7.—w Ps 33:2; Job 38:12.

57:2 *Who fulfills [his purpose] for me:* an allusion to God's providence; another translation given is: "who puts an end to my troubles."

57:5 The psalmist asks that the kingdom of God may be manifested (see Ps 72:19; Nu 14:21; 1 Ch 29:11; Isa 6:3; 33:10; Hab 2:14) by the deliverance of the faithful and the ruin of the wicked (see Ps 79:9; 102:15f; 138:5).

57:6 The psalmist's enemies have made use of any means to bring him down. Like hunters, they sought to trap him with a net or by digging a pit (see Ps 7:15; 9:15), but they were caught in their own devices and the psalmist, although hard pressed, escaped.

57:7-11 These verses (with slight variations) are the same as vv. 1-5 of Ps 108.

57:7 The psalmist is at peace because of his trust in the Lord. *Heart:* see note on Ps 4:7.

57:8 *Dawn:* personified as in Ps 139:9; Job 3:9; 38:12. The "night" (v. 4: "lie") symbolizes trials; deliverance comes with the "dawn" (see Ps 17:15).

⁹ I will praise you, O LORD, among the na-
    tions;*
    I will sing of you among the peoples.ˣ
¹⁰ For great is your love, reaching to the heav-
    ens;
    your faithfulness reaches to the skies.ʸ

¹¹ Be exalted, O God, above the heavens;
    let your glory be over all the earth.

PSALM 58*

Against Unjust Rulers

For the director of music. [To the tune of] "Do Not
    Destroy." Of David. A *miktam.*ᶠ

¹ Do you rulers* indeed speak justly?
    Do you judge uprightly among men?ᶻ
² No, in your heart* you devise injustice,
    and your hands mete out violence on the
    earth.

---

f Probably a literary or musical term.

x Ps 9:11; 18:49.—y Ps 36:5; 71:19.—z Ps 82:2; Dt 16:19.

57:9-10 A vow to offer ritual praise to the Lord for his goodness (see note on Ps 7:17).

Ps 58 This is one of the so-called imprecatory (or cursing) psalms (see introduction to Ps 35) that call upon God to mete out justice to enemies. In their thirst for justice, the authors of these psalms use hyperbole (or overstatement) in order to move others to oppose sin and evil. Such impassioned expressions may seem vengeful to a Western audience not used to the diatribes and curses of Eastern-ers. And the joy exhibited over the justice to be meted out seems ferocious to us. However, we must realize above all that the psalmists were desiring only true justice, a justice that could not be derailed, denied, or mocked—because it was God's justice.

The psalmist and all Israel regard judges as well as princes to be divine beings (see Ps 45:6; 82:6; Ex 21:6; Dt 19:17), for judging, like ruling, is a power of God. This psalm wars against those who pervert such a divine power.

The early Church applied this psalm to the trial of Jesus before the Sanhedrin (see Mt 26:57-68 par).

The words *For the director of music* in the superscription are thought to be a musical or liturgical notation; for *Do not destroy,* see introduction to Ps 57; for *miktam,* see introduction to Ps 16.

58:1 *Rulers:* literally, "gods"; see introduction.

58:2 *Heart:* see note on Ps 4:7.

³ Even from birth the wicked go astray;
>   from the womb they are wayward and
>   speak lies.*
⁴ Their venom is like the venom of a snake,
>   like that of a cobra that has stopped its
>   ears,ᵃ
⁵ that will not heed the tune of the charmer,
>   however skillful the enchanter may be.*

⁶ Break the teeth in their mouths, O God;*
>   tear out, O LORD, the fangs of the lions!ᵇ
⁷ * Let them vanish like water that flows away;ᶜ
>   when they draw the bow, let their arrows
>   be blunted.* ᵈ
⁸ Like a slug* melting away as it moves along,
>   like a stillborn child, may they not see the
>   sun.ᵉ

⁹ Before your pots can feel [the heat of] the
>   thorns—* ᶠ
>   whether they be green or dry—the wicked
>   will be swept away.ᵍ

---

g The meaning of the Hebrew for this verse is uncertain.

a Ps 64:3; 140:3; Dt 32:33; Ro 3:13.—b Ps 3:7; 35:17.—c Job 11:16; Wis
16:29.—d Ps 11:2; 57:4; 64:3.—e Job 3:16; Ecc 6:3.—f Ps 21:18; Job
21:18; Hos 13:13; Na 1:10.

58:3 The evil ways of the wicked (see Ps 10) are theirs from birth.
58:5 The roles of charmers and enchanters are frequently alluded to in the Old
Testament (see Dt 18:11; Ecc 10:11; Isa 3:3; Jer 8:17).
58:6 The psalmist regards teeth as weapons of the mouths by which the
wicked harass the righteous (see Ps 57:4); so he begs God to destroy them.
58:7-11 See introduction above and introduction to Ps 35.
58:7b *When . . . blunted:* the meaning of the Hebrew is unclear. The NIV translation likens the psalmist's foes to archers who shoot blunted arrows. Another
common translation is: "like grass let them be trodden down and wither" (see Ps
37:2).
58:8 *Slug:* the ancients believed that slugs dried up in the sun and evaporated.
58:9 The meaning of the Hebrew for this verse is uncertain. Another translation given is: "Before they sprout thorns like the bramble . . . swept away."
The translation above is in accord with the fact that twigs from wild
bushes ("thorns") were used to start quick fires for cooking (see Ps 118:12; Ecc
7:6).

¹⁰ The righteous will be glad when they are
   avenged,
      when they bathe their feet in the blood* of
      the wicked.ᵍ
¹¹ Then men will say,
      "Surely the righteous still are rewarded;
      surely there is a God who judges the earth."

PSALM 59*

Against Wicked Enemies

For the director of music. [To the tune of] "Do Not Destroy." Of David. A *miktam*.ʰ When Saul had sent men to
watch David's house in order to kill him.ʰ

¹ Deliver me from my enemies, O God;
      protect me* from those who rise up against
      me.
² Deliver me from evildoers
      and save me from bloodthirsty men.

---

h Probably a literary or musical term.

g Ps 68:23; Isa 63:1-6; Mal 3:18.—h 1 Sa 19:11.

58:10 *Bathe their feet in the blood:* a vivid expression indicating complete victory over one's foes that was common in the Near East (see Ps 68:23; Isa 63:1-6).
   Ps 59 The most realistic situation for this psalm is as follows: a believer, a
Jewish group, or the whole people is exposed to persecution; it comes from forces
that wish to impose paganism on the exiles or perhaps on Jerusalem itself. Like
raging dogs that prowl the night in the cities of the East in search of prey, evil-
intentioned persons attack the innocent victim with slander and curses, seeking
to destroy his reputation and ultimately his life. The description is ferocious and
the imprecation vehement and vengeful; but God will not tolerate lying and perfidy without end; the Almighty One cannot let himself be mocked, for his honor is
at stake (v. 13).
   We can pray this psalm to God and to Christ in our name in all our temporal
struggles, and even more in the bitter spiritual struggles we must constantly
wage against our powerful spiritual enemies in the footsteps and image of our
Master.
   The words *For the director of music* in the superscription are thought to be a
musical or liturgical notation; for *Do not destroy,* see introduction to Ps 57; for
miktam, see introduction to Ps 16. The superscription imagines that the occasion
for this psalm was the narrative in 1 Sa 19:11-17. Some believe it might have
been when Jerusalem was under siege as at the time of Hezekiah (see 2 Ki
18:19), while others point to the time of Nehemiah (see Ne 4).
   59:1 *Protect me:* literally, "lift me to a high, safe place."

³ See how they lie in wait for me!
    Fierce men conspire against me
    for no offense or sin of mine, O LORD.
⁴ I have done no wrong, yet they are ready to
       attack me.
    Arise to help me; look on my plight!
⁵ O LORD God Almighty,* the God of Israel,
    rouse yourself to punish all the nations;
    show no mercy to wicked traitors.
                                Selah

⁶ They return at evening,
    snarling like dogs,
    and prowl about the city.ⁱ
⁷ See what they spew from their mouths—
    they spew out swords from their lips,
    and they say, "Who can hear us?"*
⁸ But you, O LORD, laugh at them;
    you scoff at all those nations.ʲ

⁹ O my Strength, I watch for you;
    you, O God, are my fortress, ¹⁰my loving
       God.

    God will go before me
       and will let me gloat over those who slan-
       der me.
¹¹ But do not kill them, O LORD our shield,ⁱ
    or my people will forget.

---

i Or *sovereign*.

i Ps 22:16; 55:10.—j Ps 2:4; 37:13; Pr 1:26; Wis 4:18.

59:5 LORD *God Almighty:* an expression used first in 1 Sa 1:3 to designate the Lord as the sovereign over all powers in the universe—the God of all armies, both the heavenly army (see Ps 68:17; Dt 33:2; Jos 5:14; Hab 3:8) and the army of Israel (see 1 Sa 17:45). See also note on Ps 24:10. *God of Israel . . . punish all the nations:* seems to indicate an attack on Israel by the nations.
59:7-8 The wicked curse God as if he cannot see and hear and will not respond. But God laughs at them (see Ps 2:4; 37:13) and listens until the day of reckoning when the curses will fall back in judgment on the wicked themselves.

In your might make them wander about,
and bring them down.*
12 For the sins of their mouths,
for the words of their lips,
let them be caught in their pride.
For the curses and lies they utter,[k]
13   consume them in wrath,
consume them till they are no more.
Then it will be known to the ends of the
earth
that God rules over Jacob.* [l]   *Selah*

14 They return at evening,*
snarling like dogs,
and prowl about the city.
15 They wander about for food
and howl if not satisfied.
16 But I will sing of your strength,
in the morning I will sing of your love;
for you are my fortress,
my refuge in times of trouble.*

17 O my Strength, I sing praise to you;
you, O God, are my fortress, my loving
God.*

---

k Ps 10:7; Pr 12:13; 18:7.—l Ps 46:9-10; 83:17-18; Eze 5:13.

59:11 The psalmist asks God not to kill his foes but to prolong their chastisement; in this way the people will remember this particular saving act longer than they have remembered others (see Ps 78:11; 106:13).

59:13 God's punishment of the nations will show that God, the King of Israel (see Ps 24:1, 6; Isa 41:21ff; 63:19), is also the Master of the universe (see Ps 46:10f; 83:18).

59:14-17 The wicked wreak havoc like a pack of dogs, snarling and howling as they prowl about the city. The godly take courage in the vision of God's laughter (v. 8) and the assurance of his love (vv. 9-10). For the Lord is their Strength and their fortress, who will deliver them from all their enemies and whom they will praise.

59:16 After the night of danger (vv. 6, 14), the psalmist will sing to God on the morning of deliverance (see introduction to Ps 57 and note on Ps 57:8).

59:17 The psalmist vows to offer ritual praise for his deliverance (see note on Ps 7:17).

PSALM 60*

Prayer To End Wars

For the director of music. To [the tune of] "The Lily of the Covenant." A *miktam*[j] of David. For teaching. When he fought Aram Naharaim[k] and Aram Zobah,[l] and when Joab returned and struck down twelve thousand Edomites in the Valley of Salt.[m]

1 You have rejected us, O God, and burst forth
    upon us;
    you have been angry—now restore us!
2 You have shaken the land* and torn it open;
    mend its fractures, for it is quaking.[n]
3 You have shown your people desperate
    times;[o]
    you have given us wine that makes us stag-
    ger.*

---

j Probably a literary or musical term.—k That is, Arameans of Northwest Mesopotamia.—l That is, Arameans of central Syria.

m 2 Sa 8:2, 3, 13; 1 Ch 18:2, 3, 12.—n Ps 18:7; 75:3; Isa 24:19.—o Ps 71:20; 75:8; Isa 51:17, 21-22.

Ps 60 God responds to the supplication of the nation of Israel, which is suffering because it has neglected the covenant. The cry of a holy war sounds forth. God mobilizes Israel from one end to the other (vv. 6-7) to wreak judgment on enemy territory—one feels as if carried back to the time of the Exodus and the Conquest of Canaan. After the Exile, this psalm could have been chanted during a penitential liturgy. Verses 5-12 are also found in Ps 108 as vv. 6-13.

The military casualties and temporal disasters of ancient Israel typify the spiritual disasters that the Church, the new Israel, sometimes suffers. In union with Christ, her risen Head, the Church directs this supplication to the Father in critical moments of her history.

The words *For the director of music* in the superscription are thought to be a musical or liturgical notation; the meaning of *To [the tune of]* . . . is unknown; for *miktam,* see introduction to Ps 16. The superscription refers to events that are found in 2 Sa 8:1; 1 Ch 18. However, the accounts make no mention of Edom or of the fact that David's forces met stiff resistance (Ps 60:1-3) and even a temporary defeat (Ps 60:9f). The *Valley of Salt* is unknown (see 2 Sa 8:13).

60:2 *Shaken the land:* the defeat is likened to an earthquake, which is an apocalyptic characteristic (see Isa 24:20).

60:3 *Wine that makes us stagger:* God has given them drink from the cup of the divine wrath (see Ps 75:8; Isa 51:17, 22; Jer 25:15) rather than the cup of the divine blessings (see Ps 16:5, including note; 23:5; 116:13).

4 But for those who fear you,
you have raised a banner
to be unfurled against the bow.* *Selah*

5 Save us and help us with your right hand,*
that those you love may be delivered.
6 God has spoken from his sanctuary:*
"In triumph I will parcel out Shechem
and measure off the Valley of Succoth.
7 Gilead is mine, and Manasseh is mine;
Ephraim is my helmet,*
Judah my scepter.
8 Moab is my washbasin,*
upon Edom I toss my sandal;
over Philistia I shout in triumph."[p]

9 * Who will bring me to the fortified city?*
Who will lead me to Edom?
10 Is it not you, O God, you who have rejected us
and no longer go out with our armies?[q]
11 Give us aid against the enemy,
for the help of man is worthless.
12 With God we will gain the victory,
and he will trample down our enemies.

---

p Ps 137:7; Dt 2:5; Ru 4:7-8.—q Ps 44:9; 68:7.

60:4 *Bow:* symbol of the enemy, which relied on its bows.

60:5-12 These verses occur again as vv. 6-13 of Ps 108.

60:6-8 The Lord gives his people an oracle of hope, reminding them of his promises that the earth is his and no enemy can stand against him. *Shechem* was west of the Jordan, and *Succoth* east of it; therefore, they indicated dominion over all of Palestine. Next are named four Israelite tribes; hence, there are three regions in all that must be reduced to subjection.

60:7 *Helmet:* a symbol of the strength exhibited by the tribe of Ephraim (see Dt 33:17; Jdg 7:24—8:3). *Scepter:* a symbol of the King-Messiah who had been promised from Judah (see Ge 49:10).

60:8 *Moab is my washbasin:* i.e., its people will do menial work for the Israelites (see Ge 18:4). *Toss my sandal:* an Eastern way of signifying possession.

60:9-12 The psalmist asks the Lord to lead him to victory even though the pain of defeat and God's apparent rejection are still with him. For he knows that the Lord remains with his people and will ensure a joyous and victorious outcome (see Ps 44:5; 118:15f).

60:9 *Fortified city:* doubtless Bozrah in Idumea (see Isa 34:6; 63:1; Am 1:12). It was from this inaccessible refuge that the Edomites sent incursions into Judea.

PSALM 61*

Prayer of One in Exile

For the director of music. With stringed instruments.
Of David.

¹ Hear my cry, O God;
    listen to my prayer.

² From the ends of the earth* I call to you,
    I call as my heart grows faint;
    lead me to the rock that is higher than I.
³ For you have been my refuge,
    a strong tower against the foe.ʳ

⁴ I long to dwell in your tent foreverˢ
    and take refuge in the shelter of your
        wings.*   *Selah*

⁵ For you have heard my vows, O God;
    you have given me the heritage of those
        who fear your name.*

---

r Ps 46:1; Pr 18:10.—s Ps 15:1; 17:8; 36:7; 57:2.

Ps 61 The psalmist, a Levite deported to Babylon along with the elite of the Jewish people in 598 B.C., voices his ardent desire to return to the holy city and resume his service in the temple. Added to this lament of the exiled Levite is a prayer for the king, probably on behalf of Zedekiah, the last to sit on the throne of David after the first deportation of 598 B.C. This prayer also calls upon the Messiah, who is to come from the royal line (see 2 Sa 7; 1 Ch 17:14), to reign forever, and whose coming Israel awaits.

This prayer beautifully expresses our hope as Christians. Sent by the Father and anointed by the Holy Spirit, Christ has become our Head, our guide and leader to the Father, provided we keep our eyes fixed on him by faith (see Ac 3:15; 5:31; Heb 2:10; 12:2). Long live Christ the King!

The words *For the director of music* in the superscription are thought to be a musical or liturgical notation.

61:2 *Ends of the earth:* the phrase can also be translated as "from the brink of the netherworld," i.e., the grave. *Heart:* see note on Ps 4:7. *Higher than I:* a reference to God, the psalmist's "rock of refuge" (Ps 31:2; 71:3; see also Ps 18:2; 62:2, 6f; 94:22) or God's sanctuary (see Ps 27:5).

61:4 *Shelter of your wings:* see note on Ps 17:8.

61:5 The psalmist is certain of being heard (see Ps 56:13; 66:19) and resuming his functions (see Ps 16:5), for he is among those who fear God (see Mal 3:16; 4:2).

⁶ Increase the days of the king's life,*
   his years for many generations.ᵗ
⁷ May he be enthroned in God's presence forever;ᵘ
   appoint your love and faithfulness to protect him.ᵛ

⁸ Then will I ever sing praise to your name
   and fulfill my vows day after day.*

PSALM 62*

Trust in God Alone

For the director of music. For Jeduthun. A psalm of David.

¹ My soul* finds rest in God alone;ʷ
   my salvation comes from him.

---

t Ps 21:4; 1 Ki 3:14.—u Ps 72:5; 89:4.—v Ps 40:11; 85:10; 89:14, 24; Pr 20:28.—w 1-2, 5-6: Ps 18:2; 31:2-3; 42:9; 118:8; 146:3; Mic 7:7.

61:6-7 As in Ps 85:10f and 89:14, 24, these personified divine attributes were thought to accompany the Messiah just as they protect the king (see Pr 20:28) or the simple Levite (see Ps 40:11). They were then applied to Christ, "Son of David," by the Fathers of the Church. The insistence on an eternal reign recalls the prophecy of Nathan (see 2 Sa 7:16; 1 Ch 17:14), which is frequently alluded to in the Psalter (see Ps 18:50; 45:17; 72:5, 17; 89:4; 132:12).

61:8 See note on Ps 7:17. To fulfill one's vows meant to make an offering or sacrifice promised to God, normally in a single ceremony. To do so *day after day* shows a commitment to a debt that could never be paid off or an awareness that God's blessings are new every morning.

Ps 62 This psalm recalls the malice of human beings (see Ps 4:2), the noth-ingness of creatures (see Ps 39:5f; Isa 40:15), the vanity of riches (see Ps 49:12; Pr 11:28; 27:24), and the impartiality of the heavenly Judge (see Ps 9:7f, 16; 11:7; 33:5; 140:12). It provides an unsurpassable lesson of wisdom and simple trust in God to those who are deeply hurt and deceived (see Ps 31). Human beings seek success in wickedness, falsehood, and violence. The believer knows the futility of this manner of acting; it is of no avail in the sight of God's judg-ment. Entirely different is the strength of the faithful: the Lord, who renders to each what they merit (Job 34:11; Pr 24:12; Sir 16:14; Eze 18), will never fail them—and he is the only one who will never do so.

At the invitation of Christ and in union with him, we must learn to abandon ourselves to the heavenly Father in all the trials and difficulties of life and seek in him our rest and inner peace. We could thus recite this entire psalm to cele-brate the wonderful fruits of this filial confidence and to exhort our life compan-ions to practice similar abandonment.

The words *For the director of music* in the superscription are thought to be a musical or liturgical notation; for *Jeduthun,* see introduction to Ps 39.

62:1 *Soul:* see note on Ps 6:3.

2 He alone is my rock and my salvation;
    he is my fortress, I will never be shaken.

3 How long will you assault a man?
    Would all of you throw him down—
    this leaning wall, this tottering fence?*
4 They fully intend to topple him
    from his lofty place;*
    they take delight in lies.
  With their mouths they bless,
    but in their hearts they curse.ˣ   *Selah*

5 Find rest,* O my soul, in God alone;
    my hope comes from him.
6 He alone is my rock and my salvation;
    he is my fortress, I will not be shaken.
7 My salvation and my honor depend on God;ᵐ
    he is my mighty rock, my refuge.ʸ
8 Trust in him at all times, O people;
    pour out your hearts to him,*
    for God is our refuge.   *Selah*

9 Lowborn men are but a breath,
    the highborn are but a lie;
  if weighed on a balance, they are nothing;ᶻ
    together they are only a breath.*
10 Do not trust in extortion
    or take pride in stolen goods;*

---

m Or / *God Most High is my salvation and my honor.*

x Ps 12:2; 28:3; 55:21; Pr 26:24-25.—y Ps 3:3; Isa 26:4; 60:19; Jer 3:23.—z Ps 39:5-6; 144:4; Job 7:16; Wis 2:15; Isa 40:15.

62:3 *Leaning wall . . . tottering fence:* metaphor for the psalmist's state of weakness—real (in God's eyes) or imagined (by his enemies).
62:4 *Lofty place:* either a throne in the case of David or a place of safety such as a fortress on a cliff in the case of another psalmist.
62:5 *Find rest:* see Ps 27:13f; 42:5, 11; 43:5.
62:8 *Pour out your hearts to him:* a call for true prayer and meditation with God (see La 2:19). *Hearts:* see note on Ps 4:7.
62:9 A reference to the manner of weighing precious objects; the lighter one would rise. On God's scale, the wicked are a puff of air. The image of the scale recurs in Job 31:6; Pr 16:2; 21:2; 24:12; Isa 40:15.
62:10 The Prophets inveighed against social crimes (see Isa 30:12; Eze 22:29). The consequence was the recommendation to be detached from riches (see Job 27:12ff; 31:25; Ecc 5:8ff; Jer 17:11; Mt 6:19f, 24).

though your riches increase,[a]
do not set your heart on them.*

[11] One thing God has spoken,
two things have I heard:
that you, O God, are strong,[b]
[12]   and that you, O LORD, are loving.
Surely you will reward each person[c]
according to what he has done.*

PSALM 63*

Thirst for God

A psalm of David. When he was in the Desert of Judah.[d]

[1] O God, you are my God,
earnestly* I seek you;
my soul thirsts for you,
my body longs for you,
in a dry and weary land
where there is no water.[e]

---

a Job 31:25; Ecc 5:9; Jer 17:11; Eze 22:29; Mt 6:19-21, 24.—b Job 40:5; Rev 19:1.—c Ps 28:4; 31:23; 86:5; 2 Sa 3:39; Job 34:11; Jer 17:10; Mt 16:27; Ro 2:6; 2 Ti 4:14; Rev 22:12.—d 1 Sa 24; 2 Sa 15:23-28.—e Ps 36:7-9; 42:2; 143:6; Isa 26:9.

62:12 The doctrine of personal retribution, taught by the Prophets, above all Ezekiel (see Eze 18), is taken up by the sages and the psalmists (see Ps 28:4; 31:23; Job 34:11; Pr 24:12; Sir 16:13) and passes into the New Testament (see Mt 16:27; Ro 2:6; 2 Ti 4:14; Rev 2:23)—but only good deeds have eternal value.

Ps 63 A deported Levite thinks back to the time when he lived in the temple, close to God; in the silence of the night he meditates on those happy hours, the remembrance of which comforts him. And the desire rises in him and becomes more and more intense; already it is as if he is once again in the sanctuary with no other occupation than to offer unceasing praise to the One whose love surpasses every other good. In that time of deliverance the king will be filled with blessings by God while the oppressors will receive the severest of chastisements.

By its movement and style, this engaging prayer finds a place among the most beautiful psalms of longing (see Ps 42; 61; 73; 84). It enables us to rediscover—amid the difficulties of daily life and all that distracts us from the spiritual life—the longing for God, whose love is the only thing that makes life worth living. It can also serve as the song of the prodigal son (see Lk 15), enabling us to put into words the distress, hope, and penitence of the repentant sinner.

The superscription ascribes this psalm to a time when David was in the desert (see 1 Sa 24; 2 Sa 15:23-28; 16:2, 14; 17:16, 29).

63:1 *Earnestly:* literally, "in the morning" (see introduction to Ps 57 and note to Ps 57:8). *My soul . . . my body:* i.e., my whole being.

² I have seen you in the sanctuary
　　and beheld your power and your glory.
³ Because your love* is better than life,
　　my lips will glorify you.
⁴ I will praise you as long as I live,
　　and in your name* I will lift up my hands.
⁵ My soul* will be satisfied as with the richest
　　　of foods;
　　with singing lips my mouth will praise you.

⁶ On my bed* I remember you;
　　I think of you through the watches of the
　　　night.
⁷ Because you are my help,ᶠ
　　I sing in the shadow of your wings.*
⁸ My soul clings to you;
　　your right hand upholds me.

⁹ * They who seek my life will be destroyed;*
　　they will go down to the depths of the
　　　earth.
¹⁰ They will be given over to the sword
　　and become food for jackals.

---

f Ps 17:8; 27:9; 36:7.

63:3 *Love:* see note on Ps 6:4. For the Old Testament, the greatest good was earthly life; but God's love is better even than life.

63:4 *Name:* see note on Ps 8:1. *Lift up my hands:* in a gesture of prayerful praise.

63:5 *Soul:* see note on Ps 6:3. *Richest of foods:* literally, "marrow and fat," the preferred meats of the Palestinian Arabs and a symbol of the best of foods (see Ps 36:8).

63:6 *On my bed:* during the night of darkness, the psalmist anxiously looks for the morning of God's deliverance (see introduction to Ps 57 and note on Ps 57:8). *Watches of the night:* the night was divided into three watches, and if someone were aware of all three of them he was passing a sleepless night—in this case on prayer (see Ps 119:148; La 2:19).

63:7 See note on Ps 17:8.

63:9-11 See note on Ps 5:10 and introduction to Ps 35.

63:9-10 The psalmist's enemies will lose their lives for having sought to kill him, and they will become *food for jackals,* i.e., they will remain unburied, a cause for shame (see note on Ps 53:5).

¹¹ But the king will rejoice in God;
    all who swear by God's name* will praise
      him,
    while the mouths of liars will be silenced.ᵍ

PSALM 64*

Thanksgiving for Recovery from Illness

For the director of music. A psalm of David.

¹ Hear me, O God, as I voice my complaint;
    protect my life from the threat of the
      enemy.
² Hide me from the conspiracy of the wicked,
    from that noisy crowd of evildoers.

³ They sharpen their tongues* like swords
    and aim their words like deadly arrows.ʰ
⁴ They shoot from ambush at the innocent
      man;
    they shoot at him suddenly, without fear.

---

g Ps 21:1; 107:42.—h Ps 11:2; 37:14; 55:21; 57:4; Jer 9:3.

63:11 *All who swear by God's name:* to swear by God's name signified devoted adherence to him (see Isa 45:23; 48:1; Zep 1:5). God will acquit his followers (see Dt 6:13; Jer 12:16; Da 13:42, 60) but will chastise the wicked (see Ps 52:1-5).

Ps 64 The psalmist shows that the righteous are often defenseless before the cynicism of the machinations and calumnies to which they are prey. Those who weave their intrigues act in shadows and believe they are hidden from view. However, God sees everything, even secret human actions and designs. His judgment overtakes those who evade justice. Basing himself on the law of talion ("an eye for an eye"), the author imagines that, even here below, God will turn their evil against the wicked while publicly acquitting the righteous. Each life will be brought before the judgment of God; the righteous will find their joy in the Lord. Such is the lesson of the psalm, even though the ways of God follow a more mysterious course than its author yet suspected.

This psalm was applied to the Passion of Jesus by St. Augustine. It also finds a ready place in the prayer of the Church and the faithful who experience the physical and spiritual attacks of the world, the flesh, and the devil as we await the coming of Christ to dispense true justice (see Rev 19:1f).

The words *For the director of music* in the superscription are thought to be a musical or liturgical notation.

64:3 *Tongues:* see note on Ps 5:9.

5 They encourage each other in evil plans,*
    they talk about hiding their snares;
    they say, "Who will see them?"[n]
6 They plot injustice and say,
    "We have devised a perfect plan!"
    Surely the mind and heart* of man are
    cunning.[i]

7 * But God will shoot them with arrows;*
    suddenly they will be struck down.[j]
8 He will turn their own tongues against them
    and bring them to ruin;[k]
    all who see them will shake their heads in
    scorn.*

9 All mankind will fear;*
    they will proclaim the works of God
    and ponder what he has done.*
10 Let the righteous rejoice in the LORD
    and take refuge in him;
    let all the upright in heart praise him![l]

---

n Or *us.*

i Ps 140:2; Pr 6:14; Jer 11:20f.—j Ps 7:12-13; 38:2; Dt 32:42.—k Ps
5:10; 44:14; 52:4; 59:12.—l Ps 5:11; 36:7; 57:1.

64:5-6 These verses enlarge the portrait of the wicked set forth in vv. 2-4;
there the wicked are shown opposing the innocent, while here their common plot-
ting is shown. The wicked lay snares to trap their victims (see Ps 35:7; 119:110;
140:5; 142:3; Dt 7:16; Pr 22:24f; Jer 7:9f).
64:6 *Heart:* see note on Ps 4:7. *Cunning:* literally, "deep" (see Pr 18:4; 20:5).
64:7-9 See note on Ps 5:10 and introduction to Ps 35.
64:7-8 God will turn on the wicked the harm they wanted to do to the psalmist,
as demanded by the law of talion (see Ps 7:12f; 9:15f; 35:7f; 37:15; 59:12f;
140:9). He will shoot his arrows at them (see Ps 38:2; Dt 32:42). The shame they
had intended to bring upon the godly will fall back upon themselves (see Ps 22:7;
52:6f; 59:10; Jer 48:26).
64:8 *Shake their heads in scorn:* a common gesture of ridicule (see Ps 22:7;
44:14; 109:25; Jer 48:27).
64:9-10 The psalmist encourages all to proclaim and ponder the acts of God
(see Ps 2:10; Isa 41:20) and to turn to him in adversity. He will vindicate his servants who are righteous (see Ps 7:10; 11:2-7), and they will be in a position to
give him praise (see Ps 7:17).
64:9 The wicked asked derisively, "Who will see us?" (v. 5) and were unafraid
of the consequences of their actions. But when all humanity sees the power of
God, fear will come upon everyone.

PSALM 65*

Thanksgiving for Divine Blessings

For the director of music. A psalm of David. A song.

1 Praise awaits* o you, O God, in Zion;
   to you our vows will be fulfilled.
2 O you who hear prayer,
   to you all men* will come.m
3 When we were overwhelmed by sins,n
   you forgavep our transgressions.*
4 Blessed* are those you choose
   and bring near to live in your courts!

---

o Or *befits;* the meaning of the Hebrew for this word is uncertain.—p Or *made atonement for.*

m Ps 86:9; Isa 66:23.—n Ps 32:1-2; 40:12; 78:38; Isa 1:18.

Ps 65 In Israel, the harvest feast (see Lev 23:29) directly follows the Day of Atonement (to which reference is made in v. 3; see Lev 16). This time the people are celebrating a season of abundance. Joy and gratitude pervade this poem. At the beginning, there is a first acclamation to the Lord who dwells in Zion; in this privileged place God receives worship and dispenses pardon while the Levites are overwhelmed with joy and filled with grace. Then the horizon is expanded to include the very ends of the earth: the people praise the Master of the world whose exploits are proclaimed by all creation and history. Lastly, gratitude is offered for the huge harvest: the poet evokes the miracle that comes in the form of rain for these regions ever threatened by drought; the springtime of Judea shines forth, and the country experiences a sumptuous rebirth.

The modern—scientific—way in which we look at the succession of the seasons and harvests need not deprive us of the wisdom of the ancients, which saw God at work and extolled his splendor and goodness. It is God who acts through the regular course of nature (see Mt 6:26, 30).

This psalm reminds us to offer God unceasing praise and thanksgiving (see Col 3:16f; Eph 5:19f).

The words *For the director of music* in the superscription are thought to be a musical or liturgical notation.

65:1 *Awaits:* or "befits" (as in NIV textual note). The debt of giving praise to God is fulfilled when people carry out the vows they made in time of need (see note on Ps 7:17).

65:2 *All men:* literally, "all flesh"; all humankind will come to God. It recalls the universalism of the psalmists (see Ps 64:9; 66:1, 4, 8; 67:3-5) and of Isaiah (see Isa 17:12; 26:15; 66:19, 23).

65:3 *Forgave our transgressions:* or "made atonement for our transgressions" (as in NIV textual note). God forgives sins when his people repent and observe his rules for pardon (as he did for the Israelites who observed the Day of Atonement—see Lev 16:20-30).

65:4 *Blessed:* see note on Ps 1:1.

We are filled with the good things of your
    house,*
  of your holy temple.

5 You answer us with awesome deeds* of righ-
    teousness,
    O God our Savior,
  the hope of all the ends of the earth
  and of the farthest seas,o
6 who formed the mountains by your power,
    having armed yourself with strength,
7 who stilled the roaring of the seas,
    the roaring of their waves,p
  and the turmoil of the nations.* q

8 Those living far away fear your wonders;*
    where morning dawns and evening fades
  you call forth songs of joy.

9 You care for the land and water it;
    you enrich it abundantly.r
The streams of God* are filled with water
  to provide the people with grain,
  for so you have ordained it.q
10 You drench its furrows
    and level its ridges;
  you soften it with showers
    and bless its crops.

---

q Or *for that is how you prepare the land.*

---

o Ps 18:46; Isa 66:19.—p Ps 89:9; 93:3-4; 107:29; Job 26:12; 38:11; Mt 8:26.—q Isa 17:12.—r Ps 68:9-10; Lev 26:4; Isa 30:23, 25; Joel 2:22-23.

65:4 *Good things of your house:* see note on Ps 36:8.
65:5 *Awesome deeds:* God's creative acts as reflected in the beauty and bounty of Nature and his saving acts as seen in the deliverance of Israel from Egypt and its establishment in the promised land (see Ps 106:22; 145:6; Dt 10:21; 2 Sa 7:23; Isa 64:3).
65:7 Just as God tamed the turbulence of the primeval waters of chaos (see notes on Ps 32:6 and 33:7), so he brings to an end the *turmoil of the nations* (see Isa 2:4f; 11:6-9; Mic 4:3f).
65:8 *Wonders:* the great saving acts of God indicated in note to v. 5.
65:9 *Streams of God:* the poet evokes the means by which God brings forth the rain out of his "storehouses" (Ps 33:7), which flow into the water sources on earth and give life to creatures, not the symbolic streams of Zion (see Ps 46:4; Isa 33:21).

11 You crown the year with your bounty,*
    and your carts overflow with abundance.
12 The grasslands of the desert overflow;
    the hills are clothed with gladness.
13 The meadows are covered with flocks
    and the valleys are mantled with grain;
    they shout for joy and sing.* s

PSALM 66*

Thanksgiving for God's Deliverance

For the director of music. A song. A psalm.

1 Shout with joy to God, all the earth!*
2   Sing the glory of his name;*
    make his praise glorious!t

---

s Ps 66:1; Isa 44:23. —t Ps 65:13; 79:9; Isa 44:23.

65:11 *Bounty:* literally, "goodness"; the reference is to both material and spiritual gifts, God's covenant promises. God's royal chariot tours the heavens dispensing his abundance throughout the earth (see Ps 18:10; 68:4; Dt 33:26; Isa 66:15; Am 9:13).

65:13 *They shout for joy and sing:* all creation joins in the praise of God for his goodness (see Ps 89:12; 96:11-13; 98:8f; 103:22; 145:10; 148:3f, 7-10; Job 38:7; Isa 44:23; 49:13; 55:12).

Ps 66 This psalm is made up of two wholly autonomous parts: in the first, Israel praises God for his saving acts on its behalf, and in the second, an individual fulfills his vow to God for some favor. In its liturgy, Israel always contemplates anew the great days of the past: the Exodus from Egypt and the passage of the Jordan (v. 5). This does not constitute nostalgia for a past favor; yesterday's event is to act as the sign of God's presence today. For God always manifests himself as the savior of his people: now he delivers them from the distress of an invasion or possibly from the great trial of the Exile (vv. 8-11). A spirit of universalism pervades the first part of this poem: the whole earth is invited to proclaim the deliverances of God.

In the individual's prayer of thanksgiving, a man saved from a great trial comes to give praise by his offerings and his proclamation amidst his friends. The person who announces a deliverance at God's hands makes himself the spokesman of the community of believers.

This psalm is an apt reminder to offer God a fitting sacrifice of thanksgiving in the Eucharist. Such is the living sacrifice we offer God, placing ourselves in it as other living victims (see Ro 12:1) in order to thank him for the wonders accomplished in our souls, especially for our spiritual resurrection achieved in union with Christ's Resurrection (see Ro 6:5-8).

The words *For the director of music* in the superscription are thought to be a musical or liturgical notation.

66:1 *All the earth:* see note on Ps 65:2.

66:2 *Name:* see note on Ps 8:1.

3 Say to God, "How awesome are your deeds!ᵘ
    So great is your power
    that your enemies cringe before you.
4 All the earth bows down to you;
    they sing praise to you,
    they sing praise to your name."   *Selah*

5 Come and see* what God has done,
    how awesome his works in man's behalf!
6 He turned the sea into dry land,
    they passed through the waters* on foot—
    come, let us rejoice in him.ᵛ
7 He rules forever by his power,
    his eyes watch the nations—
    let not the rebellious rise up against him.
                                          Selah

8 Praise our God, O peoples,*
    let the sound of his praise be heard;
9 he has preserved our lives*
    and kept our feet from slipping.ʷ
10 For you, O God, tested us;
    you refined us like silver.ˣ
11 You brought us into prison*
    and laid burdens on our backs.

---

u 3-4: Ps 18:44; 81:15; Mic 7:17.—v Ps 74:15; 114:3; Ge 8:1; Ex 14:21f;
Jos 3:14ff; Isa 44:27; 1 Co 10:1.—w Ps 30:3; 91:12; 121:3; 1 Sa 2:9; Pr
3:23.—x Ex 15:25; Isa 48:10.

66:5 *Come and see:* in the eyes of the psalmist, God's saving acts are present
and can be seen in the liturgical celebration in the temple.

66:6 *Sea . . . waters:* the passages through the Red Sea (see Ex 14:1—15:21)
and through the Jordan (see Jos 3:11—4:24) became typical of God's power and
wondrous deeds in the history of Israel (see Ps 114:3; Isa 44:27; 50:2).

66:8-12 Praise for a new deliverance that God has worked on his people's behalf.

66:9 *Preserved our lives:* sometimes translated as "brought us to life," which
accounts for the name "Resurrection Psalm" given this psalm in Greek and Latin
manuscripts and its use in the Easter Liturgy.

66:11-12 The Israelites experienced imprisonment, slavery, and total defeat
before being delivered by God and brought into a place of abundance (see Ps
18:19; 23:4-6; 119:45). For the Lord does not permit his people to succumb to
their trials (see Ps 37:24; 1 Co 10:13) and rewards a persevering faith (see 1 Pe
1:7).

12 You let men ride over our heads;*
   we went through fire and water,
      but you brought us to a place of abun-
         dance.*y*

13 I will come to your temple with burnt offer-
      ings*
   and fulfill my vows to you—
14 vows my lips promised and my mouth spoke
   when I was in trouble.
15 I will sacrifice fat animals to you
   and an offering of rams;
   I will offer bulls and goats.   *Selah*

16 Come and listen, all you who fear God;
   let me tell you what he has done for me.
17 * I cried out to him with my mouth;
   his praise* was on my tongue.
18 If I had cherished sin in my heart,
   the LORD would not have listened;*
19 but God has surely listened
   and heard my voice in prayer.
20 Praise be to God,
   who has not rejected my prayer
   or withheld his love from me!

y Ps 32:6; Isa 43:2.

66:12 *You let men ride over our heads:* literally, "you let men mount our head," which suggests the ancient practice of victors in war placing their feet on the necks of their enemies as a sign of total subjugation (see Isa 51:23). *Fire and water:* conventional metaphors for the gravest of trials (see Ps 8:7; 32:6; Isa 43:2; 51:22f).

66:13-20 An individual fulfills the vows he promised to God when he was in trouble (see note on Ps 7:17; Ps 50:14; 116:17-19).

66:17-20 The psalmist's celebration of his deliverance includes a lament ("I cried out," v. 17), a profession of commitment ("his praise was on my tongue," v. 17), a protestation of innocence ("if I had cherished sin," v. 18; see Ps 17:1f; 18:20f; 59:3f; Jn 9:31), and praise ("God has surely listened," v. 19; see Ps 28:6; 31:21; 68:19, 35).

66:17 *I cried out . . . his praise:* prayer always entails praise in both the Old Testament and the New (see Php 4:6; 1 Ti 2:1). Even while the psalmist was praying for help, he was also praising God for his goodness and mercy.

66:18 Because the psalmist acknowledged his sin, he was forgiven by God, and his prayer was heard.

PSALM 67*

Prayer That All May Worship God

For the director of music. With stringed instruments.
A psalm. A song.

¹ May God be gracious to us and bless us[z]
 and make his face shine upon us,*   *Selah*
² that your ways may be known on earth,[a]
 your salvation among all nations.*

³ May the peoples praise you, O God;
 may all the peoples praise you.
⁴ May the nations be glad and sing for joy,*
 for you rule the peoples justly
 and guide the nations of the earth.[b]   *Selah*
⁵ May the peoples praise you, O God;
 may all the peoples praise you.

⁶ Then the land will yield its harvest,
 and God, our God, will bless us.[c]

---

z Ps 4:6; 31:6; 44:3; 80:3; Nu 6:24-25; Da 9:17.—a Isa 40:5; Jer 33:9.—
b Ps 82:8; 98:9.—c Ps 85:12; Lev 26:4; Isa 55:10; Eze 34:27; Hos 2:23-24.

Ps 67 This psalm recounts the assembly of the people for the feast of the harvest (see Ex 23:16; Lev 26:4) and their prayers of praise to God. They recall first all that he has done in Israel; the abundance of the fruits of the earth is like a new sign of his power and goodness. And more and more, they want the whole world to take part in this thanksgiving to God. The Lord is no longer merely the God of Israel; he is the Master and Judge of the whole world and all its peoples.

This psalm enables us to thank God for his material blessings on us. However, it also reminds us to ask God to continue to shower upon us his spiritual blessings so as to elicit admiration, envy, and divine praises even from nonbelievers.

The words *For the director of music* in the superscription are thought to be a musical or liturgical notation.

67:1 This verse was inspired by the priestly blessing (see Ps 31:16; Nu 6:24-26). *Face shine upon us:* a radiant face is the sign of a joyous and benevolent heart (see Ps 4:6; 31:16; 44:3; 67:1; 80:3; 119:135; see also note on Ps 13:1).

67:2-3 The history of the chosen people is a lesson that God gives to the pagan nations, enabling them to discover his power and goodness. They too are called to serve the one God and must join their praises to those of the people of Israel. The refrain of the psalm (vv. 3, 5) insists on the universalism that the Prophets (see Jer 33:9) and above all the second part of Isaiah, have impressed on the religious conscience of Israel. Many psalms bear witness to this spirit.

67:4 The psalmist prays that the nations may see the goodness of God's rule and react with joy and praise (see Ps 98:4-6; 100:1).

⁷ God will bless us,
   and all the ends of the earth will fear him.

PSALM 68*

Song of Victory

For the director of music. Of David. A psalm. A song.

¹ May God arise, may his enemies be scattered;*
   may his foes flee before him.*ᵈ*
² As smoke is blown away by the wind,
   may you blow them away;

---

d Nu 10:35; Isa 33:3.

Ps 68 This psalm may have been used in a processional liturgy celebrating the triumphal march of Israel's God to his sanctuary, possibly as part of the Feast of Booths or Tabernacles that included a procession of the tribes (vv. 24-27). With the words "May God arise . . .," the poet sets in motion the procession with the ark, as at the time when it went before the marches of the people (v. 1; see Nu 10:35). And he lets the whole history of Israel unfold before our eyes like a grand march of God, like his procession into the heart of Jerusalem. God rises, and the darkness dissipates; he takes the head of his people, and the adversaries are thrown into disorder. This epic poem assembles a series of allusive images, many of which remain obscure for us.

In this coming of God, however, we will recognize stirring moments in the destiny of Israel: the Exodus from Egypt and the divine manifestation at Sinai (vv. 7-8; see Ex 19:16), the wonders of the Exodus (vv. 9-10), the exploits of the Judges (vv. 11-14; see Book of Judges), the Conquest of Jerusalem (vv. 14-18), the sad fate of the criminal Ahab (v. 23; see 1 Ki 21:19), and the solemn Passover of Hezekiah who had reunited all the tribes of Israel (vv. 24-37; see 2 Ch 30), which foreshadowed the gathering in the holy city of the pagans who had finally come to render homage to the Lord of all nations.

The important thing in this psalm is not so much to grasp all the allusions as it is to let ourselves be carried along by the rhythm of the chant; we should listen to it as to an heroic march, as the glorious epic that draws Israel out of the dreary atmosphere of everyday life. It is the ideal psalm for processions to the temple.

In the ascent of God, who rises to take possession of the sacred hill of Jerusalem, the apostle Paul sees the Ascension of Christ, who draws after him the redeemed people, the Church that is filled with the gifts of the Holy Spirit (v. 18; see Eph 4:8-11). When Christians sing this hymn, they recall the presence of God in the working out of the world's destiny and the march of humanity, which is continually called by God until it is made one again in glory.

The words *For the director of music* in the superscription are thought to be a musical or liturgical notation.

68:1-3 This first of nine stanzas prays that God will come at the head of his people to defeat their enemies and enter his sanctuary in triumph.

as wax melts before the fire,
  may the wicked perish before God.*e*
³ But may the righteous be glad
  and rejoice before God;
  may they be happy and joyful.

⁴ Sing to God, sing praise to his name,*
  extol him who rides on the clouds—*r*
his name is the LORD—*f*
  and rejoice before him.*
⁵ A father to the fatherless, a defender of widows,*g*
  is God in his holy dwelling.
⁶ God sets the lonely in families,*s*
  he leads forth the prisoners with singing;
  but the rebellious live in a sun-scorched land.

⁷ When you went out before your people, O God,*
  when you marched through the wasteland,*h*   *Selah*
⁸ the earth shook,*
  the heavens poured down rain,

---

r Or / *prepare the way for him who rides through the deserts.*—s Or *the desolate in a homeland.*

e Ps 9:3; 37:20; 97:5; Jud 16:15; Wis 5:14; Mic 1:4.—f Ps 7:17; 18:9; 104:3; Dt 33:26; Isa 19:1.—g 5-6: Ps 10:14; 25:16; 103:6; 146:7, 9; Ex 22:21; Bar 6:37.—h 7-8: Ps 44:9; 114:4, 7; Ex 13:21; Dt 33:2; Jdg 5:4-5; Heb 12:26.

68:4-6 This second stanza calls for God to be praised as the savior.
68:4 *Name:* see note on Ps 8:1. *Who rides on the clouds:* the psalmist applies to Yahweh the image of the Canaanite storm-god Baal riding to battle on storm clouds; he thus stresses that Yahweh rather than Baal is the exalted God who makes the storm clouds his chariot (see v. 33; Ps 18:9f; 104:3; Dt 33:26; Isa 19:1; Hab 3:8; Mt 26:64).
68:7-10 This third stanza recalls God's march at the head of his people from Egypt, through the desert of Sinai, and into the promised land (see Ps 60:12; Ex 13:21; 19:16; Nu 14:14; Dt 33:2; Hab 3:3).
68:8 *Earth shook:* a reference to the "trembling" of Mount Sinai (see Ex 19:18). *Heavens poured down rain:* although there is no record of rain in the Sinai story, there is mention of "thunder and lightning, with a thick cloud" (see Ex 19:16), which would usually indicate rain. In addition, rain is connected with the shaking of the earth (see Jdg 5:4).

before God, the One of Sinai,
before God, the God of Israel.
9 You gave abundant showers, O God;*
you refreshed your weary inheritance.
10 Your people settled in it,
and from your bounty, O God, you provided for the poor.

11 * The LORD announced the word,*
and great was the company of those who
proclaimed it:
12 "Kings and armies flee in haste;
in the camps men divide the plunder.*i*
13 Even while you sleep among the campfires,**t**
the wings of [my] dove are sheathed* with
silver,
its feathers with shining gold."*j*
14 When the Almighty***u** scattered the kings in
the land,
it was like snow fallen on Zalmon.

15 The mountains of Bashan are majestic mountains;*
rugged are the mountains of Bashan.

---

t Or *saddlebags.*—u Hebrew *Shaddai.*

---

i Jos 10:16; Jdg 5:19.—j Ge 49:14; Jdg 5:16.

68:9-10 These two verses evoke the miracles of the Exodus: the cloud (see Ex 13:21; Nu 14:14), the manna and quail (see Ps 78:24f; Ex 16:4f), and the entrance into the promised land (v. 10: "it").
68:11-14 This fourth stanza recalls the defeat of the Canaanite kings by God.
68:11 *Announced the word:* God foretold his victory over the Canaanites (see Ex 23:22f, 27f, 31; Dt 7:10-24; 11:23-25; Jos 1:2-6).
68:13 *Wings of [my] dove are sheathed:* even while in camp, before the battle, Israel (God's "dove": see Ps 74:19; Hos 7:11) is already assured of enjoying the booty ("silver and gold") of the Canaanite kings, for God had guaranteed it (see Jos 2:8-11; 5:1; 6:16).
68:14 *Almighty:* the Hebrew is *Shaddai,* "the Mountain One." The name by which God revealed himself to the patriarchs was *El-Shaddai:* "God Almighty" (see Ge 17:1), which stressed God's power or his home in the mountains (see Ps 121:1). *Zalmon:* a mountain near Shechem (see Jdg 9:46-48) or a dark volcanic mountain in Bashan or Hauran east of the Sea of Galilee. It was known as the "dark one" in opposition to the "white one," Lebanon.
68:15-18 This fifth stanza celebrates the taking of Jerusalem to which God as-
cends and from which he will rule the world.

16 Why gaze in envy, O rugged mountains,
  at the mountain* where God chooses to
    reign,
  where the LORD himself will dwell forever?*k*
17 The chariots of God* are tens of thousands
  and thousands of thousands;
  the LORD [has come] from Sinai into his
    sanctuary.
18 When you ascended on high,
  you led captives in your train;
  you received gifts from men,
  even from*v* the rebellious—*l*
  that you,*w* O LORD God, might dwell there.*

19 Praise be to the LORD, to God our Savior,*
  who daily bears our burdens.*m*   *Selah*
20 Our God is a God who saves;
  from the Sovereign LORD comes escape
    from death.*

21 Surely God will crush the heads of his enemies,
  the hairy crowns of those who go on in
    their sins.*n*
22 The LORD says, "I will bring them from
  Bashan;

---

v Or *gifts for men, / even.*—w Or *they.*

k Ps 132:13-14; Dt 12:5; Eze 43:7.—l Ps 7:7; 47:5; Eph 4:8-10.—m Ps
34:1; 145:2; Dt 32:11; Isa 46:3-4; 63:8.—n Ps 74:14; Dt 32:42.

68:16 *The mountain:* Mount Zion, a little mount, which God has made the
highest mountain because he has placed his temple there and dwells in it.
68:17 *Chariots of God:* the heavenly hosts (see Hab 3:8, 15), later termed "le-
gions" by Jesus (see Mt 26:53). It may also refer to the heavenly chariots seen by
Elisha (see 2 Ki 6:17) rather than the chariots of Solomon (see 1 Ki 10:26).
68:18 When God went up to his place of enthronement on Mount Zion (see Ps
47:5f), he had captives in his train and received gifts like a victor in battle. The
apostle Paul applies this verse in its Greek translation to the ministry of the ascended Christ (Eph 4:8: "When he ascended on high/he led captives in his
train/and gave gifts to men"). It assures all who believe in Christ that by trusting
him we can overcome evil.
68:19-23 This sixth stanza offers joyous praise and the fervent hope that
God's victories will continue.
68:20 *Escape from death:* see notes on Ps 6:5; 11:7; 16:9-11.

I will bring them from the depths of the sea,*
23 that you may plunge your feet in the blood of your foes,[o]
while the tongues of your dogs have their share."*

24 Your procession has come into view, O God,*
the procession of my God and King into the sanctuary.
25 In front are the singers, after them the musicians;[p]
with them are the maidens playing tambourines.*
26 Praise God in the great congregation;
praise the LORD in the assembly of Israel.
27 There is the little tribe of Benjamin, leading them,
there the great throng of Judah's princes,
and there the princes of Zebulun and of Naphtali.[q]

28 Summon your power, O God;[x]
show us your strength, O God, as you have done before.*

---

x Many Hebrew manuscripts, Septuagint and Syriac; most Hebrew manuscripts *Your God has summoned power for you.*

---

o Ps 58:10; 1 Ki 21:19; 22:38; Isa 63:1-6.—p Ps 81:2-3; 87:7; 149:3; 150:3-5; 2 Sa 6:5; Rev 18:22.—q 1 Sa 9:21; Isa 9:1.

68:22 *From Bashan . . . from the depths of the sea:* i.e., the heights and the depths, the farthest places to which enemies might flee.

68:23 A vivid expression indicating complete victory over one's foes that was common in the Near East (see Ps 58:10). It alludes to the predictions of Elijah (1 Ki 21:19f) about the death of Ahab (1 Ki 22:38), his son Joram, wounded at Ramoth Gilead and brought back to Jezreel (2 Ki 8:29; 9:15), and Jezebel (2 Ki 9:36).

68:24-27 This seventh stanza describes the procession as it approaches the temple and renews God's taking up residence there (see Ps 24; 47) in the presence of all Israel, both north and south. It also alludes to the Passover of Hezekiah in which all the tribes participated (see Ps 80:1f; 2 Ch 30:1ff; Isa 9:1).

68:25 *Tambourines:* instruments played especially after a victory in battle (see Ex 15:20; 1 Sa 10:5; 18:6; 2 Sa 6:5; Jer 31:4).

68:28-31 This eighth stanza gives the prayer that God may continue to rule over the enemies of his people and exact tribute from them.

29 Because of your temple at Jerusalem
     kings will bring you gifts.*
30 Rebuke the beast among the reeds,
     the herd of bulls among the calves of the
       nations.
   Humbled, may it bring bars of silver.
   Scatter the nations who delight in war.*
31 Envoys will come from Egypt;*r*
     Cush*y* will submit herself to God.**s*

32 Sing to God, O kingdoms of the earth,*
     sing praise to the LORD,*t*   *Selah*
33 to him who rides the ancient skies above,
     who thunders with mighty voice.*
34 Proclaim the power of God,
     whose majesty is over Israel,
     whose power is in the skies.
35 You are awesome, O God, in your sanctuary;
     the God of Israel gives power and strength
       to his people.**u*

   Praise be to God!

---

y That is, the upper Nile region.

r Eze 29:2ff.—s Isa 18:7; 45:14; Zep 3:10.—t Ps 67:4; 138:4.—u Ps 18:1;
28:8; 29:11.

68:29 The defeated nations, led by their kings, will bring tribute to the Lord
who has established his majesty in his temple at Jerusalem (see Ps 76:11; Isa
18:7; 60:3-7; 66:20; Hag 2:7; Zec 2:11-13; 6:15; 8:21f; Rev 21:24).
68:30 The prayer contains a petition to strike the nations that will not submit
to the Lord. *Beast among the reeds:* the crocodile, a symbol for Egypt (see Eze
29:3), which in turn stands for all the hostile nations. *Herd of bulls among the
calves:* the bulls are leaders, the calves their subjects. *Bars of silver:* tribute from
the foreign nations brought to Zion.
68:31 Egypt will submit, as will Cush who usually formed an alliance with
Egypt (see Isa 18:1—19:15; 20:1-6).
68:32-35 This ninth stanza calls upon all nations to praise the God of Israel
who dwells in the temple and acclaim him as the God of all nations (see Ps 47).
68:33 The words "who rides the ancient skies above" indicate the Lord's
majesty, for he rules the highest heavens (see Dt 10:14; 1 Ki 8:27). The thunder
symbolizes the power and majesty of his rule (see Ps 18:13; 29:3) on behalf of his
people (see Dt 33:26).
68:35 Although the Lord is awesome in his deeds (see Ps 47:2; 65:5; Ex 15:11;
Dt 10:17; Rev 15:3f), he condescends to be present to his people in the sanctuary
in order to aid them.

PSALM 69*

Cry of Anguish in Distress

For the director of music. To [the tune of] "Lilies."
Of David.

¹ Save me, O God,
for the waters have come up to my neck.ᵛ
² I sink in the miry depths,
where there is no foothold.
I have come into the deep waters;
the floods* engulf me.ʷ
³ I am worn out calling for help;
my throat is parched.
My eyes fail,
looking for my God.ˣ
⁴ Those who hate me without reason*
outnumber the hairs of my head;
many are my enemies without cause,
those who seek to destroy me.ʸ
I am forced to restore
what I did not steal.

---

v Ps 18:4; 93:3-4; Job 22:11; Jnh 2:5.—w Ps 40:2; 124:4-5; Job 30:19.—
x Ps 6:6; 25:15; 119:82; 123:2; 141:8; Isa 38:14.—y Ps 35:19; 40:12; La
3:52; Jn 15:25.

Ps 69 This Messianic psalm encompasses the laments of two different people in distress; the first may have been accused of thievery (v. 4), and the second may have been tormented because of his piety and derided for his faith. The swamp in which they are sinking and the waters by which they are engulfed are the images of the despair that afflicts a person facing death. The tragic state of the suppliants resembles that of the righteous person whom we have encountered in Ps 22 and who makes us think of the prophet Jeremiah (see Jer 15:15) and the Suffering Servant (see Is 53:10). Their prayer, which appeals to God's justice as well as his compassion, concludes with a vast thanksgiving; the salvation that they await must be extended to all the lowly who rely only on God.

In their sufferings, Jesus sees his own suffering (Jn 15:25), and the evangelists have applied themselves to underscore this likeness (see Mt 27:46; Jn 2:17; 19:28; etc.). No psalm except Ps 22 is cited more often in the New Testament, a fact that led the Fathers of the Church to classify this psalm as Messianic.

The words *For the director of music* in the superscription are thought to be a musical or liturgical notation; nothing is known about "*To [the tune of]. . .*"

69:1-2 *Waters . . . miry depths . . . deep waters . . . floods:* a common means of indicating extreme distress (see note on Ps 30:1).

69:4 *Hate me without reason:* see note on Ps 35:19. These words were completely fulfilled in the hatred his enemies had for Jesus (see Jn 15:25).

⁵ You know my folly, O God;
    my guilt is not hidden from you.*

⁶ May those who hope in you
    not be disgraced because of me,
    O Lord, the LORD Almighty;
  may those who seek you
    not be put to shame because of me,
    O God of Israel.ᶻ
⁷ For I endure scorn for your sake,
    and shame covers my face.ᵃ
⁸ I am a stranger to my brothers,*
    an alien to my own mother's sons;ᵇ
⁹ for zeal for your house* consumes me,
    and the insults of those who insult you fall
        on me.ᶜ
¹⁰ When I weep and fast,ᵈ
    I must endure scorn;
¹¹ when I put on sackcloth,
    people make sport of me.
¹² Those who sit at the gate mock me,
    and I am the song of the drunkards.

¹³ But I pray to you, O LORD,
    in the time of your favor;*
  in your great love, O God,
    answer me with your sure salvation.ᵉ
¹⁴ Rescue me from the mire,ᶠ
    do not let me sink;

---

z Ps 40:16.—a Ps 44:15; Jer 15:15.—b Ps 31:11; Job 19:13-15.—c Ps 89:50-51; 119:139; Ro 15:3; Jn 2:17.—d 10-12: Ps 35:13; 109:24-25; Job 30:9; La 3:14.—e Ps 32:6; 102:13; Isa 49:8.—f 14-15: Ps 28:1; 30:3; 32:6; 40:2; 88:4; 144:7; Nu 16:33; Pr 1:12.

69:5 The psalmist admits his guilt, but he is innocent of the great crimes attributed to him by his enemies. This verse can be applied to Jesus only as an indication of the sins of the world that he took upon himself.

69:8 *Stranger to my brothers:* i.e., he is mocked by them; this text lies behind Jn 7:5, where Jesus' relatives ("brothers") do not believe in him.

69:9 *Zeal for your house:* cited in Jn 2:17 with reference to Jesus. *Insults of those who insult you:* cited in Ro 15:3 as an example of Jesus' selflessness.

69:13 *Time of your favor:* i.e., the special time when God is very near (see Ps 32:6; Isa 49:8; 61:2; 2 Co 6:2). *Love:* see note on Ps 6:4.

deliver me from those who hate me,
  from the deep waters.
¹⁵ Do not let the floodwaters engulf me
  or the depths swallow me up
  or the pit close its mouth over me.
¹⁶ Answer me, O Lᴏʀᴅ, out of the goodness of
      your love;
  in your great mercy turn to me.
¹⁷ Do not hide your face* from your servant;
  answer me quickly, for I am in trouble.ᵍ
¹⁸ Come near and rescue me;
  redeem me because of my foes.

¹⁹ You know how I am scorned, disgraced and
      shamed;
  all my enemies are before you.
²⁰ Scorn has broken my heart
  and has left me helpless;
  I looked for sympathy, but there was none,ʰ
  for comforters, but I found none.*
²¹ They put gall in my food
  and gave me vinegar* for my thirst.ⁱ

²² May the table set before them become a
      snare;* ʲ
  may it become retribution andᶻ a trap.*
²³ May their eyes be darkened so they cannot see,
  and their backs be bent forever.

---

z Or *snare / and their fellowship become.*

---

g Ps 22:24; 102:2; 143:7. —h Job 6:14ff; La 1:2. —i La 3:15; Mt 27:34,
48; Mk 15:23; Jn 19:28-30. —j Job 18:10; Ro 11:9-10.

69:17 *Hide your face:* see note on Ps 13:1.
  69:20 *I looked for . . . comforters, but I found none:* see Job 6:14ff; 16:2; La
1:2; and in reference to Jesus, see Mt 26:40; Jn 16:32.
  69:21 *Gall . . . vinegar:* the evangelists suggest that the sufferings of the
psalmist as described in this verse foreshadowed the sufferings of Jesus on the
cross (see Mt 27:34, 48; Mk 15:23; Lk 23:36; Jn 19:29).
  69:22-28 Prayer for divine justice to prevail (see note on Ps 5:10 and introduction to Ps 35).
  69:22-23 These two verses are applied by Paul to the divine hardening of sinners' hearts that God allows (see Ro 11:9f). *Table:* a single tablecloth spread on
the ground; hence the possibility of tripping over it.

24 Pour out your wrath on them;
     let your fierce anger overtake them.
25 May their place be deserted;*k*
     let there be no one to dwell in their tents.*
26 For they persecute those you wound
     and talk about the pain of those you hurt.
27 Charge them with crime upon crime;
     do not let them share in your salvation.
28 May they be blotted out of the book of life*
     and not be listed with the righteous.*l*

29 I am in pain and distress;
     may your salvation, O God, protect me.

30 I will praise God's name in song*
     and glorify him with thanksgiving.
31 This will please the LORD more than an ox,*m*
     more than a bull with its horns and hoofs.*
32 The poor* will see and be glad—
     you who seek God, may your hearts live!*n*
33 The LORD hears the needy
     and does not despise his captive people.

34 Let heaven and earth praise him,
     the seas and all that move in them,
35 for God will save Zion
     and rebuild the cities of Judah.*o*

---

k Ac 1:20; Mt 23:38.—l Ps 139:16; Ex 32:32; Isa 4:3; Eze 13:9; Da 12:1;
Mal 3:16; Rev 3:5; 20:12.—m Ps 40:6; 50:8-9, 14; 51:16; Isa 1:11-15; Hos
6:6; Am 5:21-22; Heb 10:5-8.—n Ps 22:26; 35:27; 70:4; 119:144.—o Ps
102:21-22; Isa 44:26; Eze 36:10.

69:25 Peter applies this verse to the replacement of Judas (see Ac 1:20).
69:28 *Book of life:* a figurative expression denoting God's record of the righteous (see note on Ps 51:1). From the human point of view, individuals may be
blotted out of that book, but from the divine point of view it contains only the
names of the elect who will not be blotted out (see Php 4:3; Rev 3:5; 13:8; 17:8;
20:15).
69:30-33 A vow to praise God for hearing his prayer (see note on Ps 7:17).
69:31 Prayer is worth more than the sacrifice of animals (see Ps 40:6; 50:13f;
51:16f), even the most perfect ones (see Lev 11:3; 1 Sa 1:24). See notes on Ps
40:6 and 50:7-15.
69:32 *Poor:* see note on Ps 22:26.

Then people will settle there and possess it;
36   the children of his servants will inherit it,
and those who love his name will dwell
there.*p*

PSALM 70*

Insistent Prayer for Divine Assistance

For the director of music. Of David. A petition.

1 Hasten, O God, to save me;* *q*
   O LORD, come quickly to help me.*r*
2 May those who seek my life*
   be put to shame and confusion;
   may all who desire my ruin
   be turned back in disgrace.*s*
3 May those who say to me, "Aha! Aha!"*
   turn back because of their shame.*t*
4 But may all who seek you
   rejoice and be glad in you;
   may those who love your salvation always
   say,
   "Let God be exalted!"* *u*

---

p Ps 25:13; 102:28; Isa 65:9.—q 1-5: Ps 40:13-17.—r Ps 22:19; 71:12.—
s Ps 6:10; 35:4, 26.—t Ps 35:21, 25.—u Ps 35:27.

Ps 70 The psalmist's cry is that of all who cannot endure suffering any longer
and have no hope except in God. He calls upon God to come to his aid quickly. It
is a slightly revised duplicate of Ps 40:13-17.

Every Christian (and the whole Church) can naturally recite this psalm in his
or her own right as one really (though not yet completely) saved.

The words *For the director of music* in the superscription are thought to be a
musical or liturgical notation; for *A petition,* see introduction to Ps 38.

70:1-5 Distress can remind a person of his attachment to sin. Is there any
reason why people should vilify the person who acknowledges his faults? Realiz-
ing his incoercible attraction toward evil, the psalmist cries out to God, and the
poor man rediscovers with astonishment the joyous assurance that God thinks
about him.

70:2-3 The psalmist prays for the downfall of his enemies, somewhat as
Christians pray for the kingdom of God to come, which includes the petition that
the Lord will come to vindicate his own and avenge the wrongs done by his enemies (see 2 Th 1:5-10; see also note on Ps 5:10 and introduction to Ps 35).

70:3 *Aha! Aha!:* the mocking words of the psalmist's adversaries.

70:4 When the Lord works his deliverance, his people will rejoice in his salvation (see Ps 35:27) and give him praise.

⁵ Yet I am poor and needy;*
  come quickly to me, O God.
You are my help and my deliverer;
  O LORD, do not delay.

PSALM 71*

Prayer of the Righteous in Old Age

¹ In you, O LORD, I have taken refuge;ᵛ
  let me never be put to shame.ʷ
² Rescue me and deliver me in your righteous-
    ness;
  turn your ear to me and save me.
³ Be my rock of refuge,
    to which I can always go;
  give the command to save me,
    for you are my rock and my fortress.ˣ
⁴ Deliver me, O my God, from the hand of the
    wicked,
    from the grasp of evil and cruel men.ʸ

⁵ For you have been my hope, O Sovereign
    LORD,
  my confidence since my youth.

---

v 1-3: Ps 31:1-3.—w Ps 22:5; 25:2.—x Ps 18:2.—y Ps 140:1; 2 Ki 19:19.

70:5 *Poor and needy:* see note on Ps 22:26. *My help and my deliverer:* the salvation promised the faithful (see Isa 25:9), first conceived as natural with reference to the Exodus or the return from the Exile, was later conceived as spiritual
without restriction of space or time (see, e.g., Ps 18: superscription; 19:14).

Ps 71 Accustomed to being exposed to malevolence, an aged person, probably
a cantor in the service of the temple, casts a look backward. From his childhood,
every day of his long life he has endeavored to remain faithful to the Lord and to
live close to him; he has made praise of God his life companion. Profoundly confident, he begs God to come to his aid, resolute in his will to praise him with all his
might. This lament resembles the "confessions" of the prophet Jeremiah (Jer
17:14-18) and could have been later applied to Israel itself. We could regard it as
primarily a prayer of fidelity in difficult moments of old age; it is a fine prayer for
the evening of life.

This supplication can find place on the lips of many Christians in their temporal and spiritual trials, and even more on the lips of the Church who is looked
upon by her enemies as old, failing, and suitable to receive the finishing blow.

⁶ From birth I have relied on you;
　　you brought me forth from my mother's
　　　womb.
　　I will ever praise you.ᶻ
⁷ I have become like a portent to many,*
　　but you are my strong refuge.
⁸ My mouth is filled with your praise,
　　declaring your splendor all day long.

⁹ Do not cast me away when I am old;
　　do not forsake me when my strength is
　　　gone.
¹⁰ For my enemies speak against me;
　　those who wait to kill me conspire to-
　　　gether.ᵃ
¹¹ They say, "God has forsaken him;
　　pursue him and seize him,
　　for no one will rescue him."
¹² Be not far from me, O God;
　　come quickly, O my God, to help me.ᵇ
¹³ May my accusers perish in shame;ᶜ
　　may those who want to harm me
　　be covered with scorn and disgrace.*

¹⁴ But as for me, I will always have hope;
　　I will praise you more and more.
¹⁵ My mouth will tell of your righteousness,*
　　of your salvation all day long,ᵈ
　　though I know not its measure.*

---

z Ps 22:10; Jer 17:14.—a Ps 3:1; 10:8; 22:7.—b Ps 22:19; 38:22.—c Ps 25:3; 35:4; 40:14; 70:2.—d Ps 35:28; 109:30.

71:7 *Like a portent to many:* more by his trials (see Ps 31:11; Dt 28:46; Isa 52:14) than by the benefits received from God, for people are surprised to see a righteous person suffering.

71:13 A prayer for the divine justice to be done (see note on Ps 5:10 and introduction to Ps 35).

71:15-18 A vow to offer praise to God for his help (see note on Ps 7:17).

71:15 The psalmist himself does not know the full extent of God's goodness toward him. For God's acts of "salvation," consisting of his "mighty acts" (v. 16) and "marvelous deeds" (v. 17), are too numerous to count (see Ps 40:5; 139:17f).

16 I will come and proclaim your mighty acts, O
Sovereign LORD;
I will proclaim your righteousness, yours
alone.
17 Since my youth, O God, you have taught me,
and to this day I declare your marvelous
deeds.
18 Even when I am old and gray,*
do not forsake me, O God,*e*
till I declare your power to the next generation,*f*
your might to all who are to come.

19 Your righteousness reaches to the skies, O
God,
you who have done great things.*g*
Who, O God, is like you?*h*
20 Though you have made me see troubles,
many and bitter,
you will restore my life again;
from the depths of the earth*
you will again bring me up.
21 You will increase my honor
and comfort me once again.

22 I will praise* you with the harp
for your faithfulness, O my God;
I will sing praise to you with the lyre,
O Holy One of Israel.

---

e Isa 46:4.—f Ps 22:30-31; 48:13-14; 145:4; Job 8:8.—g Ps 36:5;
72:18.—h Ps 86:8.

71:17-18 *Youth . . . old and gray:* this passage can be applied without difficulty to Israel to whom the Prophets apply images of youth (see Jer 2:2; Hos 2:15)
and old age (see Isa 46:4; Hos 7:9); see also Ps 129:1f. *Power:* literally, "arm," a
prophetic image (see Isa 51:9; 53:1), used often with respect to the miracles of
the Exodus. This passage (see Ps 22:30f; 78:5f; 102:18) shows how conscious the
psalmists were of being bearers of tradition.
71:20 *From the depths of the earth:* the realm of the dead, which is entered by
the grave (see note on Ps 30:1).
71:22 *I will praise:* a vow to praise God for his help (see note on Ps 7:17). *Holy
One of Israel:* a frequent expression of the Book of Isaiah but used infrequently in
the Psalter (see Ps 78:41; 89:18).

²³ My lips will shout for joy
when I sing praise to you—
I, whom you have redeemed.
²⁴ My tongue will tell of your righteous acts
all day long,
for those who wanted to harm me
have been put to shame and confusion.

PSALM 72*

The Kingdom of the Messiah

Of Solomon.

¹ Endow the king with your justice, O God,
the royal son with your righteousness.ⁱ
² He willᵃ judge your people in righteousness,*
your afflicted ones with justice.ʲ
³ The mountains will bring prosperity to the
people,
the hills the fruit of righteousness.ᵏ

---

a Or *May he;* similarly in verses 3-11 and 17.

i Ps 9:8; 99:4; Jer 23:5.—j Pr 31:8-9; Isa 9:7.—k Isa 45:8; 52:7; 55:12.

Ps 72 Only the expected Savior will fulfill all the hopes placed on the ideal leader described in this psalm, of whom the Prophets also speak (see Isa 9:7; 11:1-9; Jer 23:5f; 33:15f; Zec 9:9-17). The portrait bears more than one facet of King Solomon the Sage, but it is Messianic, i.e., it sketches a mysterious King who is to come. Promised a reign without end (v. 5), he will rescue the needy and poor from oppression and uphold their rights (vv. 12-14). He will establish definitive peace (v. 7), and the pagan nations that he subdues—even the most distant—will come to do homage to him (vv. 10-11). Finally, he will rule over the idealized promised land (v. 8) and transform it into a new heavenly paradise (vv. 6, 16).

Since Israel has never yielded to the temptation to make gods out of its kings, this king, too, is not divinized; the psalmist prays for him. This psalm is like a chart or mirror for a true reign in the name of God. It will be marked by the work of justice and peace, the effort for the deliverance of the poor and needy.

In proclaiming the beatitudes, Jesus was to provide the authentic content of this perfect happiness that is promised for the reign of the Messiah. In the adoration of the Magi, Matthew (2:11) sees a visit from pagan kings who prostrate themselves at the feet of the promised Savior (vv. 10-11); hence, this psalm is read in the Liturgy during the Epiphany time.

72:2-3 Righteousness will rain down God's blessings on the people (see Ps 5:12; 65:9-13; 133:3; Lev 25:19; Dt 28:8).

⁴ He will defend the afflicted among the people
   and save the children of the needy;
   he will crush the oppressor.

⁵ He will endure[b] as long as the sun,
   as long as the moon, through all generations.[l]

⁶ He will be like rain falling on a mown field,
   like showers watering the earth.[m]

⁷ In his days the righteous will flourish;
   prosperity will abound till the moon is no
   more.

⁸ He will rule from sea to sea*
   and from the River[c] to the ends of the
   earth.[n] [d]

⁹ The desert tribes* will bow before him
   and his enemies will lick the dust.[o]

¹⁰ The kings of Tarshish and of distant shores
    will bring tribute to him;
    the kings of Sheba and Seba [p]
    will present him gifts.*

¹¹ All kings will bow down to him
    and all nations will serve him.[q]

¹² For he will deliver the needy who cry out,
    the afflicted who have no one to help.

¹³ He will take pity on the weak and the needy
    and save the needy from death.[r]

---

b Septuagint; Hebrew *You will be feared.*—c That is, the Euphrates.—d
Or *the end of the land.*

l Ps 61:7; 89:36-37; Jer 31:35.—m Dt 32:2; Isa 45:8; Hos 6:3.—n Ex
23:31; Dt 11:24; Zec 9:10.—o Isa 49:23; Mic 7:17.—p Ps 68:29; 1 Ki 10:1ff;
Est 10:1; Isa 60:5-6.—q Ps 47:7; Ezr 1:2.—r Pr 31:9; Lk 10:33.

72:8 *From sea to sea:* the Red Sea and the Mediterranean. The *River* is the Euphrates. Both details indicate the universality of the Messianic reign.
72:9 *Desert tribes:* the tribes of the Arabian Desert, east of the promised land.
Lick the dust: a sign of abject fear and defeat (see Mic 7:17).
72:10 All kings, whether near or far, will acknowledge the Messiah's rule.
Tarshish: a seaport located in southern Spain, hence to the far west; *Sheba:* a
city of southwest Arabia, hence to the far south; *Seba:* probably a region in modern Sudan, south of Egypt (see Ge 10:7; Isa 43:3). This verse is applied by Matthew to the visit of the Magi at Christ's birth (see Mt 2:11).

¹⁴ He will rescue them from oppression and vio-
lence,
for precious is their blood in his sight.

¹⁵ Long may he live!*
May gold from Sheba be given him.
May people ever pray for him
and bless* him all day long.
¹⁶ Let grain abound throughout the land;
on the tops of the hills may it sway.
Let its fruit flourish like Lebanon;^s
let it thrive like the grass of the field.*
¹⁷ May his name endure forever;
may it continue as long as the sun.^t

All nations* will be blessed through him,
and they will call him blessed.^u

¹⁸ Praise be to the LORD God, the God of Israel,*
who alone does marvelous deeds.^v
¹⁹ Praise be to his glorious name forever;
may the whole earth be filled with his
glory. Amen and Amen.^w

²⁰ This concludes the prayers of David son of
Jesse.*

---

s Ps 4:7; Isa 27:6; Hos 14:6-8; Am 9:13.—t Ps 89:36.—u Ge 12:3; Zec 8:13.—v Ps 41:13; 89:52; 106:48; 136:4.—w Ps 57:5; Nu 14:21; Hab 3:3.

72:15-17 The psalmist prays that the Messiah-King may enjoy a long and prosperous reign acknowledged by the whole world and a blessing for all the nations.
72:15 *May people ever pray . . . and bless:* an obscure passage. As it is translated, it means: may the people pray for the Messiah that he will benefit the poor with the treasures he has received, and may they bless and thank him. But Israel could also pray to ask God for a perfect Messiah and so offer vows for the extension of the Messianic kingdom (see Ps 61:7f). Hence, one could also translate: "He [the Messiah] will pray [intercede] for him [the poor] and bless him" (see 1 Ki 8:14, 28).
72:16 Fertility of the land was one of the blessings of the Messianic age (see Hos 14:6f; Am 9:13). *Flourish like Lebanon:* with the same vital power that the majestic cedars of Lebanon display.
72:17 *All nations:* an echo of the promise to the patriarchs (see Ge 12:3; 18:18; 22:18; 26:4; 28:14).
72:18-19 This doxology is not part of the psalm; it concludes the second of the five books of the Psalter (see Ps 41:13; 89:52; 106:48; 150). Praise of the Lord is the most profound religious attitude and ends every authentic prayer.
72:20 Colophon added by a redactor.

BOOK III—PSALMS 73–89*

PSALM 73*

False Happiness of the Wicked

A psalm of Asaph.

¹ Surely God is good to Israel,*
to those who are pure in heart.

² * But as for me, my feet had almost slipped;*
I had nearly lost my foothold.

³ For I envied the arrogant
when I saw the prosperity of the wicked.ˣ

---

x Ps 37:1; Job 21:13; Pr 3:31.

Ps 73—89 This third book of the Psalter combines the collections of psalms of Asaph (probably a choral leader in the Jerusalem temple; see 1 Ch 25:2-6; 2 Ch 29:30) with the end of the Psalter of the Sons of Korah, which began in the second book (Ps 41—49). The prayers are varied in accord with the experience of believers; we pass from the lament of the innocent to the exultation after victory. We read, by turns, canticles of Zion, chants of joy and hope, and historical retrospectives that often take the tone of great national lamentations. Each prayer expresses in a new way the longing for God and his salvation.

Ps 73 The psalmist is taken back by the prosperity of the wicked and the sufferings of the righteous (see Job; Ecc 7:15; Jer 12:1; Mal 3:15). Those who make sport of God seem to succeed in life much more then believers, and their example becomes a scandal for the righteous and the wise: what is the good of remaining faithful? Still he knows that no one should deny God. Tempted by doubt, the faithful psalmist reflects and seeks light in God's presence; in such a meditation, his faith deepens and a conviction imposes itself on him with new force: human glory has no tomorrow, but the friendship of God remains forever precious; it cannot end or deceive. The psalmist-sage who expresses himself here begins to suspect that the joy of being with the Lord could become eternal happiness (v. 24).

In times of trouble, at moments when people grow weary of being faithful, this psalm brings the grace of refreshment to the interior life.

For *Asaph* in the superscription, see introduction to Ps 73—89.

73:1 *Israel:* i.e., the group of the "poor" (see v. 15; Ps 72:2ff; 149:4; 1 Mac 1:53; Isa 49:3, 13). *Pure in heart:* see note on Ps 24:4. *Heart:* see note on Ps 4:7.

73:2-3 Like many of the godly, the psalmist envied the prosperity of the wicked and their arrogance. Everything seemed to go well for them. They experienced "prosperity," i.e., well-being, full family life, and success in business. Hence, the psalmist was miserable, filled with self-pity and discontent with God's justice. But, although he almost lost his foothold on the "way" of the Lord, he righted himself with the help of the Lord, who sustains his saints (see Ps 37:23ff).

73:2 *Feet had almost slipped:* see note on Ps 37:3.

⁴ They have no struggles;*
   their bodies are healthy and strong.ᵉ
⁵ They are free from the burdens common to
      man;
   they are not plagued by human ills.
⁶ Therefore pride is their necklace;
   they clothe themselves with violence.
⁷ From their callous hearts comes iniquity;ᶠ
   the evil conceits of their minds know no
      limits.ʸ
⁸ They scoff, and speak with malice;
   in their arrogance they threaten oppres-
      sion.ᶻ
⁹ Their mouths lay claim to heaven,
   and their tongues take possession of the
      earth.
¹⁰ Therefore their people turn to them
   and drink up waters in abundance.ᵍ
¹¹ They say, "How can God know?
   Does the Most High have knowledge?"ᵃ

¹² This is what the wicked are like—
   always carefree, they increase in wealth.

¹³ Surely in vain have I kept my heart pure;*
   in vain have I washed my hands in inno-
      cence.ᵇ

---

e With a different word division of the Hebrew; Masoretic Text *struggles
at their death; / their bodies are healthy.*—f Syriac (see also Septuagint);
Hebrew *Their eyes bulge with fat.*—g The meaning of the Hebrew for this
verse is uncertain.

y Ps 17:10; Job 15:27.—z Ps 17:10; 41:5.—a Ps 10:11; Job 22:13.—b Ps
26:6; Job 9:29-31; Mal 3:14.

73:4-12 The psalmist describes the reasons that led the godly to envy the
wicked. Evildoers seem to be carefree and unconcerned for the future. They have
wealth and power and enjoy freedom of movement and speech. They appear un-
touched by life's frustrations: frailty, adversities, diseases, and hard labor. They
disregard God and his laws with apparent impunity. They decree what can be
done on earth and even what God can do in heaven. In short, it seems that God
lets the wicked get away with their wickedness.
73:13-14 The psalmist began to have doubts about his concern to keep himself holy (see Ps 24:4; 119:9). He questioned himself about the troubles and sufferings that he experienced while the wicked seemed to have no such problems.

¹⁴ All day long I have been plagued;
    I have been punished every morning.

¹⁵ If I had said, "I will speak thus,"
    I would have betrayed your children.*
¹⁶ When I tried to understand all this,*
    it was oppressive to me
¹⁷ till I entered the sanctuary of God;*
    then I understood their final destiny.

¹⁸ Surely you place them on slippery ground;*
    you cast them down to ruin.
¹⁹ How suddenly are they destroyed,
    completely swept away by terrors!
²⁰ As a dream when one awakes,
    so when you arise, O LORD,
    you will despise them as fantasies.^c

²¹ When my heart was grieved*
    and my spirit embittered,
²² I was senseless and ignorant;
    I was a brute beast before you.

---

c Ps 49:14; Job 20:8.

73:15 If he had expressed in public what he had been thinking, the psalmist would have denied the ancestral traditions and beliefs (Ps 139:24) and betrayed the "poor." For the Lord is a father to Israel (Ex 4:22; Isa 63:16; Hos 11:1).

73:16-17 Understanding did not come to the psalmist until he entered into the "sanctuary of God." There he regained his perspective in the light of God's greatness, glory, and majesty. He realized once again that the Lord is just and will judge the wicked in accord with their evil deeds.

73:17 *Sanctuary of God:* literally, "the divine sanctuaries." Rather than the temple (see Jer 51:51) where he would have been enlightened by God, or the divine mysteries (see Wis 2:22) in which he would have received revelation, this expression indicates the teaching contained in the Scriptures, the abode of wisdom (see Ps 119:130; Pr 9:1ff; Sir 39:1).

73:18-20 In reality, God makes the state of the wicked so precarious that they will not be stable but will vanish like the figures of a dream. The assurance of Scripture is that the wicked will incur sudden and complete judgment. They will be assailed by all kinds of terrors and death itself.

73:21-22 The psalmist stresses his former embittered state once again. In his grief he was irrational (see Ps 94:8) and not ruled by wisdom; he was like the fools who are compared to brute beasts (see Ps 49:12, 20; Isa 1:2f). He was assailed by doubt and mired in self-pity—but God used this experience to make him a better person and bring him closer to himself.

²³ Yet I am always with you;*
    you hold me by my right hand.^d
²⁴ You guide me with your counsel,
    and afterward you will take me into glory.*
²⁵ Whom have I in heaven but you?
    And earth has nothing I desire besides you.
²⁶ My flesh and my heart* may fail,
    but God is the strength of my heart
    and my portion forever.

²⁷ Those who are far from you will perish;*
    you destroy all who are unfaithful to you.
²⁸ But as for me, it is good to be near God.
    I have made the Sovereign LORD my
        refuge;
    I will tell of all your deeds.*

---

d Ps 121:5; Ge 48:13.

73:23-26 The psalmist's experience of anguish is transformed into the joy of God's presence and his greatness. God protects him by holding his "right hand" (v. 23; see Ps 63:8; Isa 41:10, 13; 42:6; Jer 31:32), by strengthening his resolve ("strength," v. 26; see Ps 18:2), and by taking care of all his needs ("portion," v. 26; see Ps 16:5). God gives his servant wisdom and insight ("counsel") as he journeys toward everlasting glory (v. 24; see Ps 32:8; 73:24).

73:24 *Take me into glory:* is it a question here of heavenly glory? The text does not make clear. It states that God will preserve the righteous from a brutal and premature death and rehabilitate them (see Job 19:9; 29:18; 42:7), while he despises the wicked who will suddenly disappear (vv. 18f). Nothing obliges us to give the verb "take" a stronger meaning than in Ps 18:16 and 49:15 based on the assumption into heaven of Enoch (Ge 5:24; Sir 44:16) and Elijah (2 Ki 2:3; Sir 48:9). However, as in Ps 16:9f, the psalmist's fervor and the demands of his love for God lead him to long never to be separated from him; it constitutes a stage in the explicit belief in the resurrection, attested in Da 12:2.

73:26 *My flesh . . . heart:* the whole being (see Ps 84:2). *Heart:* see note on Ps 4:7. *Portion:* as a Levite, the psalmist has the Lord for his portion (or inheritance) of the promised land, i.e., he lives off the tithes that the people present to the Lord (see Nu 18:21-24; Dt 10:9; 18:1-8).

73:27-28 The psalmist now understands that all who are unfaithful to God must perish. Their judgment is a consequence not only of their failure to profess faith in God but also of their immoral and unjust practices.

73:28 *I will tell of all your deeds:* the psalmist expresses the vow to praise the Lord's mercies (see note on Ps 7:17). The Septuagint adds to this phrase a final line taken from Ps 9:14: "in the gates of the Daughter of Jerusalem [Zion]," which may be a liturgical adaptation.

PSALM 74*

Prayer in Time of Calamity

A *maskil* [h] of Asaph.

1 Why have you rejected us forever, O God?[e]
   Why * does your anger smolder against the
      sheep of your pasture?[f]
2 Remember the people you purchased of old,
   the tribe of your inheritance, whom you re-
      deemed—[g]
   Mount Zion, where you dwell.*
3 Turn your steps toward these everlasting
      ruins,
   all this destruction the enemy has brought
      on the sanctuary.

---

h Probably a literary or musical term.

e Ps 10:1; 43:2; 44:23; 77:7.—f Ps 80:4.—g Ps 68:16; 132:13; Ex 15:16;
Dt 7:6; Isa 63:17; Jer 10:16; 51:19.

Ps 74 This lamentation expresses the soul of a stricken people who feel abandoned even by God. The deportees who have returned from the Exile (538-529
B.C.) or else the Jews persecuted by Antiochus IV Epiphanes (167-164 B.C.)
mourn over their sanctuary, which the pagans have profaned (see 2 Ki 25:9-12;
Isa 64:10 for the former and 1 Mac 4:38; 2 Mac 1:8 for the latter). Has the Lord
forgotten the covenant and the wonders he once accomplished to free his people
(vv. 13-14), to sustain them in the journey through the desert, and to open the
promised land for them (v. 15)?

Rightly, the past prevents the psalmist from despairing and enables him to
believe in a better future. Israel has now lost all pretense of power; it is the community of the poor (vv. 19-21), conscious of its weakness; it is like the timid dove
that God cannot abandon to the ferocity of the beasts (v. 19).

Prolonging Christ and even identifying mysteriously with him, the Church is
now God's people on earth (see 1 Pe 2:9f). She is also the earthly visible temple
of God, his city and the spiritual capital of the world (see 1 Co 3:16; 1 Pe 2:4-6).
Hence, her members can pray this psalm in trials when Christ seems to have delivered them over to persecution without end.

For the term *maskil* in the superscription, see introduction to Ps 32; for *Asaph*,
see introduction to Ps 73—89.

74:1 *Why . . .? Why . . .?:* see note on Ps 6:3. *Forever:* figuratively speaking; it
seemed like forever. *Sheep of your pasture:* see introduction to Ps 23.

74:2 In this time of great calamity, the psalmist begs God to recall his exploits
at the Exodus, the Conquest, and the establishment of the temple. *Your inheritance:* see Dt 9:29.

⁴ Your foes roared in the place where you met
   with us;
   they set up their standards as signs.
⁵ They behaved like men wielding axes
   to cut through a thicket of trees.
⁶ They smashed all the carved paneling
   with their axes and hatchets.
⁷ They burned your sanctuary to the ground;
   they defiled the dwelling place of your
   Name.ʰ
⁸ They said in their hearts, "We will crush
   them completely!"
   They burned every place where God was
   worshiped* in the land.
⁹ We are given no miraculous signs;
   no prophets are left,ⁱ
   and none of us knows how long this will
   be.*

¹⁰ How long will the enemy mock you, O God? ʲ
   Will the foe revile your name forever?*
¹¹ Why do you hold back your hand, your right
   hand?
   Take it from the folds of your garment and
   destroy them!*

¹² But you, O God, are my king from of old;
   you bring salvation upon the earth.

---

h Ps 79:1; Isa 64:10; Ac 21:28.—i Ps 77:8; La 2:9; Eze 7:26.—j Ps 6:3;
89:46.

74:8 *Every place where God was worshiped:* i.e., shrines, whether legitimate or
not (see 1 Ki 3:2; 2 Ki 18:4).
74:9 The people were used to asking the Prophets how long a divine punishment would last (see 2 Sa 24:13). In this case, they have had *no miraculous
signs* of any kind, and the voice of the Prophets is absent as it has been for some
time (see Ps 77:8; 1 Mac 4:46; 9:27; 14:41; La 2:9; Eze 7:26).
74:10 Jeremiah had announced that there would be 70 years of exile (see Jer
25:11; 29:10), a round figure symbolizing a very long time (see Ps 6:3; 89:46).
74:11 To do battle, the warrior bared his arm from his garment (see Isa
52:10).

13 It was you who split open the sea by your
      power;* [k]
    you broke the heads of the monster in the
      waters.[l]
14 It was you who crushed the heads of
      Leviathan[m]
    and gave him as food to the creatures of
      the desert.
15 It was you who opened up springs and
      streams;
    you dried up the ever flowing rivers.*
16 The day is yours, and yours also the night;[n]
    you established the sun and moon.
17 It was you who set all the boundaries of the
      earth;
    you made both summer and winter.

18 Remember how the enemy has mocked you,
      O LORD,
    how foolish people have reviled your
      name.
19 Do not hand over the life of your dove* to
      wild beasts;
    do not forget the lives of your afflicted peo-
      ple forever.
20 Have regard for your covenant,
    because haunts of violence fill the dark
      places of the land.

---

k Ps 89:9.—l Isa 51:9-10; Eze 29:3.—m Job 3:8; 41:1; Isa 27:1; Jer
50:39.—n 16-17: Ps 136:7-9; Ge 1:16.

74:13-14 Allusion to the crossing of the Red Sea (see Ex 14:30) and the defeat
of the Egyptians (see Isa 27:1; Eze 29:3; 32:4). *Leviathan:* a mythological multi-
headed monster of chaos; here it seems to stand especially for Egypt (for Egypt's
crocodiles, see Job 40:25f).
74:15 Allusion to the miracles of the Exodus (see Ex 17:6; Nu 20:11) and the
crossing of the Jordan (see Jos 3:15f) where God's creative power is exercised
(see Ps 89:10).
74:19 *Your dove:* a term of endearment for "Israel" (see Ps 68:13; SS 2:14;
5:2; 6:9; Hos 7:11; 11:11).

21 Do not let the oppressed retreat in disgrace;
      may the poor and needy* praise your name.

22 Rise up, O God, and defend your cause;
      remember how fools mock you all day long.
23 Do not ignore the clamor of your adversaries,
      the uproar of your enemies, which rises
      continually.

PSALM 75*

God Is Judge of the World

For the director of music. [To the tune of] "Do Not
    Destroy." A psalm of Asaph. A song.

1 We give thanks* to you, O God,
      we give thanks, for your Name is near;
      men tell of your wonderful deeds.

2 You say, "I choose the appointed time;*
      it is I who judge uprightly.
3 When the earth and all its people quake,°
      it is I who hold its pillars firm.*   *Selah*

---

o Ps 46:2; 60:2; 93:1; 96:10; 104:5; 1 Sa 2:8; 2 Sa 22:8; Isa 24:19.

74:21 *Poor and needy:* see note on Ps 22:26.
   Ps 75 This psalm has parallels to the Song of Hannah (see 1 Sa 2:1-10). Freed from the Exile but always dependent on and pestered by those who had taken their place in the land, the People of God give thanks to the Lord. They know that in the end God will make right triumph on earth; the righteous will obtain glory and the wicked will receive the chastisement they deserve. These oracles proclaim once again the reversal worked by true justice: the proud will be abased, and the humble will be lifted up.
   We can pray this psalm with the same sentiments of the psalmist and apply the role of Judge to the risen Christ, to whom the Father has given it. We can proclaim the wondrous deeds of our Savior, who will come to save the righteous and punish the wicked on the last day.
   The words *For the director of music* in the superscription are thought to be a musical or liturgical notation; for *Do Not Destroy,* see introduction to Ps 57; for *Asaph,* see introduction to Ps 73—89.
   75:1 *Give thanks:* this is given in the form of praise (see Ps 7:17; 28:7; 30:12; 35:18). *Name:* see note on Ps 5:11. *Wonderful deeds:* see note on Ps 9:1.
   75:2-5 This is a reassuring word from God possibly through prophetic words already uttered by the Prophets (e.g., Isaiah in 2 Ki 19:21-34).
   75:3 God is the Master of the moral order as well as the physical universe, and he keeps them stable (see Ps 93:1f; 96:10; 1 Sa 2:8) or makes them quake (see Ps 18:7; Job 26:11); no cataclysm escapes his will (see Ps 46:2f; 60:2); and he alone establishes the hour of the judgment (see Hab 2:3).

4 To the arrogant I say, 'Boast no more,'*
and to the wicked, 'Do not lift up your horns.*[p]
5 Do not lift your horns against heaven;[q]
do not speak with outstretched neck.' "*

6 No one from the east or the west*
or from the desert can exalt a man.* [r]
7 But it is God who judges:[s]
He brings one down, he exalts another.*
8 In the hand of the LORD is a cup
full of foaming wine mixed with spices;
he pours it out, and all the wicked of the earth[t]
drink it down to its very dregs.*

---

p Ps 5:5; 1 Sa 2:3; Zec 1:21.—q Ps 94:4; Job 15:25.—r Mt 24:23-27.—s Job 5:11; 1 Sa 2:7; Da 2:21.—t Ps 60:3; Job 21:20; Pr 23:30; Isa 51:17, 21-22; Jer 25:15ff; Hab 2:16.

75:4-5 This passage recalls Ps 94:4; 1 Sa 2:3; Job 15:25f. The wicked are fools (see Ps 14:1; 94:7). The horn is the symbol of arrogant and aggressive force (see Ps 89:17; 92:10; Dt 33:17; 1 Ki 22:11); it will be broken (see Jer 48:25; Zec 1:19).

75:4 The Lord speaks to those who incite chaos and immorality: "the arrogant" and "the wicked" who live without God and his laws (see Ps 52:1; 73:3ff).

75:5 The wicked even dare to place themselves in direct opposition to God by raising their "horns against heaven" and speaking "with outstretched neck"—a common gesture of opposition.

75:6-7 Concerning these first two verses of the response from earth (vv. 6-8), possibly by a Levite, see 1 Sa 2:7; Da 2:21. The oracles against the nations envisaged such or such a power, in the north (see Zep 2:13), in the south (see Isa 30:6), or in the desert (Isa 21:1); other oracles were directed against the mountains of Israel (see Eze 6:2; 36:1), or the forests of the south (see Eze 21:2f). Here the desert represents the south and the mountains (Lebanon) stand for the north (see note on v. 6, below). As in Zec 1:16, the accent is placed on the universality of the divine judgment (see v. 8) on the Day of the Lord (see Mt 24:23ff).

75:6 *No one . . . a man:* a more common translation is: "For judgment does not come from east or west/nor from the desert or the mountains." In other words, search where we may, there is no other arbiter but God; therefore, no earthly honor is anything but provisional. Furthermore, no one can escape God's judgment (see Ps 139); God will bring down anyone who exalts himself.

75:7 Indeed, judgment belongs to God alone, for he is sovereign in judgment and in redemption.

75:8 All the wicked will be vanquished by God. The image of the cup full of foaming and dizzying wine is taken from the Prophets (see Isa 51:17; Jer 25:15; 49:12; La 4:21; Eze 23:31; Hab 2:15); it has already appeared in Ps 60:3 (see Job 21:20) and will reappear in Rev 14:10. See also note on Ps 16:5.

⁹ As for me, I will declare this forever;
  I will sing praise to the God of Jacob.*
¹⁰ I will cut off the horns of all the wicked,ᵘ
   but the horns of the righteous will be lifted
   up.*

PSALM 76*

God, Defender of Zion

For the director of music. With stringed instruments.
A psalm of Asaph. A song.

¹ In Judah God is known;*
  his name is great in Israel.ᵛ
² His tent is in Salem,
  his dwelling place in Zion.

---

u Ps 89:17; 92:10.—v Ps 99:3; Hab 3:2.

75:9 It is unclear who is speaking in this verse. It may be the Levite in his own name or as a representative of his people. *Sing praise:* see note on Ps 7:17. *Jacob:* i.e., Israel (see Ge 32:28).

75:10 This verse appears to be another word from the Lord to go with v. 2, above. He indicates that even if godlessness now triumphs and justice is subverted, at the end of time the Messiah will come to judge the nations in fulfillment of the promise about the victory of the righteous.

Ps 76 In 701 B.C., the mighty army of Sennacherib had camped beneath the walls of Jerusalem. One night the attacker suddenly lifted the siege. What mysterious terror did the Lord employ to put to rout the forces of that haughty ruler? It is the victory of God at Jerusalem; and in the holy city, God reveals himself through his triumphs (see 2 Ki 19:35). The memory of this event remained engraved in the minds of the people (see 2 Mac 8:19; Sir 48:21) and became the symbol for the salvation awaited by the poor, the remnant of God.

Like Ps 46, this hymn to the glory of Zion is doubtless inspired by that event; it restores the courage and hope of the exiles returning from Babylon after 538 B.C. The fearsome God prostrates the powerful of the world and saves the lowly. This confidence of the poor will continuously rise from the heart of humankind in protest against haughty dominators as an announcement of the judgment of God.

It is by the glorious Christ that God the Father dwells in and protects his new People, the Church. With this psalm, we can rightly celebrate our Savior, who is terrible for his enemies: the devil, sin, and death.

The words *For the director of music* in the superscription are thought to be a musical or liturgical notation; for *Asaph,* see introduction to Ps 73—89.

76:1-2 The Lord has chosen "Salem" (ancient name for Jerusalem; see Ge 14:18; Heb 7:1-3) as his royal city so that both the southern kingdom ("Judah") and the northern kingdom ("Israel") may gain reassurance that God is in their midst (see Ps 46).

3 There he broke the flashing arrows,
    the shields and the swords, the weapons of
       war.[w]   *Selah*

4 You are resplendent with light,*
    more majestic than mountains rich with
      game.
5 Valiant men lie plundered,
    they sleep their last sleep;*
not one of the warriors
    can lift his hands.[x]
6 At your rebuke, O God of Jacob,
    both horse and chariot lie still.
7 You alone are to be feared.
    Who can stand before you when you are
      angry?[y]
8 From heaven you pronounced judgment,
    and the land feared and was quiet—
9 when you, O God, rose up to judge,
    to save all the afflicted of the land.*   *Selah*
10 Surely your wrath against men brings you
      praise,*
    and the survivors of your wrath are re-
      strained.[i]

---

i Or *Surely the wrath of men brings you praise, / and with the remainder of wrath you arm yourself.*

---

w Ps 46:9; 48:3-7; 122:6-9.—x Jdg 20:44; 2 Ki 19:35; Jer 51:39; Na 3:18.—y Dt 7:21; 1 Sa 6:20; Na 1:6; Mal 3:2; Rev 6:17.

76:4-10 Praise of God's mighty deed against the Assyrians and his judgment of evildoers.

76:5 *Last sleep:* allusion to the night of which 2 Ki 19:35 speaks (see Ps 13:4; Jer 51:39, 57; Na 3:18).

76:9 *Save all the afflicted of the land:* the psalmist widens his perspectives to include not only the inhabitants of Zion but also all the lowly who will be saved by God's defeat of the rulers and war leaders.

76:10-12 Everyone must give honor to the Most High—even those who rebel against the Lord and his kingdom must contribute to his honor and glory. In his wrath he brings down the wicked and praise from those he has thus rescued. The same theme is found in the alternative translation given in the NIV textual note: *Surely the wrath of men brings you praise*; when wrath leads men to do evil, it also leads to God's praise when he defeats them. Furthermore, God's wrath against evil is never exhausted. This should gain him the praise and fear of all peoples.

¹¹ Make vows to the LORD your God and fulfill
          them;
    let all the neighboring lands
    bring gifts to the One to be feared.^z
¹² He breaks the spirit of rulers;
    he is feared by the kings of the earth.

PSALM 77*

Lament and Consolation in Distress

For the director of music. For Jeduthun.
Of Asaph. A psalm.

¹ I cried out to God for help;*
    I cried out to God to hear me.*
² When I was in distress, I sought the LORD;
    at night I stretched out untiring hands
    and my soul refused to be comforted.^a

---

z Nu 30:3; Ecc 5:4-5. —a Ps 50:15; 88:1; Isa 26:16.

Ps 77 During a difficult period that the people of Israel are experiencing after the return from exile, more than one fervent Israelite can believe that God has abandoned his own. But the Lord does not act after the fashion of human beings: has he not from Egypt to Canaan by means of the wonders of the Exodus (vv. 14-20) transformed a motley group of slaves into a people of his own?

The striking evocation of the passage through the Red Sea and the coming of God at Sinai enables the psalmist to rediscover the great certitude that God still guides his people. Such a certitude is present even when one must realize that God's ways have become mysterious. Hope is reborn, purified by adversity and more unshakable than ever.

This psalm is a reminder of the Father's faithfulness toward Christ and calls us to remain faithful ourselves in times of distress and spiritual dryness. "Let us hold unswervingly to the hope we profess, for he who promised is faithful" (Heb 10:23). We must imitate the ancients and, even more, Christ by remaining faithful even in the darkest of times, for "we are not of those who shrink back and are destroyed, but of those who believe and are saved" (Heb 10:39).

The words *For the director of music* in the superscription are thought to be a musical or liturgical notation; for *Jeduthun,* see introduction to Ps 39; for *Asaph*, see introduction to Ps 73—89.

77:1-9 To the psalmist, God seems to have deserted his people; he no longer responds to appeals for help in time of distress and intense prayer.

77:1-2 The psalmist looked to God as the the sole comforter of his distressed soul (see Ge 37:35; Jer 31:15). He cried out ceaselessly in prayer with hands out-stretched—but remained uncomforted. *Soul:* see note on Ps 6:3.

3 I remembered you, O God, and I groaned;*
    I mused, and my spirit grew faint.*b*   *Selah*
4 You kept my eyes from closing;
    I was too troubled to speak.
5 I thought about the former days,
    the years of long ago;
6 I remembered my songs in the night.
    My heart* mused and my spirit inquired:*c*

7 "Will the LORD reject forever?*
    Will he never show his favor again?*d*
8 Has his unfailing love* vanished forever?
    Has his promise failed for all time?
9 Has God forgotten to be merciful?
    Has he in anger withheld his compassion?"
                           Selah

10 Then I thought, "To this I will appeal:*
    the years of the right hand of the Most
    High."* *e*
11 I will remember the deeds of the LORD;
    yes, I will remember your miracles of long
    ago.*f*

---

b Ps 78:35; Jnh 2:7.—c Ps 143:5; Dt 32:7.—d 7-9: Ps 13:1; 44:23; 74:1; 80:4; 89:46; 102:13; La 3:31.—e Ps 17:7; 18:35; Ex 15:6, 12.—f Ps 143:5; Ne 9:17.

77:3-6 Sleeplessness and dryness in prayer lead the psalmist's faith to be shaken, but he puts his mind on the origins of his people as God's people and attempts to rediscover hope (see Ps 119:52; Dt 32:7ff).

77:6 *Heart:* see note on Ps 4:7.

77:7-9 These verses follow the style of laments (see Ps 74:1; 89:46ff; Isa 63:15; La 3:21-24, 31ff). The prophetic word had ceased (see Ps 74:9); still God remained faithful to his promises, inscribed in the ancient writings on which the psalmist meditated endlessly (see Ps 1:2; 105:3ff) to convince himself that God had not changed in his love for his people (see Isa 49:14ff; Mal 3:6).

77:8 *Unfailing love:* see note on Ps 6:4.

77:10-20 The psalmist takes up the Book of History, so to speak, and meditates upon the great deeds of the Lord, the miracles he wrought in the past. He is so captivated by the reading that in meditating on the glorious deeds that the Lord did for Israel in former times he obtains peace of mind and forgets his present distress.

77:10 *The years of the right hand of the Most High:* the years when God—by means of his right hand—provided strong guidance and protection for his people (see Ps 17:7; 18:35; Isa 41:10).

¹² I will meditate on all your works
    and consider all your mighty deeds.

¹³ Your ways, O God, are holy.*
    What god is so great as our God?ᵍ
¹⁴ You are the God who performs miracles;
    you display your power among the peo-
    ples.ʰ
¹⁵ With your mighty arm you redeemed your
    people,ⁱ
    the descendants of Jacob and Joseph.*
                                    Selah

¹⁶ The waters saw you, O God,*
    the waters saw you and writhed;*
    the very depths were convulsed.ʲ
¹⁷ The clouds poured down water,
    the skies resounded with thunder;ᵏ
    your arrows flashed back and forth.*
¹⁸ Your thunder was heard in the whirlwind,
    your lightning lit up the world;ˡ
    the earth trembled and quaked.*

---

g Ps 18:30; Ex 15:11.—h Ps 86:10; 89:6; Ex 3:20.—i Ge 46:26-27; Ex
6:6; Ne 1:10.—j Ps 18:15; 114:3; Na 1:4; Hab 3:10.—k Ps 18:13-14; 29:3;
144:6; Dt 32:23; Job 37:3-4; Wis 5:21; Zec 9:14.—l Ps 18:7;
97:4; 99:1; Ex 19:16; Jdg 5:4-5; 2 Sa 22:13.

77:13 *Your ways . . . are holy:* see Ps 18:30; Dt 32:4. Another translation is:
"Your ways . . . are seen in the sanctuary" (see Ps 63:2).

77:15 *Descendants of Jacob and Joseph:* those who emigrated to Egypt
("Jacob") and those who were born there ("Joseph") (see Ps 81:4ff; Ge 46:26f;
48:5).

77:16-19 The miracle of the crossing of the Red Sea is presented in a cosmic
perspective, possibly to heighten the description of God's majesty in bringing his
people from slavery to freedom, which led to the Passover. For Christians, the
culminating miracle was God's deed in bringing Jesus from death to life after the
crucifixion (see Mt 28:2; Eph 1:18-22), which led to the Christian Passover,
Easter.

77:16 The waters are at the mercy of the Creator (see Ps 89:9; 93:3f; 104:7;
106:9; 114:3; Job 7:12; 38:10; Na 1:4; Hab 3:10).

77:17 This verse is inspired by Hab 3:11. See also Ps 18:15; 68:8; 144:6.
Arrows: i.e., lightning bolts.

77:18 This verse evokes the theophany at Sinai (see Ps 97:4; Ex 19:18).

¹⁹ Your path led through the sea,
  your way through the mighty waters,[m]
  though your footprints were not seen.*

²⁰ You led your people like a flock[n]
  by the hand of Moses and Aaron.*

PSALM 78*

God's Goodness in the Face of Ingratitude

A *maskil* [j] of Asaph.

¹ O my people, hear my teaching;*
  listen to the words of my mouth.

j Probably a literary or musical term.

m Ne 9:11; Wis 14:3; Isa 43:16; 51:10; Hab 3:15.—n Ps 78:52; Nu 33:1; Isa 63:11-14; Hos 12:13; Mic 6:4.

77:19 See Ne 9:11; Wis 14:3; Isa 43:16; 51:10. God's action reveals his invisible presence as Shepherd and Savior (see Ps 78:52; Is 63:11ff; Mic 6:4).

77:20 The conclusion to the thought expressed in v. 15: God led his people through the desert under the care of Moses and Aaron.

Ps 78 This lengthy sermon is given us as a lesson in wisdom: if the People of God wish to understand their destiny, they must reflect on their origins and meditate on the Exodus, which is a history of divine grace and human infidelity. In effect, their ancestors never responded with anything but ingratitude to the miracles that God multiplied for them. He rolls back the sea and brings water from a rock; the people already clamor for another prodigy (vv. 12-20). Filled with the manna and the quail, the people still murmur (vv. 23-30)! Then the Lord becomes angry and metes out punishment, but he soon grants pardon to them out of pity for their human weakness (vv. 31-39). On their behalf, he had also brought about the plagues (vv. 43-51), and guided them through the desert and into the promised land (vv. 52-56). Still, offenses multiplied; so he also resorted anew to chastisement. But ultimately he reserved for his people the privileged holy place, Zion, and the shepherd after his own heart, David (vv. 59-72).

Thus, the psalm emphasizes the infidelity of Ephraim (the ancestor of the Samaritans), the choice of Judah, and the call of David. Its lesson is that in spite of the successive about-faces of the people, God accomplished his design.

Is this not also our history? To acknowledge God's love does not keep us from infidelities; at such times, the word of God challenges us but also brings pardon, and the Eucharist is given us to sustain our steps. In Jesus, the new David and Good Shepherd, the People of God find a model and perfect guide to the new promised land, the heavenly Jerusalem, where the Father awaits all persons.

For the term *maskil* in the superscription, see introduction to Ps 32; for *Asaph*, see introduction to Ps 73—89.

78:1-8 Remembrance of the great deeds of the Lord should serve to strengthen the people's faith in his power and fidelity. Thus, they will not forget what the Lord has done for their ancestors, which was a blessing for their descendants, and what God has demanded from his covenant people.

2 I will open my mouth in parables,[o]
I will utter hidden things, things from of old—*
3 what we have heard and known,*
what our fathers have told us.[p]
4 We will not hide them from their children;
we will tell the next generation
the praiseworthy deeds of the LORD,
his power, and the wonders he has done.[q]
5 He decreed statutes for Jacob
and established the law in Israel,
which he commanded our forefathers
to teach their children,[r]
6 so the next generation would know them,
even the children yet to be born,
and they in turn would tell their children.[s]
7 Then they would put their trust in God
and would not forget his deeds
but would keep his commands.
8 They would not be like their forefathers—
a stubborn and rebellious generation,[t]
whose hearts* were not loyal to God,
whose spirits were not faithful to him.[u]

9 The men of Ephraim, though armed with bows,*
turned back on the day of battle;*

o Ps 49:4; Mt 13:35.—p Ps 44:1; 145:4.—q Ex 10:2; Dt 4:9; Job 8:8; 15:18.—r Ps 19:7; 147:19; Dt 33:4.—s Ps 22:31-32; Dt 4:9; 6:7.—t Dt 31:27; 32:5; Isa 30:9.—u Ps 95:10.

78:2 *Parable* in Hebrew means a comparison, or any saying with a deeper meaning, which is to be understood via the hidden comparison; in this case, the parable is the whole psalm. This passage is used by Mt 13:35 as a foreshadowing of Christ's teaching in parables (see also Ps 49:4; Eze 17:2; 24:3).

78:3-5 Israel is the people of tradition (see Dt 4:9; 32:7; Job 8:8; 15:18; Isa 38:19; Joel 1:3); what its people hand down is above all the remembrance of the Exodus (see Ex 10:2; 13:14) and the covenant statutes (Dt 4:9-14; 6:20-25).

78:8 *Hearts:* see note on Ps 4:7.

78:9-16 The psalmist stresses that the northern kingdom, in which Ephraim had the lead, has been unfaithful to the covenant (a theme of the prophets Amos and Hosea). It constitutes the last in a series of infidelities committed by Israel.

78:9 There is no record of flight from battle on the part of Ephraimites; it may be a metaphor for Ephraim's failure to keep the covenant.

¹⁰ they did not keep God's covenant
　　　and refused to live by his law.
¹¹ They forgot what he had done,
　　　the wonders he had shown them.
¹² He did miracles in the sight of their fathers ᵛ
　　　in the land of Egypt, in the region of
　　　Zoan.*
¹³ He divided the sea and led them through;ʷ
　　　he made the water stand firm like a wall.ˣ
¹⁴ He guided them with the cloud by day
　　　and with light from the fire all night.ʸ
¹⁵ He split the rocks in the desert
　　　and gave them water as abundant as the
　　　seas;ᶻ
¹⁶ he brought streams out of a rocky crag
　　　and made water flow down like rivers.

¹⁷ * But they continued to sin* against him,
　　　rebelling in the desert against the Most
　　　High.ᵃ
¹⁸ They willfully put God to the test ᵇ
　　　by demanding the food they craved.*
¹⁹ They spoke against God, saying,
　　　"Can God spread a table in the desert?ᶜ
²⁰ When he struck the rock, water gushed out,
　　　and streams flowed abundantly.
　　But can he also give us food?
　　　Can he supply meat for his people?"*

---

v Ps 106:7; Ne 9:17.—w 13-14: Ps 136:13; Ex 14—15.—x Ps 66:6; Ex
14:21; 15:8.—y Ps 105:39; Ex 13:21; Wis 18:3.—z Ps 105:41; 114:8; Ex
17:1-7; Nu 20:2-13; Dt 8:15; Wis 11:4; Isa 48:21; 1 Co 10:4.—a Dt 9:7; Eze
20:13.—b Ps 106:14; Ex 16:2-36; 1 Co 10:9.—c Ps 23:5; Nu 21:5.

78:12 *Zoan:* a city in the Nile delta, capital of Egypt at the time of the Exodus.
78:17-31 The psalmist indicates that the Israelites rebelled against the Lord
in the desert despite all kinds of marvels that he worked on their behalf. This led
to the Lord's anger against them.
78:17 *Continued to sin:* the psalmist has mentioned no sin, but because of the
theme of water in v. 16 he is reminded of the people's murmuring over the lack of
water at Marah (see Ex 15:24).
78:18 See Ex 16:2f.
78:20 See Ex 16:2f and Nu 11:4.

²¹ When the L**ORD** heard them, he was very
  angry;*d*
    his fire broke out against Jacob,
    and his wrath rose against Israel,
²² for they did not believe in God
    or trust in his deliverance.
²³ Yet he gave a command to the skies above
    and opened the doors of the heavens;
²⁴ he rained down manna for the people to eat,
    he gave them the grain of heaven.*e*
²⁵ Men ate the bread of angels;*
    he sent them all the food they could eat.
²⁶ He let loose the east wind from the heavens
    and led forth the south wind by his power.
²⁷ He rained meat down on them like dust,
    flying birds like sand on the seashore.
²⁸ He made them come down inside their camp,
    all around their tents.
²⁹ They ate till they had more than enough,
    for he had given them what they craved.
³⁰ But before they turned from the food they
  craved,
    even while it was still in their mouths,
³¹ God's anger rose against them;
    he put to death the sturdiest among them,
    cutting down the young men of Israel.*f*

³² In spite of all this, they kept on sinning;*
    in spite of his wonders, they did not be-
    lieve.

---

d 21f: Nu 11; Dt 32:22.—e Ps 105:40; Ex 16:4, 14; Dt 8:3; Wis 16:20; Jn
6:31.—f Nu 14:29; Isa 10:16.

78:25 *Bread of angels:* literally, "bread of mighty ones," which clearly refers to
angels (see Ps 103:20; Wis 16:20; see also Jn 6:32, 50; 1 Co 10:3). Ps 105:40
speaks of "the bread of heaven" (see Dt 8:3).
78:32-39 The people's infidelity to the Lord continued unabated throughout
the entire sojourn in the desert (see Isa 26:16; 29:13; Hos 5:15; 8:1). However,
the Lord tempered his punishment, for he knew they shared the inherent weakness of human beings (see Ps 65:3; 85:3; 103:14; Ex 32:14; Nu 14:20; 21:7ff; Isa
48:9; Eze 20:22).

³³ So he ended their days in futility
   and their years in terror.*
³⁴ Whenever God slew them, they would seek
      him;
   they eagerly turned to him again.ᵍ
³⁵ They remembered that God was their Rock,*
   that God Most High was their Redeemer.
³⁶ But then they would flatter him with their
      mouths,
   lying to him with their tongues;
³⁷ their hearts* were not loyal to him,
   they were not faithful to his covenant.ʰ
³⁸ Yet he was merciful;
   he forgave their iniquities
   and did not destroy them.
   Time after time he restrained his anger
   and did not stir up his full wrath.ⁱ
³⁹ He remembered that they were but flesh,
   a passing breeze that does not return.

⁴⁰ How often they rebelled against him in the
      desert*
   and grieved him in the wasteland!
⁴¹ Again and again they put God to the test;
   they vexed the Holy One of Israel.*
⁴² They did not remember his power—
   the day he redeemed them from the op-
      pressor,ʲ

---

g Nu 21:7; Dt 32:15, 18; Isa 26:16.—h Ps 95:10; Isa 29:13; Hos 8:1.—i
Ps 85:3; Ex 32:14; Nu 14:20; Isa 48:9; Eze 20:22; Hos 11:8-9.—j Ps
106:21; Jdg 3:7.

78:33 Nonetheless, the Lord decreed that the faithless generation of the Exodus would never set foot on the promised land (see Nu 14:22f, 28-35).
78:35 *Rock:* see note on Ps 18:2.
78:37 *Hearts:* see note on Ps 4:7.
78:40-55 The Israelites continued to rebel against God in the desert. They failed to recall how he had delivered them from Egypt by such wonders as the plagues and the passage through the Red Sea. Nonetheless, the Lord went on to lead them to the conquest and settlement of the promised land.
78:41 *Holy One of Israel:* see note on Ps 71:22.

43 the day he displayed his miraculous signs in
Egypt,[k]
his wonders in the region of Zoan.
44 He turned their rivers to blood;*
they could not drink from their streams.
45 He sent swarms of flies that devoured them,
and frogs that devastated them.[l]
46 He gave their crops to the grasshopper,
their produce to the locust.
47 He destroyed their vines with hail
and their sycamore-figs with sleet.[m]
48 He gave over their cattle to the hail,
their livestock to bolts of lightning.[n]
49 He unleashed against them his hot anger,
his wrath, indignation and hostility—
a band of destroying angels.*
50 He prepared a path for his anger;
he did not spare them from death
but gave them over to the plague.
51 He struck down all the firstborn of Egypt,[o]
the firstfruits of manhood in the tents of
Ham.*
52 But he brought his people out like a flock;
he led them like sheep through the desert.[p]
53 He guided them safely, so they were unafraid;
but the sea engulfed their enemies.[q]

k 43f: Ps 105:27-36; 135:9; Ex 7:14—11:10; 12:29-36; Wis 16—18.—l Ps 105:31; Ex 8:17.—m Ps 147:17; Wis 16:16.—n Ex 9:3, 25.—o Ps 105:36; 135:8; 136:10; Ex 12:29.—p Ps 28:9; 77:20.—q Ps 106:10-11; Ex 14:26-28.

78:44-51 The psalmist is not concerned about a complete, chronological, and exact narrative of the plagues. He gives them in a different order and enumeration, while also omitting the third, fifth, sixth, and ninth (see Ex 7—12).

78:49 *Destroying angels:* the psalmist here generalizes the theme of the "destroyer" of the firstborn (see Ex 12:23), personifying the Lord's wrath, indignation, and hostility as agents of his anger (see Ex 9:14; Dt 32:24; Job 20:23).

78:51 *Tents of Ham:* usually linked with Egypt (see Ps 105:23, 27; 106:21f; Ge 10:6).

⁵⁴ Thus he brought them to the border of his
          holy land,
       to the hill country his right hand had
          taken.ʳ
⁵⁵ He drove out nations before them
       and allotted their lands to them as an in-
          heritance;
       he settled the tribes of Israel in their
          homes.*

⁵⁶ But they put God to the test*
       and rebelled against the Most High;
       they did not keep his statutes.
⁵⁷ Like their fathers they were disloyal and
          faithless,
       as unreliable as a faulty bow.
⁵⁸ They angered him with their high places;*
       they aroused his jealousy with their idols.ˢ
⁵⁹ When God heard them, he was very angry;
       he rejected Israel completely.*
⁶⁰ He abandoned the tabernacle of Shiloh,*
       the tent he had set up among men.ᵗ
⁶¹ He sent [the ark of] his might into captivity,
       his splendor* into the hands of the enemy.ᵘ

---

r Ps 44:3; Ex 15:17.—s Ex 20:4; Dt 32:16, 21.—t Jos 18:1; 1 Sa 1:3; Jer
7:12; 26:6; Eze 8:6.—u Ps 132:8; 1 Sa 4:11, 22.

78:55 The psalmist here summarizes the story of the Conquest told in Joshua.
78:56-64 This part, like its predecessors, begins with the remembrance of Israel's sins and evokes the time of Samuel and Saul in the Book of Judges. Because of the people's infidelity, God rejected Israel (see Jer 7:12ff).
78:58 *High places:* the Canaanites were accustomed to build altars to their
gods on hills ("high places"), a custom followed by the Israelites who built altars
to Yahweh on hills. However, this led to the adoption of pagan practices and idols
by God's people. *Jealousy:* see Ex 20:5 ("I . . . am a jealous God").
78:59 The psalmist is here not speaking of a permanent abandonment of Israel by God.
78:60 *Shiloh:* a shrine located in Ephraim (see Jdg 21:19) that was the center
of Israelite worship from the time of Joshua (see Jos 18:1, 8; 21:1f; Jdg 18:31; 1
Sa 1:3; Jer 7:12; 26:6). It was destroyed by the Philistines when the ark of the
covenant was captured (see 1 Sa 4:1-11).
78:61 *His might . . . his splendor:* the divine attributes of which the ark of the
covenant was the symbol (see Ps 132:17; 1 Sa 4:19ff; 2 Ch 6:41).

62 He gave his people over to the sword;
      he was very angry with his inheritance.
63 Fire consumed their young men,
      and their maidens had no wedding songs;v
64 their priests were put to the sword,
      and their widows could not weep.

65 Then the Lord awoke as from sleep,*
      as a man wakes from the stupor of wine.
66 He beat back his enemies;
      he put them to everlasting shame.
67 Then he rejected the tents of Joseph,
      he did not choose the tribe of Ephraim;
68 but he chose the tribe of Judah,
      Mount Zion,* which he loved.w
69 He built his sanctuary like the heights,
      like the earth* that he established forever.
70 He chose David* his servant
      and took him from the sheep pens;x
71 from tending the sheep he brought him
      to be the shepherd of his people Jacob,
      of Israel his inheritance.y
72 And David shepherded them with integrity of
        heart;
      with skillful hands he led them.*

---

v Nu 11:1; Dt 32:25; Jer 7:34.—w Ps 48:1; 50:2; 87:2; 108:8; La 2:15.—
x Ps 89:20; 1 Sa 13:14; 2 Ch 6:6; Ez 34:23; 37:24.—y Ge 37:2; 1 Sa 16:11-
13; 2 Sa 7:8.

78:65-72 After the Israelites had been cleansed by the divine chastisement, the Lord had mercy on them and fought by their side once more in vanquishing their enemies. But afterward God chose Judah instead of Ephraim as the leading tribe, Mount Zion instead of Shiloh as the royal seat (the place of his sanctuary), and David instead of Saul as his king and regent. David is the ideal shepherd (see Eze 34:23; 37:24), the Lord's anointed (see Ps 89:20), and the type of the Messiah to come (see Ps 110). What the Lord did for the people in the desert, David did in his name for the people of Judah.

78:68 *He chose . . . Mount Zion:* see Ps 132:11, 17.

78:69 *Heights . . . earth:* the Lord built his sanctuary to last like the heavens and the earth (see note on Ps 24:2) and to reflect his glory as they do (see Ps 19:1; 29:9; 97:6).

78:70 *He chose David:* see Ps 132.

78:72 The Prophets regarded Israel led by David as the hope of God's people (see Eze 34:23; 37:24; Mic 5:2—fulfilled in Jesus: see Mt 2:6; Jn 10:11; Rev 7:17).

PSALM 79*

Prayer for Restoration

A psalm of Asaph.

¹ O God, the nations have invaded your inheri-
     tance;*
     they have defiled your holy temple,
     they have reduced Jerusalem to rubble.ᶻ
² They have given the dead bodies of your ser-
     vants
     as food to the birds of the air,
     the flesh of your saints to the beasts of the
     earth.ᵃ
³ They have poured out blood like water ᵇ
     all around Jerusalem,
     and there is no one to bury the dead.*
⁴ We are objects of reproach to our neighbors,ᶜ
     of scorn and derision to those around us.*

---

z 2 Ki 25:9-10; Jer 26:18; La 1:10.—a Ps 80:12-13; Jer 7:33.—b 1 Mac
7:17; Jer 14:16; Zep 1:17.—c Ps 39:8; 44:13; 80:6; 123:3-4; Job 12:4; Da
9:16; Zep 2:8.

Ps 79 In this poem the psalmist is speaking of the darkest days of Israel's
history: in 587 B.C. the Chaldeans captured and sacked Jerusalem; the neighboring Moabites and Edomites then attacked this people that was in its death-
throes. Israel is aware now that it deserved to be punished for its infidelities, and
it appeals to God's mercy. In this lamentation, the distress of the oppressed calls
upon the Lord for redress. The pagans dishonor the divine name; this is tantamount to a defeat for the Lord. In avenging his own, God must first save his
honor in the eyes of the world, and his people will be grateful to him. Such is the
theme of this national lamentation.
    Must vengeance be paid back seven times (i.e., in full measure) upon one's
neighbors? Christ has told us to pardon seventy times seven (Mt 18:22)—so that
we cannot take this psalm literally. Still it remains a poignant appeal to God's
mercy, an act of faith in the Lord when everything seems to be collapsing around
us. We do not demand the total destruction of our enemies but a salutary punishment, in keeping with the divine justice, which brings evildoers low in order to
pardon and save them.
    For *Asaph* in the superscription, see introduction to Ps 73—89.
    79:1-4 God's city and temple have been desecrated and so have his wor-
shipers, whose dead bodies have been left unburied.
    79:2-3 *They have given . . . the flesh . . . to bury the dead:* these verses are
cited freely in 1 Mac 7:17 in application to the massacre of sixty pious Jews in
Jerusalem during the Maccabean wars.
    79:4 A secular hostility opposed Israel to its neighbors, as is shown by the ora-
cles of the Prophets against the nations (see La 3:45; Zep 2:8).

5 * How long, O LORD?* Will you be angry forever?

How long will your jealousy burn like
fire?*d*

6 Pour out your wrath on the nations*
that do not acknowledge you,*e*
on the kingdoms
that do not call on your name;*

7 for they have devoured Jacob
and destroyed his homeland.

8 Do not hold against us the sins of the fathers;
may your mercy come quickly to meet us,*f*
for we are in desperate need.*

9 Help us, O God our Savior,*
for the glory of your name;*g*
deliver us and forgive our sins
for your name's sake.*

10 Why should the nations say,
"Where is their God?"*h*

Before our eyes, make known among the nations
that you avenge* the outpoured blood of
your servants.*i*

---

d Ps 13:1; 44:23; 74:1; 89:46; Dt 4:24.—e Ps 14:4; Sir 36:1-5; Jer
10:25.—f Ps 116:6; 142:6.—g Ps 25:11; Eze 20:44; 36:22.—h Ps 42:3;
115:2; Joel 2:17.—i Dt 32:43; Joel 3:2.

79:5-8 The divine justice cannot remain inactive in the case of such wickedness, which calls out for retribution.

79:5 *How long . . . ?:* see note on Ps 6:3. *Jealousy:* see note on Ps 78:58. *Burn
like fire:* see Dt 4:24; 6:15; Zep 1:18; 3:8.

79:6-7 Cited in Jer 10:25. Concerning the call for redress, see note on Ps
65:10.

79:6, 12 See note on Ps 5:10 and introduction to Ps 35.

79:8 The exiles beg God to show mercy on them and not hold the sins of their
ancestors against them (see 2 Ki 17:7-23; 23:26f; 24:3f; Da 9:4-14).

79:9-13 The psalmist beseeches God to pardon Israel for his name's sake so
that the Most High may no longer be dishonored and blasphemed by the nations.
Then the people of God will praise him from generation to generation.

79:9 The divine pardon is always gratuitous; it is the effect of his mercy and
love (see Ps 78:38; Eze 20:44; 36:22; see also note on Ps 65:3).

79:10 *You avenge:* God is the avenger of blood in Israel (see Ps 18:47; 19:14;
58:10f; 94:1; 149:7; Dt 32:43).

11 May the groans of the prisoners come before
   you;^j
     by the strength of your arm
     preserve those condemned to die.*

12 Pay back into the laps of our neighbors seven
   times*
     the reproach they have hurled at you, O
     LORD.^k
13 Then we your people, the sheep of your pasture,
     will praise you* forever;
   from generation to generation
     we will recount your praise.

PSALM 80*

Prayer for the Persecuted People

For the director of music. To [the tune of] "The Lilies
of the Covenant." Of Asaph. A psalm.

1 * Hear us, O Shepherd of Israel,*
     you who lead Joseph like a flock;

---

j Ps 102-20; 126:2.—k Ps 89:50-51; Isa 65:6.

79:11 *Prisoners . . . those condemned to die:* i.e., the exiles in Babylonia (see
Ps 102:20) who are under threat of death if they seek to escape.
   79:12 *Seven times:* a symbolic phrase meaning fullness or superabundance
(see Ps 12:6; Ge 4:24; Lev 26:21).
   79:13 *Praise you:* see note on Ps 7:17.
   Ps 80 At the time of this psalmist, the northern kingdom of Israel and the
southern kingdom of Judah have disappeared in turn (721 and 587 B.C.). For the
time being, Israel will be nothing but a scattered flock, a ruined vineyard. Whence
can restoration come if not from God? This psalm is well adapted to our prayer
during Advent: so deep is our wretchedness that we await the coming of God; he
alone can turn us to himself by his presence and convert us.
   The words *For the director of music* in the superscription are thought to be a
musical or liturgical notation; nothing is known about *To [the tune of] . . . ;* for
Asaph, see introduction to Ps 73.
   80:1-7 God is the Shepherd of Israel (see Isa 40:11; Jer 31:10; Eze 34:31), and
Jesus will call himself the Good Shepherd (see Jn 10). This image evokes profound links between Israel and God—affectionate solicitude on one side and
confident belonging on the other. Hence, those who are in distress do not address
an unknown and distant God.
   80:1 *Shepherd of Israel:* see Ps 74:1; 77:20; 78:52, 71f; 79:13. *Joseph:* see
note on Ps 77:15. *Cherubim:* see note on Ps 18:10.

you who sit enthroned between the cherubim,
      shine forth [l]
2   before Ephraim, Benjamin and Manasseh.*
Awaken your might;
      come and save us.

3 Restore us, O God;
      make your face shine* upon us,
      that we may be saved.[m]

4 O Lord God Almighty,*
      how long will your anger smolder
      against the prayers of your people?[n]
5 You have fed them with the bread of tears;
      you have made them drink tears by the
         bowlful.[o]
6 You have made us a source of contention to
         our neighbors,
      and our enemies mock us.[p]

7 Restore us, O God Almighty;
      make your face shine upon us,
      that we may be saved.

8 * You brought a vine* out of Egypt;
      you drove out the nations and planted it.

---

l Ps 23:1-3; 77:20; 95:7; 100:3; Ge 48:15; Ex 25:22; 1 Sa 4:4; 2 Sa 6:2;
Eze 34:2; Mic 7:14.—m 3, 7, 19: Ps 4:6; 31:16; 67:1; 85:4; Nu 6:25; Jer
31:18.—n Ps 13:1; 44:23; 74:1; 79:5; 89:46; Dt 4:24; 29:20.—o Ps 42:3;
102:9.—p Ps 44:13; 79:4; 123:3-4; Job 12:4; Da 9:16; Zep 2:8.

80:2 *Before Ephraim, Benjamin and Manasseh:* Ephraim and Manasseh were
the two principal tribes of the northern kingdom, with which Benjamin was at
times associated (see Nu 2:18f). It was also in front of these three tribes that the
ark of the covenant advanced during the sojourn from Sinai to the promised land
(see Nu 10:21-24).
  80:3 *Make your face shine:* see notes on Ps 4:6 and 13:1.
  80:4 *Lord . . . Almighty:* see note on Ps 59:5. *How long. . . ?:* see note on Ps 6:3.
  80:8-16 Israel is God's magnificent garden whose ideal limits extend as far as
the Euphrates ("River" of v. 11). God is like the vinedresser who cherishes his
vine-vineyard and takes pleasure in it. How could he not be saddened to see it
devastated (see Isa 5:1-7; 27:2-5; Jer 2:21; 12:10)? This image will pass into the
New Testament (see Mt 20:1; 21:33-41; Jn 15:1-5).
  80:8 *Vine:* a familiar allegory in the Prophets (see Isa 5:1; 27:2; Jer 2:21;
12:10; Eze 17:6-8; 19:10-14; Hos 10:1; 14:7; Mic 7:1), as is that of the shepherd
(see Ps 23:1; Ge 48:15; Eze 34:11). See also Mt 20:1; Jn 15:1.

9 You cleared the ground for it,
and it took root and filled the land.
10 The mountains were covered with its shade,
the mighty cedars* with its branches.
11 It sent out its boughs to the Sea,[k]
its shoots as far as the River.*[l]

12 * Why * have you broken down its walls
so that all who pass by pick its grapes?[q]
13 Boars from the forest ravage it
and the creatures of the field feed on it.[r]
14 Return to us, O God Almighty!*
Look down from heaven and see!
Watch over this vine,
15 the root your right hand has planted,
the son*[m] you have raised up for yourself.

16 Your vine is cut down, it is burned with fire;
at your rebuke your people perish.
17 Let your hand rest on the man at your right hand,*
the son of man you have raised up for yourself.
18 Then we will not turn away from you;
revive us, and we will call on your name.*

19 Restore us, O LORD God Almighty;
make your face shine upon us,
that we may be saved.

---

k Probably the Mediterranean.—l That is, the Euphrates.—m Or *branch*.

q Ps 89:40; Jer 12:7-13.—r Jer 5:6; Hos 2:12.

80:10 *Mighty cedars:* literally, "cedars of God," which were so huge that they were regarded as being planted by God.

80:11 *Sea . . . River:* see NIV textual notes.

80:12-19 The psalmist begs God to attend once again to his wasted vine. Then the people will once again praise their savior.

80:12 *Why. . . ?:* see note on Ps 6:3.

80:14 *God Almighty:* see note on Ps 59:5.

80:15 *Son:* i.e., Israel; but see NIV textual note.

80:17 *Man at your right hand:* probably a reference to Israel, beloved son of the Lord (see Ex 4:22) or to the Davidic king who will lead the army in battle. Others put forth by scholars are Zerubbabel and Ezra who presided over the restoration. *Son of man:* another word for "man" in the first half of this verse.

80:18 A vow to offer praise to God's name (see note on Ps 7:17).

PSALM 81*

Exhortation To Worship Worthily

For the director of music. According to *gittith*.[n] Of Asaph.

[1] Sing for joy to God our strength;[s]
    shout aloud to the God of Jacob!*
[2] Begin the music, strike the tambourine,
    play the melodious harp and lyre.

[3] Sound the ram's horn at the New Moon,[t]
    and when the moon is full, on the day of
    our Feast;*

---

n Probably a musical term.

s Ps 43:4; 66:1; 68:26; 149:3; 150:3-4; Jud 16:1.—t Ex 19:13; Lev 23:24; Nu 29:1.

Ps 81 The blasts of the trumpet call Israel to an assembly. The time is the full moon of September, the feast of Booths or Tabernacles (see Nu 10:10; Lev 23:34, 39-43). The covenant is renewed. At such a time, it is also important to rediscover the demands of fidelity. The psalmist, who is completely pervaded by the spirit of Deuteronomy, makes everyone aware of them. Let the people be on guard not to close their hearts to God. Today (v. 13) as yesterday (vv. 7, 11-12) the fidelity of God is checkmated by the infidelity of human beings.

In the last verse (v. 16) of this psalm, Christians cannot fail to be reminded of the blessings of the Eucharist in which we are filled with the "finest of wheat" (words found in the Mass texts of the Holy Thursday Evening Mass and the Easter Season), with bread that has become the Body and Blood, Soul, and Divinity of our Lord Jesus Christ. Each Eucharist is a renewal of the New Covenant, enabling us to relive the saving events of Christ's Passion and Resurrection. And in each Eucharist we pledge ourselves to Christ by hearing and keeping his word proclaimed and by receiving his Body and Blood.

The words *For the director of music* in the superscription are thought to be a musical or liturgical notation; for *gittith,* see introduction to Ps 8; for *Asaph,* see introduction to Ps 73—89.

81:1 *Jacob:* i.e., Israel (see Ge 32:28). Concerning the ritual "shout," see Ps 33:3.

81:3 The first day of the lunar month (New Moon) was for a long time celebrated as a feast (see 2 Ki 4:23; Isa 1:13; Hos 2:11; Am 8:5). Here it is a question of the beginning of the seventh month, long considered as the New Year (see Lev 23:24; Nu 29:1); on the following full moon (on the fifteenth of the month) the feast of Tabernacles was celebrated (see Lev 23:34; Nu 29:12), five days after the Day of Atonement (see Lev 16:29). It concluded the cycle of feasts that began with the Passover and Unleavened Bread six months before (see Ex 23:14-17; Lev 23; Dt 16:13-15). Every seventh year the covenant law was to be read to all the people (see Dt 31:9-13; Ne 8:2-15).

⁴ this is a decree for Israel,
  an ordinance of the God of Jacob.ᵘ
⁵ He established it as a statute for Joseph*
  when he went out against Egypt,
  where we heard a language we did not understand.ᵒ

⁶ He says, "I removed the burden from their shoulders;ᵛ
  their hands were set free from the basket.*
⁷ In your distress you called and I rescued you,*
  I answered you out of a thundercloud;
  I tested you at the waters of Meribah.ʷ
                              Selah

⁸ "Hear, O my people, and I will warn you—
  if you would but listen to me, O Israel!ˣ
⁹ You shall have no foreign god among you;ʸ
  you shall not bow down to an alien god.
¹⁰ I am the LORD your God,
  who brought you up out of Egypt.
  Open wide your mouth and I will fill it.*

---

o Or / *and we heard a voice we had not known.*

u Ex 23:14ff.—v Ex 1:14; 6:6; Isa 9:4.—w Ps 95:8; Ex 2:23ff; 17:7; 19:16; Nu 20:13; 27:14; Dt 33:8.—x Ps 50:7; Ex 15:26; Isa 55:2-3.—y 9-10: Ex 20:2-6; Dt 5:6-10; Eze 2:8.

81:5 *Joseph:* see note on Ps 77:15. *Heard a language we did not understand:* i.e., the people were aliens in a foreign land (see Ps 114:1; Dt 28:49; 33:19). Some regard this as a reference to inspiration. See NIV textual note for alternative translation, in which case the "voice" is the "thunder" of God's judgment against Egypt (v. 7).
81:6 *Burden . . . basket:* allusion to the forced labor that the Israelites had to endure in Egypt (see Ex 1:11-14).
81:7 *You called and I rescued you:* see Ex 3:7-10; see also Ps 106:9; Ex 14:21, 24; 15:8, 10). *Out of a thundercloud:* allusion to the theophany at Sinai (see Ex 19:16ff). *I tested you . . . Meribah:* see Ps 95:8; Ex 17:1-7.
81:10 The Lord challenges Israel to obey the first commandment of fidelity to God after the proclamation of the Exodus (see Ps 78:23-29; Dt 11:13-15; 28:1-4).

11 "But my people would not listen to me;
    Israel would not submit to me.*
12 So I gave them over to their stubborn hearts *z*
    to follow their own devices.*

13 "If my people would but listen to me,* *a*
    if Israel would follow my ways,*
14 how quickly would I subdue their enemies*
    and turn my hand against their foes!*b*
15 Those who hate the LORD would cringe be-
        fore him,
    and their punishment would last forever.*
16 But you would be fed with the finest of
        wheat;*
    with honey from the rock I would satisfy
        you."*c*

---

z Jer 3:17; 7:24; Ac 7:42.—a Dt 5:29; Isa 48:18.—b Lev 26:7-8; Am 1:8.—c Ps 147:14; Dt 32:13-14.

81:11 Instead of remaining loyal to the Lord out of gratitude for their redemption and his promise of the future, the people continued to rebel against him—a characteristic typical of their history beginning with the generation in the desert (see Ps 78; 95; 106).

81:12 God gives the people over to their sins (see Ps 78:29; Isa 6:9f; 29:10; 63:17; see also Ro 1:24, 26, 28) because of their hardness of heart; but he always reserves the right to "circumcise" their hearts and bring them back to him (see Dt 30:6; 1 Ki 8:58; Jer 31:33; Eze 11:19; 36:26).

81:13-16 An allusion to the covenant blessings; the era of wars and persecutions will cease (see Lk 21:24), their enemies will be vanquished, and the people will enjoy the best of everything.

81:13 The Lord cannot abandon his people completely. He calls them to return to him and follow his "ways," i.e., his commandments (see Ps 27:11; 86:11; 128:1; 143:8). For if they listen to God's word, they will respond by faith and repentance, and carry out his will rather than their own.

81:14 If his people return to him, the Lord will quickly come to their aid with his "hand" pressing hard against their enemies.

81:15 If his people return to him, the Lord will mete out to their enemies—"those who hate the LORD"—their just desserts, inflicting on them an everlasting punishment.

81:16 *Finest of wheat:* a staple of life. For Christians, of course, wheat is associated with the Eucharist, and this phrase has given rise to one of the finest modern Eucharistic hymns: *Gift of Finest Wheat,* composed for the 1976 Eucharistic Congress that took place in the United States. *Honey from the rock:* the purest of honey, since it came from places usually not attainable (from a cleft of rock in which bees in Canaan sometimes built their hives). The phrase is reminiscent of God's promise to Moses of a "land flowing with milk and honey" (Ex 3:8).

PSALM 82*

Judgment on Abuse of Authority

A psalm of Asaph.

¹ God presides in the great assembly;*
     he gives judgment among the "gods":*d*

² "How long will youᵖ defend the unjust*e*
     and show partiality to the wicked?*   *Selah*
³ Defend the cause of the weak and fatherless;*
     maintain the rights of the poor and op-
     pressed.

---

p The Hebrew is plural.

---

d Ps 7:8; Isa 3:13-14.—e Ps 58:2; Pr 18:5.

Ps 82 The psalmist sets forth a word about just and unjust judges (somewhat similar to Ps 58). He reminds rulers and magistrates that they are members on earth of God's tribunal, associated in the government of the world, and in this respect "gods" (v. 5). Why then does the cause of the poor find such little regard among them! By establishing injustice rather than justice, these powerful people disturb the very order of the world (v. 5). They themselves will therefore be judged by the great King (see Ps 47) and Judge of all the earth (see Ps 94:2; Ge 18:25; 1 Sa 2:10) who "loves justice" (Ps 99:4) and judges the nations in righteousness (see Ps 9:8; 96:13; 98:9). Furthermore, God's justice turns human judgments topsy-turvy; the kingdom of God and his justice will succeed to the fall of evildoers and the powers of oppression (see Isa 24:21f).

Even in nations that are not concerned with God or openly deny him, rulers and judges receive their powers from God and are bound to exercise them for justice in accord with his will: "[Civil authority] is God's servant to do ... good ... to bring punishment on the wrongdoer" (Ro 13:4). This same truth is proclaimed by 1 Pe 2:13f.

For the term *Asaph* in the superscription, see introduction to Ps 73—89.

82:1 *Great assembly:* the psalmist pictures a kind of heavenly assembly (see Ps 89:5; 1 Ki 22:19; Job 1:6; 2:1; Isa 6:1-4) in the Hall of Justice, patterned after the Solomonic one (see 1 Ki 7:7), in which God is dispensing justice. *Gods:* a word applied to rulers and judges who are "godlike" in their function of establishing justice on the earth (see note on Ps 45:6).

82:2 Like other authors of the Old Testament, the psalmist reproaches those in power with the sin of administering justice inequitably and showing partiality toward the wicked (see Ex 23:6; Lev 19:15; Dt 1:17; 2 Ch 19:7; Pr 18:5; Mic 3:1-12).

82:3-4 Rulers and judges are exhorted to protect the powerless against exploiters and oppressors (see Ps 72:2, 4, 12-14; Job 29:11f; Pr 31:8f; Isa 11:4; Jer 22:3, 16; Eze 22:27, 29; Zec 7:9f). Indeed, to see to it that the weak do not fall into the hands of unscrupulous exploiters is one of the most important functions of government.

4 Rescue the weak and needy;*f*
    deliver them from the hand of the wicked.*

5 "They know nothing, they understand noth-
    ing.
    They walk about in darkness;
    all the foundations of the earth are
    shaken.*

6 * "I said, 'You are "gods";
    you are all sons of the Most High.'*

7 But you will die like mere men;
    you will fall like every other ruler."*

8 Rise up, O God, judge the earth,
    for all the nations are your inheritance.*

---

f Dt 1:17.

82:4 This verse can also be looked upon as the end of a two-verse didactic poem, in which the Lord reminds his people of his expectations for them under the covenant (see Isa 1:16f; Zec 7:7-10; Mal 3:9; Jas 1:27). Failure to live up to those expectations on their part leads to condemnation (see Isa 10:1-3).

82:5 When those in authority, instead of sharing in God's wisdom (see 1 Ki 3:9; Pr 8:14-16; Isa 11:2), have no understanding of their most important duty or of the divine norm and standard and do not walk in the light of the revealed will of the eternal Judge (see Job 21:22), then all the supports upon which a well-ordered State rests will crumble (see Ps 11:3; 75:3). *Foundations of the earth:* a metaphor for God's rule on earth (see Ps 11:3; 75:3; 96:10). Even in pagan nations the Lord has established some order, and he condemns the ungodly for undermining that order for their own ends.

82:6-7 These verses can be interpreted to apply to judges or rulers but also to pagan gods. The Lord pronounces sentence and dethrones such gods. Indeed, his judgment is pronounced upon all manifestations of evil both in the human world and in the angelic world (see Mt 25:41; Rev 20:10, 14f; 21:8).

82:6 Rulers and judges are representatives of God, appointed by him (see Ps 2:7; Isa 44:28; Jer 27:6; Da 2:21; 4:17, 32; 5:18; Jn 19:11; Ro 13:1). *Gods:* see note on v. 1. This passage is applied by Christ, in an entirely different context, to Jews instructed by the word of God (see Jn 10:34; see also Ac 17:28; 2 Co 6:18).

82:7 These corrupt rulers will see death like all other human beings and be judged in the same way. *You will fall like every other ruler:* another possible translation is: "as one man, rulers, you will fall." God will humble the great of the world as he annihilated the false gods likened to personages of the ancient mythology (see Isa 14:12; Eze 28:11ff).

82:8 The psalmist prays that God's just judgment (see Ps 9:20; 10:12-15; 76:9) will come soon. This verse can be fittingly applied to Christ, to whom all judgment has been entrusted by the Father (see Jn 5:22).

PSALM 83*

Against a Hostile Alliance

A song. A psalm of Asaph.

1 O God, do not keep silent;*
    be not quiet, O God, be not still.*g*
2 See how your enemies are astir,*
    how your foes rear their heads.
3 With cunning they conspire against your peo-
        ple;
    they plot against those you cherish.*h*
4 "Come," they say, "let us destroy them as a
        nation,
    that the name of Israel be remembered no
        more."

---

g Ps 10:1; 44:23; 50:3; 109:1.—h Ps 17:14; Jer 11:9.

Ps 83 After the deportation in 587 B.C., the people have lost their political existence. The community that has been reestablished in Jerusalem after the return is subjected to the tutelage of great powers and the vexation of their neighbors. The communities that had been scattered among foreign peoples have already experienced more than one persecution. In their struggles with pagan religions and cultures, believers feel threatened in their faith. It seems that all forces have formed a coalition to destroy Israel because it wishes to remain faithful to its vocation as the People of God. As a result the psalmist directs the following challenge to the Lord: May he let himself be known by crushing the pride of the nations; indeed, may the latter meet the cruel fate of the petty kings who wanted to destroy Israel at the time of the Judges (see note on Ps 5:10 and introduction to Ps 35).

Obviously, this is a prayer of vengeance, but even more of salvation. It wishes to provoke Heaven: how could a polytheistic and idolatrous world come to worship the one and all-powerful God if he abandons his people? The chosen people could never resign themselves to such a collapse; that would be tantamount to the defeat of the Lord himself.

Although as Christians we are constantly under threat from the godless, we can ceaselessly implore God the Father (by this psalm) to grant his new People a complete victory over our enemies. We do not desire the eternal death of our foes but ask that God will bring them low and lead them to himself as God and Father.

For the term *Asaph* in the superscription, see introduction to Ps 73—89.

83:1 *Do not keep silent:* i.e., spring into action (see Ps 35:22; 109:1).

83:2-4 The words "Come . . . let us" are the very ones used by the leaders of the rebels at the tower of Babel when humanity attempted to usurp the power of the Lord (see Ge 11:3f). They obviously identify the enemies of God and of his people who cunningly plot to show their independence from the Lord and to exterminate Israel as a nation.

5 With one mind they plot together;[i]
they form an alliance* against you—
6 the tents of Edom and the Ishmaelites,*
of Moab and the Hagrites,[j]
7 Gebal,[q] Ammon and Amalek,[k]
Philistia, with the people of Tyre.[l]
8 Even Assyria has joined them
to lend strength to the descendants of Lot.
Selah
9 * Do to them as you did to Midian,*
as you did to Sisera and Jabin at the river
Kishon,* [m]
10 who perished at Endor
and became like refuse on the ground.[n]

---

q That is, Byblos.

---

i Ps 2:2.—j Nu 20:23; Dt 2:5; 1 Ch 5:10, 19.—k Ex 17:8.—l Jos 13:2; Isa 23:3.—m Ex 2:15; Jdg 4:2; Isa 9:3; 10:26.—n 1 Sa 28:7; Jer 8:2.

83:5 *Alliance:* there is no record of such a vast alliance of nations ever arrayed against Israel at one time. It may be that only some of them were attacking at the moment while passively being supported by the others. Some point to the time when Moab, Ammon, and Edom were invading Judah during the reign of King Jehoshaphat (see 2 Ch 20). *Against you:* the invaders acknowledge openly that the war is intended not only against the people but also against their God.

83:6-8 The members of the hostile alliance are all well-known foes of Israel. The psalmist alludes to the *Edomites,* descendants of Esau, the son of the patriarch Isaac (see Ge 36), and the *Ishmaelites* who descended from Ishmael, the son of Abraham and Hagar (see Ge 16:15f); he also mentions the *Moabites* (see 2 Ch 20:1) and *Ammonites,* descendants of Lot, the nephew of Abraham (see Ge 19:38); next he includes the *Hagrites,* an Arabian bedouin tribe that was encamped on the border of the Syro-Arabian desert (see 1 Ch 5:10, 19f). Other members were the inhabitants of *Gebal,* in the territory of the Edomites south of the Dead Sea (see Jos 13:5), and the *Amalekites* (see Ge 14:7). The *Philistines,* Israel's foes along the Mediterranean coast of Palestine (see Ex 15:14), were also part of the alliance as were the inhabitants of *Tyre* (see Isa 23:3). *Assyria* (see Ge 10:11) is mentioned as rendering assistance to the alliance.

83:9-18 See note on Ps 5:10 and introduction to Ps 35.

83:9-12 The psalmist takes heart by recalling two great victories won with God's help against superior forces during the time of the Judges: the victory of Gideon over the Midianites (see Jdg 7) and the defeat of King Jabin (see Jdg 4). He knows that in order for God's kingdom of righteousness and peace to come his foes must be defeated (see note on Ps 5:10).

83:9 *Midian:* it was at Midian (see Ex 2:15) that Gideon defeated the Midianites and slew the leaders named in v. 11 (see Jdg 7:25; 8:5). *Sisera and Jabin:* commander and king, respectively, of the army defeated by Deborah and Barak in the plain of Esdraelon near Endor at the foot of Mount Tabor (see Jdg 4—5).

11 Make their nobles like Oreb and Zeeb,*
all their princes like Zebah and Zalmunna,
12 who said, "Let us take possession
of the pasturelands of God."

13 Make them like tumbleweed, O my God,*
like chaff before the wind.[o]
14 As fire consumes the forest
or a flame sets the mountains ablaze,[p]
15 so pursue them with your tempest [q]
and terrify them with your storm.*
16 Cover their faces with shame
so that men will seek your name,* O LORD.

17 May they ever be ashamed and dismayed;*
may they perish in disgrace.
18 Let them know that you, whose name is the LORD—
that you alone are the Most High over all the earth.[r]

---

o Ps 1:4; 35:5; 58:9; Job 27:21; Isa 5:24; 10:17; 17:13; 29:5; Eze 21:3.—p Ps 50:3; Dt 32:22.—q Job 9:17; 27:20; Jer 25:32.—r Ps 46:10; 97:9; Dt 4:39; Da 3:45.

83:11-12 The Midianites had despoiled the land of crops (v. 12: "Let us take possession of the pasturelands of God") and driven fear into the hearts of the Israelites. In their defeat at the hands of the Lord through Gideon, their leaders Oreb, Zeeb, Zebah, and Zalmunna were captured and put to death (see Jdg 7:25; 8:21).

83:13-14 The psalmist likens the fate of the enemies to that of "tumbleweed" and "chaff" carried away by the wind and a "forest" or "mountains" destroyed by fire (common figures of destruction at the hand of the Lord: see Ps 1:4; 35:5; Isa 5:24; 10:17; 17:13; 29:5; Jer 13:24).

83:15 *Tempest . . . storm:* for God in the thunderstorm, see Ps 18:7-15; 68:33; 77:17f; Ex 15:7-10; Jos 10:11; Jdg 5:4, 20f; 1 Sa 2:10; 7:10; Isa 29:5f; 33:3). See also note on Ps 68:4.

83:16 *Men will seek your name:* the psalmist prays that God will humiliate the enemies and lead men to seek his name, i.e., realize and accept that the Lord alone is God (see v. 18).

83:17-18 The Chronicler (2 Ch 20:22-29) records the defeat of the alliance and mentions that all the nations were terrified when they learned that the Lord fought on the side of the Israelites. This is precisely what the psalmist asks so that his people will be saved and the Lord will be praised by the whole world.

PSALM 84*

Longing for God's Dwelling

For the director of music. According to *gittith*.[r]
Of the Sons of Korah. A psalm.

1 How lovely is your dwelling place,[s]
   O LORD Almighty!*
2 My soul* yearns, even faints,
   for the courts of the LORD;
   my heart and my flesh cry out
   for the living God.[t]

3 Even the sparrow has found a home,
   and the swallow a nest for herself,
   where she may have her young—
   a place near your altar,*
   O LORD Almighty, my King and my God.[u]
4 Blessed* are those who dwell in your house;
   they are ever praising you.   *Selah*

---

r Probably a musical term.

s Ps 27:4; 43:3; 122:1.—t Ps 42:1-2; 63:1-2; 143:6; Job 19:27; Isa
26:9.—u Ps 5:2; 43:4.

Ps 84 During one of the pilgrimages prescribed by the Mosaic Law (see Ex
23:17; 1 Sa 1:3; Lk 2:42), perhaps the one for the harvest, a pilgrim expresses his
joy at finding himself near God in the temple. At the last stage, the Lord has already manifested his favor to the faithful pilgrims (vv. 5-6). He reserves even
more happiness for those who follow his Law. Another opinion holds that this
psalm recalls Ps 42 and reflects its circumstances. The psalmist is a Levite who
has no access to God's house, possibly at the time when Sennacherib was over-
running Judah (see 2 Ki 18:13-16), and expresses his longing for the closeness in
the temple that he experienced in the past.

This pilgrim song, overflowing with the desire for and joy of God, becomes the
song of hope and confidence for all Christians en route to the house of the Father
where they will sing an Alleluia (or Hallelujah) without end. It also translates the
sentiments of all who love Christ's Eucharistic Presence in the tabernacle. Those
who in one way or another have consecrated their life to the Lord will find herein
words to express their deepest aspirations.

The words *For the director of music* in the superscription are thought to be a
musical or liturgical notation; for the term *gittith,* see introduction to Ps 8; for *the
Sons of Korah,* see introduction to Ps 42.

84:1 LORD *Almighty:* see note on Ps 24:10.

84:2 *Soul:* see note on Ps 6:3. *Heart . . . flesh:* i.e., entire being (see Ps 73:26).

84:3 God sees to it that even the "birds of the air have nests" (Mt 8:20);
hence, he will welcome his faithful to the shelter of his altars.

84:4 *Blessed:* see note on Ps 1:1.

5 Blessed are those whose strength is in you,
  who have set their hearts on pilgrimage.*
6 As they pass through the Valley of Baca,
  they make it a place of springs;ˢ
  the autumn rains also cover it with pools.*
7 They go from strength to strength,
  till each appears before God in Zion.*

8 Hear my prayer, O LORD God Almighty;*
  listen to me, O God of Jacob.   *Selah*
9 Look upon our shield,* ᵗ O God;
  look with favor on your anointed one.ᵛ

10 Better is one day in your courts
   than a thousand elsewhere;
   I would rather be a doorkeeper* in the house
     of my God
   than dwell in the tents of the wicked.
11 For the LORD God is a sun and shield;
   the LORD bestows favor and honor;
   no good thing does he withhold
     from those whose walk is blameless.*

12 O LORD Almighty,
   blessed is the man who trusts in you.

---

s Or *blessings.*—t Or *sovereign.*

v Ps 59:11; 89:18.

84:5 *Who have set their hearts on pilgrimage:* literally, "in whose hearts are the open roads."

84:6 Through God's care, even the most fearsome path becomes a path of blessings and praise (see 2 Ch 20:26). *Valley of Baca:* valley of "weeping" or "balsam trees"; in the Vulgate, it is called "the Valley of Tears," which gave rise, in the ascetical and preaching tradition, to the familiar expression, "vale of tears," for our earthly pilgrimage (see the popular Marian prayer "Hail, Holy Queen"). *Pools:* or "blessings" (see NIV textual note).

84:7 *Zion:* see note on Ps 9:11.

84:8 *LORD God Almighty:* see note on Ps 59:5. *Jacob:* i.e., Israel (see Ge 32:28).

84:9 *Our shield:* the king (see Ps 89:18). *Anointed one:* either the king (who was God's earthly regent over his people) or the high priest (who led the community of Israel after the disappearance of the royalty).

84:10 *Doorkeeper:* some of the Sons of Korah (see the superscription) were doorkeepers or gatekeepers in the temple (see 1 Ch 26:1).

84:11 There is no joy of the world that can outweigh and replace supernatural joys that have their source in God alone. For he denies no grace to his faithful ones. *Sun:* see note on Ps 27:1.

PSALM 85*

Prayer for the People's Salvation

For the director of music. Of the Sons of Korah.
A psalm.

¹ You showed favor to your land, O Lord;ʷ
   you restored the fortunes of Jacob.*
² You forgave the iniquity of your people
   and covered all their sins.   *Selah*
³ You set aside all your wrath
   and turned from your fierce anger.ˣ

⁴ Restore us again, O God our Savior,*
   and put away your displeasure toward us.ʸ
⁵ Will you be angry with us forever?
   Will you prolong your anger through all
   generations?ᶻ
⁶ Will you not revive us again,
   that your people may rejoice in you?
⁷ Show us your unfailing love,* O Lord,
   and grant us your salvation.

---

w Ps 14:7; 126:4; Dt 30:3.—x Ps 78:38; 106:23; Ex 32:14; Isa 48:9.—y
Ps 71:20; 80:3.—z Ps 50:21; 79:5; 89:46.

Ps 85 This psalm is a national lament recalling God's goodwill in bringing his people back from exile to their homeland (538 B.C.) but also indicating that the repatriates are having difficulty in reestablishing themselves in Judea. The psalmist as much as says: "You have enabled us to come back to our land; now let us come back to our lives." The lament becomes a prayer of hope, for the Prophets had announced a better future (see Isa 58:8; Zec 8:12). The temple of Jerusalem is being rebuilt (520-515 B.C.) and will be a visible sign of the presence of God, of his "glory" (v. 9; see Eze 43:2). Happiness is promised to those who remain faithful. All these thoughts are similar to those expressed by the postexilic Prophets (see Hag 1:5-11; 2:6-9; Mal 3:13-21).

In praying this psalm, we can keep in mind that in Jesus, the Son of God, the promise becomes reality (see Jn 14:27; Col 1:20). When love and truth, justice and peace dwell on the earth, a new world is being born and God is there.

The words *For the director of music* in the superscription are thought to be a musical or liturgical notation; for *the Sons of Korah,* see introduction to Ps 42.

85:1 *Restored the fortunes of Jacob:* another translation possible is: "brought Jacob back from exile." *Jacob:* i.e., Israel (see Ge 32:28).

85:4-7 The psalmist begs God to favor his penitent people with pardon and peace.

85:7 *Unfailing love:* see note on Ps 6:4.

8 I will listen to what God the LORD will say;*
   he promises peace to his people, his
     saints—*
   but let them not return to folly.
9 Surely his salvation is near those who fear
     him,
   that his glory may dwell in our land.*

10 * Love and faithfulness* meet together;
   righteousness and peace kiss each other.*a*
11 Faithfulness springs forth from the earth,
   and righteousness* looks down from
     heaven.*b*
12 * The LORD will indeed give what is good,*
   and our land will yield its harvest.*c*
13 Righteousness goes before him
   and prepares the way for his steps.

---

a Ps 61:7; 89:14; 97:2.—b Isa 45:8.—c Ps 67:6; Lev 26:4; Eze 34:27; Hos
2:22-23; Zec 8:12; Jas 1:17.

85:8-13 God answers the prayer through a reassuring word of a priest or Levite.
  85:8 *Saints:* see notes on Ps 4:3 and 34:9. *But . . . to folly:* another translation
possible is: "and to those who turn from folly" (the Hebrew word for "folly" includes the connotation of moral deficiency: see NIV textual note on Ps 14:1).
  85:9 Only those who fear God in the spirit of wisdom (in contrast to the spirit
of folly, v. 8) will inherit his benefits, which will be their glory. They will experience a renewed spirit since they are the heirs of the new age of restoration, which
is described by various terms: salvation and glory (v. 9), love, faithfulness, righteousness, and peace (vv. 10-11), good and harvest (v. 12). *Glory:* the Lord's
glory—a visible manifestation of his power and divinity—had left the temple
and the holy city (see Eze 11:23); it would return there once the temple was restored (see Eze 43:2; Hag 2:9). See also Jn 1:14.
  85:10-11 People will regulate their lives by the divine norms. The divine attributes as well as the moral virtues that correspond to them are here personified
(see Ps 89:14; 97:2) as courtiers of the returning king.
  85:10 *Love and faithfulness:* often found together to express God's loyalty (see
Ps 25:10; 40:10f; 57:10; 61:7; Ex 34:6).
  85:11 *Righteousness:* personification of God's attribute, which expresses his
kingship in and over his people (see Ps 4:1; 22:31).
  85:12-13 The goodness and blessings that the psalmist sees in a vision of the
future are, for Christians, fulfilled in Christ. Yet the completion of salvation is
also for Christians an object of promise and of longing expectation.
  85:12 *What is good:* the benefits of God's kingdom enjoyed by those who fear
him: forgiveness (v. 2), reconciliation, renewal of covenant status (vv. 8-9), and
fullness of restoration (vv. 9-13). Thus, faith in God leads to hope in a new age of
righteousness (see Gal 5:5; 2 Pe 3:13).

PSALM 86*

Prayer in Suffering and Distress

A prayer of David.

¹ Hear, O LORD, and answer me,
   for I am poor and needy.*
² Guard my life, for I am devoted to you.
   You are my God;* save your servant
   who trusts in you.
³ Have mercy on me, O LORD,
   for I call to you all day long.
⁴ Bring joy to your servant,*d*
   for to you, O LORD,
   I lift up my soul.*

⁵ You are forgiving and good, O LORD,
   abounding in love* to all who call to you.*e*
⁶ Hear my prayer, O LORD;
   listen to my cry for mercy.*f*
⁷ In the day of my trouble I will call to you,
   for you will answer me.

⁸ Among the gods there is none like you, O
   LORD;*g*
   no deeds can compare with yours.

---

d Ps 25:1; 143:8.—e Ex 34:6; Joel 2:13.—f Ps 5:2; 17:1; 130:1-2.—g Ps 35:10; 89:8; Ex 15:11; Dt 3:24; Job 21:22; Jer 10:6.

Ps 86 The psalmist passes in turn from supplication to an act of trust and gratitude toward God. This poem, composed most likely after the Exile, is the prayer of devout Israelites who believe in the Lord's goodness as a result of their own experience. After all, he brought Israel back to life in the most somber moment of her history! The Lord seemed so close to them as to be able to listen, pardon, and save; the psalmist contemplates the mystical experience of Moses encountering God (see Ex 34:6). The conviction of God's goodness overwhelms us by its evidence and its simplicity of expression. It already paves the way for a "missionary" sensitivity. The imprecations against the pagans lose their vehemence and one foresees the day when, touched by the Lord, they will render glory to the only God.

By means of this psalm, Christians can pray for their well-being in this world and beyond. Prolonging Christ's Passion, the Church and Christians experience the same anguish he did and seek to take refuge in the same heavenly Father.

86:1 *Poor and needy:* see note on Ps 22:26.

86:2 *You are my God:* indeed, God himself has chosen David to be his servant (see 1 Sa 13:14; 15:28; 16:12; 2 Sa 7:8).

86:4 *My soul:* see note on Ps 6:3.

86:5 *Love:* see note on Ps 6:4.

⁹ All the nations* you have made
will come and worship before you, O LORD;
they will bring glory to your name.*h*

¹⁰ For you are great and do marvelous deeds;*
you alone are God.

¹¹ Teach me your way, O LORD,
and I will walk in your truth;*i*
give me an undivided heart,
that I may fear your name.*

¹² I will praise you, O LORD my God, with all my
heart;*j*
I will glorify your name forever.*

¹³ For great is your love toward me;*
you have delivered me from the depths of
the grave.*u*

¹⁴ The arrogant are attacking me, O God;
a band of ruthless men seeks my life—
men without regard for you.*

¹⁵ But you, O LORD, are a compassionate and
gracious God,*k*
slow to anger, abounding in love and faithfulness.*

¹⁶ Turn to me and have mercy on me;
grant your strength to your servant *l*
and save the son of your maidservant.* **v**

---

u Hebrew *Sheol.*—v Or *save your faithful son.*

h Ps 22:27; 66:4; Zec 14:16; Rev 15:4.—i Ps 25:4; 26:3; 27:11; 119:12,
35; 143:8, 10; Jer 24:7; 32:39.—j Ps 30:3; 40:2; 88:6; Jnh 2:7.—k Ps
103:8; 111:4; 130:7; 145:8; Ex 34:6.—l Ps 18:1; 25:16; 116:16; Wis 9:5.

86:9 *All the nations:* see note on Ps 46:10. *Your name:* see note on Ps 8:1.
86:10 *Marvelous deeds:* see note on Ps 9:1.
86:11 The psalmist asks God to save him from his enemies and also from
himself (see Ps 25:5; 51:7, 10). *Undivided heart:* see Eze 11:19 as well as 1 Ch
12:33; 1 Co 7:35. *Heart:* see note on Ps 4:7.
86:12 The psalmist vows to praise the Lord for his help (see note on Ps 7:17).
86:13 The psalmist anticipates being heard. *Depths:* see note on Ps 30:1.
86:14 These haughty foes disregard God—to their ruin (see Ps 54:3; Jer 20:11).
86:15 This verse recalls Ex 34:6.
85:16 *Son of your maidservant:* see NIV textual note; see also Ps 116:16 and
NIV textual note there.

¹⁷ Give me a sign of your goodness,*
     that my enemies may see it and be put to
          shame,
     for you, O LORD, have helped me and com-
          forted me.

PSALM 87*

Zion, Home of All Nations

Of the Sons of Korah. A psalm. A song.

¹ He has set his foundation* on the holy moun-
          tain;^m
²   the LORD loves the gates of Zion
     more than* all the dwellings of Jacob.

---

m 1-2: Ps 76:1-2; 78:68-69; Zec 2:13.

86:17 *Goodness:* the good things promised in the covenant (see notes on Ps 27:13 and 31:19). *Enemies . . . put to shame:* the imprecations against enemies that conclude a good number of the psalms are here kept to a minimum.

Ps 87 The psalmist here paints a picture of Jerusalem as the spiritual mother of all peoples and thus prefigures the Church of Christ (see Ac 2:5ff; Gal 4:26). No other canticle has given greater exaltation to the holy city, Zion, the chosen city of God. Not only is she at the heart of Israel, but in her God lays the basis for the spiritual rebirth of all peoples, even the sworn enemies of Israel such as Egypt and Chaldea, through their worship of the true God (see Ps 45:14f; Zec 2:15; 8:23). All will be admitted into her bosom, and God will declare her mother of all peoples.

After having encountered, in so many psalms, the conflicts of peoples and the persecution of Israel, here is a symphony with unforgettable melodies. We are enchanted by this universalist aspect and the perspective of a humanity reunited by God in his presence, in accord with the vision of the Prophets (see Isa 2:2-4; 19:19-25; 25:6; 45:14, 22-24; 56:6-8; 60:3; 66:23; Da 7:14; Mic 4:1-3; Zec 8:23; 14:16). Such is also the vocation of the Church, the new Jerusalem, to be a leaven for the ingathering of all peoples.

Thus, in praying this psalm, Christians keep in mind not only the earthly Zion with its fulfillment, the Church, but also the heavenly Jerusalem, the heavenly Church, which is our true and definitive home, the source of eternal life and perfect blessedness. At the end of time, this new Jerusalem will come down out of heaven from God, prepared as a bride for her husband (see Rev 21:2, 24).

For *the Sons of Korah* in the superscription, see introduction to Ps 42.

87:1 *His foundation:* it is the Lord himself who has made Zion his city (see Isa 14:32) and the temple his dwelling. *Mountain:* see notes on Ps 2:6 and 48:2.

87:2 *Loves . . . more than:* Zion is more cherished by the Lord than any other Israelite city or town (see Ps 9:11; 78:68; 132:12-14). *The gates of Zion:* a common Hebrew idiom for the city. *Jacob:* i.e., Israel (see Ge 32:28).

3 Glorious things are said of you,
O city of God: *Selah*
4 * "I will record Rahab [w] and Babylon*
among those who acknowledge me—
Philistia too, and Tyre, along with Cush—[x]
and will say, 'This [y] one was born in Zion.' "

5 Indeed, of Zion it will be said,
"This one and that one were born in her,[n]
and the Most High himself will establish her."* [o]
6 The LORD will write in the register of the peoples:[p]
"This one was born in Zion." * *Selah*
7 As they make music they will sing,*
"All my fountains are in you."[q]

w A poetic name for Egypt.—x That is, the upper Nile region.—y Or *"O Rahab and Babylon, / Philistia, Tyre and Cush, / I will record concerning those who acknowledge me: / 'This.*

n Gal 4:26.—o Ps 48:8; Isa 62:4-5.—p Isa 4:3; Eze 13:9.—q Ps 36:9; 68:25; 149:3.

87:4-5 These verses foresee a wholesale conversion to the Lord on the part of peoples who were longtime enemies of God and his kingdom (see Isa 19:21).

87:4 The Gentiles will be incorporated into the People of God and adopted by Zion, their religious homeland. As the representatives of all the Gentile nations, the psalmist mentions the arrogant Egypt ("Rahab") and Babylon, the two world kingdoms on the Nile and Euphrates, both of which had fought for centuries for the possession of Palestine, as well as the Philistines, archenemy of Israel, wealthy Tyre proud of its independence, and the ambitious Ethiopians. *Rahab:* the name of an ocean monster used poetically for Egypt.

87:5 The privileges of the holy city and her spiritual motherhood are divine in origin and hence indefectible. The eschatological community of the faithful is established by the Lord (see Ps 48:8; Isa 14:32; 28:16; 54:11f).

87:6 Here it is a case simply of a list ("register") of the citizens of Zion (see Isa 4:3; Eze 13:9) rather than the apocalyptic book of destinies (see Ps 69:28). Each people will thus have two homelands—one material and one spiritual. The basis for the people's security and inclusion in Zion lies in the promise of the Lord and the fact that he is its builder (see Heb 11:10, 16).

87:7 Zion is associated with "the fountain of life" (Jer 2:13), of "salvation" (Isa 12:3), "a river whose streams make glad the city of God" (Ps 46:4; see Eze 47; Rev 22:1-5). *As they make music they will sing:* an alternative translation is: "So all sing in their festive dance." Hence, the peoples will be admitted to the official liturgical worship (see Isa 66:21) and will at least be able to participate in the ritual dances (see Ps 149:3; 150:4; 2 Sa 6:5).

PSALM 88*

Prayer in Affliction

A song. A psalm of the Sons of Korah. For the director of
music. According to *mahalath leannoth.*[z] A *maskil* [a]
of Heman the Ezrahite.

1 O LORD, the God who saves me,*
   day and night I cry out before you.[r]
2 May my prayer come before you;
   turn your ear to my cry.[s]

3 * For my soul* is full of trouble [t]
   and my life draws near the grave.[b]

---

z Possibly a tune, "The Suffering of Affliction."—a Probably a literary or
musical term.—b Hebrew *Sheol.*

---

r Ps 3:4; 77:2.—s Ps 119:170.—t 3-6: Ps 6:3; 28:1; 30:3; 40:2; 86:13;
143:7; Nu 16:33; Job 17:1; La 3:55; Jnh 2:6.

Ps 88 The anguish of death has rarely found expression in such touching images as those of the present psalm: prison, shipwreck, solitude, and darkness.
The suppliant has experienced the depths of misfortune. Has God abandoned
him? Despite the depths of his distress, the believer refuses to admit such a
thing; he puts down all thought of rebellion within himself. For although no expressions of hopeful expectation (as in most psalms) are present and the last
word speaks of darkness as "my closest friend," the psalmist firmly believes that
the Lord is "the God who saves."

This psalm illustrates the hazy ideas that the ancients harbored about survival
after death before they arrived at faith in the resurrection: in the grave ("Sheol"),
in the subterranean pit, the dead have no more communication with God; they are
no more than dull shadows of themselves in the land of no recall. It is a prayer of
a man who experiences the depths of human misery, a prayer of Israel at the edge
of collapse, but also a prayer of everyone on the brink of hopelessness.

This psalm furnishes Christians with a prayer during times of spiritual dryness as well as human calamities of all kinds. We can then express to the heavenly Father our sufferings and distresses in the face of hostility, the weight of our
spiritual and human solitude, and our fear in the light of his persistent silence. It
will enable us to accept our cup without recrimination and to renew our trust in
our God.

For *the Sons of Korah* in the superscription, see introduction to Ps 42; the words
For the director of music are thought to be a musical or liturgical notation; *mahalath leannoth* may be a tune; for *maskil,* see introduction to Ps 32. *Heman the
Ezrahite* is thought to be the son of Zerah (hence, Ezrahite) and member of the tribe
of Judah (see 1 Ch 2:6) as well as leader of the Korahite guild (see 1 Ch 6:33, 37).

88:1-2 The psalmist, despite his wretched state, has not lost hope; he believes
that the Lord is the God who saves and so he cries out to him for help.

88:3-5 His soul is full of troubles; indeed, he is accounted as one already in
the grave and cut off from God (see Ps 143:7; Job 10:15; 17:1).

88:3 *Soul:* see note on Ps 6:3.

⁴ I am counted among those who go down to
     the pit;*
  I am like a man without strength.
⁵ I am set apart with the dead,
     like the slain who lie in the grave,
  whom you remember no more,
     who are cut off from your care.*

⁶ You have put me in the lowest pit,*
     in the darkest depths.
⁷ Your wrath lies heavily upon me;
     you have overwhelmed me with all your
        waves.ᵘ   *Selah*
⁸ You have taken from me my closest friends ᵛ
     and have made me repulsive to them.*
  I am confined and cannot escape;
⁹   my eyes are dim* with grief.

  I call to you, O Lᴏʀᴅ, every day;*
     I spread out my hands to you.
¹⁰ Do you show your wonders* to the dead?
     Do those who are dead rise up and praise
        you?ʷ   *Selah*

---

u Ps 7:11; 18:4; 32:6; 42:7; 69:1; Jnh 2:3.—v Ps 31:1 38:11; 79:4; 80:6;
123:3-4; 142:8; Job 12:4; 19:13; La 3:7; Da 9:16.—w Ps 6:5; 30:9; 115:17;
Isa 38:18.

88:4 The psalmist is alive but dead (see Ps 6:5; 107:18) as to his contempo-
raries (see Ps 22:29; 28:1; 143:7; Pr 1:12). He is like a shade, "a man without
strength" (see Isa 14:19f). *Pit:* see note on Ps 30:1.

88:5 As far as the psalmist is concerned, he is already in the pit (see note on
Ps 6:5), where he cannot call upon God to remember him and come to his aid
(see Ps 25:7; 74:2; 106:4).

88:6-9a For some reason God has let a flood of troubles overwhelm the suppliant so that he remains deprived of all human consolation (see Ps 142:7; La 3:7).

88:8 Friends interpret the suffering of the suppliant as a punishment from
God and remain aloof from him lest they also be struck with it.

88:9a *Eyes are dim:* see note on Ps 6:7.

88:9b-12 The psalmist prays to be saved in order to continue to praise the
Lord for his wondrous deeds, for those in the grave can no longer do so (see notes
on Ps 6:5 and 9:1).

88:10 *Wonders:* see note on Ps 9:1. *Rise up:* i.e., a simple act of rising to give
praise in the kingdom of the dead (see Isa 14:9)—not a bona fide resurrection
from the dead.

11 Is your love declared in the grave,*
    your faithfulness in Destruction?c
12 Are your wonders known in the place of
    darkness,
      or your righteous deeds in the land of
      oblivion?

13 But I cry to you for help, O LORD;*
    in the morning my prayer comes before
    you.
14 Why, O LORD, do you reject me
    and hide your face from me?*

15 From my youth I have been afflicted and
    close to death;
      I have suffered your terrors and am in de-
      spair.
16 Your wrath has swept over me;
    your terrors have destroyed me.x
17 All day long they surround me like a flood;
    they have completely engulfed me.
18 You have taken my companions and loved
    ones from me;y
      the darkness is my closest friend.*

---

c Hebrew *Abaddon.*

---

x Ps 7:11; Job 6:4; 20:25.—y Job 17:13-14; 19:13.

88:11 The psalmist would be unable to render praise to God if he were to go to the "grave," also known as the "pit." *Love . . . faithfulness:* see notes on Ps 6:4 and 36:5f. *Destruction:* another name for the grave or the pit; in Hebrew it is *Abaddon* (see Job 26:6; 28:22; Pr 15:11; Rev 9:11).
88:12 The psalmist speaks of death as a place of total darkness, also known as the "land of oblivion" in contrast with the "land of the living" (Ps 27:13; 52:5; 116:9; 142:5), because those who die are quickly forgotten by the living (see Ps 6:5; 31:12; Ecc 9:5).
88:13-18 Even when human consolation is lacking, suffering can still be bearable if God gives his perceptible consolation; however, the psalmist also feels himself abandoned by God.
88:14 *Why . . . ?:* see note on Ps 6:3. *Hide your face:* see note on Ps 13:1.
88:18 The lamentation ends on a cry of sadness, like Ps 39. However, it is not a cry of despair, for God cannot remain deaf to the prayers of his faithful ones (see Ps 79:9-11; Job 16:18-20).

PSALM 89*

Prayer for the Fulfillment of
God's Promise

A *maskil* [d] of Ethan the Ezrahite.

¹ * I will sing of the LORD's great love forever;
with my mouth I will make your faithfulness* known through all generations.[z]
² I will declare that your love stands firm forever,
that you established your faithfulness in
heaven itself.

³ You said, "I have made a covenant with my
chosen one,
I have sworn to David my servant,

---

d Probably a literary or musical term.

---

z Ps 59:16; Isa 63:7.

Ps 89 This psalm constitutes a beautiful hymn to God the Creator and a grand
acclamation to the Lord who has given his word and his promise to Israel. And
although the facts in Israel's history seem to give the lie to such splendid visions, the believer refuses to rely on appearances. God's word and his promise
are solid in spite of a temporary present roadblock, as a long history bears witness. The temporary roadblock may have been the attack on Jerusalem by Neb-
uchadnezzar and the exile of King Jehoiachin in 597 B.C. (see 2 Ki 24:8-17) or the
disappearance of the Davidic dynasty after the Exile (from the sixth century on).

The psalmist draws out wonderful coherences in God's work: the origins of the
world and the election of David; the order of the cosmos and the stability of the
royal throne; heaven and earth and the present, past, and future. In time of un-
certitude, one must make use of this sublime contemplation and continue to believe in the faithfulness of God. Then the Messianic Hope will be renewed; it is
the expectation of the coming of the Lord by his "anointed," the Messiah.

Through David, it is principally to his Son Jesus Christ that God the Father
promised love and faithfulness, prosperity and perpetual royal stability upon the
new Israel, the Church. Even though catastrophes of all kind seem to belie God's
loving faithfulness, we can pray this psalm with complete confidence.

For the word *maskil* in the superscription, see introduction to Ps 32. *Ethan the
Ezrahite* is thought to be the son of Zerah (hence, Ezrahite) and member of the
tribe of Judah (see 1 Ch 2:6) as well as founder of one of the three choirs (see 1
Ch 15:19) and identical with the *Jeduthun* of Ps 39 (see 2 Ch 5:12).

89:1-4 God is true. If anything is certain, it is his love and faithfulness. They
endure without fail in creation and they endure in the covenant with David (see 2
Sa 7:8-16; 1 Ch 17:10-15), on which Israel's Messianic Hope is based.

89:1 *Love . . . faithfulness:* see notes on Ps 6:4 and 36:5f. These words are
each repeated seven times in the psalm.

⁴ 'I will establish your line forever*ᵃ*
   and make your throne firm through all
   generations.' "*   *Selah*

⁵ * The heavens* praise your wonders, O LORD,
   your faithfulness too, in the assembly of
   the holy ones.*ᵇ*

⁶ For who in the skies above can compare with
   the LORD?*ᶜ*
   Who is like the LORD among the heavenly
   beings?*

⁷ In the council of the holy ones God is greatly
   feared;
   he is more awesome than all who surround
   him.

⁸ O LORD God Almighty,* who is like you?
   You are mighty, O LORD, and your faithfulness surrounds you.

⁹ You rule over the surging sea;*
   when its waves mount up, you still them.*ᵈ*

¹⁰ You crushed Rahab* like one of the slain;
   with your strong arm you scattered your
   enemies.

---

a Ps 61:6-7; 132:11; 2 Sa 7:8-16; 1 Ki 8:16.—b Ps 19:1; 29:1; 82:1; Job
1:6; 5:1.—c 6-8: Ps 35:10; 86:8; 111:1; 113:5; Ex 15:11; Isa 6:3; Jer
10:6.—d 9-10: Ps 65:7; 68:1; 74:13-15; 107:29; Job 7:12; Isa 51:9-10.

89:4 Despite the fall of the Davidic monarchy, God remains faithful to his
covenant, which is an eternal covenant (see 2 Sa 7:16; Isa 54:10; 55:3; 61:8; Jer
31:31-34; Eze 16:60; 37:26) and the foundation of the Messianic Hope.
89:5-18 The psalmist sings of God's greatness in the secret of heaven where
he is surrounded by angels (the "holy ones" and the "heavenly beings," vv. 5-6).
He declares the power of the One who created the earth and rules the primitive
chaos, symbolized by the mythological monster Rahab. The more deeply the believer divines the mystery of God, the more overwhelmed he becomes with joy.
89:5 *The heavens:* i.e., all beings who are part of God's heavenly kingdom.
Wonders: see note on Ps 9:1. *Assembly of the holy ones:* the great council in
heaven (see Ps 82:1).
89:6 *Heavenly beings:* literally, "sons of God(s)" (see note on Ps 29:1).
89:8 *Lord . . . Almighty:* see note on Ps 59:5.
89:9 *Sea:* see note on Ps 65:7.
89:10 *Rahab:* a mythical sea monster that may be another name for Leviathan
(see Ps 74:14; 104:26) and is used in the Old Testament primarily as a personification of the primeval chaos. Here it is a symbol of God's dominance of the sea
and all rebellious creatures. *With . . . enemies:* cited in Lk 1:51.

11 The heavens are yours, and yours also the
     earth;
     you founded the world* and all that is in it.*e*
12 You created the north and the south;*
     Tabor and Hermon sing for joy at your
     name.
13 Your arm is endued with power;
     your hand is strong, your right hand exalted.

14 Righteousness and justice are the foundation
     of your throne;*f*
     love and faithfulness go before you.*
15 Blessed* are those who have learned to ac-
     claim you,
     who walk in the light of your presence, O
     LORD.
16 They rejoice in your name all day long;
     they exult in your righteousness.*g*
17 For you are their glory and strength,* *h*
     and by your favor you exalt our horn.* *e*
18 Indeed, our shield*f* belongs to the LORD,
     our king to the Holy One of Israel.*i*

---

e *Horn* here symbolizes strong one.—f Or *sovereign.*

e Ps 24:1-2; 50:12; Dt 10:14; 1 Ch 29:11; 1 Co 10:26.—f Ps 85:10-11;
97:2; Ex 34:6-7.—g Ps 30:4; 47:1; Zep 3:14.—h Ps 18:1; 112:9; 148:14.—i
Ps 18:2; 47:9; 96:10; 97:1; 99:1; Isa 6:3.

89:11 *Heavens . . . earth . . . world:* the Lord is the almighty Creator of the
heavens and the earth as well as everything in them. At the same time, he is the
benign Ruler of these same areas with a love that extends through them to the
Messianic kingdom, symbolized by David (vv. 3, 20). Thus, he not only created
but also redeemed them.
    89:12 *The north and the south:* some believe that the Hebrew words for these
two geographical poles (*saphon* and *yamin*) are the names of two sacred mountains in northern Syria: Mount Zaphon (see Ps 48:2 and note; Isa 14:13) and
Mount Amana (see SS 4:8), paralleling the mountains Tabor and Hermon (which
also stand for east and west). *Tabor:* a low mountain in the Valley of Jezreel in
northern Israel. *Hermon:* a tall mountain in Lebanon that marks the southern
limit of the Anti-Lebanon range. *Sing for joy:* see note on Ps 65:13.
    89:14 The divine attributes are personified (see Ps 85:10; 97:2).
    89:15 *Blessed:* see note on Ps 1:1.
    89:17-18 These verses serve as a transition to the great oracle that follows.
On the Lord depend completely the lot of the Davidic dynasty and the coming of
the Messiah-King.
    89:17 *Horn:* symbolizes strong one (see also Ps 18:2, with note, and Ps 75:10).

¹⁹ * Once you spoke in a vision,*
    to your faithful people you said:^j
"I have bestowed strength on a warrior;
    I have exalted a young man from among
    the people.
²⁰ I have found David my servant;
    with my sacred oil I have anointed him.
²¹ My hand will sustain him;^k
    surely my arm will strengthen him.
²² No enemy will subject him to tribute;
    no wicked man will oppress him.
²³ I will crush his foes before him
    and strike down his adversaries.
²⁴ My faithful love will be with him,
    and through my name his horn^g will be ex-
    alted.
²⁵ I will set his hand over the sea,
    his right hand over the rivers.*
²⁶ He will call out to me, 'You are my Father,^l
    my God, the Rock my Savior.'
²⁷ I will also appoint him my firstborn,*
    the most exalted of the kings of the earth.
²⁸ I will maintain my love to him forever,^m
    and my covenant with him will never fail.
²⁹ I will establish his line forever,
    his throne as long as the heavens endure.

---

g *Horn* here symbolizes strength.

j 19-20: Ps 78:70; 132:11-12; Ex 29:7; 2 Sa 7:4, 8:16; 1 Ki 1:39; 1 Ch 17:3, 7-14; Isa 42:1; Ac 13:22.—k 21-24: Ps 18:35; 1 Sa 2:9-10.—l 26-27: Ps 2:6; 110:2-3; 2 Sa 7:9, 14; Jer 3:19; Col 1:15; Jn 20:17; Rev 1:15.—m 28-29: Ps 18:50; 61:7; 144:10, 2 Sa 7:11; Isa 55:3.

89:19-37 This powerful and faithful God has revealed to his "faithful people" (the prophets Samuel and Nathan) his plan for David and his posterity. It is a promise that cannot be effaced, a covenant that will never be revoked. It is guaranteed by God's love and faithfulness.
89:19 *Vision:* the revelation made to Samuel (see 1 Sa 16:12) or to Nathan (see 2 Sa 7:4-16). *Faithful people:* those faithful to his covenant.
89:25 *Sea . . . rivers:* David's dominion would extend from the Mediterranean Sea (west) to the Tigris and Euphrates rivers (east) (see Ps 72:8; 80:11).
89:27-29 The only one in whom these promises are fulfilled is Jesus Christ. This is hinted at by the use of *firstborn* and *most exalted,* which in Hebrew is *elyon,* a divine name (see Ps 83:18), applied to the Messiah, the Son of God (see 2 Sa 7:14; Jn 20:17) and supreme king (see Col 1:18; Rev 1:5).

30 "If his sons forsake my law*
    and do not follow my statutes,*n*
31 if they violate my decrees
    and fail to keep my commands,
32 I will punish their sin with the rod,
    their iniquity with flogging;
33 but I will not take my love from him,*
    nor will I ever betray my faithfulness.*o*
34 I will not violate my covenant.*
    or alter what my lips have uttered.*p*
35 Once for all, I have sworn by my holiness—
    and I will not lie to David—*q*
36 that his line will continue forever *r*
    and his throne endure before me like the
        sun;
37 it will be established forever like the moon,
    the faithful witness in the sky."   *Selah*

38 But you have rejected, you have spurned,*
    you have been very angry with your
        anointed one.*s*
39 You have renounced the covenant with your
        servant
    and have defiled his crown in the dust.
40 You have broken through all his walls *t*
    and reduced his strongholds to ruins.
41 All who pass by have plundered him;
    he has become the scorn of his neighbors.

---

n 30-32: Lev 26:14-33; 2 Sa 7:14.—o Ps 40:11; 2 Sa 7:15; Sir 47:22.—p
Nu 23:19; Jer 33:20-21.—q Ps 110:4; Am 4:2.—r 36-37: Ps 61:7; 72:5; Sir
43:6.—s 38-46: Ps 44:9-24.—t 40-41: Ps 80:12-13; Isa 22:5.

89:30-37 God's promises can be said to be partly provisional and partly absolute. As provisional promises, they were not fulfilled in David's descendants who
did not carry out the conditions of the covenant (vv. 30-32). As absolute promises
they were fulfilled in the Son of God who is also the Son of David (vv. 33-37).

89:33 *Not take my love from him:* see 2 Sa 7:15.

89:34-35 See Ps 110:4; Isa 31:2; 55:3; Jer 33:20ff; Am 4:2.

89:38-45 Seemingly, God has renounced his covenant. The temple is sacked,
the village ruined, the kingship laid open to scorn contrary to the word given to
David. It is of little import as to why such an evil has occurred; the important
thing is that God seems inconsistent.

⁴² You have exalted the right hand of his foes;
   you have made all his enemies rejoice.ᵘ
⁴³ You have turned back the edge of his sword
   and have not supported him in battle.
⁴⁴ You have put an end to his splendor
   and cast his throne to the ground.
⁴⁵ You have cut short the days of his youth;*
   you have covered him with a mantle of
   shame.   *Selah*

⁴⁶ * How long, O LORD? Will you hide yourself
   forever?*
   How long will your wrath burn like fire?ᵛ
⁴⁷ Remember how fleeting is my life.
   For what futility you have created all men!ʷ
⁴⁸ What man can live and not see death,ˣ
   or save himself from the power of the
   grave?ʰ   *Selah*
⁴⁹ O LORD, where is your former great love,*
   which in your faithfulness you swore to
   David?
⁵⁰ Remember, LORD, how your servant hasⁱ
   been mocked,
   how I bear in my heart the taunts of all the
   nations,ʸ
⁵¹ the taunts with which your enemies have
   mocked, O LORD,
   with which they have mocked every step of
   your anointed one.

---

h Hebrew *Sheol.*—i Or *your servants have.*

u Ps 13:2; La 1:15.—v Ps 13:1; 44:24; 74:10; 79:5; Dt 4:24.—w Ps 39:4-5; 62:9; 90:9-10; 144:4; Job 7:6, 16; 14:1, 5; Wis 2:5; Ecc 6:12; 1 Pe 1:24.—x Ps 22:29; 90:3.—y Ps 69:19; 79:12.

89:45 *Cut short the days of his youth:* the Israelite royalty enjoyed only four and a half centuries of independence: this was the time of its youth (see Ps 129:1) after its birth in the desert (see Isa 46:3; Jer 2:2; Hos 11:1).

89:46-48 To give himself hope, the psalmist begs God not to let him die without having assisted at the renewal of the covenant. *How long:* see note on Ps 6:3.

89:49-51 May the God who made the promise to David not prove insensitive to the king removed from his throne and the people expatriated from their kingdom and forced to experience the taunts of the Gentiles. The believer awaits a new discovery of God, as happened in days gone by at the beginnings of love.

⁵² Praise be to the LORD forever! Amen and
   Amen.*ᶻ

BOOK IV—PSALMS 90–106*

PSALM 90*

Prayer To Use Time Wisely

A prayer of Moses the man of God.

¹ LORD, you have been our dwelling place
     throughout all generations.
² Before the mountains were born
     or you brought forth the earth and the
       world,
     from everlasting to everlasting you are
       God.ᵃ

---

z Ps 41:13; 72:18; 106:48.—a Ps 48:14; 55:19; 93:2; 102:12; Ge 1:1; Pr
8:25; Hab 1:12.

89:52 This doxology is not a part of the psalm but a conclusion to Book III of
the Psalter added by a redactor (see note on Ps 41:13).

Ps 90—106 Joined to a series of very diverse psalms, many of which lack superscription or indication of origin, is a well-defined group: the psalms of the
kingdom of God (Ps 93; 96-99). In this part of the Psalter, praise comes to the
fore. The psalmists acclaim the Creator who brought the world into being, the
Lord who intervenes in history. They await the God who comes to make all things
new.

Ps 90 The psalmist (who is well versed in the Scriptures) herein depicts the
dismal human condition as contrasted with the majesty and eternity of God. The
Lord alone remains. Man passes away, a derisory creature undermined by sin;
even if his life is lengthy, it remains precarious. The ancient account of the fall
and the malediction of Adam (see Ge 3:19) illustrates the origin of our human
condition: the ancients accept it with some distress and resignation (see the
Book of Ecclesiastes). Man's days are numbered, and it is wisdom to reflect on
this fact.

However, such lucidity does not exclude the joy that comes when God's presence illumines the days that he accords to each one and the times that he prepares for his people. This meditation of wisdom becomes a prayer of conversion.

Praying with the expressive formulas of the psalmist will teach us to contemplate the eternity of God and aid us to be detached from the present life, sin, and
death, which can prevent us from entering into eternal life.

The phrase *man of God* in the superscription is usually applied to prophets
(see 1 Sa 2:27), including Moses (see Dt 33:1; Jos 14:6).

3 You turn men back to dust,
   saying, "Return to dust,* O sons of men."*b*
4 For a thousand years in your sight
   are like a day that has just gone by,*c*
   or like a watch in the night.*
5 You sweep men away in the sleep of death;*d*
   they are like the new grass of the morning—*
6 though in the morning it springs up new,
   by evening it is dry and withered.*e*

7 We are consumed by your anger*
   and terrified by your indignation.
8 You have set our iniquities before you,
   our secret sins in the light of your presence.*f*
9 All our days pass away under your wrath;*g*
   we finish our years with a moan.
10 The length of our days is seventy years—
   or eighty, if we have the strength;
   yet their span*j* is but trouble and sorrow,*
   for they quickly pass, and we fly away.

---

j Or *yet the best of them.*

b Ps 103:14; 104:29; 146:4; Ge 3:19; 1 Mac 2:63; Job 34:14-15; Ecc 3:20; 12:7; Sir 40:11; 1 Co 15:47.—c Job 10:5; 2 Pe 3:8.—d Ps 89:47; Ge 19:15.—e Ps 37:2; 102:11; 103:15-16; Job 14:1-2; Isa 40:6-8; Mt 6:30; Jas 1:10.—f Ps 109:14-15; Hos 7:2; Eph 5:12.—g 9-10: Ps 39:4-6; 62:9; 78:33; 102:23-24; 144:4; Ge 6:3; 2 Sa 19:35; Job 7:6, 16; 14:5; Pr 10:27; Wis 2:5; Ecc 6:12; Sir 18:8; Isa 65:20.

90:3 *Return to dust:* by a word of the Lord, human beings return to the dust from which they were made (see Ge 2:7; 3:19).

90:4 A thousand years are for God like one day or, even less, like a fraction of one night—like one of the three watches into which the night was divided (see Jdg 7:19). This verse is cited by 2 Pe 3:8.

90:5 The life of people is like that of the new grass that appears in the morning and disappears by nightfall under the burning rays of the sun (see Ps 103:15f; 129:6; Job 14:1f; Isa 40:6f). They have no longevity.

90:7-10 Short though it is, human life is filled with trouble because of sin and God's righteous wrath.

90:10 *Yet their span is but trouble and sorrow:* an alternative translation (see NIV textual note) is: "yet the best of them are but trouble and sorrow" (see Ge 6:3; Job 20:8; Pr 10:27; Ecc 12:1ff; Sir 18:8f).

11 Who knows the power of your anger?*
   For your wrath is as great as the fear that
      is due you.
12 Teach us to number our days aright,
   that we may gain a heart of wisdom.

13 Relent, O LORD! How long will it be?
   Have compassion on your servants.*
14 Satisfy us in the morning with your unfailing
      love,*h*
   that we may sing for joy and be glad all
      our days.*
15 Make us glad for as many days as you have
      afflicted us,
   for as many years as we have seen
      trouble.*i*
16 May your deeds be shown to your servants,
   your splendor to their children.

17 May the favor* k of the LORD our God rest
      upon us;
   establish the work of our hands for us—
   yes, establish the work of our hands.*j*

---

k Or *beauty.*

h Ps 17:15; 103:5.—i Nu 14:34; Jer 31:13.—j Ps 33:22; Isa 26:12.

90:11-12 The psalmist prays that God may teach his people to appreciate the number of years given them and to use them in doing God's will. He asks that they may acquire a correct view of life so as not to challenge God's wrath but rather work out their salvation throughout their life. All this is given us in wisdom, which discerns the true values and gives the righteous a realistic attitude in accord with the divine will and adapted to circumstances (see Dt 4:6; 32:29).

90:13 The psalmist now extends to Israel the meditation and prayer that concerned all humanity. *Relent:* literally, "Turn." *How long . . .?:* see note on Ps 6:3.

90:14 The psalmist prays that *in the morning* (the typical time for deliverance and salvation: see note on Ps 49:14) God's love will put an end to the long night of their trial. The fulfillment of this prayer is found in the resurrection (see Ro 5:2-5; 8:18; 2 Co 4:16-18). *Unfailing love:* see note on Ps 6:4.

90:17 *Favor:* another translation (see NIV textual note) is "beauty," which constitutes the Lord's "goodness" (see Ps 90:17). Thus, the psalmist asks for God's loving help to his people, so that their work may be effective and enduring, even though the workers are apt to disappear quickly. *Yes, establish the work of our hands:* this second occurrence of these words may be an accidental repetition.

PSALM 91*

Security under God's Protection

1 He who dwells in the shelter of the Most
    High*
        will rest in the shadow of the Almighty.[1]
2 I will say[m] of the LORD, "He is my refuge and
    my fortress,
        my God, in whom I trust."[k]

3 Surely he will save you from the fowler's
    snare*
        and from the deadly pestilence.
4 He will cover you with his feathers,
        and under his wings you will find refuge;
    his faithfulness will be your shield and
        rampart.[l]

---

l Hebrew *Shaddai.*—m Or *He says.*

k Ps 9:9; 18:2; 31:2-3; 42:9; 142:5; 2 Sa 22:2.—l Ps 17:8; 35:2; 36:7;
57:1; 63:7; Dt 32:10; Ru 2:12; Isa 31:5; Mt 23:37.

Ps 91 This pilgrimage psalm is a glowing testimony to the security that God
bestows on those who come to the temple to place themselves under his protection. They will be strengthened by God and his angels all along the path of life in
which perils and snares proliferate on every side: the terror of night, the arrow by
day, the fowler's snare, pestilence, and plague as well as the lion and cobra,
great lion and serpent—in a word, every possible threat. Death itself seems to
retreat and one gets a glimpse of the peace and joy of the Messianic Age.

En route toward Jerusalem, or toward God, every believer is a pilgrim. The
itinerary is not an idyllic dream; rather, amidst risks and dangers, the Lord delivers us from fear and leads us to salvation, to life in his presence. This peaceful
psalm is especially suited to be an evening prayer.

We can regard this psalm as an exhortation of Christ developing the invitation
that he addressed to his disciples after the Last Supper: "Do not let your hearts
be troubled. Trust in God [the Father]; trust also in me" (Jn 14:1). We are to journey along the path of life with the constant certitude that the divine Persons surround us with a never-ending solicitude.

91:1 *The shelter of the Most High:* a designation in the psalms for the temple
(see Ps 27:5; 31:20; 61:4). *The shadow of the Almighty:* literally, "the shadow of
the wings of the Almighty" (see Ps 17:8; 36:7; 57:1; 63:7). As indicated by v. 4,
the shadow is an image of the safety to be found under the outstretched wings of
the cherubim in the holy of holies. *Almighty:* literally, "Shaddai," an ancient
name for God (see note on Ps 68:14).

91:3 *Fowler's snare:* a proverbial phrase for danger (see Ps 124:7; Pr 6:5; Hos
9:8).

5 You will not fear the terror of night,*
nor the arrow that flies by day,[m]
6 nor the pestilence that stalks in the darkness,
nor the plague* that destroys at midday.[n]
7 A thousand may fall at your side,
ten thousand at your right hand,
but it will not come near you.
8 You will only observe with your eyes*
and see the punishment of the wicked.[o]

9 If you make the Most High your dwelling—
even the LORD, who is my refuge—
10 then no harm will befall you,
no disaster will come near your tent.[p]
11 * For he will command his angels* concerning you[q]
to guard you in all your ways;[r]
12 they will lift you up in their hands,[s]
so that you will not strike your foot against a stone.*
13 You will tread upon the lion and the cobra;[t]
you will trample the great lion and the serpent.*

---

m Job 5:21; Pr 3:25; SS 3:8.—n Dt 32:24; Jer 15:8.—o Ps 37:34; 92:11.—p Dt 7:15; Pr 12:21.—q 11-12: Mt 4-6; Lk 4:10f.—r Ps 34:7; Heb 1:14.—s Ps 121:3; Pr 3:23.—t Job 5:22; Isa 11:8; Da 6:22; Lk 10:19.

91:5 *Terror of night:* resulting from true or false alerts of enemy attacks; attacks by day were announced by flying *arrows.*

91:6 *Pestilence . . . plague:* dreaded mortal diseases that frequently grew into epidemics (see Dt 32:24; Hos 13:14; Hab 3:5). In place of the "plague that destroys at midday" the versions have: "devil at noon" or the "noonday devil" (apparently a mythological expression for a contagious disease presumed to be caused by the noonday sun).

91:8 *Only observe with your eyes:* the righteous will be merely a spectator to the threats mentioned and not be harmed by them.

91:11-12 These words were cited by Satan when tempting Christ to presumption against divine providence (Mt 4:6; Lk 4:10f). They hold only in cases where the danger is not of one's own doing.

91:11 *His angels:* the teaching on guardian angels is common in the Old Testament (see Ps 34:7; Ge 24:7; Ex 23:20).

91:12 *Against a stone:* along the stony paths of Canaan (see Ps 23:3).

91:13 *Lion . . . cobra . . . great lion . . . serpent:* these terms correspond to the references found in vv. 5-6 and complete the list of deadly threats against God's servants (see Am 5:19).

¹⁴ "Because he loves me," says the LORD, "I will
     rescue him;*
     I will protect him,* for he acknowledges
     my name.ᵘ
¹⁵ He will call upon me, and I will answer him;
     I will be with him in trouble,
     I will deliver him and honor him.ᵛ
¹⁶ With long life will I satisfy himʷ
     and show him my salvation."*

PSALM 92*

Praise of God's Just Rule

A psalm. A song. For the Sabbath day.

¹ It is good to praise the LORD*ˣ
     and make music to your name, O Most
     High,*

---

u Ps 9:10; 119:132.—v Isa 43:2; Jer 33:3; Zec 13:9; Jn 12:26.—w Ps
50:23; Pr 3:2.—x Ps 33:1; 135:3; 147:1.

91:14-16 The psalmist reinforces his message by utilizing the form of a
prophetic oracle in which God promises Messianic blessings to all who put their
trust in him (see Ps 50:15, 23; Ro 8:30).

91:14 *Protect him:* literally, "raise him to a high, safe place." *My name:* see
note on Ps 5:11.

91:16 *With long life . . . my salvation:* for the sages of Israel, a long life is the
reward of the righteous (see Ex 23:26; Dt 4:40; 1 Sa 2:30; Job 5:26; Pr 3:2, 16;
10:27).

Ps 92 This is a didactic psalm, that is, both a praise of the Lord and an instruction for the faithful. The psalmist meditates on God's way of acting. His love
and faithfulness are reflected in everything he does, but they must be compre-
hended. Ultimately the happiness of the wicked will fade like seasonal grass,
whereas the lot of the righteous will be like the great trees whose roots are
planted in solid ground. For the latter, new seasons are promised in the courts of
God. God's joy is like a new spring in the life of believers.

We can make use of this psalm in following Christ's lead to praise the triune
God, to sing of the wondrous divine work that delivers us from our spiritual enemies and mysteriously introduces us into eternal life.

The words *For the Sabbath day* in the superscription indicate that in the
postexilic temple liturgy this psalm was sung at the time of the morning sacrifice
on the Sabbath or seventh day. Psalms sung on the other days were: Ps 24: first
day; Ps 48: second day; Ps 82: third day; Ps 94: fourth day; Ps 81: fifth day; and
Ps 93: Sixth day.

92:1 Human beings have the duty to praise the Lord Most High (see note on Ps
7:17). *Name:* see note on Ps 5:11.

2 to proclaim your love* in the morning
and your faithfulness at night,
3 to the music of the ten-stringed lyre
and the melody of the harp.*y*

4 For you make me glad by your deeds, O
LORD;*
I sing for joy at the works of your hands.
5 How great are your works, O LORD,*z*
how profound your thoughts!
6 * The senseless man does not know,
fools* do not understand,
7 that though the wicked spring up like grass
and all evildoers flourish,*a*
they will be forever destroyed.

8 But you, O LORD, are exalted forever.*

9 For surely your enemies, O LORD,
surely your enemies will perish;
all evildoers will be scattered.*b*
10 You have exalted my horn*n* like that of a wild
ox;*c*
fine oils have been poured upon me.*d*
11 My eyes have seen the defeat of my adversaries;
my ears have heard the rout of my wicked
foes.*e*

---

n *Horn* here symbolizes strength.

y Ps 33:2; 71:22; 144:9.—z 5-6: Ps 111:2; 131:1; 139:6, 17; Wis 13:1;
17:1; Rev 15:3.—a Ps 37:2, 35.—b Ps 45:5; 68:1-2; 125:5.—c Ps 75:10;
89:17; Dt 33:17.—d Ps 23:5.—e Ps 54:7; 91:8.

92:2 *Love:* see note on Ps 6:4.
92:4-5 God's great deeds (of creating, redeeming, and ruling human beings)
bring joy to the psalmist and all who have understanding through his grace.
92:6-9 Evildoers have no knowledge of the Lord's deeds or his dispensing of
justice; they are seemingly happy and prosperous now, but they will soon perish
under the just judgment of the Lord.
92:6 *Senseless man . . . fools:* enemies of God and his faithful (see notes on
Ps 14:1 and 14:2; see also Ps 37:33ff; 68:2; 83:3; 94:8-11).
92:8 *Exalted forever:* since God reigns forever, there is no hope of escape for
the senseless.

¹² The righteous will flourish like a palm tree,*
    they will grow like a cedar of Lebanon;*f*

¹³ planted in the house of the LORD,*
    they will flourish in the courts of our God.

¹⁴ They will still bear fruit in old age,
    they will stay fresh and green,

¹⁵ proclaiming, "The LORD is upright;
    he is my Rock, and there is no wickedness
    in him."*g*

PSALM 93*

Glory of the Lord's Kingdom

¹ The LORD reigns,* he is robed in majesty;
    the LORD is robed in majesty
    and is armed with strength.

---

f Ps 1:3; 52:8; Jer 17:8; Hos 14:6. — g Dt 32:4; Job 34:10.

92:12-15 In contrast to the lot of the wicked, the righteous are exalted and renewed in their strength and happiness.

92:13 *Planted in the house of the LORD:* the righteous are likened to trees growing in the temple itself, which is a source of life and fertility because of the divine presence (see Ps 36:7-9; Eze 47:1-12).

Ps 93 This is one of the nine psalms of the kingdom (Ps 47; 93-100), most of which feature the liturgical acclamation "The Lord reigns," in which is centered the whole faith of Israel. All these hymns exalt the kingdom of God that extends over the entire universe and dominates the course of time. God reveals his kingship when he brings forth the world; he does so even more when he chooses Israel. Nonetheless, creation and history are still only the beginning and promise; the kingdom of God will be manifested in all its glory at the end of time (see Rev 4:11; 11:15-17): a new heaven, a new earth, and a new Jerusalem—such are the images that allow us to glimpse the joy of a new humanity gathered together in the glory of God (see Rev 21:1—22:5). The acclamation of the psalms of the kingdom already vibrates with this ineffable hope.

Psalm 93 exalts the Lord who reigns, robed in majesty. He affirms his greatness by the forces of creation that he rules, by the Law—or "statutes"—that he gives to his people, and by the temple of Jerusalem that he consecrates to his mysterious presence. From his earthly experience, the believer acclaims the splendor of a kingdom that can have no end.

In all truth, we can regard this psalm as applicable to Christ's kingship and sing: "Christ reigns." For he vanquishes in himself and in his followers all hostile powers (Satan, death, and sin), delivering the believers from the empire of death and transferring them into his kingdom (see Eph 1:2). This is the extraordinary wonder that he continues across the centuries until the full deliverance of his Church and the definitive destruction of his enemies will occur (see Rev 20—22).

93:1a-c *The LORD reigns:* a liturgical acclamation that sums up the entire faith of Israel (see Ps 96:10; 97:1; 99:1; see also Zec 14:9).

The world is firmly established;*
    it cannot be moved.[h]

2 Your throne was established long ago;
    you are from all eternity.[i]

3 The seas* have lifted up, O LORD,
    the seas have lifted up their voice;
    the seas have lifted up their pounding
      waves.

4 Mightier than the thunder of the great wa-
    ters,
    mightier than the breakers of the sea—[j]
    the LORD on high is mighty.*

5 Your statutes* stand firm;
    holiness adorns your house
    for endless days, O LORD.

---

h Ps 47:7; 75:3; 96:10; 97:1; 99:1; 104:5; Isa 52:7.—i Ps 55:19; 90:2; 102:12; 2 Sa 7:16; Hab 1:12.—j Mk 8:39.

93:1d-2 The Lord established his kingdom on earth when he created the world and everything in it (see Ps 24:1). Hence, the world will not be moved no matter what pressure is brought to bear on it by hostile forces (see Ps 10:6; 104:5), because the Lord has established his rule over it. Indeed, the Lord is eternal (see Ps 90:2), but his rule was established when his throne was set up at the beginning of history with the creation ("long ago"; see Isa 44:8; 45:21; 48:3-8).

93:3 *Seas:* the waters of the primeval chaos that the Lord mastered through his creative word (see Ps 33:7; 104:7-9; Ge 1:6-10; Job 38:8-11; see also note on Ps 65:7). They can also stand for the enemies of God and his people (see Job 7:12; Isa 8:7; 17:12; Jer 46:8; Da 7:2; Rev 17:15) as well as the ocean currents, whose powers were feared by the pagan nations as indicated in the mythical account of Baal's victory over the sea god Yamm.

93:4 The Lord is the Master of the thundering storms and surging waves by his simple word (see Christ's calming of the storm by a single word in Mk 4:39).

93:5 *Statutes:* these divine judgments constitute revelation in the wide sense insofar as they are the norm of human life (see Ps 119). As stable (see Ps 19:7) as the physical universe and as inviolable (see Ps 95:8-11) as the sanctuary of Jerusalem, this revelation will be the foundation of the Lord's definitive kingdom, inaugurated from the creation and already effective in Israel (see Isa 51:9f, 13; 52:7). *Holiness adorns your house for endless days:* the temple, home of the King of Israel, is consecrated forever (1 Ki 8:13; 9:3; Jud 9:18; Eze 42:13f; Rev 21:27). Those who approach the most holy God (see Ps 99) are also consecrated (see Ex 19:6; Lev 10:3; 19:2).

PSALM 94*

God, Judge and Avenger

1 O LORD, the God who avenges,*
    O God who avenges, shine forth.[k]
2 Rise up, O Judge of the earth;
    pay back* to the proud what they deserve.[l]
3 How long will the wicked, O LORD,[m]
    how long will the wicked be jubilant?*

4 They pour out arrogant words;*
    all the evildoers are full of boasting.[n]
5 They crush your people, O LORD;
    they oppress your inheritance.
6 They slay the widow and the alien;
    they murder the fatherless.[o]

---

k Dt 32:35; Na 1:2.—l Nu 10:35; Jer 51:56; La 3:64.—m Ps 13:2; 75:4; Jer 12:1—n Ps 73:7-12; Jer 43:2; Mal 2:17; 3:14.—o Ex 22:21-22; Dt 24:17-22; Isa 1:17.

Ps 94 Distressed at the delays by God in dispensing justice, the psalmist utters this cry of impatience. Why does God not intervene immediately against the wickedness that crushes the lowly? The reflection of this sage tells him that despite appearances the lot of the righteous is in the final analysis the only one that matters. Certainly God's hour will come when the Lord will avenge his "inheritance," the true Israel, that is, the people of the poor. He cannot remain indifferent to wrongs and evils that the innocent endure nor suffer the scorn of haughty spirits and wicked hearts. As the "God who avenges," he authorizes no one to launch individual reprisals; it is he himself who reestablishes a justice that is troubled by the arrogance of men to the scorn of the poor. These comparative tableaus of the arrogant and the innocent have the astonishing power to challenge us: is our life marked by the sense of justice?

Placed in a condition similar to that of the psalmist, we can pray this psalm to implore the divine intervention against those who exploit our brothers and sisters. At the same time, we can use it to proclaim that trials, far from crushing us, instruct us and enable us to discover true joy and happiness in the love of God (see Jn 15:9-11).

94:1 *Avenges:* i.e., redresses wrongs (see Dt 32:35, 41). It is God's prerogative to avenge as Paul declares in Ro 12:19.

94:2 *Pay back:* the central theme of the psalm: God is righteous and repays both the good and the bad as they deserve (see Ps 7:6; 28:4; 62:12; La 3:64; Joel 3:4).

94:3 *How long . . . ?:* see note on Ps 6:3.

94:4-7 Not only do the wicked hurl arrogant words, but they also attack God's people, especially those to whom the Lord has promised his protection: the widows, orphans, and aliens (see Ex 22:21; Dt 24:17; Isa 1:17; 10:2; Eze 22:7). They no longer believe that God is concerned with their activities or demands an accounting from them (see Ps 10:2-11).

7 They say, "The LORD does not see;
the God of Jacob* pays no heed."[p]

8 Take heed, you senseless ones among the people;*
you fools, when will you become wise?[q]
9 Does he who implanted the ear not hear?
Does he who formed the eye not see?[r]
10 Does he who disciplines nations* not punish?
Does he who teaches man lack knowledge?
11 The LORD knows the thoughts of man;*
he knows that they are futile.[s]

12 * Blessed* is the man you discipline, O LORD,
the man you teach from your law;[t]
13 you grant him relief from days of trouble,
till a pit is dug for the wicked.
14 For the LORD will not reject his people;[u]
he will never forsake his inheritance.*
15 Judgment will again be founded on righteousness,
and all the upright in heart will follow it.

---

p Ps 10:11; 64:5; 73:11; Job 22:13-14; Eze 9:9.—q Dt 32:6; Pr 1:22; 8:5.—r Ex 4:11; Pr 20:12.—s Ps 33:15; Ecc 1:2; 1 Co 3:20.—t Ps 119:71; Job 5:17; Heb 12:5.—u 1 Sa 12:22; Sir 47:22; Ro 11:2.

94:7 *Jacob:* i.e., Israel (see Ge 32:28).

94:8-11 The wicked are "senseless" like animals (see Ps 92:6), "fools" (see Ps 49:10) without understanding. The Lord not only hears and sees and knows everything that takes place on earth but also metes out punishment for all wicked deeds.

94:10 *Disciplines nations:* through chastisement (see Lev 26:18; Jer 31:18). *Teaches man:* about the natural and the supernatural order (see Dt 20:1-17; Isa 28:26).

94:11 *The LORD knows the thoughts of man:* contrary to what the proud profess to believe. This verse is cited by Paul in 1 Co 3:20.

94:12-15 Blessed are those who are instructed by God, for they know that God sees all and rewards and punishes in his own good time.

94:12 *Blessed:* see note on Ps 1:1. *Law:* in the wide sense, revelation and moral doctrine, as often used in the wisdom writings. This verse recalls Ps 119:71 and Job 5:17.

94:14 God guides his people, especially the powerless, through difficult times because they are his possession, and he never rescinds his promises. On the Day of the Lord, divine retribution will be meted out and persecuted justice will triumph. This verse is cited by Paul in Ro 11:1f.

¹⁶ Who will rise up for me against the wicked?*
    Who will take a stand for me against evil-
        doers?
¹⁷ Unless the LORD had given me help,^v
    I would soon have dwelt in the silence of
        death.*
¹⁸ When I said, "My foot is slipping,"
    your love,* O LORD, supported me.^w
¹⁹ When anxiety was great within me,
    your consolation brought joy to my soul.*

²⁰ Can a corrupt throne be allied with you—*
    one that brings on misery by its decrees?*
²¹ They band together against the righteous*
    and condemn the innocent to death.
²² But the LORD has become my fortress,*
    and my God the rock in whom I take
        refuge.
²³ He will repay them for their sins
    and destroy them for their wickedness;^x
    the LORD our God will destroy them.^y

---

v Ps 115:17; 124:2.—w Ps 145:14; Dt 32:35.—x Ps 7:15; 9:15; 35:8;
57:6; Pr 5:22; 26:27; Ecc 10:8; Sir 27:26.—y Ps 107:42; 145:20.

94:16-19 The faithful psalmist puts his trust only in God. When he was bur-
dened with cares, temptations, difficulties, and trials, God was always there to
help, console, and encourage him and bring joy to his soul.
94:17 *Silence of death:* i.e., the silence of the netherworld (see Ps 88:3-5;
115:17).
94:18 The psalmist experienced the Lord's presence (see Ps 24:1) through the
support of God's "love" (see note on Ps 6:4).
94:19 The psalmist was overcome with anxiety and close to despair because of
his situation, but the Lord came to his aid and infused him with consolation and
joy (see 2 Co 1:5). *Soul:* see note on Ps 6:3.
94:20-23 The psalmist is confident that the Lord will save his people and call
the wicked to account.
94:20 The Lord will never allow evil to be victorious over himself and his faithful ones for a long period of time.
94:21 *Righteous:* see note on Ps 5:1.
94:22-23 The Lord is the "fortress" and "rock" of those who take refuge in him
(see Ps 18:1f; 59:1) and the judge and chastiser of those who do evil (see Ps
7:11-16).

PSALM 95*

A Call To Praise and Obey God

1 Come, let us sing for joy to the LORD;*
    let us shout aloud to the Rock of our salva-
    tion.[z]
2 Let us come before him with thanksgiving
    and extol him with music and song.

3 For the LORD is the great God,[a]
    the great King above all gods.*
4 In his hand are the depths of the earth,
    and the mountain peaks belong to him.
5 The sea is his, for he made it,[b]
    and his hands formed the dry land.*

6 Come, let us bow down in worship,
    let us kneel before the LORD our Maker;

---

z Ps 5:11; Dt 32:15.—a Ps 47:2; 96:4; 135:5.—b Ps 24:1-2; 146:6.

Ps 95 This psalm calls upon the Israelites assembled at the temple to worship the Lord: "Come, let us sing for joy to the LORD." All are invited to give praise, and all acclaim the God of the covenant. He is the Creator and sovereign Ruler of the world; he is the Shepherd who loves and saves Israel, his flock (see Eze 34:11, 31; Jn 10).

The Prophets address their oracle to the crowd: "Today, if you hear his voice. . . ." It is an exhortation to faithfulness, placing them on guard against the sins of yesteryear. The spirit of rebellion has no place in God's land (see Ex 17:1-7; Nu 20:13; Dt 6:16; 33:8).

The Letter to the Hebrews gives a long commentary on this exhortation (3:7—4:11), and this invitation to praise God opens the Church's official prayer, the Liturgy of the Hours. Like Israel in the desert, the Church journeys on earth. Christians know God's promises but they are equally familiar with temptation. If we wish to enter into the new promised land, that is, share God's life, we must persevere in the struggle for fidelity. Each day is the "today" in which we must heed the voice of God.

95:1-2 The first duty of his faithful toward God is one of praise and adoration (see Isa 66:18-23; Zec 14:16-21). *Rock:* see note on Ps 18:2.

95:3 As the pagans had different gods for different peoples, regions of the earth and sky, and spheres of life (war, fertility), so, the psalmist indicates, do the Israelites. However, in their case, it is only the Lord who is God of every one of these spheres ("above all gods") (see Ps 47:2; 96:4; Job 36:22; Da 2:47).

95:4-5 *Depths . . . mountain peaks . . . sea . . . dry land:* depths, heights, waters, and dry land—all are God's as well as everything in them.

⁷ for he is our God
   and we are the people of his pasture,*
   the flock under his care.ᶜ

   Today, if you hear his voice,ᵈ
⁸   do not harden your hearts as you did at
        Meribah,* ᵒ
        as you did that day at Massahᵖ in the
        desert,
⁹ where your fathers tested and tried me,ᵉ
   though they had seen what I did.*
¹⁰ For forty years* I was angry with that generation;
        I said, "They are a people whose hearts go
        astray,
        and they have not known my ways."ᶠ
¹¹ So I declared on oath in my anger,
   "They shall never enter my rest."*

---

o *Meribah* means *quarreling.*—p *Massah* means *testing.*

c Ps 23:1-3; 80:1; 100:3; Eze 34:1; Mic 7:14.—d 7c-11: Ps 81:7; 106:32;
Ex 19:5; Dt 12:9; Heb 3:7-11, 15; 4:3, 5, 7.—e Ex 17:1-7; Nu 14:22; 20:2-
13; Dt 6:16; 33:8.—f Ps 78:8; Nu 14:34; Dt 32:5; Job 21:14.

95:7 As the "Maker" of his people (v. 6) because he has brought them into
being as his covenant people (see Dt 32:6, 15, 18; Isa 44:2; 54:5), the Lord is
also their shepherd, and they are "the people of his pasture" (see Ps 23:1; 79:13;
100:3; Jer 23:1; 25:36; Eze 34:21; Jn 10:11-14). *Today, if you hear his voice:* see
Ps 81:8, 13; Ex 19:5; beginning with these words, vv. 7-11 are cited in Heb 3:
7-11.

95:8 *Meribah:* the place during the journey in the desert where the Israelites
quarreled with the Lord; *Massah:* the place where they *tested* the Lord (see NIV
textual notes and Ex 17:7; Nu 20:13). Scholars assign the first episode to a place
near and to the southwest of Sinai and the second to a place near Kadesh Barnea
in southern Palestine.

95:9 *Had seen what I did:* God's wonders in Egypt, at the Red Sea, and in the
desert (see Ex 16; Nu 14:11, 22).

95:10 *Forty years:* Israel was condemned to wander forty years in the desert
when the people refused to advance into Canaan and opted to return to Egypt instead (see Nu 14:1-4, 34). *That generation:* the adults who were freed from Egypt
and made a covenant with the Lord at Sinai (see Nu 32:13). *Hearts:* see note on
Ps 4:7. *My ways:* see note on Ps 25:4-7.

95:11 *My rest:* where the Lord has his dwelling (see Ps 132:7, 14) in the land
of Canaan (see Dt 12:9; Eze 20:15). In Heb 3:7ff, this rest is interpreted in the
spiritual sense of heavenly beatitude.

PSALM 96*

God, Sovereign and Judge of the Universe

1 Sing to the LORD a new song;*
   sing to the LORD, all the earth.^{g}
2 Sing to the LORD, praise his name;*
   proclaim his salvation day after day.
3 Declare his glory* among the nations,
   his marvelous deeds among all peoples.^{h}

4 For great is the LORD and most worthy of
   praise;
   he is to be feared above all gods.^{i}
5 For all the gods of the nations are idols,^{j}
   but the LORD made the heavens.*

---

g Ps 30:4; 98:1; Isa 42:10.—h Ps 98:4; 105:1; Rev 15:3.—i Ps 48:1;
89:7; 95:3; 145:3.—j Ps 97:7; Lev 19:4; Isa 40:17; 1 Co 8:4.

Ps 96 Partially cited in 1 Ch 16:23-33, this hymn is comprised of Old Testament reminiscences, especially from the Psalter and Isaiah (e.g., 42:10; 55:12). The peoples and nations of which it speaks were originally the neighbors who attempted to prevent Israel from becoming established in Canaan; later, they were all the peoples of the world who failed to recognize the one true God. Israel, which had been saved at the time of the Judges and brought back from an exile through which she had suffered a kind of annihilation, had experienced the Lord's deliverance more than once. She could well bear witness before the whole world of the power and superiority of the one sole God: the Lord had created the world and had given his people new life.

All peoples are invited to acknowledge him as the sovereign Master; all are summoned to the liturgy, to adoration. Deep emotion will grip the entire universe when God comes as Judge; he who has brought into being an unshakable world will establish all human beings in justice and righteousness.

This song of universal joy is always new with the newness of God himself; the New Testament (see Ac 17:31; Rev 19:11) refers to v. 13 in announcing the final coming of Christ on the day of judgment, when he will renew all things. Thus, by means of it Christians call upon the whole universe to praise God the Father as well as the risen Jesus, whom the Father has made "Lord and Christ" (Ac 2:36), "Prince and Savior" (Ac 5:31), and "ruler of the kings of the earth" (Rev 1:5).

According to the superscription in the Septuagint and Vulgate, this psalm was sung at the dedication of the postexilic temple. Its Messianic content made it suitable for that occasion.

96:1 *New song:* see note on Ps 33:3. *All the earth:* see note on Ps 9:1; see also Ps 97:1; 100:1.

96:2 *Name:* see note on Ps 5:11. *Proclaim his salvation:* see note on Ps 67:2-3.

96:3 *Glory:* see note on Ps 85:9.

96:5 *Made the heavens:* since the Lord made the heavens, which were supposedly the home of the gods, it follows that he is far greater than all the gods; but he is also greater because they are nothing more than idols.

6 Splendor and majesty are before him;
strength and glory are in his sanctuary.*

7 Ascribe to the LORD, O families of nations,[k]
ascribe to the LORD glory and strength.*
8 Ascribe to the LORD the glory due his name;
bring an offering and come into his courts.*
9 Worship the LORD in the splendor of his[q] holiness;
tremble before him, all the earth.

10 Say among the nations, "The LORD reigns."*
The world is firmly established, it cannot be moved;
he will judge the peoples with equity.[l]
11 Let the heavens rejoice, let the earth be glad;
let the sea resound, and all that is in it;[m]
12 let the fields be jubilant, and everything in them.
Then all the trees* of the forest will sing for joy;

q Or *LORD with the splendor of.*

k Ps 22:27; 29:1.—l Ps 75:3; 93:1; 97:1.—m Ps 98:7; Isa 49:13.

96:6 The Lord is surrounded by personifications of divine attributes ("splendor and majesty . . . strength and glory") that extol his universal kingship.

96:7 The psalmist makes use of Ps 29:1f, eliminating any allusion to the theme of "mighty ones" (i.e., "sons of God") and accentuating the universalist tone (see Ps 47:9; Zec 14:17). All peoples are specifically summoned to pledge their obedience to the Lord.

96:8 *Courts:* i.e., of the temple where the Lord dwells (see Ps 84:2, 10; 2 Ki 21:5; 23:11f). The psalmist may have been thinking of the outermost court of the temple, which was the court of the Gentiles.

96:10 *The LORD reigns:* see note on Ps 93:1a-c. Not only is the Lord the Creator of all (as well as the Redeemer of all) but also the Judge of all. Greek and Latin mss have a Christian addition: "from the wood" [of the cross]—a splendid expression of the theology of the cross found in the Gospel of John.

96:11-12 *Heavens . . . sea . . . fields . . . trees:* i.e., the whole world. By being what it is, God's creation gives him glory. However, it will rejoice even more when the fullness of redemption is attained, which it is presently awaiting together with all humanity (see Ro 8:21f).

13   they will sing before the LORD, for he comes,
      he comes to judge the earth.[n]
He will judge the world in righteousness
      and the peoples in his truth.*

PSALM 97*

Divine King and Universal Judge

1 The LORD reigns,* let the earth be glad;
      let the distant shores rejoice.[o]

2 * Clouds and thick darkness* surround him;
      righteousness and justice are the founda-
      tion of his throne.[p]

---

n Ps 98:9; Rev 19:11.—o Ps 75:3; 93:1; 96:10; Ex 15:18.—p Ps 85:10;
89:14; Ex 19:16; Dt 4:11; 5:22; 1 Ki 8:12; Job 22:14.

96:13 The psalmist may have been thinking of the Lord's coming as the one in
which he led the exiles back to Jerusalem. But the Lord comes in many ways. In
Christ, the Lord came to fulfill the words of this psalm, bringing all peoples back
to God, and he will come again at the end of time to judge the living and the
dead (Ac 10:42; 17:31). His judgment is righteousness and truth.

Ps 97 Here is another hymn to King Yahweh, the sole Lord and Savior. His
coming is described with the grandiose and traditional images of divine manifestations (see Ex 19:16-20). These produce terror among idolaters and joy in Israel. When this song was imposed, all fear of foreign deities had disappeared
among the Israelites; the gods themselves, or at least their worshipers, are invited to come and prostrate themselves before the Sole God. The people's faith in
the only Lord is henceforth unshakable.

This majestic Lord is also the God who comes, the one who loves every righteous heart. Furthermore, this God of the universe who is praised is the very same
God who is close to us along the paths of life.

The theme of the kingdom of God was dominant in the teaching of Jesus. According to John's Gospel, Jesus was enthroned on the cross and in his Resurrec-
tion-Ascension. Hence, as Christians pray this psalm, we can rejoice in Christ's
rule.

According to the superscription in the Septuagint and Vulgate, this psalm was
sung when David's land was established, hence after the return from the Exile.

97:1 *The LORD reigns:* see note on Ps 93:1a-c. *The distant shores:* distant
countries accessible only by sea (see 1 Ki 9:26-28; 10:22; Isa 60:9; Jnh 1:3).

97:2-6 The psalmist portrays the Lord's appearance by traditional signs of his
manifestation at Sinai. These went on to become the signs used to describe the
future Day of the Lord, when he would come in glory to establish true justice on
the earth (see note on Ps 18:7).

97:2 *Clouds and thick darkness:* these served to veil God's ineffable glory from
human eyes (see Ex 19:9; 1 Ki 8:12). *Righteousness and justice:* divine attributes
personified (see Ps 61:7; 85:11; Pr 16:12; 25:5).

3 Fire* goes before him
   and consumes his foes on every side.
4 His lightning lights up the world;
   the earth sees and trembles.q
5 The mountains melt like wax before the LORD,
   before the LORD of all the earth.r
6 The heavens proclaim his righteousness,*
   and all the peoples see his glory.s
7 All who worship images are put to shame,t
   those who boast in idols—
   worship him, all you gods!*
8 Zion hears and rejoices
   and the villages of Judah* are glad
   because of your judgments, O LORD.u
9 For you, O LORD, are the Most High over all
   the earth;
   you are exalted far above all gods.v
10 Let those who love the LORD hate evil,*
   for he guards the lives of his faithful ones
   and delivers them from the hand of the
   wicked.w
11 Light* is shed upon the righteous
   and joy on the upright in heart.x
12 Rejoice in the LORD, you who are righteous,y
   and praise his holy name.*

---

q Ps 18:7; 50:3; 77:18; 99:1; 104:32; Jdg 5:4-5.—r Ps 68:2; Jud 16:15;
Mic 1:4.—s Ps 50:6; 98:2.—t Ps 96:5; Jer 10:14.—u Ps 9:2; 48:11.—v Ps
7:8; 83:18.—w Ps 121:7; Pr 8:13.—x Ps 4:6; 112:4.—y Ps 30:4; 104:34.

97:3 *Fire:* symbol of God's wrath (see Ps 21:9; 50:3; 83:14; Dt 4:24; 1 Ki 19:12;
Isa 10:17).

97:6 *Proclaim his righteousness:* the heavens show forth the glory of their Creator to all peoples (see Ps 19:1-4a).

97:7 Those who trust in false gods are put to shame. For "our God is in
heaven; he does whatever pleases him. But their gods are silver and gold, made
by the hands of men" (Ps 115:3f).

97:8 *Villages of Judah:* literally, "Daughters of Judah." *Judgments:* see note on
Ps 48:11.

97:10-12 Those who are loyal to the covenant (the righteous) live in the light
of God's presence, where there is fullness of joy. They glorify his holy name, that
is, they honor him by their lives.

97:11 *Light:* see notes on Ps 27:1 and 36:9.

97:12 *Name:* see note on Ps 5:11.

PSALM 98*

Praise of the Lord, King and Judge

A psalm.

1 Sing to the LORD a new song,[z]
   for he has done marvelous things;
 his right hand and his holy arm[a]
   have worked salvation for him.*
2 The LORD has made his salvation known
   and revealed his righteousness to the na-
     tions.*
3 He has remembered his love
   and his faithfulness to the house of Israel;
 all the ends of the earth have seen
   the salvation of our God.*

4 Shout for joy to the LORD, all the earth,
   burst into jubilant song with music;
5 make music to the LORD with the harp,
   with the harp and the sound of singing,

---

z Ps 96:1; Isa 42:10.—a Isa 59:16; 63:5; Lk 1:51.

Ps 98 Israel has returned from the Exile; God has saved her, and the whole world is a witness of it. Hence, the Lord is pursuing his project of salvation. Let all peoples acclaim him as their sovereign and let joy burst out over the whole face of the earth, for God comes to inaugurate a kingdom of peace and justice for all humanity. The same worldwide perspective is glimpsed in the second part of the Book of Isaiah (Isa 40—55) with which the psalms of the kingdom have much in common.

The previous psalm brought to mind the second coming of Christ. This psalm recalls the first coming of the Lord and the faith of all peoples. Hence, the Christian Liturgy uses it during the Christmas season, since the latter is so shot through with joy at the coming of the Lord, the Savior of all human beings.

98:1 God's deliverance of Israel from exile, a type of the Messianic redemption, is such a wondrous deed that it deserves to be praised in song. *New song:* see note on Ps 33:3. *Marvelous things:* see note on Ps 9:1. *His right hand and his holy arm:* God is portrayed as a champion warrior.

98:2 In this new act, reminiscent of his wonders during the Exodus, God has revealed his infinite power and greatness (see note on Ps 46:10; see also Isa 52:10).

98:3 God has kept his promise made to the house of Israel, and it is fully visible to all nations. The complete fulfillment of this promise was the wondrous act God performed in the redemption worked by his Son Jesus Christ—which also was seen by all nations.

⁶ with trumpets and the blast of the ram's
   horn—*b*
   shout for joy before the LORD, the King.*

⁷ Let the sea resound, and everything in it,*
   the world,* and all who live in it.*c*

⁸ Let the rivers clap their hands,
   let the mountains sing together for joy;*d*

⁹ let them sing before the LORD,
   for he comes to judge the earth.*e*
   He will judge the world in righteousness*f*
   and the peoples with equity.*

PSALM 99*

God, King of Justice and Holiness

¹ The LORD reigns,*
   let the nations tremble;
   he sits enthroned between the cherubim,
   let the earth shake.*g*

---

b Ps 47:5-6; Ex 19:16.—c Ps 93:3; 96:11.—d Ps 148:9; Isa 44:23;
55:12.—e Ps 96:13.—f Ps 67:4.—g Ps 18:7-10; 48:1; 80:1; 93:1; Ex 25:22;
1 Sa 4:4; 2 Sa 6:2.

98:6 The whole of creation is summoned to acclaim the Lord as King, as Israel
acclaimed her kings at their coronation, with trumpets and horns (see 1 Ki 1:34).
98:7-9 All creation is exhorted to honor its King (see note on Ps 96:11-12).
98:7 *Sea . . . world:* the two major areas that contain living things.
98:9 The Lord will come to judge everyone impartially. Jesus announced that
the long-awaited coming of the Lord to judge the earth had begun in his ministry
(see Mk 1:15: "The kingdom of God is near"). See also note on Ps 96:13.
Ps 99 Each of the two parts of this eschatological hymn is followed by a refrain (vv. 5, 9) that stresses the holiness of the King of Israel (see Isa 6:3-5). In
the temple at Jerusalem, on the ark of the covenant two winged creatures, the
cherubim, support the throne of God: a weak image of the greatness of the
Almighty, for whom Mount Zion is a "footstool." God is so holy that he infinitely
transcends all the realities of the universe. However, his holiness is not a far-off
greatness, indifferent to human life. In adoring him we are brought face to face
with difficult demands called justice, right, and faith. The holiness of a God who
is accessible to sinful human beings is truly astounding. In the final analysis, it
constitutes God's intimate presence in our lives.
We can pray this psalm in honor of Christ the King who is all-holy and in full
accord with the will of his Father (see Jn 4:34; 14:31). His whole life was one long
obedient carrying out of what the Father had given him to accomplish, one
lengthy self-sacrifice for the salvation of the world (Heb 7:27; 9:28).
99:1 *The LORD reigns:* see note on Ps 93:1a-c. *Cherubim:* see note on Ps 18:10.

² Great is the LORD in Zion;
    he is exalted over all the nations.
³ Let them praise your great and awesome
    name—*
    he is holy.ʰ

⁴ The King is mighty, he loves justice—
    you have established equity;ⁱ
in Jacob you have done
    what is just and right.*
⁵ Exalt the LORD our God
    and worship at his footstool;ʲ
    he is holy.*

⁶ Moses and Aaron were among his priests,
    Samuel was among those who called on
    his name;ᵏ
they called on the LORD
    and he answered them.*
⁷ He spoke to them from the pillar of cloud;*
    they kept his statutes and the decrees he
    gave them.ˡ

---

h Ps 33:21; Isa 6:3.—i Ps 2:6; 72:1; Jer 23:5.—j Ps 132:7; Ex 15:2.—k 1 Sa 7:5; Jer 15:1.—l Ps 19:9; Ex 19:18-19; 33:9; Nu 12:5.

99:3 *Name:* see note on Ps 5:11. *He is holy:* God is so holy that he infinitely transcends all the realities of our universe; furthermore, because he is holy himself, God calls upon his people to be holy too (see Lev 11:44). They must consecrate themselves wholly to him (see also Mt 5:48; Ro 12:1).

99:4 God is completely just by nature. He gave the Law to his people so that equity would reign. Paul characterizes the Gospel as the revelation of the justice ("righteousness") of God (see Ro 1:17). *Jacob:* i.e., Israel (see Ge 32:28).

99:5 God is portrayed seated in heaven with his feet resting on the earth as on a footstool (see Isa 66:1), and more specifically on Mount Zion (see Ps 132:7; 1 Ch 28:2; La 2:1). The people are to praise and worship the Lord at his footstool.

99:6 The psalmist wishes to show that the Lord is a gracious King who hears the prayers of all who come to him with the right disposition. To do so, he mentions three great figures who at various stages interceded with the Lord for the nation (see Ex 32:30; Nu 16:47f; 1 Sa 7:2-11).

99:7 *Spoke to them from the pillar of cloud:* the pillar of cloud was the symbol of God's presence with his people during the Exodus (see Ex 13:21ff), and God spoke to Moses (see Ex 33:9) and to Aaron (see Nu 12:5) in the pillar of cloud. But though he spoke to Samuel, we have no record of it being in the pillar of cloud. Hence, the psalmist may here be alluding to the communication itself rather than the environment in which God communicated.

8 O LORD our God,
   you answered them;
  you were to Israel[r] a forgiving God,[m]
   though you punished their misdeeds.*[s]
9 Exalt the LORD our God
   and worship at his holy mountain,
   for the LORD our God is holy.*

PSALM 100*

Processional Entrance Hymn

A psalm. For giving thanks.

1 Shout for joy to the LORD,* all the earth.
2   Worship the LORD* with gladness;
   come before him with joyful songs.

---

r Hebrew *them.*—s Or *an avenger of the wrongs done to them.*

m Ex 32:11; Lev 26:18; Nu 20:12.

99:8 *Punished their misdeeds:* among those punished for misdeeds were Moses and Aaron, neither of whom was allowed to enter the promised land (see Ps 106:22f; Nu 27:14; Dt 3:26).

99:9 Refrain similar to that in v. 5.

Ps 100 Although it does not explicitly mention the theme of the Lord as King, this psalm is linked with the group of psalms of the kingdom by its style and ideas and serves as a kind of general conclusion for them. The Lord is King of the world and especially of Israel his flock. This is the Good News that calls for praise and joy.

The psalmist intimates that in a few brief moments, the sacrifice will be offered by which the people enter into communion with God (see Lev 7:11-15). He invites the throng to celebrate the one God and his providence for the people he has created and chosen for himself. Although this hymn is short, it must have filled the hearts of believers with great wonder since they knew themselves to be in the hand of God. The entire universe is invited to share this endless joy of Israel.

By this hymn, the Church calls Christians to sing to the Lord Jesus with a similar enthusiastic joy, for he too is our Lord and God (see Jn 20:28). In cooperation with his Father he has created and then recreated us (see Jn 1:1-3, 12). Because of this, we belong entirely to him (see 1 Cor 3:22f).

The word *thanks* in the superscription may indicate that the psalm was to be used in conjunction with a "thank offering" (see Lev 7:12).

100:1 *Shout . . . LORD:* a similar opening phrase occurs in Ps 66; 81; and 95. *All the earth:* the entire world is to worship God for all that he is and all that he has done for his people (see Ps 47:1f; 66:1, 4; 97:1; 117:1 for this theme of universalism).

100:2 *Worship the LORD:* the psalmist reminds the people that their first duty is to worship the Lord with mind, heart, and voice in complete gladness.

³ Know that the LORD is God.*
It is he who made us, and we are his;[t]
we are his people, the sheep of his pasture.[n]

⁴ Enter his gates* with thanksgiving[o]
and his courts with praise;
give thanks to him and praise his name.

⁵ For the LORD is good and his love endures
forever;
his faithfulness continues through all generations.*

PSALM 101*

Norm of Life for a Good Ruler

Of David. A psalm.

¹ I will sing of your love and justice;
to you, O LORD, I will sing praise.[p]

---

t Or *and not we ourselves.*

---

n Ps 23:1; 95:7; Dt 32:39; Isa 64:8; Mic 7:14.—o 4-5: Ps 42:4; 106:1; 107:1; 118:1; 136:1; 138:8; Ezr 3:11; Jer 33:11.—p Pss 33:1; 51:17; 89:2; 145:7.

100:3 *Know . . . God:* acknowledge that the Lord is God and be faithful to him; it is a statement of monotheism (see Dt 4:39; 32:39; Isa 43:10, 13). *Made us . . . his people:* through his choice and the wonders he did for them (see Ps 95:6). *Sheep of his pasture:* see note on Ps 95:7. Christians know that God made us his people through Jesus the Good Shepherd who gave his life for his sheep (see Jn 10:11).

100:4 *His gates:* of the temple (see note on Ps 24:7, 9). *Courts:* of the temple (see Ps 84:2, 10; 2 Ki 21:5; 23:11f).

100:5 The psalm concludes with the reasons why the Lord is to be praised: he is good (i.e., generous), loving (i.e., merciful), and faithful to his promises from generation to generation (see Ps 106:1; 107:1; 118:1; 2 Ch 5:13; 1 Mac 4:24; Jer 33:11; Mic 7:18-20; Mt 19:17; 1 Jn 4:7ff).

Ps 101 The Lord's covenant comprises a rule of life for every Israelite, including the king. This psalm constitutes the mirror of the ruler in whom it inculcates essential resolutions: personal integrity, choice of loyal counselors, ferreting out the arrogant, the deceitful, and the slanderous from the royal court, and the battle against injustice. The teaching is classic in the Bible, but its application is rarely carried out. Nonetheless, its main ideas continue to be vitally relevant.

We can pray this psalm in honor of Christ the King, constituted by the Father as supreme Head of the Church and of the world (Eph 1:20-23), who alone has perfectly fulfilled the commitments mentioned herein. He is thus the invisible Suzerain from whom all visible leaders (both spiritual and temporal) derive their powers (see Jn 21:15-17; Rev 1:5). Since Christ makes them his representatives, all these leaders must be loving and faithful images before their subjects.

2 I will be careful to lead a blameless life—
   when will you come to me?*

I will walk in my house*
   with blameless heart.q
3 I will set before my eyes
   no vile thing.

The deeds of faithless men I hate;*
   they will not cling to me.r
4 Men of perverse heart shall be far from me;
   I will have nothing to do with evil.

5 Whoever slanders his neighbor in secret,s
   him will I put to silence;*
whoever has haughty eyes and a proud heart,
   him will I not endure.t

6 My eyes will be on the faithful in the land,
   that they may dwell with me;u
he whose walk is blameless
   will minister to me.*

7 No one who practices deceit
   will dwell in my house;
no one who speaks falsely
   will stand in my presence.v

---

q Pss 26:11; 119:32; 1 Ki 3:14; 9:4; Isa 33:15.—r Pr 11:20; Jer 16:18.—s
Ex 20:16; Pr 17:20; 30:10.—t Pr 21:4.—u Ps 26:11; 119:1; Pr 20:7.—v Ps
5:5; Pr 25:5.

101:2b In imitation of the heavenly King, the psalmist himself will lead a
blameless life. But to do so he will need God's help, which he prays will be forthcoming (see 1 Ki 3:7-9; see also Ps 72). *When will you come to me?:* some see in
these words an allusion to the awaited coming of the Messiah, who was at times
called "He who comes" (see Mt 11:3; Jn 4:25). Others offer an alternative translation: "I will attend to the wholehearted man whenever he comes to me."
   101:2c-3b *House:* the king promises to make his household free of those who
abuse power. *Heart . . . eyes:* in the Old Testament, people were thought to act
after inner ("heart") and/or external ("eye") influence (see note on Ps 4:7; see
also Ps 119:36f; Nu 15:39; Job 31:7; Pr 21:4; Ecc 2:10; Jer 22:17).
   101:3c-4 The psalmist will not desire or do evil himself nor condone it in
others and will avoid all evildoers.
   101:5 *Put to silence:* i.e., destroy (see Ps 54:5; 94:23). *Proud:* see note on Ps
31:23.
   101:6 The norms of the king's private life are also the fundamental principles of
his governing. He will bring into his service only the "faithful" and the "blameless."

⁸ Every morning I will put to silence
   all the wicked in the land;
I will cut off every evildoer
   from the city of the LORD.*

PSALM 102*

Prayer of an Exile

A prayer of an afflicted man. When he is faint and
pours out his lament before the LORD.

¹ Hear my prayer, O LORD;*
   let my cry for help come to you.
² Do not hide your face* from me
   when I am in distress.
Turn your ear to me;
   when I call, answer me quickly.ʷ

³ For my days vanish like smoke;ˣ
   my bones burn like glowing embers.

---

w Ps 31:2; 69:17; 143:7. — x 3-4: Ps 38:3-4; La 1:13.

101:8 Evildoers will be eradicated from the kingdom. *Every morning:* the customary time for administering justice (see 2 Sa 15:2; Jer 21:12) and for receiving God's help (see Ps 59:16; 143:7; Isa 33:2). *City of the LORD:* see Ps 46:4f; 48:1f, 8; 87:3).

Ps 102 Known as the fifth of the seven Penitential Psalms (Ps 6; 32; 38; 51; 102; 130; 143), this psalm combines the lament of an afflicted person overwhelmed with pain and the prayer of the community of poor returned exiles waiting to be able to rebuild the walls of Jerusalem, their holy city. It shows that humanity and the universe pass away, while God remains (vv. 11, 12, 25, 27). This is the proof of the Lord's power and the reason for their hopes.

It is also the reason for the hopes of Christians, since we know that in Jesus and in his Church God has built for his people an imperishable dwelling place, a point emphasized by the Letter to the Hebrews (1:10-12) when it comments on vv. 25-27 of this psalm.

The superscription to this psalm is unique, giving neither author nor liturgical or historical note; instead it assigns the prayer to a life situation—when an afflicted person is close to giving up, i.e., *faint* (see Ps 61:2; 77:3; 142:3; 143:4).

102:1-11 One day, possibly during a grave sickness, the psalmist reaches the bitter conclusion of the inconsistency of human life. And the supreme outrage is that all who see him attribute his sad state to punishment sent by God, for his prayer and repentance receive no answer. The poor man experiences the depths of anguish where everything is falling apart; he can do nothing except cry out to God.

102:2 *Hide your face:* see note on Ps 13:1.

⁴ My heart* is blighted and withered like grass;
   I forget to eat my food.
⁵ Because of my loud groaning
   I am reduced to skin and bones.
⁶ I am like a desert owl,*
   like an owl among the ruins.
⁷ I lie awake;* I have become
   like a bird alone on a roof.
⁸ All day long my enemies taunt me;*
   those who rail against me use my name as
      a curse.
⁹ For I eat ashes as my food*
   and mingle my drink with tears ʸ
¹⁰ because of your great wrath,
   for you have taken me up and thrown me
      aside.
¹¹ My days are like the evening shadow;ᶻ
   I wither away like grass.ᵃ

¹² But you, O Lᴏʀᴅ, sit enthroned forever;*
   your renown endures through all genera-
      tions.ᵇ

---

y Ps 42:3; 80:5; Isa 44:20.—z Ps 109:23; 144:4; 1 Ch 29:15; Job 8:9;
14:2; Wis 2:5; Ecc 6:12.—a Ps 90:5-6; Jas 1:10.—b Ps 55:19; 90:2; 93:2;
135:13; 145:13; Isa 55:13; La 5:19; Hab 1:12.

102:4 *Heart:* see note on Ps 4:7. *Withered like grass:* see note on Ps 90:5.
102:6 *Owl:* a symbol of desolateness and destruction (see Isa 34:11, 15; Jer 50:39; Zep 2:14).
102:7 *I lie awake:* some translations add here: "and I moan."
102:8 *Enemies taunt me:* see note on Ps 5:9; see also Ps 109:25. *Use my name as a curse:* his enemies point him out as an example of divine malediction, saying: "May you become as wretched as so-and-so."
102:9-11 The Israelites indicated their penance externally by covering their heads with ashes and uttering lamentation accompanied by copious tears. To move the divine pity, the sick psalmist does not hold back. He covers himself with such an abundance of ashes that they are interspersed with his food, and he gives way to so many tears that they mingle with his drink. All the same, he is inexorably on his way toward death.
102:12-22 The people thus experience the time of scorn. Uprooted from their temple and their land, they are too overwhelmed by the loss of what they most cherish for them to think of revenge. They have recourse to God's tender mercies. In their misfortune, they fall back on a single certitude—the goodness of the Lord. At once, hope of restoration begins shining forth, for "the appointed time has come"—so much so that they do not stop at imagining the sole reestablishment of Israel but their perspective of renewed happiness embraces all humanity.

13 You will arise and have compassion on Zion,
   for it is time to show favor to her;
   the appointed time* has come.
14 For her stones are dear to your servants;
   her very dust moves them to pity.*
15 The nations will fear the name of the LORD,[c]
   all the kings of the earth will revere your
      glory.*
16 For the LORD will rebuild Zion
   and appear in his glory.*
17 He will respond to the prayer of the destitute;
   he will not despise their plea.

18 Let this be written* for a future generation,
   that a people not yet created may praise
      the LORD:[d]
19 "The LORD looked down from his sanctuary
      on high,
   from heaven he viewed the earth,[e]
20 to hear the groans of the prisoners[f]
   and release those condemned to death."*
21 So the name of the LORD will be declared in
      Zion
   and his praise* in Jerusalem
22 when the peoples and the kingdoms[g]
   assemble to worship the LORD.*

---

c 1 Ki 8:43; Isa 59:19; 66:18.—d Ps 22:30-31.—e Ps 11:4; 14:2; 53:2.—f Ps 79:11; Lk 4:18.—g Ps 22:27; Isa 60:3-4; Zec 2:11; 8:22.

102:13 *Appointed time:* the time established by God for judgment and salvation (see Ps 75:2; Ex 9:5; 2 Sa 24:15; Da 11:27, 35).
102:14 The psalmist intimates that Zion must be highly cherished by the Lord for she is so dear to his servants.
102:15 See note on Ps 46:10. *Name:* see note on Ps 5:11.
102:16 *And appear in his glory:* may also be translated as: "and thus appear in his glory" (see v. 15 and note on Ps 46:10; see also Isa 40:1-5). The ultimate fulfillment of this hope will occur in the "new Jerusalem" (see Rev 21).
102:18 *Written:* this is the only place in the Psalter that calls for a written record of God's saving deed. The usual reference is to an oral record (see Ps 22:30; 44:1; 78:1-4).
102:20 *Prisoners . . . those condemned to death:* see note on Ps 79:11.
102:21 *Praise:* see note on Ps 9:1.
102:22 See notes on Ps 46:10 and 47:9; see also Ps 96; 98; 100; Isa 2:2-4; Mic 4:1-3.

²³ In the course of my life^u he broke my
     strength;*
     he cut short my days.
²⁴ So I said:
     "Do not take me away, O my God, in the
     midst of my days;*
     your years go on through all generations.^h
²⁵ In the beginning you laid the foundations of
     the earth,*
     and the heavens are the work of your
     hands.ⁱ
²⁶ They will perish, but you remain;
     they will all wear out like a garment.
     Like clothing you will change them
     and they will be discarded.*
²⁷ But you remain the same,
     and your years will never end.*
²⁸ The children of your servants will live in your
     presence;^j
     their descendants will be established be-
     fore you."*

---

u Or *By his power.*

---

h Ps 39:4; 90:10; Job 14:5; 36:26.—i 25:27: Isa 51:6; Heb 1:10-12.—j Ps
25:13; 69:36.

102:23-28 Here the individual lament and the national supplication are combined. Upon meditating on the precariousness of existence before the God who
endures forever, a hope arises, the hope of not being abandoned. The Letter to
the Hebrews (13:8) will proclaim: "Jesus Christ is the same yesterday and today
and forever."

102:24 *In the midst of my days:* when the normal life span is only half-com-
pleted (see Isa 38:10; Jer 17:11).

102:25-27 This passage is inspired by Isa 51:6-8 and applied to the Messiah
(Heb 1:10-12). The restoration of Israel and the coming of the Messiah will be the
preface to the eschatological renewal or regeneration that will accompany the
end of time (see Isa 65:17; 66:22; Rev 20:11; 21:1).

102:26 Both the "foundations of the earth" and the "heavens" (which the
ever-living God has made) will perish (see Ps 1:6; 90:4; 2 Pe 3:8) and be of no
use, like discarded clothing (see Isa 51:6).

102:27 By contrast, the Lord remains forever the same (see Heb 13:8); he is
the "first and the last" (see Dt 32:39; Isa 41:4; 46:4; 48:12).

102:28 Because God does not change, the children of his people will be secure
in the Lord (see Mal 3:6). *Live in your presence:* another translation is: "dwell in
the [promised] land" (see Ps 69:36; see also Ps 37:3, 29; Isa 65:9).

PSALM 103*

Praise of God's Providence

Of David.

1 Praise the LORD, O my soul;*
   all my inmost being, praise his holy name.
2 Praise the LORD, O my soul,
   and forget not all his benefits—
3 who forgives all your sins
   and heals all your diseases,*
4 who redeems* your life from the pit
   and crowns you with love and compassion,^{k}
5 who satisfies your desires with good things
   so that your youth is renewed like the eagle's.*

---

k Ps 28:1; 30:3; 34:22; 40:2; 69:15; 88:4; 143:7; Pr 1:12; Jnh 2:6.

Ps 103 In its literary construction and sublime concepts, this psalm is one of the most pure and joyous of the Psalter. Healed of a grave sickness that he considers to have been caused by sin, the psalmist regards this cure doubled by God's pardon as a privileged experience of the love of the Lord. By this favor, God has shown his love for the psalmist in concrete fashion, thus forcefully confirming for him the revelation he made of this love to Israel through the Exodus and to Moses in the meeting on Sinai.

God's love is boundless for the righteous and magnanimous for sinners, disconcerting for the ephemeral creatures that we are and long-suffering to the point of extending to the far-off descendants of his faithful ones. Such is the love of the infinite God whose name is holy, whose throne is in heaven, and whose reign is eternal. He is the Father who will reveal Jesus and whose ineffable goodness Paul will proclaim (see 1 Co 2:9). We can thus understand how right the psalmist is in calling upon heaven itself to celebrate such a God.

The signal corporal and spiritual cure obtained by the psalmist constitutes only a pale figure of the Resurrection that definitively snatches Jesus from corporal death and the sinful world and shows him his Father's love with incomparable force. By sharing in the Resurrection of Christ through the sacraments, Christians discover that "God is love" in an experience derived from that of Christ and far superior to that of the psalmist. In all truth every Christian can recite this psalm to praise this God who is love.

103:1 *Soul:* see note on Ps 6:3. *Name:* see note on Ps 5:11.

103:3 Following the Old Testament understanding, the psalmist considers sufferings as the punishment for sin (see Ps 41:4; Ex 15:26).

103:4 *Redeems:* i.e., "delivers." *Pit:* i.e., the grave (see note on Ps 30:1).

103:5 *Like the eagle's:* because of its acknowledged long span of life, which at times reaches one hundred years, the eagle was regarded as a symbol of perennial youth and vigor (see Isa 40:31).

⁶ The LORD works righteousness
      and justice for all the oppressed.[l]

⁷ * He made known his ways* to Moses,
      his deeds to the people of Israel:
⁸ The LORD is compassionate and gracious,
      slow to anger, abounding in love.[m]
⁹ He will not always accuse,
      nor will he harbor his anger forever;*
¹⁰ he does not treat us as our sins deserve
      or repay us according to our iniquities.
¹¹ For as high as the heavens are above the
      earth,[n]
      so great is his love for those who fear him;*
¹² as far as the east is from the west,
      so far has he removed our transgressions
      from us.*
¹³ As a father has compassion on his chil-
      dren,*
      so the LORD has compassion on those who
      fear him;

---

l Ps 9:8; 146:6-7.— m Ps 86:15; 145:8; Ex 34:6-7; Nu 14:18; Jer 3:12; Joel 2:13; Jnh 4:2; Mic 7:18-19; Jas 5:11.— n Ps 13:5; Isa 55:9.

103:7-12 Already on Mount Sinai, God made known his ways to Moses, telling him that his attitude toward human beings and his great works find their inspiration in his loving kindness. Passing mysteriously before Moses, God cried out: "The LORD, the LORD, the compassionate and gracious God, slow to anger, abounding in love and faithfulness, maintaining love to thousands, and forgiving wickedness, rebellion, and sin. Yet he does not leave the guilty unpunished" (Ex 34:6f).

103:7 *His ways:* see note on Ps 25:10.

103:9 God pardons sinners who repent, a truth often affirmed (see Ps 86:15; 145:8; Ex 34:6; Ne 9:17; Isa 57:16; Jer 3:12; Joel 2:13; Jnh 4:2).

103:11 *Those who fear him:* see note on Ps 15:2-5.

103:12 God places a huge gulf between his faithful and their sins, extending, as it were, from one end of the earth to the other (see Isa 1:18; 43:25; Jer 31:34; 50:20; Mic 7:18f).

103:13-17 What an amazing condescension on the part of God's love. Although he is well aware that we are fragile and ephemeral creatures who, like grass or flowers, are carried off by the slightest breeze, God keeps in his love the whole lives of his servants. He presents a just account of their merits and blesses their descendants who are faithful to his covenant.

14 for he knows how we are formed,*o*
     he remembers that we are dust.*
15 As for man, his days are like grass,
     he flourishes like a flower of the field;*p*
16 the wind blows over it and it is gone,
     and its place remembers it no more.
17 But from everlasting to everlasting
     the LORD's love is with those who fear him,
     and his righteousness with their children's
       children—
18 with those who keep his covenant
     and remember to obey his precepts.*

19 The LORD has established his throne in
       heaven,
     and his kingdom rules over all.*

20 Praise the LORD, you his angels,*
     you mighty ones who do his bidding,*q*
     who obey his word.*
21 Praise the LORD, all his heavenly hosts,
     you his servants who do his will.
22 Praise the LORD, all his works
     everywhere in his dominion.

     Praise the LORD, O my soul.*

---

o Ps 90:3; 119:73.—p Ps 37:2; 90:5-6; Job 14:2; Isa 40:6.—q Ps 28:6;
148:2; Da 3:58.

103:14 The Lord has compassion on those "who fear him" (v. 13) because he
knows their frailty, that they are but "dust" (see Ge 2:7; 3:19; Job 4:19; Ecc 3:20;
12:7).
103:18 Keeping the covenant entails obeying the Lord's precepts (see Ex 20:6;
Dt 7:9), i.e., doing the will of God (see Mt 6:9-15).
103:19 *His kingdom rules over all:* see Ps 22:28; 145:11-13. The Book of Obadiah concludes with this cry of triumphant eschatology (v. 21: "And the kingdom
will be the LORD's").
103:20-22 The psalmist calls upon all creatures to join him in praising the
heavenly King who rules all things with love (see note on Ps 9:1).
103:20 The angels are God's messengers (see Ps 91:11).
103:22c *Praise the LORD, O my soul:* this last line was probably added by the
redactors of the Psalter to show that the divine word is efficacious by itself and
needs no intermediary.

PSALM 104*

Praise of God the Creator

¹ Praise the LORD, O my soul.

O LORD my God, you are very great;
  you are clothed with splendor and majesty.
² He wraps himself in light* as with a garment;
  he stretches out the heavens like a tent^r
³   and lays the beams of his upper chambers
    on their waters.
  He makes the clouds his chariot
    and rides on the wings of the wind.*

r Ps 19:1; Ge 1:6-7; Job 9:8; Pr 8:27-28; Isa 40:2; Am 9:6.

Ps 104 This hymn calls to mind the majestic poem that opens the Book of Genesis (see Ge 1); perhaps it is even older. The text seems to have undergone the influence of an Egyptian hymn to the sun. It is a rarity at this period for the author to look at the world with the curious eyes of a scientist who is seeking the cause of things and the laws that govern them. The author nevertheless conceives of the universe primarily as a song to God who gives it life. While Ps 103 celebrates the Lord insofar as he shows himself animated by a powerful love in the moral and spiritual order, this psalm—possibly composed by the same poet—invites us to praise him insofar as he reveals himself as a prodigious artist in the initial creation and a benevolent organizer in the governance of the universe.

The power of the creative act brings worlds forth: perfectly mastered, nature and creatures come alive. Divine providence has foreseen everything and organized it all: the seasons, the rhythm of existence, nourishment, and the home of animals and humans. Animated by the Spirit, that is, the divine Breath, creatures sing of the glory of their Creator. The only shadow in this tableau is sin, which risks destroying such a beautiful harmony; hence, the author prays that it be eliminated. In the creative Breath (v. 30), the Church sees the Spirit of Pentecost who renews the broken harmony and gives rise to the new creation, "the new human being" who is reborn in Christ (see 2 Co 5:17).

Enlightened by science concerning the unsuspected and amazing wonders of the material universe, all Christians sing to their heavenly Father this psalm of enthusiastic praise. They will also sing it to Christ, intimately associated with the Father both in the creation of these wonders and in their continuance in being (see Col 1:16f). We will praise above all the eminent greatness and power of Father and Son in sending their Spirit to recreate sinful human beings and to renew the spiritual cosmos, the Church (v. 30).

104:2 *Light:* created on the first day (see Ge 1:3-5). In general, the psalmist follows the order of creation found in Ge 1. *Heavens:* created on the second day (see Ge 1:6-8).

104:3 As the ancients represented the world, the rains were stored in reservoirs in the vault of the heavens, which they thought were solid. *Upper chambers:* God's heavenly dwelling above the upper waters of the sky (see notes on Ps 29:10 and 36:8; see also Ge 1:6f). *Clouds his chariot:* see note on Ps 68:4.

⁴ He makes winds his messengers,ᵛ
  flames of fire his servants.*ˢ

⁵ He set the earth on its foundations;
  it can never be moved.*
⁶ You covered it with the deep as with a garment;
  the waters stood above the mountains.
⁷ But at your rebuke* the waters fled,
  at the sound of your thunder they took to
  flight;ᵗ
⁸ they flowed over the mountains,
  they went down into the valleys,*
  to the place you assigned for them.
⁹ You set a boundary they cannot cross;
  never again will they cover the earth.ᵘ

¹⁰ He makes springs pour water into the ravines;*
  it flows between the mountains.
¹¹ They give water to all the beasts of the field;ᵛ
  the wild donkeys quench their thirst.
¹² The birds of the air nest by the waters;
  they sing among the branches.

---

v Or *angels.*

s Ps 148:8; Heb 1:7.—t Ps 29:3; Job 7:12.—u Ge 9:11-15; Job 38:8-11;
Jer 5:22.—v 11-14: Ps 135:7; 147:8-9; Ge 1:11-12.

104:4 The Letter to the Hebrews cites this verse to show that Christ is superior
to the angels. Since God makes use of mere wind and lightning ("flames of fire")
as his messengers and servants, the ministering spirits in heaven that he also
uses as his messengers must be infinitely inferior to the eternal Son of God. The
cogency of the argument is much greater in Greek (in which the Letter was written) because the word *pneuma* means both "wind" and "spirit" while the word
angelos means both "messenger" and "angel."
  104:5 The ancients regarded the earth as resting upon firm foundations (see
note on Ps 24:2).
  104:7 *Rebuke:* see Ps 76:6. *Waters fled:* poetic description of what took place
on the third day of creation (see Ge 1:9f).
  104:8 *They flowed . . . into the valleys:* the sources of the Jordan and the other
great rivers of the Near East are in the mountains. Another translation offered is:
"the mountains rose high and the valleys went down."
  104:10-12 God refreshes the ravines by means of the lower waters.

¹³ He waters the mountains from his upper
       chambers;*
    the earth is satisfied by the fruit of his work.
¹⁴ He makes grass grow for the cattle,
       and plants for man to cultivate—
    bringing forth food from the earth:
¹⁵ wine that gladdens the heart* of man,
       oil to make his face shine,
    and bread that sustains his heart.
¹⁶ The trees of the LORD are well watered,
       the cedars of Lebanon* that he planted.
¹⁷ There the birds make their nests;
       the stork has its home in the pine trees.ʷ
¹⁸ The high mountains belong to the wild goats;
       the crags are a refuge for the coneys.*ʷ

¹⁹ The moon marks off the seasons,ˣ
       and the sun knows when to go down.*
²⁰ You bring darkness, it becomes night,
       and all the beasts of the forest prowl.
²¹ The lions roar for their prey
       and seek their food from God.ʸ
²² The sun rises, and they steal away;
       they return and lie down in their dens.
²³ Then man* goes out to his work,
       to his labor until evening.

---

w That is, the hyrax or rock badger.

w Eze 31:6, 13.—x Ps 19:6; Sir 43:6.—y Job 38:39; Am 3:4.

104:13-15 God refreshes his creatures by means of the reservoir of upper waters (see v. 3 above and Ge 7:11; Job 38:22; Sir 43:14).

104:15 *Heart:* see note on Ps 4:7.

104:16 *Cedars of Lebanon:* see note on Ps 80:10.

104:18 *Coneys:* the hyrax or rock badger, a small, harelike, ungulate mammal (see Lev 11:5; Dt 14:7; Pr 30:26).

104:19 The ancients governed their lives by the cycles of the sun and moon, which God created on the fourth day for that purpose (see Ge 1:14-19).

104:21-23 *Lions . . . man:* representing the animal and the human kingdom. The psalmist, in accord with the life of his day, postulates that animals come out at night to search for their food and humans do their working and eating by day. See Jn 9:4, where Jesus uses the inability of humans to work at night (because of the circumstances of his time—absence of light at night) to impart a greater spiritual truth.

²⁴ How many are your works, O LORD!*
  In wisdom you made them all;
    the earth is full of your creatures.ᶻ
²⁵ There is the sea, vast and spacious,
    teeming with creatures beyond number—
    living things both large and small.ᵃ
²⁶ There the ships go to and fro,ᵇ
    and the leviathan, which you formed to
    frolic there.*

²⁷ These all look to you*
    to give them their food at the proper time.* ᶜ
²⁸ When you give it to them,*
    they gather it up;
  when you open your hand,
    they are satisfied with good things.
²⁹ When you hide your face,*
    they are terrified;
  when you take away their breath,
    they die and return to the dust.* ᵈ

---

z Ps 8:1; 92:5; Sir 39:16.—a Ps 69:34; Sir 43:26.—b Job 3:8; 40:20; Eze 27:9.—c Ps 136:25; 145:15-16; Job 36:31.—d Ps 90:3; Ge 3:19; Job 34:14-15; Ecc 3:20.

104:24-26 The psalmist now takes up God's creation of the sea and everything in it on the fifth day (see Ge 1:20-23). He calls upon the people to worship the Lord's wisdom and creative diversity. Here he emphasizes sea creatures to complement the wild and domesticated animals as well as man mentioned in vv. 10-18.

104:26 See note on Ps 74:14. Here "leviathan" is a whale or large cetacean. The name is that of a fabled dragon and is already found in Ugaritic poems of the fifteenth century B.C.

104:27-30 On the sixth day, God enabled everything he had made to fructify (see Ge 1:24-31). All living things on earth and in the sea, whether wild or domesticated, birds, sea creatures, and human beings have some idea of the living Presence by whom they exist (see Ps 145:15f; 147:9). They have their being in God (see Ac 17:24f), and the Lord gives and sustains life by his Spirit. Indeed, God has supreme power over the universe, creating, preserving, and governing all. The lives of all creatures are in his hands.

104:27 All nature depends on its Creator for provisions, and he has arranged for everyone to have enough food.

104:28-29 The experiences of creatures are governed by the Lord; they are gladdened by his provisions, terrified by his absence, and encounter death by the withdrawal of his breath.

104:29 *Hide your face:* see note on Ps 13:1. *Return to dust:* see note on Ps 90:3.

³⁰ When you send your Spirit,*
    they are created,
    and you renew the face of the earth.

³¹ * May the glory of the LORD endure forever;
    may the LORD rejoice in his works—*
³² he who looks at the earth, and it trembles,ᵉ
    who touches the mountains, and they
        smoke.*

³³ I will sing to the LORD all my life;*
    I will sing praise to my God as long as I
        live.ᶠ
³⁴ May my meditation be pleasing to him,
    as I rejoice in the LORD.
³⁵ But may sinners vanish from the earth*
    and the wicked be no more.

    Praise the LORD, O my soul.

    Praise the LORD.ˣ

---

x Hebrew *Hallelu Yah;* in the Septuagint this line stands at the beginning
of Psalm 105.

---

e Ps 97:4; 144:5.—f Ps 7:17; 146:2.

104:30 *Your Spirit:* the Spirit or "Breath" of God is the divine creative power,
source of all natural life (see Ge 1:2; 2:7). So also the Holy Spirit is the source of
all supernatural life (see Jn 3:5f). Hence, this verse is applied by the Church to
the third Person of the Blessed Trinity.

104:31-34 The psalmist concludes the psalm the way it began—with praise
(vv. 1-4). The Lord, who reveals himself in creation in all his splendor (vv. 1-4)
has bestowed his glory on it (see Ps 19:1; Isa 6:3), and his handiwork will endure
as long as he undergirds it. Hence, his faithful should respond with praise, devotion, and an intention to please the Lord (see Ps 19:14).

104:31 *Rejoice in his works:* as he did at the end of creation (see Ge 1:31).

104:32 The Lord is so much greater than his creation that even a mere look or
touch on his part is enough to wreak havoc in it.

104:33 *I will sing . . . all my life:* a perpetual vow to praise the Lord (see note
on Ps 7:17).

104:35 Before concluding, the psalmist prays that sin may disappear from
creation because it is the only mar on it. However, because the hymn cannot end
with a malediction (see Ps 139:19), he repeats the words of v. 1 as a refrain:
"Praise the LORD, O my soul." *Praise the LORD:* i.e., "Hallelujah" or "Alleluia,"
which most likely belongs to the beginning of Ps 105 (see NIV textual note and Ps
105:45; 106:1, 48).

PSALM 105*

God's Faithfulness to the Covenant

1 Give thanks to the Lord, call on his name;*g
    make known among the nations what he
        has done.h

2 Sing to him, sing praise to him;
    tell of all his wonderful acts.

3 Glory in his holy name;
    let the hearts* of those who seek the Lord
        rejoice.

4 Look to the Lord and his strength;
    seek his face always.i

5 Remember the wonders he has done,
    his miracles, and the judgments* he pro-
        nounced,

---

g 1-15: 1 Ch 16:8-22.—h Ps 18:49; 96:3; 145:5; Isa 12:4-5; Ac 2:21.—i
Ps 24:6; 27:8; Dt 4:29.

Ps 105 The magnificent hymn in praise of God for creation (see Ps 104) does
not suffice for believers. God is he who comes among human beings; hence, they
proclaim God's greatness in history by delivering the human race from slavery
and leading it to salvation. In order to voice its joy and thanks, Israel loves to recall the events that marked the beginnings of its adventure: the promise made to
Abraham and renewed to the patriarchs (vv. 8-15), the adventure of Joseph (vv.
16-23; see Ge 37—50), Moses and the plagues in Egypt (vv. 24-36; see Ex 1—
13), the Exodus and the miracles in the wilderness (vv. 37-43; see Ex 14—15),
and lastly the entrance into Canaan, the land promised as an inheritance (v. 44).

Contrary to the following psalm (Ps 106), the author is silent about Israel's
sins; he wishes to sing of nothing but the action of God. The Lord has always kept
his word; he has multiplied wonders for his people, and his providence has guided
their steps. Now he has a right to expect them to be faithful to him (v. 45).

This psalm becomes the song of the Church, a people chosen by God in Christ
and saved by his Passover (see Eph 1). Since our God is the God of Abraham,
Isaac, and Jacob (see Mk 12:26), unchanged and also faithful, we can legitimately base our confidence in him on the promises and proofs he gave to our distant spiritual ancestors. Let us not forget, however, that these promises have received eminent confirmation in the life of Christ, whom God has led—through
the dreadful detour of death—from this exile to the true promised land. This last
proof constitutes the primary foundation of our enthusiasm and confidence.

The first fifteen verses of this psalm are found again in 1 Ch 16:8-22.

105:1 *Name:* see note on Ps 5:11. *Make known among the nations:* see note on
Ps 9:1.

105:3 *Hearts:* see note on Ps 4:7.

105:5 *Judgments:* see note on Ps 48:11.

⁶ O descendants of Abraham his servant,
  O sons of Jacob, his chosen ones.*
⁷ He is the LORD our God;
  his judgments are in all the earth.

⁸ He remembers his covenant* forever,
    the word he commanded, for a thousand
      generations,
⁹ the covenant he made with Abraham,ʲ
  the oath he swore to Isaac.*
¹⁰ He confirmed it to Jacob as a decree,*
  to Israel as an everlasting covenant:
¹¹ "To you I will give the land of Canaan
  as the portion you will inherit."ᵏ

¹² When they were but few in number,
  few indeed, and strangers in it,ˡ
¹³ they wandered from nation to nation,
  from one kingdom to another.
¹⁴ He allowed no one to oppress them;
  for their sake he rebuked kings:*
¹⁵ "Do not touch my anointed ones;
  do my prophets* no harm."

¹⁶ He called down famine on the land
  and destroyed all their supplies of food;ᵐ

---

j Ge 15:1ff; 26:3; Lk 1:73.—k Ge 12:7; 15:18; Nu 34:2.—l 12-13: Dt 4:27; 26:5; Heb 11:9.—m Ge 41:54; 57; Lev 26:26.

105:6 Here begin the allusions to Genesis (22:17; see Isa 51:2). *O sons of Jacob, his chosen ones:* most manuscripts read instead: "O sons of Jacob his chosen one," which seems to fit better with the previous line.
  105:8 *Covenant:* see Ge 15:9-21. This verse (and v. 9) are alluded to in Lk 1:72f.
  105:9 *The oath he swore to Isaac:* another possible translation is "the oath concerning Isaac."
  105:10-11 These verses recall the promise (see Ge 15:18) on which rest the hopes of Israel (see Ps 47:4; 72:8; Dt 4:31, 40).
  105:12-41 The psalmist recapitulates God's saving acts for Israel from the making of the covenant (see Ge 15:9-21) to its fulfillment (see Jos 21:43). In this connection, see the short summary of salvation prescribed to be said by the individual Israelite reaching the promised land (see Dt 26:1-11).
  105:14 *He rebuked kings:* see Ge 12:11ff; 20:7; 26:7ff.
  105:15 *My anointed ones . . . my prophets:* the patriarchs, Abraham, Isaac, and Jacob, who were in a sense "anointed," that is, consecrated to God, and the recipients of his revelations.

17 and he sent a man before them—
   Joseph, sold as a slave.[n]
18 They bruised his feet with shackles,
   his neck was put in irons,[o]
19 till what he foretold came to pass,
   till the word of the LORD proved him true.[p]
20 The king sent and released him,
   the ruler of peoples set him free.[q]
21 He made him master of his household,
   ruler over all he possessed,[r]
22 to instruct his princes as he pleased
   and teach his elders wisdom.

23 Then Israel entered Egypt;[s]
   Jacob lived as an alien in the land of Ham.*
24 The LORD made his people very fruitful;
   he made them too numerous for their foes,[t]
25 whose hearts he turned* to hate his people,
   to conspire against his servants.[u]
26 He sent Moses his servant,
   and Aaron, whom he had chosen.[v]
27 They performed his miraculous signs among
   them,
   his wonders in the land of Ham.[w]
28 He sent darkness and made the land dark—*
   for had they not rebelled against his words?
29 He turned their waters into blood,
   causing their fish to die.
30 Their land teemed with frogs,
   which went up into the bedrooms of their
   rulers.

---

n Ge 37:28, 36; 45:5; Ac 7:9.—o Ge 39:20; 40:15.—p Ge 40:20-22; 41:9-13.—q Ge 41:14.—r Ge 41:41-44.—s Ps 78:51; Ge 46:1—47:12; Ac 7:15.—t Ex 1:7-9; Ac 7:17.—u Ex 1:8-14; Ac 7:19.—v Ex 3:10; 4:27; Nu 33:1.—w 27-36: Ps 78:43-51; Ex 7:8—12:51.

105:23 *Land of Ham:* i.e., Egypt.
105:25 *Whose hearts he turned:* the ancients regarded every happening as coming from God, even evil (see Ex 4:21; 7:3; Jos 11:20; 2 Sa 24:1; Isa 10:5-7; 37:26f; Jer 34:22).
105:28-38 As in Ps 78:43-51, here also the plagues of Egypt are recalled with poetic license so that their order and number are different from Ex 7:14—12:30.

³¹ He spoke, and there came swarms of flies,
    and gnats throughout their country.
³² He turned their rain into hail,
    with lightning throughout their land;
³³ he struck down their vines and fig trees
    and shattered the trees of their country.
³⁴ He spoke, and the locusts came,
    grasshoppers without number;^x
³⁵ they ate up every green thing in their land,
    ate up the produce of their soil.
³⁶ Then he struck down all the firstborn in their land,
    the firstfruits of all their manhood.

³⁷ He brought out Israel, laden with silver and gold,
    and from among their tribes no one faltered.^y
³⁸ Egypt was glad when they left,
    because dread of Israel had fallen on them.
³⁹ He spread out a cloud as a covering,*
    and a fire to give light at night.^z
⁴⁰ They asked, and he brought them quail^a
    and satisfied them with the bread of heaven.*
⁴¹ He opened the rock, and water gushed out;^b
    like a river it flowed in the desert.*

---

x Ex 10:1-20; Joel 1:4.—y Ex 3:21-22; 12:33-36.—z Ps 78:14; Ex 13:21-22; Wis 18:3; 1 Co 10:1.—a Ps 78:24-28; Ex 16:13-15; Nu 11:31ff; Wis 16:20; Jn 6:31.—b Ps 78:15-16; Ex 17:1-7; Nu 20:11; 1 Co 10:4.

105:39 *As a covering:* the psalmist indicates that the cloud symbolizing God's presence served as a protection for the people against the sun, somewhat like his shading wings (see note on Ps 17:8). Other functions of the cloud given are: to guide the people in the wilderness (see Ps 78:14; Ex 13:21; Nu 9:17; Ne 9:12), to protect the people from the Egyptians as a cover of darkness (see Ex 14:19f), and to insulate them from the glorious manifestations of God's overwhelming presence (see Ex 16:10; Nu 11:25; Dt 31:15; 1 Ki 8:11).

105:40 *Bread of heaven:* the psalmist names it thusly because it was the immediate gift of the heavenly Father in contrast to the ordinary natural bread. See also note on Ps 78:25 and Christ's use of this phrase in Jn 6:31.

105:41 The psalmist concludes his account of God's saving deeds for Israel with one of the most admired of them: creating a river of water from a rock in the wilderness (see Ps 114:8; Isa 43:19f).

⁴² For he remembered his holy promise
    given to his servant Abraham.
⁴³ He brought out his people with rejoicing,
    his chosen ones with shouts of joy;*
⁴⁴ he gave them the lands of the nations,ᶜ
    and they fell heir to what others had toiled
        for—
⁴⁵ that they might keep his preceptsᵈ
    and observe his laws.

Praise the LORD.ʸ

PSALM 106*

Israel's Confession of Sin and
God's Mercy

¹ Praise the LORD.ᶻ

Give thanks* to the LORD, for he is good;
    his love endures forever.ᵉ

---

y Hebrew *Hallelu Yah.*—z Hebrew *Hallelu Yah*; also in verse 48.

---

c Dt 4:37-40; Jos 11:16-23.—d Ps 78:5-7; Dt 6:20-25; 7:8-11.—e Ps
100:5; 103:2; 107:1; 1 Ch 16:34; Jer 33:11; Da 3:89.

105:43 An allusion to the song of victory of Ex 15.
Ps 106 A beautiful acclamation opens this psalm, but from v. 6 onward the
tone changes. We enter into a liturgy of grief and take part in a national confession. It is, especially after the Exile, a psalm for times of distress (see Isa 63:7—
64:11; Ne 9:5-37). A repentant Israel evokes the sin of the ancestors, but only to
confess its own sin. The people continue the long succession of infidelities of
yesteryear. The meditation on Israel's history contrasts with the beautiful hymn of
Psalm 105. Taking his inspiration from Nu and Dt, the psalmist retains from the
past only the concatenation of sins: the ancestors doubted God (v. 7; see Ex
14:12), murmured in the wilderness (v. 14; see Ex 15:24; 16:3; 17:2), adored the
golden calf (v. 19; see Ex 32), balked at conquering the promised land (v. 24; see
Nu 14:3f), adopted pagan practices (vv. 28-35; see Nu 25; Jdg 2:1-5), and sacrificed to idols (vv. 36-38; see 1 Ki 16:34).
   Paul will later evoke how the flood of sin submerges humanity (see Ro 3:23).
But the history of sin is opposed to that of the love of God; the Lord always pardons and delivers his people. On recalling such goodness, the community of his
people gathered together acknowledges its sins and begs God to save it.
   In praying this psalm, Christians recall that the wonders of God's mercy in
favor of his chosen people were simple preludes to the works of mercy that he accomplishes in Christ on behalf of sinful but believing humankind (see Ro 5:20).
Acknowledgment of sin opens the door to the experience of God's love.
   106:1 *Give thanks:* a liturgical call to praise (see Ps 107:1; 118:1, 29; 136:1-
3). *Love:* see note on Ps 6:4.

2 Who can proclaim the mighty acts of the
   Lord
   or fully declare his praise?*
3 Blessed are they who maintain justice,*f*
   who constantly do what is right.*
4 Remember me, O Lord, when you show
   favor to your people,*g*
   come to my aid when you save them,*
5 that I may enjoy the prosperity of your chosen ones,
   that I may share in the joy of your nation
   and join your inheritance in giving praise.

6 We have sinned, even as our fathers did;*h*
   we have done wrong and acted wickedly.*
7 When our fathers were in Egypt,
   they gave no thought to your miracles;
   they did not remember your many kind-
   nesses,
   and they rebelled by the sea, the Red Sea.*a*
8 Yet he saved them for his name's sake,*i*
   to make his mighty power known.*
9 He rebuked the Red Sea, and it dried up;
   he led them through the depths as through
   a desert.*j*

---

a Hebrew *Yam Suph*; that is, *Sea of Reeds*; also in verses 9 and 22.

f Isa 56:1-2; Hos 12:6.—g Ps 25:7; Ne 5:19; 13:14, 22, 31.—h 6-7: Ps 78:11-17; Ex 14:11; Lev 26:40; Jdg 3:7; 1 Ki 8:47; Ne 1:7; Bar 2:12; Da 9:5.—i Ps 80:3; Eze 36:20-22.—j Ps 18:15; 89:9; Ex 14:21-31; Isa 50:2; 63:11-14; Na 1:4.

106:2 *His praise:* see note on Ps 9:1.
106:3 The Lord expects his people to persevere in righteousness and justice, because they thus establish his kingdom (see Ps 15:1-5; 99:4; Isa 11:3-5; 33:15-17). *Blessed:* see note on Ps 1:1.
106:4 *When you save them:* another translation is: "with your salvation."
106:6-12 The psalmist sketches the people's lack of faith and rebellion at the Red Sea (see Ex 14—15).
106:6 This general theme (see Lev 26:40; 1 Ki 8:47; Da 9:5) is reprised by the Vulgate in Jud 7:29. *We:* the psalmist identifies himself with his sinful people.
106:8 A motive often ascribed to God by Ezekiel (see Eze 20:9, 14; 36:21f; 39:25).

10 He saved them from the hand of the foe;
     from the hand of the enemy he redeemed
       them.
11 The waters covered their adversaries;
     not one of them survived.
12 Then they believed his promises[k]
     and sang his praise.*

13 But they soon forgot what he had done*
     and did not wait for his counsel.
14 In the desert they gave in to their craving;
     in the wasteland they put God to the test.[l]
15 So he gave them what they asked for,
     but sent a wasting disease upon them.[m]

16 In the camp they grew envious of Moses*
     and of Aaron, who was consecrated to the
       LORD.[n]
17 The earth opened up and swallowed Dathan;
     it buried the company of Abiram.
18 Fire blazed among their followers;
     a flame consumed the wicked.

19 At Horeb they made a calf*
     and worshiped an idol cast from metal.[o]
20 They exchanged their Glory*
     for an image of a bull, which eats grass.

---

k Ex 14:31; 15:1-21.—l Ps 78:18; Ex 15:24; 16:3; Nu 11:1-6; 1 Co 10:9.—m Ps 78:26-31; Ex 16:13; Nu 11:33.—n 16-18: Lev 10:2; Nu 16:1-3; Dt 11:6; Isa 26:11.—o 16-20: Ex 32:1-9; Dt 9:8-21; Jer 2:11; Ac 7:41; Ro 1:23.

106:12 An allusion to Ex 15. Praise is the expression of faith in the divine word (see Ps 119:42, 65, 74, 81; 130:5).
106:13-15 The psalmist recalls the people's forgetfulness of the Lord in their craving for meat in the desert (see Nu 11).
106:16-18 The psalmist recounts the challenge to Moses' authority in the camp by Korah, Dathan, and Abiram (see Nu 16:1-35).
106:19-23 The psalmist recalls the people's worship of the golden calf at Sinai (see Ex 32; Dt 9:7-29; Hos 4:7; 9:10; 10:5).
106:20 *Glory:* none other than their Glorious one (see 1 Sa 15:29; Jer 2:11), their Savior-God (v. 21).

21 They forgot the God who saved them,
who had done great things in Egypt,[p]
22 miracles in the land of Ham*
and awesome deeds by the Red Sea.
23 So he said he would destroy them—
had not Moses, his chosen one,
stood in the breach* before him
to keep his wrath from destroying them.[q]

24 * Then they despised the pleasant land;*
they did not believe his promise.[r]
25 They grumbled in their tents
and did not obey the LORD.
26 So he swore to them with uplifted hand
that he would make them fall in the desert,
27 make their descendants fall among the nations
and scatter them throughout the lands.

28 They yoked themselves to the Baal of Peor*
and ate sacrifices offered to lifeless gods;[s]
29 they provoked the LORD to anger by their wicked deeds,
and a plague broke out among them.
30 But Phinehas stood up and intervened,
and the plague was checked.
31 This was credited to him as righteousness*
for endless generations to come.

---

p Ps 75:1; 78:42-58; Dt 32:18; Jer 2:32.—q Ex 32:11; Nu 11:2; Dt 9:25; Eze 22:30.—r 24-27: Lev 26:33; Nu 13:25—14:37; Dt 1:25-36; Eze 20:15, 23; Heb 3:18-19.—s 28-31: Ps 141:4; Nu 25; Dt 26:14; Sir 45:23-24.

106:22 *Land of Ham:* see note on Ps 78:51.

106:23 *Stood in the breach:* see Ex 32:11-14, 31f.

106:24-27 The psalmist tells of the people's refusal to capture Canaan via the southern route and their punishment of not entering the promised land (see Nu 13—14; Dt 1—2).

106:24 *Pleasant land:* see the description given in Jer 3:19; 12:10; Zec 7:14.

106:28-31 The psalmist recalls the people's apostasy and rebellion in worshiping the Baal of Peor (see Nu 25:1-10).

106:31 *Credited to him as righteousness:* reminiscent of Abraham's justification and that of the new People of God (see Ge 15:6; Ro 4:3, 23-25).

³² * By the waters of Meribah* they angered the
   LORD,ᵗ
      and trouble came to Moses because of
      them;
³³ for they rebelled against the Spirit of God,*
      and rash words came from Moses' lips.ᵇ

³⁴ They did not destroy the peoples*
      as the LORD had commanded them,ᵘ
³⁵ but they mingled with the nations
      and adopted their customs.ᵛ
³⁶ They worshiped their idols,
      which became a snare to them.ʷ
³⁷ They sacrificed their sons
      and their daughters to demons.*
³⁸ They shed innocent blood,
      the blood of their sons and daughters,
      whom they sacrificed to the idols of Canaan,
         and the land was desecrated by their
         blood.
³⁹ They defiled themselves by what they did;*
      by their deeds they prostituted themselves.

---

b Or *against his spirit. / and rash words came from his lips.*

t 32-33: Ps 95:8-9; 107:11; Ex 17:1-7; Nu 20:2-13; Dt 6:16; 33:8; Isa
63:10.—u Dt 7:1; Jos 9:15; Jdg 2:1-5.—v Lev 18:3; Jdg 1:27-35; 3:5; Ezr
9:1-2.—w 36-38: Ex 22:20; Lev 18:21; Nu 35:33; Dt 32:17; Jdg 2:11-13, 17,
19; 2 Ki 16:3; Bar 4:7; Eze 16:20-21; 1 Co 10:20.

106:32-33 The psalmist relives the people's quarreling with the Lord at
Meribah, which led Moses to sin (see Nu 20:1-13).
106:32 *Meribah:* see note on Ps 95:8. *Trouble came to Moses:* he was not allowed to enter the promised land because of his rash words (see Nu 20:12). Dt
1:37 indicates that Moses was not allowed to do so because of the people's sin,
not his own.
106:33 *Against the Spirit of God:* see NIV textual note for a literal translation.
The Old Testament indicates that the Spirit of God was present and at work in the
desert (see Ex 31:3; Nu 11:17; 24:2; Ne 9:20; Isa 63:10-14).
106:34-39 The psalmist indicts the mingling of the people with the pagan nations and their evil practices (such as idolatry, infant sacrifices, and injustice of
all kinds) from the time of the Judges to the Babylonian Exile.
106:37 *Demons:* i.e., pagan gods.
106:39 The people were made ritually unclean by the evils they practiced, and
the land was also defiled by their wickedness (see Nu 35:33f; Isa 24:5; Jer
3:1f, 9).

⁴⁰ Therefore the LORD was angry with his people*
    and abhorred his inheritance.
⁴¹ He handed them over to the nations,
    and their foes ruled over them.ˣ
⁴² Their enemies oppressed them
    and subjected them to their power.
⁴³ Many times he delivered them,
    but they were bent on rebellion
    and they wasted away in their sin.ʸ

⁴⁴ But he took note of their distress
    when he heard their cry;
⁴⁵ for their sake he remembered his covenant*
    and out of his great love he relented.ᶻ
⁴⁶ He caused them to be pitied
    by all who held them captive.

⁴⁷ Save us, O LORD our God,
    and gather us from the nations,
    that we may give thanks to your holy nameᵃ
    and glory in your praise.*

⁴⁸ Praise be to the LORD, the God of Israel,ᵇ
    from everlasting to everlasting.
    Let all the people say, "Amen!"

    Praise the LORD.*

---

x Jdg 2:14-23.—y Ne 9:28; Isa 63:7-9.—z Lev 26:42; Jer 42:10.—a Ps
28:9; 1 Ch 16:35.—b Ps 41:13; 72:18; 89:52; 1 Ch 16:36; Ne 9:5.

106:40-46 The psalmist recalls God's tempered judgment mingling chastisements and mercies.
106:45 *Remembered his covenant:* see Ps 105:8, 42; Ex 2:24; Lev 26:42, 45.
Love: see note on Ps 6:4.
106:47 The psalmist ends on a note of communal prayer for deliverance and
restoration from dispersion. The triumph of the Lord results in thanksgiving and
praise. *Praise:* see note on Ps 9:1.
106:48 This last verse does not belong to the psalm but is the doxology to
Book IV (see note on Ps 41:13). The doxology declares the praise of the Lord as
the God of Israel (see Lk 1:68). As his love endures forever (v. 1), so will his
praise from his people be "from everlasting to everlasting." In hope of deliverance and prosperity (vv. 4-5, 47), the People of God respond with an Amen (see 1
Ch 16:35f). *Praise the LORD:* i.e., "Hallelujah" or "Alleluia," which very likely belongs to the next psalm (see note on Ps 104:35).

BOOK V—PSALMS 107–150*

PSALM 107*

God, Savior of Those in Distress

¹ Give thanks to the LORD, for he is good;^c
    his love endures forever.*
² Let the redeemed of the LORD say this—
    those he redeemed from the hand of the foe,^d

---

c Ps 100:4-5; 106:1; 1 Ch 16:8; Jer 33:11.—d Ps 106:10; Isa 63:12.

Ps 107—150 Book V of the Psalter. Two collections are included in this final part: the pilgrimage chants or "Songs of Ascent" (Ps 120—134) and the Hallel or "Praise" psalms (113—118; 120—136; 146—150). In addition, we see a further group of psalms attributed to David (Ps 138—145). Jewish tradition also groups together Ps 113—118, known as the Egyptian Hallel, for use at the Passover. The "hymn" sung at the Last Supper (see Mk 14:26) was probably part of that Hallel.

Although cries of supplication still form part of the prayer of the psalmist, joy begins to radiate upon the face of the pilgrim who draws near to the Lord; the acclamation voiced in the presence of God will transform the conclusion of the Psalter into a prodigious symphony of happiness.

Ps 107 Even though this psalm is not part of Book IV, many believe that it was originally associated with Ps 105 and 106 and served as a kind of conclusion to the theme-related Ps 104—107. After the account of God's works in creation (see Ps 104:2-26) and his care for the animal world (see Ps 104:27-30) it recounts God's "wonderful deeds for men" (Ps 107:8).

Ps 107 is a thanksgiving for "God's deliverances." Persons in distress have cried out to him and obtained help: wandering voyagers (vv. 4-9), prisoners (vv. 10-16), the sick (vv. 17-22), and the shipwrecked (vv. 23-32). The Lord reverses situations as he pleases (vv. 33-41), but only the believer can discern the divine action. Beneath the concrete life of the era, evoked at times with humor (vv. 26-27 remind us that the Israelites were not very seaworthy), we see the history of the chosen people: the journeys of the Exodus and the Exile, their temptations and their sins.

Visibly the author takes his inspiration from the Book of Consolation (see Isa 40—55) and the writings of the sages (see Job; Wis 16). Thanksgivings that are at first private ultimately express the gratitude of an entire people. For the believer, the events become signs: they invite him to discover in his life and that of the community of peoples a secret presence of God.

Christians pray this psalm to praise the Father for redeeming us in Christ. We have been saved by him from the hand of the infernal oppressor, gathered by him into the Church, and delivered by his love from the spiritual death to which we were doomed by the state in which Satan bound us and which was symbolized by the image of the desert, captivity, sickness, and the storm.

107:1 A conventional cry of praise in the liturgy of the temple often cited in the Old Testament (see Ps 106:1; 118:1; 136:1; 1 Ch 16:34; 1 Mac 4:24; Jer 33:11; Da 3:89). *Love:* see note on Ps 6:4.

³ those he gathered from the lands,*ᵉ
   from east and west, from north and south.ᶜ

⁴ Some wandered in desert wastelands,*
   finding no way to a city where they could
      settle.ᶠ
⁵ They were hungry and thirsty,
   and their lives ebbed away.ᵍ
⁶ Then they cried out to the LORD in their trou-
      ble,
   and he delivered them from their distress.
⁷ He led them by a straight wayʰ
   to a city where they could settle.ⁱ
⁸ Let them give thanks to the LORD for his un-
      failing love
   and his wonderful deeds for men,*
⁹ for he satisfies the thirsty
   and fills the hungry with good things.ʲ

¹⁰ Some sat in darkness and the deepest
      gloom,*
   prisoners suffering in iron chains,*

---

c Hebrew *north and the sea.*

e Ne 1:9; Isa 43:5-6; 49:12; Zec 8:7.—f Dt 8:15; 32:10; Jos 5:6.—g Ex 16:3; Isa 49:10.—h Ezr 8:21; Isa 35:8; 40:3; 43:19.—i Dt 6:10.—j Isa 49:10; 55:1; Lk 1:53.

107:3 *From the lands:* e.g., Assyria, Babylonia, Egypt, and Moab, into which the catastrophe of 587 B.C. had dispersed the chosen people (see 2 Ki 17:6; 24:12-16; Jer 52:28-30; Isa 11:11f; 43:5f). *South:* literally, "[the] sea."
107:4-9 The psalmist evokes the Lord's deliverances of his people from the desert in which they were lost, hungry, thirsty, and exhausted, especially during the Exodus (see Jos 5:6), which prefigured the just completed return from the Exile (see Ne 1:3). Jesus would later indicate that he delivered people from the same four situations as the Way to the Father (see Jn 14:6), the Bread of Heaven (see Jn 6:41), the Water of Life (see Jn 4:14), and the Giver of Rest (see Mt 11:28).
107:8 This refrain is repeated in vv. 15, 21, 31. *Wonderful deeds:* see note on Ps 9:1 concerning God's "wonders."
107:10-16 The psalmist evokes God's deliverance of his people from foreign bondage, especially in the return from the Exile (see Isa 43:5f; 49:12; Zec 8:7f). In addition, guilt, darkness, grinding toil, and the constriction of chains, gates, and bars are apt figures for the fallen state of human beings.
107:10 See Ps 105:18; 149:8; Isa 42:7; 49:9. The Exile was a chastisement (see Lev 26:41ff; Job 33:19; 36:8ff; Pr 3:12), announced by the Prophets.

11 for they had rebelled against the words of
   God
       and despised the counsel of the Most
       High.ᵏ

12 So he subjected them to bitter labor;*
       they stumbled, and there was no one to
       help.ˡ

13 Then they cried to the LORD in their trouble,
       and he saved them from their distress.

14 He brought them out of darkness and the
   deepest gloom
       and broke away their chains.ᵐ

15 Let them give thanks to the LORD for his unfailing love
       and his wonderful deeds for men,

16 for he breaks down gates of bronze
       and cuts through bars of iron.

17 Some became fools through their rebellious
   ways*
       and suffered affliction because of their in-
       iquities.

18 They loathed all foodⁿ
       and drew near the gates of death.*

19 Then they cried to the LORD in their trouble,
       and he saved them from their distress.

20 He sent forth his word* and healed them;
       he rescued them from the grave.º

---

k Ps 5:10; Job 36:8-9; Pr 1:25; Isa 42:7, 22.—l Ps 106:43; Lev 26:40-
41.—m Isa 42:7; 49:9; 51:14; Lk 1:79.—n Job 6:6-7; 17:16; 33:20.—o Ps
147:15; Dt 32:2; Wis 16:12; Isa 55:11; Mt 8:8; Lk 7:7.

107:12 *Subjected them to bitter labor:* literally, "humbled their heart with
labor," i.e., a labor that broke their spirit.
107:17-22 The psalmist evokes God's deliverance of his people from the chastisement of sickness unto death incurred because of sin.
107:18 *Gates of death:* metaphorical description for death (see Ps 9:13; 88:3)
in keeping with the ancient custom of picturing the realm of death as a city in
the netherworld with a series of gates that prevented return to the land of the
living (see Job 38:17; Mt 16:18).
107:20 The "word" is here personified as God's messenger of healing and deliverance from the "grave" (see Ps 147:15; Job 33:23ff; Wis 16:12; Isa 55:11; Mt
8:8; Jn 1:1).

21 Let them give thanks to the LORD for his unfailing love
and his wonderful deeds for men.
22 Let them sacrifice thank offerings
and tell of his works with songs of joy.

23 Others went out on the sea in ships;*
they were merchants on the mighty waters.[p]
24 They saw the works of the LORD,*
his wonderful deeds in the deep.
25 For he spoke and stirred up a tempest
that lifted high the waves.[q]
26 They mounted up to the heavens and went down to the depths;
in their peril their courage melted away.
27 They reeled and staggered like drunken men;
they were at their wits' end.[r]
28 Then they cried out to the LORD in their trouble,
and he brought them out of their distress.
29 He stilled the storm to a whisper;
the waves of the sea were hushed.[s]
30 They were glad when it grew calm,
and he guided them to their desired haven.
31 Let them give thanks to the LORD for his unfailing love
and his wonderful deeds for men.
32 Let them exalt him in the assembly of the people
and praise him in the council of the elders.*

---

p Sir 43:25; Isa 42:10.—q Ps 93:3; Jnh 1:4.—r Isa 19:14; 29:9.—s Ps 65:7; 89:9; Isa 43:2; Mt 8:26 par.

107:23-32 The psalmist evokes God's deliverance of his people from the perils of the sea.

107:24-29 The merchants who cross the seas in search of wealth witness God's wonderful deeds at sea (see Ps 104:24-26) and his ability to calm a storm on the surging waters (see Ps 65:7; 77:19).

107:32 The merchants are urged to render worship to God by declaring, both in communal worship and in places of leadership, what he has done for them.

33 He turned rivers into a desert,*
    flowing springs into thirsty ground,*t
34 and fruitful land into a salt waste,u
    because of the wickedness of those who
        lived there.*
35 He turned the desert into pools of water
    and the parched ground into flowing
        springs;v
36 there he brought the hungry to live,*
    and they founded a city where they could
        settle.w
37 They sowed fields and planted vineyards
    that yielded a fruitful harvest;x
38 he blessed them, and their numbers greatly
        increased,
    and he did not let their herds diminish.y

39 Then their numbers decreased, and they were
        humbled
    by oppression, calamity and sorrow;
40 he who pours contempt on nobles
    made them wander in a trackless waste.z
41 But he lifted the needy out of their affliction
    and increased their families like flocks.a
42 The upright see and rejoice,
    but all the wicked* shut their mouths.b

---

t Ps 74:15; Isa 35:7; 42:15; 50:2.—u Ge 13:10; 19:23-28; Dt 29:23; Sir
39:23.—v Ps 114:8; 2 Ki 3:17; Isa 41:18.—w Eze 36:35.—x 2 Ki 19:29; Isa
65:21; Jer 31:5.—y Dt 7:13-14; Isa 49:21.—z Job 12:21, 23-25.—a Ps
113:7-9; Job 5:16.—b Ps 58:10; 63:11; Ro 3:19.

107:33-42 The psalmist evokes God's deliverance of his people by a "reversal
of fortune."
   107:33-35 Imagery like that found in Isa 35:6f; 41:18; 42:15; 43:19f; 50:2.
   107:34 Allusion to Sodom and Gomorrah (see Ge 13:10; 19; Dt 29:22; Sir
39:23). Salt was cast on cities that had been destroyed (see Jdg 9:45).
   107:36-41 These verses are written in general terms; however, scholars believe the psalmist is most likely referring here to the settlement and development
of the promised land (vv. 36ff), the hardships during the Assyrian and Babylonian invasions (v. 39), the humiliation and exile of the last kings of Judah (v. 40),
and the restoration of Zion after the Exile (v. 41).
   107:42 *Upright . . . wicked:* a comparison often made in the Old Testament
(see Pr 2:21f; 11:6f; 12:6; 14:11; 15:8; 21:18; 29:27).

⁴³ Whoever is wise, let him heed these things[c]
and consider the great love of the LORD.*

PSALM 108*

Prayer for Divine Assistance
against Enemies

A song. A psalm of David.

¹ My heart is steadfast, O God;*
I will sing and make music with all my
soul.*[d]
² Awake, harp and lyre![e]
I will awaken the dawn.*
³ I will praise you, O LORD, among the nations;*
I will sing of you among the peoples.[f]
⁴ For great is your love, higher than the heavens;
your faithfulness reaches to the skies.[g]

---

c Hos 14:9.—d 1-5: Ps 57:7-11.—e Job 21:12; 38:12.—f Ps 9:11; 18:49;
148:13.—g Ps 36:5; 71:19; Nu 14:18.

107:43 This conclusion transforms the hymn of thanksgiving and praise into a
wisdom psalm. The righteous will become wise by studying the Lord's deliverances of his people.

Ps 108 Two fragments of psalms (with very slight modifications) have been
used to make up this song of praise (Ps 57:7-11 and Ps 60:6-12), which Israel
proclaims as it awaits liberation. We see the Lord already rallying all his children
and taking the lead of their combat, as in the past, to enable them to gain redress against their enemies. This song of martial confidence will become a canticle of hope inculcating joy and praise, for the glory of God will fill all humankind.

Christians can make use of this psalm to thank God for the redemption and
for the constant victories that he enables us to obtain over our spiritual enemies
by the aid of our Redeemer.

108:1-5 The psalmist offers praise to God's love, which gives him steadfast
hope.

108:1 The psalmist is at peace because of his trust in the Lord. _Heart:_ see
note on Ps 4:7. _O God:_ after this phrase, some mss repeat the words "my heart is
steadfast." _With all my soul:_ another possible translation is: "awake, my soul."

108:2 _Dawn:_ personified as in Ps 139:9; Job 3:9; 38:12. The psalmist wishes to
waken the dawn, for that is the usual time when deliverance comes from the Lord
(see notes on Ps 17:15 and 57:8).

108:3-4 A vow to offer ritual praise to the Lord for his goodness (see note on
Ps 7:17).

5 Be exalted, O God, above the heavens,
    and let your glory be over all the earth.

6 Save us and help us with your right hand,*
    that those you love may be delivered.
7 God has spoken from his sanctuary:*h*
    "In triumph I will parcel out Shechem*
    and measure off the Valley of Succoth.
8 Gilead is mine, Manasseh is mine;
    Ephraim is my helmet,*
    Judah my scepter.
9 Moab is my washbasin,*
    upon Edom I toss my sandal;
    over Philistia I shout in triumph."*i*

10 Who will bring me to the fortified city?*
    Who will lead me to Edom?
11 Is it not you, O God, you who have rejected
    us*
    and no longer go out with our armies?*j*
12 Give us aid against the enemy,
    for the help of man is worthless.
13 With God we will gain the victory,
    and he will trample down our enemies.

---

h 7-13: Ps 60:6-12.—i Ge 19:37; Ru 4:7-8.—j Ps 44:9.

108:6-13 The psalmist prays for God's help against his enemies.

108:7-9 *Shechem* was west of the Jordan, and *Succoth* east of it; therefore, they indicate dominion over all Palestine. Next are named four Israelite tribes; hence, there are three regions in all that must be reduced to subjection.

108:8 *Helmet:* a symbol of the strength exhibited by the tribe of Ephraim (see Dt 33:17; Jdg 7:24—8:3). *Scepter:* a symbol of the King-Messiah who had been promised from Judah (see Ge 49:10).

108:9: *Moab is my washbasin:* i.e., its people will do menial work for the Israelites (see Ge 18:4). *Toss my sandal:* an Eastern way of signifying possession.

108:10 *Fortified city:* doubtless Bozrah in Idumea (see Isa 34:6; 63:1; Am 1:12). It was from this inaccessible refuge that the Edomites sent incursions into Judea.

108:11-12 The psalmist looks to the Lord rather than other human beings for an answer to the people's problems. He calls upon him to end his abandonment and lead his people to victory over their enemies. Indeed, he believes the Lord is still with them and will bring them through this trial with strength, joy, and success (see Ps 44:5; 118:15f).

PSALM 109*

Prayer for One Falsely Accused

For the director of music. Of David. A psalm.

¹ O God, whom I praise,*
    do not remain silent,ᵏ
² for wicked and deceitful men
    have opened their mouths against me;*
    they have spoken against me with lying
    tongues.
³ With words of hatred they surround me;
    they attack me without cause.
⁴ In return for my friendship they accuse me,
    but I am a man of prayer.*
⁵ They repay me evil for good,
    and hatred for my friendship.ˡ

---

k Ps 35:22; 83:1; Jer 17:14.—l Ps 35:12; 38:20; Ge 44:4; Pr 17:13; Jer 18:20.

Ps 109 The Psalter contains other cries of hatred or revenge (e.g., Ps 9; 35; 137; 139), but none is harsher than this one (vv. 6-19). It is ordinarily attributed to the psalmist who has been speaking from the beginning of the psalm. However, an attentive examination of the context leads some scholars to attribute these imprecations to another person—most likely, the leader of the psalmist's enemies.

It is a fact, of course, that in the East people enjoy exaggerated expressions, and it is also a fact that it was written before the Christian faith changed the harsh law of revenge or law of talion. But the Gospel itself contains curses (see Mt 23:13-26; Lk 6:24-26), and while it is true that Jesus and the apostles were able to forgive their enemies, they also saw the "ancient serpent" (Rev 12:9) at work, against God's will and for their destruction.

In taking up these imprecatory psalms, the Church invites Christians to commence an unceasing struggle against the spirit of evil (see Eph 6:12). Except for a few details, the formulas of this prayer were suitable for Jesus to express his own situation and sentiments and to describe the attitude and machinations of his enemies. In fact, the evangelists record that his enemies fulfilled certain passages to the letter (e.g., v. 25; see Mt 27:39; Mk 15:20).

The words *For the director of music* in the superscription are thought to be a musical or liturgical notation.

109:1-5 This psalmist has never said and done anything other than good; will betrayal, hatred, and slander be his recompense? Bitter is the calumny that crushes the righteous.

109:2 *Opened their mouths against me:* see note on Ps 5:9.

109:4 *But I am a man of prayer:* he is not a man of evil and slander; he even prays for his foes (as in Ps 35:13f).

6 * Appoint*ᵈ an evil manᵉ to oppose him;
   let an accuserᶠ stand at his right hand.
7 When he is tried, let him be found guilty,
   and may his prayers condemn him.*
8 May his days be few;
      may another take his place* of leader-
      ship.ᵐ
9 May his children be fatherless
   and his wife a widow.ⁿ
10 May his children be wandering beggars;
      may they be drivenᵍ from their ruined
      homes.
11 May a creditor seize all he has;
      may strangers plunder the fruits of his
      labor.
12 May no one extend kindness to him*
   or take pity on his fatherless children.
13 May his descendants be cut off,
      their names blotted out from the next gen-
      eration.ᵒ
14 May the iniquity of his fathers be remem-
      bered before the LORD;
      may the sin of his mother never be blotted
      out.ᵖ

---

d Or *They say:* "Appoint (with quotation marks at the end of verse 19).—
e Or *the Evil One.*—f Or *let Satan.*—g Septuagint; Hebrew *sought.*

---

m Job 15:32; Ac 1:20.—n Ex 22:24; Jer 18:21.—o Ps 21:10; Job 18:19;
Pr 10:7.—p Ex 20:5; Jer 18:23.

109:6-15 Pitiless are the words of those who curse the innocent psalmist; he
has taken them to heart and remembered every one. See note on Ps 5:10 concerning redress for wrongs.

109:6 *Appoint:* or (as in alternative translation in NIV textual note) *They say:*
"Appoint . . ." (with closing quotation marks after v. 19). *Evil man:* or "the evil
one." *Accuser:* i.e., a "satan" (see Job 1:6), a name later given to the devil (see 1
Ch 21:1). He stood as an advocate (v. 31) at the right of the accused (see Zec
3:1).

109:7 *May his prayers condemn him:* another possible translation is: "may his
pleas be in vain."

109:8 *Another take his place:* applied to Judas in Ac 1:20.

109:12-13 The Law, the Prophets, and the Gospel all give warnings of what
the sins of fathers can bring down upon the children (see Ex 20:5; 1 Sa 2:31ff; Lk
19:41ff). *Names blotted out:* see note on Ps 69:28.

15 May their sins always remain before the
LORD,[q]
that he may cut off the memory of them
from the earth.[r]

16 For he never thought of doing a kindness,*
but hounded to death the poor
and the needy and the brokenhearted.
17 He loved to pronounce a curse—*
may it[h] come on him;
he found no pleasure in blessing—
may it be[i] far from him.
18 He wore cursing as his garment;
it entered into his body like water,
into his bones like oil.
19 May it be like a cloak wrapped about him,
like a belt tied forever around him.
20 May this be the LORD's payment* to my accusers,
to those who speak evil of me.

21 But you, O Sovereign LORD,*
deal well with me for your name's sake;*
out of the goodness of your love, deliver
me.

---

h Or *curse, / and it has.*—i Or *blessing, / and it is.*

---

q Ps 90:8.—r Ps 34:16; Ex 17:14.

109:16-20 No other place expresses with such vivid intensity the terrible logic of judgment whereby what humans choose they ultimately receive to the full.

109:17 *Curse:* see note on Ps 10:7.

109:20 *Payment:* the Hebrew word means either "work done" or "wages for work done." Accordingly, the preceding curses may be understood as spoken either by the psalmist against his primary foe or by his enemies first and then willed by him to recoil against them. Another translation for the verse is also possible: "This is the work of those who wish to call down harm upon me from the LORD." In that case, the only imprecations of the psalmist would be the mild ones in v. 29.

109:21-31 The poem seems to begin again at this point. The poor man once again invokes God, reveals his distress, asks for health, cries out his imprecations, and promises to give thanks. It is the rhythm of the prayer of a persecuted person. It testifies to a conviction: in the time of God's judgment, the evil one will return in defeat to the world of darkness where he willed to swallow up everything, but the righteous will obtain access to the glory of the Lord.

109:21 *For your name's sake:* see note on Ps 5:11. *Love:* see note on Ps 6:4.

22 For I am poor and needy,*
   and my heart is wounded within me.
23 I fade away* like an evening shadow;
   I am shaken off like a locust.
24 My knees give way from fasting;*s*
   my body is thin and gaunt.
25 I am an object of scorn to my accusers;
   when they see me, they shake their heads.*

26 Help me, O Lord my God;
   save me in accordance with your love.*
27 Let them know that it is your hand,
   that you, O Lord, have done it.
28 They may curse, but you will bless;
   when they attack they will be put to
      shame,
   but your servant will rejoice.*
29 My accusers will be clothed with disgrace
   and wrapped in shame as in a cloak.

30 With my mouth I will greatly extol the Lord;*t*
   in the great throng I will praise him.*
31 For he stands at the right hand of the needy
      one,
   to save his life from those who condemn
      him.*

---

s 24-25: Ps 22:6-7; 69:10-12.—t Ps 71:22; 111:1.

109:22 *Poor and needy:* see note on Ps 22:26. *Heart:* see note on Ps 4:7.

109:23 *I fade away:* the psalmist's illness draws the scorn of enemies (see note on Ps 5:9). *Like an evening shadow:* similar to Ps 102:11. *Shaken off like a locust:* allusion to the custom of brushing locusts off the plants in order to kill them on the ground. Another translation possible is: "swept away like a locust," an image similar to Job 30:22; in Palestine a strong wind sometimes ends a plague of locusts by blowing them out into the sea (see Ex 10:19; Joel 2:20).

109:25 His accusers seek the psalmist's downfall by casting scorn on him (see Ps 31:11; 79:4; 89:41) and by rejecting him ("[shaking] their heads": see Ps 22:7; Mt 27:39).

109:26 *Love:* see note on Ps 6:4.

109:28 This is a good prayer to turn the edge of an attack (see Ro 8:31ff).

109:30 A vow to praise the Lord for his deliverance (see note on Ps 7:17).

109:31 The final verse puts everything in perspective—replacing the figure of the "accuser," who stands at the right hand of his victim to accuse him, with the figure of God who "stands at the right hand of the needy one" to save him.

PSALM 110*

The Messiah—King, Prophet, and Conqueror

Of David. A psalm.

¹ The LORD says to my Lord:
  "Sit at my right hand^u
until I make your enemies
    a footstool for your feet."*

² The LORD will extend your mighty scepter
    from Zion;
  you will rule in the midst of your enemies.*

---

u Jos 10:24; Mt 22:44; Mk 12:36; Ac 2:34-35; 1 Co 15:25; Heb 1:13; 8:1; 10:12-13; 1 Pe 3:22.

Ps 110 These few surprising verses (which comprise essentially two oracles) became the supreme Messianic psalm in both the Jewish and the Christian traditions. It was so much used and adapted down the centuries before becoming part of the Psalter that it is difficult to reconstruct completely the original text. In its oldest version it certainly goes back to the earliest times of the monarchy.

The psalm was subsequently revised, perhaps on various occasions; the song no longer refers to the kings who are passing away but to the Messiah who is to come at the end of the earthly time and restore everything in the name of God. He will be of royal birth (see 2 Sa 7:16) and will be charged with judging the nations and ruling over the entire world. He will not be counted among the princes of the nations, who have their power from human beings, for God himself will invest him as everlasting King and Priest, as is shown by the parallel with the mysterious Melchizedek, priest and king of Salem, whose earthly ancestry no one knows (see Ge 14:18; Heb 7:3).

Jesus, who claims to be the Christ, that is, the Messiah, and Son of God, fulfills the promise given in this psalm, as he hints to the Pharisees (see Mt 22:42-45; 26:64); the apostles are inspired by this passage to proclaim the glory of the risen Christ, Lord of the universe (see Mk 16:19; Ac 2:33-35; Ro 8:34; 1 Co 15:25-28; Eph 1:20; Col 3:1; Heb 10:12f; 1 Pe 3:22). The author of the Letter to the Hebrews finds in this psalm the proof that Christ is superior to the priests of the Old Testament and that he alone is the Savior of humankind (Heb 7).

110:1 The first oracle (vv. 1-3) establishes God's anointed as his regent over all (see Ps 2:7-12). *The LORD says to my Lord:* a polite form of address from an inferior to a superior (see 1 Sa 25:25; 2 Sa 1:10). By the word "Lord," the court singer is referring to the king. Jesus in interpreting this psalm takes the psalmist to be David, who was acknowledged by all to be referring to the Messiah. Hence, the Messiah must be David's superior and not merely his son or descendant (see Mt 22:41-46 par). *Right hand:* the place of honor beside a king (see Ps 45:9; 1 Ki 2:19), in this case making the Messiah second to God himself (see Mt 26:64; Mk 14:62; 16:19; Lk 22:69; Ac 2:33; 5:31; 7:55f; Ro 8:34; Eph 1:20; Col 3:1; Heb 1:3; 8:1; 10:12; 12:2). *Footstool for your feet:* see 1 Co 15:25; Eph 1:22; Heb 10:12f.

110:2 The Messiah is the Lord's regent over his emerging kingdom.

³ ᵛ Your troops will be willing
    on your day of battle.
  Arrayed in holy majesty,
    from the womb of the dawn
    you will receive the dew of your youth.*ʲ

⁴ The LORD has sworn
    and will not change his mind:
  "You are a priest forever,ʷ
    in the order of Melchizedek."*

⁵ The LORD is at your right hand;*
    he will crush kings on the day of his wrath.*ˣ

---

j Or *your young men will come to you like the dew.*

v Vulgate text (note 110:3): Ps 2:7; 89:27; Ex 15:11; Isa 49:1; Mic 5:7.—
w Ps 89:35; 132:11; Ge 14:18; Nu 23:19; Heb 5:6; 7:21.—x Ps 2:9; 16:8;
Rev 2:27; 12:5; 19:15.

110:3 The NIV translation (in contrast with most Catholic editions) follows the current Hebrew, which is obscure and seems to be corrupt. It refers to numerous royal troops at the Messiah's command. The people come voluntarily on the day of battle, as in the days of Deborah (see Jdg 5:2, 9). They consecrate themselves, are fully prepared, and place themselves at his service. They will be as abundant as the dew at dawn. The image is close to those of Paul about "living sacrifices" (Ro 12:1) or a life poured out like a "drink offering" (Php 2:17). It should be noted that, even not considering the linguistic difficulties that argue against this reading and the fact that the Septuagint of pre-Christian times already confirms the text of the Vulgate, the Hebrew reading does not fit the great theme of the psalm as well as the Latin translation does. Every connection with the central thought that speaks of the royal and priestly dignity of Melchizedek is missing.

The usual Catholic translation comes from the revised Latin Vulgate, which is based on the ancient versions: "Yours is royal dignity in the day of your birth, in holy splendor; / before the daystar, like the dew, I have begotten you." *Before the daystar:* when the sun had not yet been created, i.e., from all eternity. *Like the dew:* in a secret, mysterious manner. Hence, the Messiah and Son of God existed before the dawn of creation in eternity.

110:4 The prophet-psalmist pronounces a second divine oracle, guaranteed by an oath. The Lord makes his king his chief priest of life, according to the order and image of Melchizedek. There are three main points of resemblance between Melchizedek and Christ. Both are kings as well as priests, both offer bread and wine to God, and both have their priesthood directly from God (see Ge 14:18; Heb 7). For a prophetic vision of the glorious union of the Messiah-Priest, see Zec 6:13; for the New Testament application, see Heb 5:6-10; 7:22. *Forever:* perhaps alluded to in Jn 12:34.

110:5 *The LORD is at your right hand:* when the king goes out to battle, the Lord, as the Master of the universe, is right with him, and crushing the foes.

⁶ He* will judge the nations, heaping up the dead
   and crushing the rulers of the whole earth.
⁷ He will drink from a brook beside the way;ᵏ
   therefore he will lift up his head.*ʸ

PSALM 111*ˡ

Praise of God for His Wondrous Works

¹ Praise the LORD.ᵐ

I will extol the LORD with all my heart
   in the council of the upright* and in the as-
      sembly.ᶻ

² Great are the works of the LORD;*
   they are pondered by all who delight in
      them.

---

k Or / *The One who grants succession will set him in authority.*—l This
psalm is an acrostic poem, the lines of which begin with the successive letters of the Hebrew alphabet.—m Hebrew *Hallelu Yah.*

y Ps 3:3; 27:6.—z Ps 34:1; 138:1.

110:6 *He:* the Messiah-King. *Heaping up the dead:* gory imagery symbolizing
full victory (see Ps 2:9; Rev 19:11-21) when God's judgment comes to pass.

110:7 Figurative language of uncertain meaning. Some see an allusion to a
rite of royal consecration at the spring of Gihon (see 1 Ki 1:33, 38). Others see an
image of the Messianic King bowing down in humility to drink of the waters of divine assistance before moving on to more victories (see Isa 8:6; Jer 2:13, 17f).

Ps 111 A sage sets forth the essence of the religion of Israel: the Lord has delivered his people in order to conclude a covenant with them and to reveal his will
to them. The author contemplates the divine "righteousness" (v. 3.), i.e., everything the Lord has done in favor of his chosen ones, the wonders that in some way
are renewed when they are recalled in the liturgy (v. 4): the miracle of the manna
and the quail (v. 5), the gift of the promised land (v. 6), and the stability of the
laws of the world and the moral order (v. 7). The sages who pursue this meditation
and observe the Law will be enabled to understand who God is: holy and re-
doubtable, compassionate and tender, so that they may render thanks to him.

In praying this psalm, we should keep in mind that the wonders to which it alludes are only a pale figure of the wonders that the Father has accomplished
through and in his Incarnate Son on behalf of his new people the Church (see Jn
5:20). After various physical cures and raisings from the dead, God works the
glorious Resurrection of his Son and our own spiritual resurrection in him (see
Eph 2:5f).

111:1 *Council of the upright:* probably a circle of friends and advisors (as in
Ps 107:32). *In the assembly:* in the temple (see Ps 149:1).

111:2 *Works of the LORD:* sometimes his deeds, as in v. 6, but more often the
things he has made (e.g., the heavens, Ps 8:3; 19:1; 102:25; and the earth, Ps
104:24). Made "in wisdom" (Ps 104:24), these lend themselves to meditation
and lead to delight.

3 Glorious and majestic are his deeds,*
   and his righteousness endures forever.
4 He has caused his wonders to be remem-
      bered;*
   the LORD is gracious and compassionate.ᵃ
5 He provides food for those who fear him;*
   he remembers his covenant forever.
6 He has shown his people the power of his
      works,
   giving them the lands* of other nations.
7 The works of his hands are faithful and just;*
   all his precepts are trustworthy.
8 They are steadfast for ever and ever,
   done in faithfulness and uprightness.
9 He provided redemption for his people;
   he ordained his covenant forever—
   holy and awesome is his name.*

10 The fear of the LORD is the beginning of wis-
      dom;*
   all who follow his precepts have good un-
      derstanding.
   To him belongs eternal praise.ᵇ

---

a Ps 103:8; 112:4; Dt 4:31.—b Dt 4:6; Pr 1:7; 9:10; Sir 1:16.

111:3 *Deeds:* probably his providential acts as in Dt 32:4. We should keep in mind that, as Isa 45:9-13 indicates, God's Creation and Providence are of one piece. *Righteousness:* as embodied in his deeds.
111:4 *Caused his wonders to be remembered:* by the celebration of annual feasts (see Ex 23:14), notably the Passover (for Christians, see 1 Cor 11:23-26). See also note on Ps 9:1. *Gracious and compassionate:* classic description of the meaning of God's name (see Ps 103:8; Ex 34:6f).
111:5 *Food for those who fear him:* probably a reference to the manna in the desert (see Ex 16:1ff), which in the New Testament is seen as a type of the Eucharist (see Jn 6:31-33, 49-51). The entire verse may also refer to God's giving of our daily bread (see Mt 6:11) and his daily forbearance. *His covenant:* see Ps 105:8-11.
111:6 *Lands:* literally, "inheritance, heritage."
111:7-8 There is complete harmony between what God does and what he says, between the "works of his hands" and "his precepts."
111:9 This verse recalls the miracles of the Exodus and the theophany at Sinai. *Name:* see note on Ps 5:11.
111:10 *The fear of the LORD is the beginning of wisdom:* the motto of the Wisdom writings (see Job 28:28; Pr 1:7; 9:10; Ecc 12:13; Sir 1:18, 24; 19:18). Here it refers to God especially as Creator, Redeemer, and Provider.

PSALM 112*[n]

The Blessings of the Righteous

[1] Praise the LORD.[o]

Blessed is the man who fears the LORD,[c]
    who finds great delight in his commands.*

[2] His children will be mighty in the land;
    the generation of the upright will be
    blessed.*
[3] Wealth and riches* are in his house,
    and his righteousness endures forever.

---

n This psalm is an acrostic poem, the lines of which begin with the successive letters of the Hebrew alphabet.—o Hebrew *Hallelu Yah*.

c Ps 1:1-2; 103:11; 119:1-2; 128:1.

Ps 112 This psalm provides the same literary characteristics as the preceding one and most likely stems from the same unknown author. By their theme the two chants complete one another. The first celebrates the divine perfections and works, while the second sings of the virtues and deeds of the true righteous person and the happiness he attains.

The ancients believed that the man who faithfully observed the Law and was solicitous of his neighbor was assured prosperity, posterity, and renown. In this psalm a sage once again praises the righteous in these terms, but he adds another more mystical religious sentiment. In effect, applying to the righteous the qualities that the preceding psalm attributed to the Lord, he wishes to show that by dint of placing his delight in the will of the Lord, the righteous man ends up resembling him. Hence, the Law is not a burden imposed from without but a power that transforms the heart. To obey is to let oneself be invaded by the sentiments of God: mercy, tenderness, and righteousness. Is there any other source of happiness?

This psalm is also very suitable for describing the Christian ideal, the perfection we must achieve in the steps of the Master and the happiness we will find therein.

112:1 Blessed is the man who follows unswervingly God's will and call. *Blessed:* see note on Ps 1:1. *Fears the LORD:* see note on Ps 15:2-5.

112:2 The upright man is blessed in his children and brings blessings on them (see Ps 37:26; 127:3-5; 128:3).

112:3 *Wealth and riches:* see Ps 1:3; 128:2. *His righteousness:* i.e., his happiness, his successes, and his well-being. There is a tacit comparison of the upright person's righteousness to God's (they both "endure forever": see Ps 111:3b). Some scholars translate the word "righteousness" as "generosity," claiming that the original meaning of the Hebrew word in a later period of the language also acquired the meaning of "liberality, almsgiving" (see Sir 3:30; 7:10; Mt 6:1).

4 Even in darkness light dawns for the upright,*[d]
for the gracious and compassionate and righteous man.[p]
5 Good* will come to him who is generous and lends freely,
who conducts his affairs with justice.
6 Surely he will never be shaken;*
a righteous man will be remembered forever.[e]
7 He will have no fear of bad news;
his heart is steadfast, trusting in the LORD.
8 His heart is secure, he will have no fear;
in the end he will look in triumph on his foes.
9 He has scattered abroad his gifts to the poor,
his righteousness endures forever;[f]
his horn[q] will be lifted high in honor.*

10 The wicked man will see and be vexed,
he will gnash his teeth and waste away;
the longings of the wicked will come to nothing.*

p Or / *for the LORD is gracious and compassionate and righteous.*—q *Horn* here symbolizes dignity.

d Ps 18:28; 37:6; 97:11; Pr 13:9; Isa 58:18.—e Ps 15:5; Pr 10:7; Wis 8:13.—f Ps 89:17; Pr 22:9; 2 Co 9:9.

112:4 The goodness of the righteous man overflows to others. He acts in the same way as God does (see Ps 111:4b). This is brought out more clearly by the more usual Catholic rendition: "He dawns through the darkness, a light for the upright; / he is gracious and compassionate and righteous."

112:5 *Good:* i.e., well-being and prosperity (see Ps 34:8-14). Good is also the quality of the righteous man. He is good in that he "is generous and lends freely" (see Ps 34:8-10; 37:21). Just as the Lord is "faithful and just" in all his acts (see Ps 111:7), so the upright man "conducts his affairs with justice."

112:6-8 The righteous man observes the precepts of God that are "steadfast for ever and ever" (Ps 111:8); hence "he will never be shaken" (v. 6) and "have no fear" (v. 7), for "his heart is secure" (v. 8). His trust is in the Lord in spite of "bad news," reasons to "fear," or problems with others (vv. 7-8).

112:9 As God's name is held in holy awe (see Ps 111:9), so the righteous will be held in honor. Paul uses this verse to support the principle that "whoever sows generously will also reap generously" (2 Co 9:6, 9). *Horn:* here symbolizes dignity.

112:10 The only alternative way of life to that of the righteous is bitter, transient, and futile.

THE EGYPTIAN HALLEL—Ps 113–118*

PSALM 113*

Praise of the Lord for His Care of the Lowly

¹ Praise the LORD.ʳ

Praise, O servants of the LORD,*
praise the name of the LORD.ᵍ

---

r Hebrew *Hallelu Yah;* also in verse 9.

---

g Ps 99:2; 148:13.

Ps 113—118 The *Hallel* ("praise") psalms are found in three separate collections: the "Egyptian Hallel," also known as the "Little Hallel" (113—118), the "Great Hallel" (120—136), and the "Concluding Hallel" (146—150). The Egyptian Hallel and the Great Hallel (most of which are pilgrimage psalms: 120—134) were sung during the annual feasts (see Lev 23; Nu 10:10). The Egyptian Hallel received a special place in the Passover liturgy; by custom 113—114 were recited or sung before the festive meal and 115—118 after it (see Mt 26:30; Mk 14:26). These were probably the last psalms Jesus sang before his Passion. Only the second (114) speaks directly of the Exodus, but the themes of the others make it an appropriate series to mark the salvation that began in Egypt and would spread to the nations. The concluding Hallel psalms (146—150) were incorporated into the daily prayers in the synagogue after the destruction of the temple in 70 A.D.

Ps 113 This psalm presents a surprising contrast in the praises of Israel: the acclamation of the glory of the Almighty One attains its summit, and certitude becomes even stronger that God is near to the lowly. His tenderness reaches those whom the powerful of the earth regard as nothing. The God of justice reverses established situations, as both the canticle of Hannah (see 1 Sa 2:4-8) and the Magnificat of Mary (see Lk 1:46-55) attest with equal intensity. In celebrating the salvation of the humiliated poor man and the abandoned woman, Israel keeps alive the hope of a wondrous renewal in the Messianic age (see Ps 76; 87; Isa 49:21; 54:1-8).

In praying this psalm, we are aware that the New Testament provides us with new motives for praising God the Father for the great condescension he manifests toward Zechariah, Mary, and those known as the poor of Yahweh. We can also chant this psalm in honor of the glorified Christ. Exalted by his Father above every earthly power and introduced by him into divine glory (Php 2:9-11; Heb 2:7-9), Christ shows himself to be incomparable by uniting to his supreme transcendence an astonishing condescension. It was toward the poor and lowly that he stooped during his public ministry, eating and drinking with them (see Mk 2:16), offering them the kingdom of God (see Mt 5:3-12) with its mysteries (see Mk 4:11), and making them the princes of his new people (see Mk 3:13-19). It is on the poor and the weak in the eyes of the world that he continues to confer his spiritual riches and powers (see 1 Co 1:26-28).

113:1 *Servants of the Lord:* devout worshipers, in particular the Levites (see Ps 134:1; 135:1; Da 3:85). *Name:* see note on Ps 5:11.

2 Let the name of the LORD be praised,*
   both now and forevermore.
3 From the rising of the sun to the place where
      it sets,
   the name of the LORD is to be praised.

4 The LORD is exalted over all the nations,*
   his glory above the heavens.[h]
5 Who is like the LORD our God,[i]
   the One who sits enthroned on high,
6 who stoops down to look
   on the heavens and the earth?

7 He raises the poor from the dust*
   and lifts the needy from the ash heap;[j]
8 he seats them with princes,
   with the princes of their people.
9 He settles the barren woman* in her home
   as a happy mother of children.[k]

   Praise the LORD.

---

h Ps 99:2; 148:13.—i 5-6: Ps 11:4; 89:6-8.—j Ps 35:10; 107:41; 1 Sa 2:8.—k 1 Sa 2:5; Isa 54:1.

113:2-3 The name of the Lord is to be proclaimed so that every generation may remember what he has done and how he has revealed himself (see Ex 3:16). This praise is to extend in time ("forevermore") and in space ("from the rising of the sun to the place where it sets," i.e., from east to west; see Mal 1:11).

113:4-6 The psalmist calls attention to the contrast: the exalted rule of the Lord and his accommodation to the needs of his people. *Over all the nations:* and by implication over all their gods (see Ps 95:3; 96:4f; 97:9). *Above the heavens:* above all creation.

113:7-9 The Lord does not ally himself with the high and mighty but takes care of the poor and needy by transforming them from outcasts of society ("the dust," see Isa 47:1, or "ash heap," see La 4:5) into those who have a position of prominence ("with the princes of their people," v. 8; see 1 Sa 2:8; Job 36:7). The afflicted man will be accorded recognition and the oppressed woman will be given honor.

113:9 *Barren woman:* a barren wife was considered cursed by God and a social outcast, a disappointment to her husband, to other women, and especially to herself (see Ge 16:2; 20:18; 1 Sa 1:6; 2:5; Lk 1:25). The Lord blesses her with children (see Ps 115:14; Isa 48:19; 54:1-3). *Praise the Lord:* probably was once the first line of Ps 114.

PSALM 114*

The Lord's Wonders at the Exodus

1 When Israel came out of Egypt,*
  the house of Jacob from a people of foreign
    tongue,
2 Judah became God's sanctuary,
  Israel his dominion.*l*

3 The sea looked and fled,*
  the Jordan turned back;*m*
4 the mountains skipped like rams,
  the hills like lambs.*n*

---

l Ex 19:6; Jer 2:3.—m Ps 66:6; 74:15; 77:16; Ex 14:21f; Jos 3:14.—n Ps 29:6; Jdg 5:5; Wis 19:9.

Ps 114 By reason of its literary composition and poetic inspiration this poem constitutes a little masterpiece. Felicitously, the poet personifies herein the elements of nature led in a dance by God during the Exodus, to make them keen-eyed witnesses of the Lord's triumphal march at the head of his people. Israel belongs so strongly to God that it is like his sanctuary and his dominion (v. 2). On an epic and triumphal tone, the people underline the time beyond compare when God established this destiny for them: it is the great adventure of their deliverance.

When the Lord passes by with his people, the sea and waters flee (see Ex 14:15-31; Jos 3:7-17), Sinai thunders and smokes (see Ex 19:16-18), the source springs forth in the desert rocks (see Ex 17:1-7; Nu 20:1-13). These remembrances of the Exodus are like the prelude to the upheaval of the universe announcing the coming of God at the end of the earthly ages.

We can pray this psalm in union with the Church ceaselessly meditating on and celebrating the privileged hour of her beginnings: the Passover of Christ that opens up for humankind a destiny of salvation in a new Exodus. Nature bows down before the divine Pioneer of this Exodus. The waters become calm and peaceful in the Sea of Galilee at a word from him: "Be still!" (Mk 4:39), while the mountains tremble at the moment of his Death and Resurrection (Mt 27:51; 28:2) as well as at the moment of his great interventions in history (see Rev 11:19; 16:18).

114:1-2 The deliverance from a foreign country was only a preamble to the greater deeds: the election of the chosen people and the making of the covenant on Sinai. Judah, the province of the tribe of that name, became the sanctuary of God and all Israel his kingdom; it was a theocracy, a priestly kingdom (see Ex 19:3-6; Jer 2:3). This was a grand event prefiguring the redemption to come and the birth of the Church.

114:3-4 The wonder of Israel's election as the People of God has its effect on the world of nature. The Red Sea and the Jordan River scurry around to make way for their Creator, and the mountains and hills are all animated and agog at his majestic coming (see Ps 18:7-15; 68:7ff; 77:16-19; Jdg 5:4f; Hab 3:3-10).

5 Why was it, O sea, that you fled,*
O Jordan, that you turned back,
6 you mountains, that you skipped like rams,
you hills, like lambs?

7 Tremble, O earth, at the presence of the LORD,*
at the presence of the God of Jacob,ᵒ
8 who turned the rock into a pool,
the hard rock into springs of water.ᵖ

PSALM 115*

Hymn to the Lord, the One God

1 * Not to us, O LORD, not to us*
but to your name be the glory,
because of your love and faithfulness.ᑫ

---

o Ps 68:8; 1 Ch 16:30.—p Ex 17:6; Nu 20:11; 1 Co 10:4.—q Ps 23:3; Eze 36:22-23.

114:5-6 The psalmist calls upon the Red Sea, the Jordan, and the mountains to bear witness to the great event when God established his kingdom on earth.

114:7-8 The God of Israel ("Jacob") is none other than the Lord of the universe (see Ps 97:4-6; Rev 20:11). He is still providing streams of blessings for his people as he did at Kadesh, at the waters of Meribah (see Ps 107:35; Ex 17:6; Nu 20:8; Dt 8:15; 1 Co 10:4) and also at the return from the Exile, prefigured by the Exodus and Conquest (see Isa 41:15ff; 42:15; 43:20). On the symbolism of the waters, see Ps 46:1-6; 110:7.

Ps 115 Probably in the course of a celebration of the covenant, choir and soloists in turn voice their confidence in the Lord. Ridiculing the jerry-built gods venerated by the pagans, the community professes its attachment to the one true God, from whom it hopes to receive prosperity. The formulas are brief and striking, with a captivating rhythm; the satire against idols has the flavor of a popular caricature. This simple prayer is at the service of a deep and demanding religious thought and turns into praise. After the Exile, such a clear credo was needed for the community of Jerusalem and for the communities of the dispersion who all coexisted with pagan civilizations that welcomed countless gods. Today, it is still necessary for us to depart from idols fashioned according to our tastes and desires and to turn to the one true God.

We can pray this psalm for the Church, the new Israel, who often experiences profound misfortunes, staggering oppressions, that seem to proclaim the inferiority and impotence of her Head in the face of earthly powers and their satanic idol. We can beg Christ the Lord to intervene to restore the renown of the Church and especially his own in the world.

115:1-3 A song in praise of the living God who is faithful to his people and in derision of the pagan idols who are lifeless.

115:1 *Not to us:* God alone is responsible for Israel's covenant blessings. *Name:* see note on Ps 5:11. *Love:* see note on Ps 6:4.

² Why do the nations say,ʳ
  "Where is their God?"*
³ Our God is in heaven;ˢ
  he does whatever pleases him.*
⁴ But their idols are silver and gold,ᵗ
  made by the hands of men.*ᵘ
⁵ They have mouths, but cannot speak,
  eyes, but they cannot see;
⁶ they have ears, but cannot hear,
  noses, but they cannot smell;
⁷ they have hands, but cannot feel,
  feet, but they cannot walk;
  nor can they utter a sound with their
    throats.
⁸ Those who make them will be like them,
  and so will all who trust in them.

⁹ O house of Israel, trust in the Lord—*ᵛ
  he is their help and shield.ʷ
¹⁰ O house of Aaron, trust in the Lord—
  he is their help and shield.
¹¹ You who fear him, trust in the Lord—
  he is their help and shield.

---

r Ps 42:3; 79:10.—s Ps 135:6; Jud 9:5.—t 4-10: Ps 29:2; 135:15-19; Wis 15:15-16; Isa 44:9f; Jer 10:1-5; Bar 6:3, 7ff.—u Isa 40:19; Rev 9:20.—v Ps 118:2-4; 135:19-20.—w Ps 33:20.

115:2 *Where is their God?*: implying that God does not help his people (see Ps 42:3, 10; 79:10; Mic 7:10).

115:3 The community expresses the belief that God is supreme and present; everything that happens to Israel, good or bad, is his doing.

115:4 The theme of this verse is one that is often found in the Old Testament: idols, unlike the God of Israel, do not speak, reveal, promise, or utter any spoken word; ultimately, divine revelation is the difference between the religions made by humans and the true religion of the Lord (see Ps 135:15-18; Dt 4:16; Isa 44:9ff).

115:9-11 In a litany the various classes of people express their confidence in the Lord. The threefold division ("house of Israel," "house of Aaron," "You who fear him") occurs elsewhere (see Ps 118:2-4; 135:19f, with "Levi" instead of "Aaron"). It is unclear whether the phrase "[those] who fear him" is a synonym for "house of Israel" (see Ps 34:7, 9; 85:9) or all of Israel (laity as well as priests) or whether it identifies a separate class from the house of Israel, namely the "Godfearers" known as the proselytes in the Old Testament (see 1 Ki 8:41; Isa 56:6) and in the New (see Ac 13:16, 26; 16:14).

12 The LORD remembers us and will bless us:*
   He will bless the house of Israel,
   he will bless the house of Aaron,
13 he will bless those who fear the LORD—
   small and great alike.*

14 May the LORD make you increase,*
   both you and your children.
15 May you be blessed by the LORD,
   the Maker of heaven and earth.

16 The highest heavens belong to the LORD,*
   but the earth he has given to man.ˣ
17 It is not the dead who praise the LORD,ʸ
   those who go down to silence;*
18 it is we who extol the LORD,
   both now and forevermore.*

   Praise the LORD.ˢ

---

s Hebrew *Hallelu Yah.*

x Ps 89:11; Ge 1:28.—y Ps 6:5; 88:10ff; 94:17; Sir 17:22f; Isa 38:18.

115:12-15 Utilizing the same group of worshipers as in vv. 9-11, the thought moves forward from God's power to save to his power to enrich. The Lord does not discriminate among his people—all will be the recipients of his blessing. Although they may be put to the test by afflictions of various kinds, the Lord remembers those with whom he has made a covenant (see Ps 98:3; 136:23; Isa 49:14f) and delivers them, bringing to fulfillment the promises he has made.

115:13 *Small and great alike:* the outcasts and the powerful. All will be treated alike by the Lord (see Jer 6:13; 16:6; 31:34; Rev 19:5).

115:14-15 Through these words of blessing, the Lord renews his promise that Abraham's descendants will increase without end (see Ps 127:3-5; Dt 1:11; Isa 54:1-3; Zec 10:8-10).

115:16-18 The psalmist concludes with a short hymn of praise. In so doing he reminds his people that they have been given the earth to enjoy and care for, while praising the Lord.

115:17 The psalmist stresses that the dead cannot praise the Lord; for, according to the idea of the ancients, in the netherworld the souls of the dead had a kind of shadowy existence with no activity or lofty emotion and could not offer praise to God. *Silence:* a euphemism for the grave (see Ps 94:17; see also notes on Ps 6:5 and 30:1).

115:18 *Forevermore:* some view this as saying that those who serve the living God will themselves live on, unlike the worshipers of lifeless idols (v. 8). This would then add its witness to an afterlife to such passages as Ps 11:7; 16:8-11; 17:15; 23:6; 49:15; 73:23ff; 139:18). *Praise the Lord:* the Septuagint and Vulgate add these words as the opening of Ps 116.

PSALM 116*

Thanksgiving to God for Help Received

1 I love the LORD, for he heard my voice;
  he heard my cry for mercy.*
2 Because he turned his ear to me,
  I will call on him as long as I live.*

3 The cords of death* entangled me,
  the anguish of the grave[t] came upon me;
  I was overcome by trouble and sorrow.[z]
4 Then I called on the name* of the LORD:
  "O LORD, save me!"

5 The LORD is gracious and righteous;
  our God is full of compassion.[a]

---

t Hebrew *Sheol.*

---

z Ps 18:4-5; Jnh 2:3.—a Ex 34:6; Ezr 9:15.

Ps 116 Countless are the distresses of human beings and countless too are the deliverances worked by God. This psalm adapts itself to diverse situations; every believer knows the mortal dangers from which the Lord has extricated him in order to bring him to the joy of his presence. In a praying community, all can give thanks. In thanking the divinity it was the custom in the ancient East to pour a cup as a libation, i.e., the "cup of salvation" (that has been granted) (v. 13). The Jews certainly practiced a similar rite during the "fellowship [or: peace] offerings" (see Lev 7:11ff). By this act of thanksgiving the Israelites publicly bore witness that God had saved them; this is the loftiest expression of their religion.

It is also the loftiest expression of the Christian religion. It was certainly in this spirit that Jesus recited this psalm with his disciples after having instituted the Eucharist (see Mt 26:30). Who else could have fully relied on God even through the moment of his death? Once this psalm became the prayer of Jesus on the night in which he was betrayed, it proclaimed the hope of a life and a joy that are everlasting. The priest who mystically offers the divine victim anew still says: "We offer to you, God of glory and majesty . . . the cup of eternal salvation" (Eucharistic Prayer I) and "We offer you, Father, . . . this saving cup" (Eucharistic Prayer II).

In the Hebrew text this psalm is a single psalm, as the sense requires; in the Septuagint and Vulgate it is two distinct psalms, 114 (comprising vv. 1-9) and 115 (comprising vv. 10-19).

116:1 The psalmist expresses love for God who has heard his prayer. For a similar expression of God's care and man's love, see 1 Jn 4:19: "We love because [God] first loved us."

116:2 *I will call on him as long as I live:* a more common translation in Catholic editions is: "on the day [or: as] I called" (see Ps 4:3; 31:22; 34:4; 138:3).

116:3 *Cords of death:* see note on Ps 18:5.

116:4 *Name:* see note on Ps 5:11.

⁶ The Lord protects the simplehearted;*
    when I was in great need, he saved me.

⁷ Be at rest once more, O my soul,
    for the Lord has been good to you.ᵇ

⁸ For you, O Lord, have delivered my soul
        from death,
    my eyes from tears,ᶜ
    my feet from stumbling,*
⁹ that I may walk before the Lordᵈ
    in the land of the living.*
¹⁰ I believed; thereforeᵘ I said,*
    "I am greatly afflicted."ᵉ
¹¹ And in my dismay I said,ᶠ
    "All men are liars."*

¹² How can I repay the Lord
    for all his goodness to me?
¹³ I will lift up the cup of salvation*
    and call on the name of the Lord.
¹⁴ I will fulfill my vows* to the Lord
    in the presence of all his people.

---

u Or *believed even when.*

b Ps 13:6; Mt 11:29.—c Ps 56:13; 86:13; Isa 25:8; Rev 21:4.—d Ps 27:13; 56:13; Isa 38:11; Jer 11:9.—e Ps 9:18; 2 Co 4:13.—f Ps 12:2; 62:9.

116:6 *Simplehearted:* a person who depends on and trusts only in the Lord (see Ps 34:6).
116:8 The psalmist here spells out salvation in terms of earthly well-being, but in words that are true at the deepest level (see, e.g., Ro 8:10f; 2 Co 6:10; Jude 24). *Soul:* see note on Ps 6:3.
116:9 *The land of the living:* see note on Ps 27:13.
116:10 *I believed; therefore I said:* the psalmist kept faith even in the darkest times (see 2 Co 4:13 where this text is cited).
116:11 *All men are liars:* the psalmist avers that his enemies are telling falsehoods about him (see Ps 5:9f; 35:11, 15; 109:2-4) because all men are liars. He could also be alluding to the fact that all men offer only a false hope of deliverance. These words are cited in Ro 3:4.
116:13 *The cup of salvation:* probably the libation of wine poured out in gratitude for one's deliverance (see Ex 25:29; Nu 15:1-10). These words are used at Mass in Eucharistic Prayer I and II, as indicated in the introduction.
116:14 *Vows:* see note on Ps 7:17.

¹⁵ Precious in the sight of the LORD
   is the death* of his saints.*g*

¹⁶ O LORD, truly I am your servant;*h*
   I am your servant, the son of your maidser-
     vant;*v*
   you have freed me from my chains.

¹⁷ I will sacrifice a thank offering to you
   and call on the name of the LORD.*i*

¹⁸ I will fulfill my vows to the LORD
   in the presence of all his people,*j*

¹⁹ in the courts of the house of the LORD—
   in your midst, O Jerusalem.

Praise the LORD.**w*

PSALM 117*

Universal Praise of God

¹ Praise the LORD, all you nations;*k*
   extol him, all you peoples.*

---

v Or *servant, your faithful son.*—w Hebrew *Hallelu Yah.*

g Ps 72:14; Nu 23:10; Isa 43:4.—h Ps 86:16; 119:125; 143:12; Wis 9:5.—i Lev 7:12ff; Ezr 1:4.—j Jnh 2:9.—k Ps 103:2; Ro 15:11.

116:15 *Precious . . . is the death:* the psalmist indicates that God consents to the death of his faithful only with difficulty (see Isa 43:4), for death was regarded as taking away their relationship with him (see Ps 6:5; 72:13; 115:17). The versions interpreted this passage according to the dogma of the resurrection: "the death of the saints has worth in the eyes of God." See the analogous expression, "Precious is their blood in his sight" (Ps 72:14).

116:19 *Praise the LORD:* the Septuagint and Vulgate add these words as the opening of Ps 117.

Ps 117 This psalm is a short invitatory earnestly exhorting all peoples to praise the Lord, the God of Israel, for the signal love and faithfulness that he manifests toward his people. His goodness toward Israel should inspire admiration and enthusiastic praise among foreigners, who are simply witnesses of his wonders (see Sir 36:1-4; Eze 36).

Since God's love and faithfulness are manifested much more forcefully in the life of the Church than in the history of Israel, all people should on that account give more enthusiastic praise to the heavenly Father. Enabling his Son to vanquish his enemies (the devil and death), the Father fills him with divine riches (eternal life in glory, joy, peace, beatitude, royalty). And he has done the same for the Church and her members. Praise of God is to be unanimous (see Ro 15:11).

117:1 All nations and peoples are called to praise the Lord (see Ps 47:1; 67:3-5; 96:7; 98:4; 100:1; see also note on Ps 9:1). This verse is cited in Ro 15:11.

2 For great is his love toward us,
  and the faithfulness of the LORD endures
    forever.*

Praise the LORD.ˣ

PSALM 118*

Thanksgiving for Salvation

1 Give thanks to the LORD, for he is good;*
  his love endures forever.*ᶦ

---

x Hebrew *Hallelu Yah.*

---

l Ps 100:5; 136:1f; 1 Ch 16:8.

117:2 Universal praise is owed to the Lord because of his dealings with the covenant people. He has shown them constant love and faithfulness, that is, faithful love. Indeed, His love is not only so great in depth and height (see Ro 5:20; 1 Ti 1:14) but also lasting (see Ps 89:28); see also note on Ps 6:4. In Christ the love of God has been even more powerfully shown both to Jews and to Gentiles so that all might praise him for it (see Ro 15:8ff). *Praise the LORD:* the Septuagint and Vulgate add these words to open Ps 118.

Ps 118 This psalm brings to a close the Egyptian Hallel. As the procession of pilgrims goes up to Jerusalem for the feast of Tabernacles (vv. 15, 27; see Lev 23:39-43), the celebrants and the crowd conduct a dialogue, the rhythm of which is determined by the stages of the journey. The procession starts out with a familiar refrain (vv. 1-4) and proceeds while singing a hymn of thanksgiving (vv. 5-18); it arrives at the gates of the temple that has been rebuilt (v. 19) and has become the sign of Israel's renewal after the Exile (vv. 22-24) where the priests respond to the acclamations of the people by blessing them (vv. 25-27). Finally, with palms in hand the procession reaches the sanctuary, whose courts are illumined, and the liturgy takes place with the most solemn thanksgiving (vv. 28-29).

Songs of thanksgiving such as this one called to mind the entire history of Israel, from past to present. Israel is ceaselessly put to the test, humbled, and then delivered, and in this very experience it discovers its calling to be a people that bears witness to God in the midst of the nations and is the capstone of the world (v. 22). Jesus makes this calling his own (see Mt 21:42), and the apostles speak of it in their preaching (see Ac 4:11; 1 Pe 2:4-7). For them this psalm expresses in advance the mystery of Christ who is rejected and then exalted and who is the foundation stone of the new People of God (see 1 Co 3:11; Eph 2:20). This festal song soon became popular; we find the crowd spontaneously singing it on Palm Sunday to greet Jesus as the envoy promised by God (v. 26; see Mt 21:9; Jn 12:13). We find this same acclamation in the *Sanctus* of the Mass; in all the liturgical families the psalm has become an Easter song.

118:1-4 The liturgical call to praise that begins the procession.

118:1 A conventional call to praise (see Ps 105—107). *Love:* see note on Ps 6:4.

² Let Israel say:
  "His love endures forever."
³ Let the house of Aaron say:
  "His love endures forever."
⁴ Let those who fear the LORD* say:
  "His love endures forever."*m*

⁵ In my anguish I cried to the LORD,*
  and he answered by setting me free.
⁶ The LORD is with me; I will not be afraid.
  What can man do to me?*n*
⁷ The LORD is with me; he is my helper.
  I will look in triumph on my enemies.

⁸ It is better to take refuge in the LORD*
  than to trust in man.*o*
⁹ It is better to take refuge in the LORD
  than to trust in princes.

¹⁰ All the nations surrounded me,*
  but in the name of the LORD I cut them off.
¹¹ They surrounded me on every side,
  but in the name of the LORD I cut them off.
¹² They swarmed around me like bees,
    but they died out as quickly as burning
      thorns;
  in the name of the LORD I cut them off.*p*

¹³ I was pushed back and about to fall,
  but the LORD helped me.*q*

---

m Ps 115:9-11.—n Ps 27:1; 56:11; Heb 13:6.—o 8f: Ps 146:3; Isa 25:4.—
p Ps 58:9; Dt 1:44.—q Ps 86:17; 129:1-2.

118:2-4 *Israel . . . house of Aaron . . . those who fear the LORD:* see note on Ps 115:9-11.

118:5-18 A song of thanksgiving for deliverance of the whole nation voiced by a single individual.

118:8-9 All should be ever mindful of the motto learned through experience that it is better to have confidence in the Lord than to rely on flesh and blood (see Ps 33:16-19; see also Ps 62; 146).

118:10-13 The fury of the assault recalls the attacks experienced by Jesus at his trial (see Lk 22:63—23:25) and even during his Public Ministry (see Lk 11:53f). *Name:* see note on Ps 5:11.

¹⁴ The LORD is my strength and my song;ʳ
　　he has become my salvation.*

¹⁵ Shouts of joy and victory
　　resound in the tents of the righteous:
　"The LORD's right hand has done mighty
　　things!
¹⁶ The LORD's right hand is lifted high;
　　the LORD's right hand has done mighty
　　things!"

¹⁷ I will not die but live,
　　and will proclaim* what the LORD has
　　done.
¹⁸ The LORD has chastened me severely,
　　but he has not given me over to death.

¹⁹ Open for me the gates of righteousness;*
　　I will enter and give thanks to the LORD.ˢ
²⁰ This is the gate of the LORD
　　through which the righteous may enter.
²¹ I will give you thanks, for you answered me;
　　you have become my salvation.

²² The stone the builders rejected*
　　has become the capstone;ᵗ

---

r Ps 62:2; Ex 15:2; Isa 12:2.—s Ps 24:7; Isa 26:2.—t Isa 28:16; Zec 4:7; Mt 21:42; Lk 20:17; Ac 4:11; Ro 9:33; 1 Pe 2:7.

118:14 This verse is an exact quotation from the song of victory at the Red Sea (see Ex 15:2) and is echoed in vv. 15 ("right hand") and 28 ("exalt you"). Hence, God's saving acts throughout history bear the stamp of the Exodus events (see 1 Co 10:6) culminating in the work of Christ (see Lk 9:31: "his departure [literally, 'exodus'], which he was about to bring to fulfillment at Jerusalem").

118:17 *Live, and . . . proclaim:* see note on Ps 6:5.

118:19-21 The procession has arrived at the gates of the rebuilt temple; all the righteous may enter and give thanks.

118:22-23 The community of the righteous join in with thanksgiving. They praise the Lord that he has given prominence to his suffering servant Israel like a "capstone." It was rejected by the worldly powers but has been made the capstone for God's salvation of the world in the Messiah. These verses allude to Isa 8:14; 28:16; Jer 51:26; Zec 3:9; 4:7, passages that are interpreted in a Messianic sense. Israel is here a type of Christ, in whom these words have been most eminently fulfilled (see Mt 21:42 par; Ac 4:11; Ro 9:33; 1 Co 3:11; Eph 2:20; 1 Pe 2:7).

²³ the LORD has done this,
    and it is marvelous in our eyes.
²⁴ This is the day the LORD has made;*
    let us rejoice and be glad in it.

²⁵ O LORD, save us;*
    O LORD, grant us success.
²⁶ Blessed is he who comes in the name of the
        LORD.*ᵘ
    From the house of the LORD we bless you.ʸ
²⁷ The LORD is God,
    and he has made his light shine upon us.
    With boughs in hand, join in the festal pro-
        cession
    upᶻ to the horns of the altar.*

²⁸ You are my God, and I will give you thanks;*
    you are my God, and I will exalt you.

²⁹ Give thanks to the LORD, for he is good;
    his love endures forever.

---

y The Hebrew is plural.—z Or *Bind the festal sacrifice with ropes / and take it.*

u Mt 21:9; 23:39; Mk 11:9.

118:24 *This is the day the LORD has made:* the day given by the Lord in which joy and jubilation are appropriate, the day of thanksgiving and rejoicing because of the wondrous deed of the Lord (vv. 22-23; see Ps 71:17; Jer 32:17, 27), the day of salvation. Used by the Liturgy as an antiphon for the Easter Season, this phrase identifies the "day" as that of Christ's Resurrection.

118:25 *O LORD, save us:* the Hebrew for this cry has come into English as "Hosanna." The crowd takes it up on Palm Sunday (see Mt 21:9; 23:39; Mk 11:9; Jn 12:13). It has become part of the *Sanctus* at Mass.

118:26 *Blessed is he who comes in the name of the LORD:* words used in the Gospels to welcome Jesus entering the temple on Palm Sunday (see Mk 11:9 par).

118:27 The people respond to the blessing by confessing that the Lord alone is God. He has made his light shine upon them, protecting them from the darkness of great trials (e.g., famine, war, and exile—see Ps 43:3). Accordingly, they are here renewing their commitment to the Lord in a formal liturgical celebration. *The horns of the altar:* the four corners of the altar of holocausts (see Ex 27:2; 38:2; Lev 4:25, 30, 34).

118:28-29 The psalm concludes with the community's affirmation that the Lord alone is God, similar to the confession of Moses (see Ex 15:2).

PSALM 119* ᵃ

Praise of God's Law

Aleph

1 Blessed are they whose ways are blameless,*
   who walk according to the law of the
     LORD.*ᵛ
2 Blessed are they who keep his statutesʷ
   and seek him with all their heart.*
3 They do nothing wrong;
   they walk in his ways.

---

a This psalm is an acrostic poem; the verses of each stanza begin with the same letter of the Hebrew alphabet.

v Ps 1:1-2; 15:2; 112:1; Mt 5:3ff. —w Dt 4:29; 2 Ch 31:21.

Ps 119 This longest of the psalms is a monumental literary piece consisting of twenty-two strophes, each containing eight verses (sixteen lines) and each beginning with a letter of the Hebrew alphabet that is repeated at the beginning of each pair of verses. Each strophe is a unit, but does not have a close connection with the strophe that precedes or follows. The whole is a free-flowing meditation, now sad, now joyous, now peaceful, now passionate. It is a reflection and a prayer in which the author, a sage and a mystic who draws his inspiration from the Prophets and Deuteronomy, converses with God and voices his deepest feelings: love of true wisdom, attachment and fidelity to the word of God in spite of weakness and obstacles; desire to better understand and live the truth; joy of outdoing oneself to follow the will of God manifested in the Law.

In practically every verse, there is the word "law" or some equivalent. We can point to eight such terms—four with a more juridic nuance (statutes, precepts, decrees, commands or commandments) and four with a more religious nuance (law, promise, word, laws or judgments). These terms introduce us into the heart of the psalm, for they signify less an ensemble of laws to observe than the word of God, which sometimes ordains and judges and sometimes reveals and promises. It is a psalm of spiritual intimacy, of love for God (which means doing his will). In meditating on the Law, believers contemplate above all the visage of God and let themselves be transformed in the very depths of their hearts. Such observance becomes liberty. Understood in this fashion, the Law proclaims to us Jesus Christ, the living revelation of God, given to human beings to lead them to the Father: "I am the way and the truth and the life" (Jn 14:6).

119:1-3 Introduction to the entire psalm that stresses the theme: instruction in godly wisdom.

119:1 A beginning analogous to those of Ps 1 and 112:1 (see Ps 101:6; Mt 5:3ff). The word law and its synonyms are to be taken in the widest sense of revealed teaching, as transmitted by the Prophets. *Blessed:* see note on Ps 1:1.

119:2 This verse makes explicit what is implicit throughout the psalm: Scripture is revered because it consists in God's statutes; it is God that his servants seek and not the book for its own sake.

⁴ You have laid down precepts*
    that are to be fully obeyed.
⁵ Oh, that my ways were steadfast
    in obeying your decrees!
⁶ Then I would not be put to shame
    when I consider all your commands.
⁷ I will praise you with an upright heart
    as I learn your righteous laws.
⁸ I will obey your decrees;
    do not utterly forsake me.

Beth

⁹ How can a young man keep his way pure?*
    By living according to your word.
¹⁰ I seek you with all my heart;
    do not let me stray from your commands.*
¹¹ I have hidden your word in my heart*
    that I might not sin against you.
¹² Praise be to you, O LORD;
    teach me your decrees.ˣ
¹³ With my lips I recount
    all the laws that come from your mouth.
¹⁴ I rejoice in following your statutes
    as one rejoices in great riches.
¹⁵ I meditate on your precepts
    and consider your ways.
¹⁶ I delight in your decrees;
    I will not neglect your word.

---

x Ps 25:4; 27:11; 86:11; 143:8, 10; Ex 18:20.

119:4-8 Those who obey God's law have a right to hope that he will come to their assistance.

119:9-16 The love for God's word is love for God, expressed in one's attitude of heart, in actions, and in words. With his entire being the godly person seeks God and delights in his will. Such a sublime teaching can lead "a young man" to keep his way pure.

119:10 The psalmist seeks the God of the law and the promises; he meditates on the latter only because they constitute God's word of life for him. *Heart:* see note on Ps 4:7.

119:11 *Hidden your word in my heart:* Pr 2:10-12 and Col 3:16 show that those whose hearts are steeped in the word of God are educated by God.

Gimel

17 * Do good to your servant, and I will live;*
    I will obey your word.
18 Open my eyes that I may see
    wonderful things in your law.
19 I am a stranger on earth;^y
    do not hide your commands from me.*
20 My soul is consumed with longing
    for your laws at all times.
21 You rebuke the arrogant,* who are cursed
    and who stray from your commands.
22 Remove from me scorn and contempt,
    for I keep your statutes.
23 Though rulers sit together and slander me,
    your servant will meditate on your decrees.
24 Your statutes are my delight;
    they are my counselors.

Daleth

25 * I am laid low in the dust;*
    preserve my life according to your word.^z
26 I recounted my ways and you answered me;
    teach me your decrees.

---

y Ps 39:12; Heb 11:13. — z Ps 44:25; 143:11.

119:17-24 In difficulty and distress, the Lord and his word are a comfort to the godly. God's blessing comes to those who submit to his law, but his curse comes to those who stray deliberately from his revealed will.

119:17 *I will live:* here the psalmist is speaking of living in its fullest sense of happiness, security, prosperity—a frequent theme in Eze (3:21; 18; 33; see Ps 133:3)—and, of course, fellowship with God (see Ps 16:11; 36:9; Dt 8:3).

119:19 Though the psalmist is a stranger (or wayfarer) on earth, he is the guest of God to whom the whole universe belongs; he will learn from the Lord how to conduct himself (see note on Ps 39:12).

119:21 *The arrogant:* enemies of God and his faithful who act as though they are a law unto themselves (see notes on Ps 73:4-12 and 86:14; see also Isa 13:11; Mal 4:1). They are "cursed," i.e., ready for God's judgment.

119:25-32 Whether in distress or in prosperity, the psalmist is determined to remain close to God's law. In adversities, he becomes more teachable and his spirit is renewed in him, for the word of the Lord has the power to comfort. In prosperity, he enjoys a freedom from anxiety and care that enables him to focus on doing God's will.

119:25 *Laid low in the dust:* see note on Ps 44:25.

²⁷ Let me understand the teaching of your pre-
  cepts;
    then I will meditate on your wonders.
²⁸ My soul is weary with sorrow;
    strengthen me according to your word.
²⁹ Keep me from deceitful ways;
    be gracious to me through your law.
³⁰ I have chosen the way of truth;*
    I have set my heart on your laws.
³¹ I hold fast to your statutes, O LORD;
    do not let me be put to shame.
³² I run in the path of your commands,
    for you have set my heart free.

He

³³ Teach me, O LORD, to follow your decrees;*
    then I will keep them to the end.**a*
³⁴ Give me understanding, and I will keep your
  law
    and obey it with all my heart.*
³⁵ Direct me in the path of your commands,
    for there I find delight.*b*
³⁶ Turn my heart toward your statutes
    and not toward selfish gain.
³⁷ Turn my eyes away from worthless things;
    preserve my life according to your word.*b*

---

b Two manuscripts of the Masoretic Text and Dead Sea Scrolls; most
manuscripts of the Masoretic Text *life in your way.*

---

a Ps 19:11.—b Ps 1-2; 25:4; 27:11; 86:11; 143:8, 10.

119:30-32 Godliness is nicely summed up by the three opening verbs: choos-
ing (see Heb 11:25), holding fast (see Ac 11:23), and running (see Php 3:12-14).
119:33-40 Since God alone can interpret his revelation ("teach [it]," v. 33),
the psalmist prays that God will instruct him in his "law" (see Ps 25:4). He asks
the Lord to provide spiritual direction and motivation to direct his steps (see Pr
4:11-19) and incline his heart (see Ps 141:4) to do the divine will.
119:33 *Then I will keep them to the end:* another possible translation is: "I will
keep them as a reward" (see Ps 19:11; Pr 22:4). In both translations the godly
person finds his joy in doing the will of God.
119:34 The desire for understanding often voiced in this psalm conforms to
the ideal of the sages of Israel. *Heart:* see note on Ps 4:7.

38 Fulfill your promise to your servant,
   so that you may be feared.*
39 Take away the disgrace I dread,
   for your laws are good.
40 How I long for your precepts!
   Preserve my life in your righteousness.

Waw

41 * May your unfailing love* come to me, O
   LORD,
   your salvation according to your promise;
42 then I will answer the one who taunts me,
   for I trust in your word.
43 Do not snatch the word of truth from my
   mouth,*
   for I have put my hope in your laws.
44 I will always obey your law,
   for ever and ever.
45 I will walk about in freedom,
   for I have sought out your precepts.*
46 I will speak of your statutes before kings
   and will not be put to shame,
47 for I delight in your commands
   because I love them.

119:38 *That you may be feared:* as a result of the saving acts that the Lord does in accord with his promises, he is acknowledged as the one true God and feared (see Ps 130:4; 2 Sa 7:25f; 1 Ki 8:39f; Jer 33:8f).

119:41-48 Here the psalmist, as it were, gives Christians what is needed for them to fulfill their desire "to speak [the Lord's] word with great boldness" (Ac 4:29). In order to be spoken, the word must first be appropriated (v. 41), trusted (vv. 42f), obeyed (v. 44), sought (v. 45), and loved (vv. 47f).

119:41 *Love:* see note on Ps 6:4.

119:43 *Do not snatch the word of truth from my mouth:* for it will enable the psalmist to respond to the insults and calumnies to which he is subjected (see Ps 119:61, 85, 95, etc.).

119:45 *Sought out your precepts:* the psalmist strives to understand the meaning of the Scriptures and make them his rule of life (see Ps 119:94, 155; see also Ps 111:2; Ezr 7:10; Sir 51:23; Isa 34:16). Such a study is at the origin of the Midrashic literature.

⁴⁸ I lift up my hands* to^c your commands,
>   which I love,
>   and I meditate on your decrees.

Zayin

⁴⁹ Remember your word to your servant,*
>   for you have given me hope.
⁵⁰ My comfort in my suffering is this:
>   Your promise preserves my life.
⁵¹ The arrogant* mock me without restraint,
>   but I do not turn from your law.
⁵² I remember your ancient laws, O Lᴏʀᴅ,
>   and I find comfort in them.
⁵³ Indignation grips me because of the wicked,
>   who have forsaken your law.
⁵⁴ Your decrees are the theme of my song
>   wherever I lodge.
⁵⁵ In the night I remember your name,* O Lᴏʀᴅ,
>   and I will keep your law.
⁵⁶ This has been my practice:
>   I obey your precepts.

Heth

⁵⁷ * You are my portion,* O Lᴏʀᴅ;
>   I have promised to obey your words.

---

c Or *for*.

119:48 *I lift up my hands:* as a sign of veneration and praise (see Ps 44:20; 63:4; 134:2; Ne 8:6).

119:49-56 The word of God provides hope and consolation even in suffering. The psalmist guards the precepts of the Lord because in them he finds life, restoration, and consolation.

119:51 *The arrogant:* see note on Ps 119:21.

119:55 *Name:* see note on Ps 5:11.

119:57-64 The Lord is the portion of the psalmist, and it is God's law that fills the earth with joy and security. Hence, far from regarding obedience as a crushing, disagreeable burden, the psalmist considers it a happy lot, a privileged destiny, and a signal favor.

119:57 *You are my portion:* a familiar formula of trust (see Ps 16:5; 73:26 and note; 142:5).

58 I have sought your face with all my heart;*
    be gracious to me according to your
    promise.
59 I have considered my ways
    and have turned my steps to your statutes.
60 I will hasten and not delay
    to obey your commands.
61 Though the wicked bind me with ropes,
    I will not forget your law.
62 At midnight I rise to give you thanks
    for your righteous laws.
63 I am a friend to all who fear you,
    to all who follow your precepts.
64 The earth is filled with your love,* O LORD;
    teach me your decrees.c

Teth

65 Do good to your servant*
    according to your word, O LORD.
66 Teach me knowledge and good judgment,
    for I believe in your commands.
67 Before I was afflicted* I went astray,
    but now I obey your word.
68 You are good, and what you do is good;
    teach me your decrees.
69 Though the arrogant* have smeared me with
    lies,
    I keep your precepts with all my heart.d

---

c Ps 33:5; 108:4.—d Ps 17:10; 73:8; Job 13:4.

119:58 *Heart:* see note on Ps 4:7.
119:64 *The earth is filled with your love:* an exclamation of God's cosmic love; the world of creation witnesses to his love (see Ps 104:10-30; 136:1-9). For other glimpses of the world as God's handiwork and kingdom, see Ps 24:1; 33:5; Isa 6:3; Hab 2:14; 3:3.
119:65-72 The psalmist ascribes goodness to God in his past and present dealings, to the positive values of the trials God sent him, and to the ultimate value of God's law and divine teaching.
119:67 *Afflicted:* through God's doing (see note on Ps 119:25-32).
119:69 *The arrogant:* see note on Ps 119:21.

70 Their hearts are callous and unfeeling,*
    but I delight in your law.
71 It was good for me to be afflicted
    so that I might learn your decrees.
72 The law from your mouth is more precious to
    me
    than thousands of pieces of silver and gold.

Yodh

73 * Your hands made me and formed me;*
    give me understanding to learn your com-
    mands.
74 May those who fear you rejoice when they
    see me,
    for I have put my hope in your word.
75 I know, O LORD, that your laws are righ-
    teous,
    and in faithfulness you have afflicted me.
76 May your unfailing love* be my comfort,
    according to your promise to your servant.
77 Let your compassion come to me that I may
    live,
    for your law is my delight.
78 May the arrogant* be put to shame for
    wronging me without cause;
    but I will meditate on your precepts.
79 May those who fear you turn to me,
    those who understand your statutes.

119:70 *Callous and unfeeling:* literally, "fat as grease," i.e., incapable of understanding divine things (see Ps 17:10; 73:7; Isa 6:10; Jer 5:28).
119:73-80 The psalmist declares his experiential knowledge of God, of his
"unfailing love" and "compassion." He asks God to give the arrogant their just
deserts and so enable the godly to be encouraged and rejoice at God's vindication.
119:73 *Your hands made me and formed me:* see Dt 32:6; Job 10:8; Zec 12:1.
Give me understanding: so that the psalmist can carry out what God willed in
forming him.
119:76 *Unfailing love:* see note on Ps 6:4.
119:78 *The arrogant:* see note on Ps 119:21.

⁸⁰ May my heart* be blameless toward your decrees,
   that I may not be put to shame.

Kaph

⁸¹ * My soul* faints with longing for your salvation,
   but I have put my hope in your word.ᵉ
⁸² My eyes fail,* looking for your promise;
   I say, "When will you comfort me?"ᶠ
⁸³ Though I am like a wineskin in the smoke,*
   I do not forget your decrees.ᵍ
⁸⁴ How long must your servant wait?*
   When will you punish my persecutors?
⁸⁵ The arrogant* dig pitfalls for me,
   contrary to your law.
⁸⁶ All your commands are trustworthy;
   help me, for men persecute me without
   cause.
⁸⁷ They almost wiped me from the earth,
   but I have not forsaken your precepts.
⁸⁸ Preserve my life according to your love,*
   and I will obey the statutes of your mouth.

---

e Ps 84:2; 130:5.—f Ps 25:15; 123:1-2; 141:8; La 2:11.—g Job 30:30.

119:80 *Heart:* see note on Ps 4:7.
119:81-88 This last strophe of the first part of the psalm brings to a climax
the psalmist's need for God. In extreme distress, he looks to the Lord for his salvation as promised in his word, urgently calling upon him to come to his aid and
effect justice upon the arrogant who wrong him.
119:81 *Soul:* see note on Ps 6:3.
119:82 *My eyes fail:* see note on Ps 6:7.
119:83 *Like a wineskin in the smoke:* the psalmist feels as brittle and useless
as tanned hides holding wine that are placed near the fireplace.
119:84 *How long . . . wait?:* literally, "How many are the days of your servant?"
i.e., the psalmist does not have too much time for God to delay in punishing his
persecutors. *Punish:* literally, "effect justice upon" (see note on Ps 5:10).
119:85 *The arrogant:* see note on Ps 119:21.
119:88 *Love:* see note on Ps 6:4.

Lamedh

89 Your word, O LORD, is eternal;*
  it stands firm in the heavens.*[h]

90 Your faithfulness continues through all gen-
    erations;
  you established the earth, and it endures.

91 Your laws endure to this day,
  for all things serve you.

92 If your law had not been my delight,*
  I would have perished in my affliction.

93 I will never forget your precepts,
  for by them you have preserved my life.

94 Save me, for I am yours;
  I have sought out your precepts.

95 The wicked are waiting to destroy me,
  but I will ponder your statutes.

96 To all perfection I see a limit;
  but your commands are boundless.*

Mem

97 Oh, how I love your law!*
  I meditate on it all day long.

---

h Isa 40:8.

119:89-91 Like the first three verses of the first half of the psalm, these first three verses of the second half teach a general truth: there is constancy and order in all of creation, reflecting the "faithfulness" of the Lord (see Ps 89:2; 104; 147:7-9). Nature serves and abides by the word and the laws of the Lord (see note on Ps 93:5).

119:89 This verse is an echo of Pr 8:22ff where divine wisdom is presented as a living being existing from all eternity (see Wis 7:22—8:1; Isa 40:8).

119:92-96 The psalmist confesses that if through God's law he had not found meaning in the experience of his affliction, he would have perished. Therefore, no matter what his persecutors do, he will not forget God's precepts because they give order and preservation of life. For he knows that just as there are laws for the order in nature, so also are there laws for human conduct.

119:96 Everything on earth is limited; perfection belongs only to God and his commands.

119:97-104 God's law is heavenly wisdom, which is far greater than earthly wisdom. Meditation on it is a form of devotion to the Lord himself, and hence the psalmist regularly cultivates its practice. God's words, likened to honey, are sweet only when God's instruction is received and leads to understanding as well as an obedient life style.

⁹⁸ Your commands make me wiser than my
        enemies,*
    for they are ever with me.
⁹⁹ I have more insight than all my teachers,
    for I meditate on your statutes.
¹⁰⁰ I have more understanding than the elders,*
    for I obey your precepts.ⁱ
¹⁰¹ I have kept my feet from every evil path
    so that I might obey your word.
¹⁰² I have not departed from your laws,
    for you yourself have taught me.
¹⁰³ How sweet are your words to my taste,ʲ
    sweeter than honey to my mouth!*
¹⁰⁴ I gain understanding from your precepts;
    therefore I hate every wrong path.

Nun

¹⁰⁵ * Your word is a lamp to my feet*
    and a light for my path.ᵏ
¹⁰⁶ I have taken an oath and confirmed it,*
    that I will follow your righteous laws.
¹⁰⁷ I have suffered much;
    preserve my life, O LORD, according to
        your word.

---

i Dt 6:17; Job 32:6; Wis 4:8-9.—j Ps 19:10; Jer 15:16.—k Ps 18:28; Pr
6:23; 2 Pe 1:19.

119:98-100 These verses are illuminated by the New Testament, which shows
that heavenly wisdom is a gift to "little children," hidden from the worldly wise
(see Lk 10:21; 1 Co 1:18ff; 2:6-10).
119:100 The psalmist speaks in the same vein as Elihu (see Job 32:6ff; Wis
4:9). *Elders:* the aged, taught by experience.
119:103 *Sweeter than honey to my mouth:* see Ps 19:10; Job 23:12; Jer 15:16;
Jn 4:32, 34.
119:105-112 The word of the Lord enlightens the psalmist's path of life;
therefore, he has accepted the covenant and obeys the Lord. Even in affliction,
the psalmist has learned to give God willing praise, for his joy and determination
to please the Lord are far greater than the affliction that is constantly with him.
119:105 *Your word is a lamp to my feet:* the word of the Lord is a guide and
life-sustaining source (see Ps 18:28; 97:11; 112:4; Pr 6:23; Jn 8:12).
119:106 *Have taken an oath and confirmed it:* the psalmist has made a pact
to follow God's laws (see Ne 10:29).

108 Accept, O LORD, the willing praise of my
       mouth,
       and teach me your laws.[l]
109 Though I constantly take my life in my
       hands,*
       I will not forget your law.
110 The wicked have set a snare for me,
       but I have not strayed from your precepts.
111 Your statutes are my heritage forever;
       they are the joy of my heart.*
112 My heart is set on keeping your decrees
       to the very end.

Samekh

113 * I hate double-minded men,*
       but I love your law.
114 You are my refuge and my shield;
       I have put my hope in your word.
115 Away from me, you evildoers,
       that I may keep the commands of my
       God![m]
116 Sustain me according to your promise, and I
       will live;
       do not let my hopes be dashed.
117 Uphold me, and I will be delivered;
       I will always have regard for your de-
       crees.

---

l Ps 50:14; 23; 51:15; Heb 13:15.—m Ps 6:8; 139:19; Job 21:14.

119:109 *Take my life in my hands:* i.e., my life is constantly exposed to danger, for I am ready to risk it for God (see 1 Sa 19:5; Jdg 12:3; Est C:15=4:17[1]; Job 13:14).
119:111-112 *Heart:* see note on Ps 4:7.
119:113-120 The ways of the righteous and the wicked are completely divergent. The psalmist dissociates himself from the wicked; he hates the double-minded but loves the law of the Lord. He draws near to God, his refuge and his shield. For, unlike the wicked whom the Lord will discard, the godly have hope in and veneration for the Lord.
119:113 *Double-minded men:* those who hesitate between fidelity and infidelity to God (see 1 Ki 18:21); they are "unstable in all they do" (Jas 1:8).

118 You reject all who stray from your de-
　　crees,
　　for their deceitfulness is in vain.
119 All the wicked of the earth you discard like
　　dross;*
　　therefore I love your statutes.
120 My flesh trembles* in fear of you;
　　I stand in awe of your laws.

Ayin

121 I have done what is righteous and just;*
　　do not leave me to my oppressors.
122 Ensure your servant's well-being;
　　let not the arrogant oppress me.*
123 My eyes fail,* looking for your salvation,
　　looking for your righteous promise.
124 Deal with your servant according to your
　　love*
　　and teach me your decrees.
125 I am your servant; give me discernment
　　that I may understand your statutes.
126 It is time for you to act, O LORD;
　　your law is being broken.
127 Because I love your commands
　　more than gold, more than pure gold,*

119:119 *You discard like dross:* the Lord discards evildoers like "dross," i.e., the scum that forms in refining precious metals and is discarded (see Jer 6:28-30).

119:120 *My flesh trembles:* a reminiscence of Job 4:15; 23:15 (see Ps 88:16). It denotes the dread of the sacred, the fear of the awesome God.

119:121-128 The psalmist has entrusted himself to God's care and done what is righteous and just; now he expects the Lord to keep his promise according to which the godly will be relieved of all adversities. He prays to receive understanding and, while affirming his devotion to the Lord and his commands, calls for God to deal justly with the ungodly, who have broken his law.

119:122 This is the only verse in the psalm that lacks either a direct or an indirect reference to the law of God; some have suggested replacing "servant" by "word" as a remedy. *The arrogant:* see note on Ps 119:21.

119:123 *My eyes fail:* see note on Ps 6:7.

119:124 *Love:* see note on Ps 6:4.

119:127 The psalmist compares the Lord's commands favorably with pure gold (see Job 22:25; 28:15f; Pr 3:14; 8:10, 19; 16:16).

[128] and because I consider all your precepts
    right,
  I hate every wrong path.

Pe

[129] Your statutes are wonderful;*
    therefore I obey them.
[130] The unfolding of your words gives light;
    it gives understanding to the simple.*
[131] I open my mouth and pant,*
    longing for your commands.
[132] Turn to me and have mercy on me,* [n]
    as you always do to those who love your
    name.*
[133] Direct my footsteps according to your word;
    let no sin rule over me.
[134] Redeem me from the oppression of men,
    that I may obey your precepts.
[135] Make your face shine* upon your servant
    and teach me your decrees.
[136] Streams of tears flow from my eyes,
    for your law is not obeyed.*

---

n Ps 25:16; 86:16; 91:14.

119:129-136 God's word illumines so that even those not experienced in the realities of life (the "simple"; see Ps 116; Pr 1:4) may gain wisdom (see Ps 19:7). The psalmist longs to receive, understand, and put it into practice. So great is his zeal for God's law that he weeps over the continuance of rebellion and transgression on the part of evildoers.
119:130 The law is a luminous sanctuary that fills souls with its clarity (see Ps 73:16f) when it is explained to them. *Unfolding:* literally, "opening."
119:131 *Open my mouth and pant:* same image as in Job 29:23.
119:132-136 The psalmist asks for the Lord's blessing (see Nu 6:24-26), which brings down God's grace to enable him to direct his steps in accord with the divine law and away from sin and adversity (vv. 133-134). He also asks for the Lord's face to shine on him (v. 135), i.e., to bring him nothing but good in all circumstances of his life; for when God's face shines on people it brings deliverance and blessings.
119:132 See Ps 5:11; 25:15; 91:15. *Name:* see note on Ps 5:11.
119:135 *Make your face shine:* the psalmist asks God to smile on him with favor (see note on Ps 13:1; see also Ps 67:1; 80:3; Nu 6:25).
119:136 The godly are saddened in the face of evil (see Ezr 9:3ff; Job 16:20; Eze 9:4).

Tsadhe

137 Righteous are you, O LORD,*
and your laws are right.º
138 The statutes you have laid down are righteous;
they are fully trustworthy.
139 My zeal wears me out,
for my enemies ignore your words.
140 Your promises have been thoroughly tested,*
and your servant loves them.
141 Though I am lowly and despised,
I do not forget your precepts.
142 Your righteousness is everlasting
and your law is true.
143 Trouble and distress have come upon me,
but your commands are my delight.
144 Your statutes are forever right;
give me understanding that I may live.

Qoph

145 I call with all my heart; answer me, O LORD,*
and I will obey your decrees.
146 I call out to you; save me
and I will keep your statutes.
147 I rise before dawn and cry for help;
I have put my hope in your word.

---

o Ex 9:27; Job 3:2.

119:137-144 The troubles and disgraces of his holy ones adversely affect the excellence of the Lord and his word. Hence, the psalmist points out his sad state and prays that the Lord will establish righteousness in his world. Though he is still immersed in troubles, he knows the Lord is faithful and wholeheartedly puts his trust in him.

119:140 *Tested:* literally, "refined." God's word is fire-tried; it is genuine and reliable.

119:145-152 The psalmist urgently presents his lament before the Lord to be delivered from adversity. So intense is his longing for this salvation that he prays through the night watches. Even though his foes hunt him down, the Lord is near and faithful to rescue him, for the psalmist keeps the law.

¹⁴⁸ My eyes stay open through the watches of
  the night,*
    that I may meditate on your promises.^p
¹⁴⁹ Hear my voice in accordance with your
  love;*
    preserve my life, O LORD, according to
    your laws.
¹⁵⁰ Those who devise wicked schemes are near,
    but they are far from your law.*
¹⁵¹ Yet you are near, O LORD,
    and all your commands are true.
¹⁵² Long ago I learned from your statutes
    that you established them to last forever.

Resh

¹⁵³ Look upon my suffering and deliver me,*
    for I have not forgotten your law.
¹⁵⁴ Defend my cause and redeem me;*
    preserve my life according to your prom-
    ise.^q
¹⁵⁵ Salvation is far from the wicked,
    for they do not seek out your decrees.*
¹⁵⁶ Your compassion is great, O LORD;
    preserve my life according to your laws.
¹⁵⁷ Many are the foes who persecute me,
    but I have not turned from your statutes.

---

p Ps 63:6; 77:6.—q Ps 35:1; 43:1.

119:148 *Watches of the night:* see note on Ps 63:6.
119:149 *Love:* see note on Ps 6:4.
119:150-152 Although the wicked are closing in on the psalmist, he remains serene, for the Lord is also near to protect him (see Ps 69:18; 73:28). The wicked will get nowhere, for they break the statutes of the Lord (v. 150: "are far from your law"), which were meant to last forever.
119:153-160 The lament becomes more intense as the psalmist prays for deliverance, mercy, and life. By protesting his innocence, bringing up his affliction, and mentioning the perfidy of the wicked, he seeks to move God to act, for he alone can preserve the psalmist's full enjoyment of covenant life. The fidelity and righteousness of God's word sustain the psalmist in his belief of total vindication.
119:154 *Redeem me:* or "Be my redeemer" (see Ps 19:14; 69:18; 72:13f).
119:155 The godless haunt the psalmist, for they flaunt the commandments of the Lord. *The wicked:* see note on Ps 119:21 ("the arrogant").

¹⁵⁸ I look on the faithless with loathing,*
    for they do not obey your word.^r
¹⁵⁹ See how I love your precepts;
    preserve my life, O LORD, according to
    your love.
¹⁶⁰ All your words are true;
    all your righteous laws are eternal.*

Sin and Shin

¹⁶¹ Rulers persecute me without cause,*
    but my heart* trembles at your word.
¹⁶² I rejoice in your promise
    like one who finds great spoil.
¹⁶³ I hate and abhor falsehood
    but I love your law.
¹⁶⁴ Seven times* a day I praise you
    for your righteous laws.
¹⁶⁵ Great peace have they who love your law,^s
    and nothing can make them stumble.*
¹⁶⁶ I wait for your salvation, O LORD,
    and I follow your commands.

---

r Ps 139:22; Ex 32:19.—s Ps 37:11; 72:7.

119:158 *I look on the faithless with loathing:* i.e., they are people who have broken the covenant relationship and whose words and acts are unreliable (see Ps 25:3; Isa 48:8; Jer 5:11; Mal 2:10f).

119:160 The word ("words . . . righteous laws") of the Lord is a source of life that never languishes because it is fed by infinite truth that continues forever. Therefore, it can never be exhausted no matter how many drink from this life-giving fountain.

119:161-168 Despite the continuation of his adversity, the psalmist rejoices in the promise of the Lord, praising him many times a day for his righteous laws. The godly have peace, for they know that the Lord in his righteousness will vindicate them. While waiting for the great day of salvation, the psalmist keeps his hope alive and follows God's commands.

119:161 *Heart:* see note on Ps 4:7.

119:164 *Seven times:* a Hebrew idiom for "many times" (see Ge 4:24; Ps 12:7; Pr 24:16; Mt 18:21f; Lk 17:4).

119:165 The godly have peace, for, even surrounded by adversity, they are confident of God's loving care and his promise that they will not stumble (see Pr 4:12; 1 Jn 2:10). *Great peace:* i.e., complete security and well-being (see Ps 37:11; Isa 26:3, 12; 32:17; 54:13; 57:19).

¹⁶⁷ I obey your statutes,
  for I love them greatly.
¹⁶⁸ I obey your precepts and your statutes,
  for all my ways are known to you.*

Taw

¹⁶⁹ May my cry come before you, O LORD;*
  give me understanding according to your
  word.*^t
¹⁷⁰ May my supplication come before you;
  deliver me according to your promise.
¹⁷¹ May my lips overflow with praise,
  for you teach me your decrees.
¹⁷² May my tongue sing of your word,
  for all your commands are righteous.
¹⁷³ May your hand* be ready to help me,
  for I have chosen your precepts.
¹⁷⁴ I long for your salvation, O LORD,*
  and your law is my delight.
¹⁷⁵ Let me live that I may praise you,
  and may your laws sustain me.
¹⁷⁶ I have strayed like a lost sheep.*
  Seek your servant,
  for I have not forgotten your commands.^u

---

t Ps 88:2; Job 16:18.—u Isa 53:6; Jer 50:6; Eze 34:1ff; Lk 15:1-7.

119:168 *All my ways are known to you:* for a similar thought, see Pr 5:21.
119:169-176 In this last strophe, the psalmist offers a prayer for the Lord's salvation. Although his problems have not yet been resolved, he raises the spirit of expectation in those who love God's word. He prays for complete deliverance so that he may praise his faithful God.
119:169-173 The psalmist comes before the Lord with a broken spirit, asking for understanding and deliverance. Looking forward to the moment of redemption, he dwells on the joyful expressions of his thanksgiving.
119:173 *Your hand:* a metaphor for God's powerful deliverance (see Dt 32:39).
119:174-176 These final three verses form the conclusion to the whole. They succinctly restate and summarize the main themes.
119:176 *Lost sheep:* the Prophets' theme of lost sheep is here applied to an individual (see Isa 53:6; Jer 50:6; Eze 34:16; Zec 11:16; Mt 10:6; Lk 15:4; 1 Pe 2:25). *For I have not forgotten your commands:* this final line sums up the inner state of the psalmist, who is zealous for the knowledge and practice of the divine law.

THE SONGS OF ASCENTS AND GREAT HALLEL—Ps 120–136*

PSALM 120*

A Complaint against Treacherous Tongues

A song of ascents.

1 I call on the LORD in my distress,
   and he answers me.ᵛ
2 Save me, O LORD, from lying lipsʷ
   and from deceitful tongues.*

3 What will he* do to you,
   and what more besides, O deceitful tongue?

---

v Ps 18:6; Jnh 2:2. — w Ps 12:2-4; 52:2-4; Sir 51:3.

Ps 120—136 Human beings are born to be pilgrims in search of the Absolute, on a journey to God. We advance by way of stages, from the difficulties of life to the certitudes of hope, from the dispersion of cares to the joyous encounter with God, from daily diversions to inner recollection. The "Songs of Ascents" (Ps 120—134) are prayers for the path we travel as human beings.

This group of psalms, which forms a major part of the Great Hallel (Ps 120—136: see introduction to Ps 113—118), served as a kind of handbook for pilgrims as they went up to the holy city for the great annual feasts (see Ex 23:17; Dt 16:16; 1 Ki 12:28; Mt 20:17; Lk 2:41f). Two other explanations are offered but are regarded as less likely: namely, that they were sung by the returning exiles when they "went up" to Jerusalem from Babylon (see Ezr 7:9), or that they were sung by the Levites on the fifteen steps by which they ascended from the Court of the Women to the Court of the Israelites in the temple. The latter would account for the name "Gradual Psalms" or "Psalms of the Steps" by which they also are known. The name "gradual" may also be assigned to them because of a rhythm that consists in every other verse continuing the thought of the preceding verse.

Ps 120 Ill at ease in a hostile environment, often detested and calumniated because his faith and his Law place him apart—such is the pious Jew situated far from Palestine. Sometimes he gets the feeling of living among the savage peoples of the Caucuses and the Syrian desert (v. 5: Meshech and Kedar). We can appreciate his desire to return to Jerusalem, the city of his God.

We Christians have the same kind of feeling of nostalgia to be with God (see 2 Co 5). Without belonging to the world from which Christ's call has taken us (see Jn 15:19), we are sent by him into the world. It is in this hostile environment that we must live while continually journeying toward the Father (see Jn 17:15, 18, 24). Thus, we can in all truth make this psalm our prayer when suffering distress caused by the continuous hostile pressure of this world.

120:2 *Lying lips . . . deceitful tongues:* see note on Ps 5:9.

120:3 *He:* i.e., the Lord. *What more besides:* the full curse formula was: "May the LORD do such and such to you *and more besides*" (see 1 Sa 3:17; 14:44; 25:22; 2 Sa 3:35; 1 Ki 2:23).

⁴ He will punish you with a warrior's sharp arrows,
    with burning coals* of the broom tree.ˣ

⁵ Woe to me that I dwell in Meshech,
    that I live among the tents of Kedar!*
⁶ Too long have I lived
    among those who hate peace.
⁷ I am a man of peace;ʸ
    but when I speak, they are for war.*

PSALM 121*

God, Guardian of His People

A song of ascents.

¹ I lift up my eyes to the hills—*
    where does my help come from?ᶻ

---

x Ps 11:6; 140:10; Dt 32:23; Pr 16:27.—y Ps 35:20; 140:2-3.—z Jer 3:23.

120:4 *Sharp arrows . . . burning coals:* the evil tongue is like a sharp arrow
(see Ps 57:4; 64:3; Pr 25:18; Jer 9:8) and a scorching fire (see Pr 16:27; Jas 3:6);
but the enemies of the psalmist will be destroyed by the far more potent shafts of
God's arrows of truth (see Ps 64:7) and coals of judgment (see Ps 140:10). *Broom
tree:* apparently its roots burn well and yield coal that produces intense heat.

120:5 *Meshech . . . Kedar:* Meshech is located to the far north in Asia Minor by
the Black Sea (see Ge 10:2; Eze 38:2). Kedar stands for the Arab tribesmen of the
south in the Arabian Desert (see Isa 21:16f; Jer 2:10; 49:28; Eze 27:21). The
psalmist feels that he is dwelling among a barbarian and ungodly people.

120:7 The godly have nothing in common with the wicked. The godly speak of
peace, but the wicked sow discord and adversity (see Gal 5:19-21; Jas 3:14f).
God alone can be of help in this situation.

Ps 121 The ground of Palestine is rough, and journeys meant discomforts:
rocks, cold, nights in the open; but the pilgrim took courage, for the Lord protects
each of his own.

This psalm is a prayer for Christians in a time of uncertainty. We find ourselves engaged, like the patriarchs, in the adventure that will lead us to the
"rest" of the promised land, across the difficulties and dangers of the desert of
this world (see Heb 11). We can ask ourselves with distress whence help will
come to us that will enable us to complete our pilgrimage. We can be reassured.
Sending us into the world on mission and pilgrimage, Jesus guarantees us his
almighty assistance together with that of his Father (see Mt 28:19f; Jn 17:15-
17). To enable us to overcome the world, its seductions, and its snares, Christ
sends us the Holy Spirit, who continues the safeguarding solicitude of the Master
toward us (see Jn 14:16f; 16:8).

121:1 *Hills:* the ridge on which Mount Zion with its temple was situated (see
Ps 87:1; 125:2).

2 My help comes from the LORD,*ᵃ*
    the Maker of heaven and earth.*

3 He will not let your foot slip—*ᵇ*
    he who watches over you will not slum-
       ber;*
4 indeed, he who watches over Israel
    will neither slumber nor sleep.*

5 The LORD watches over you—*
    the LORD is your shade at your right hand;*ᶜ*
6 the sun will not harm you by day,*ᵈ*
    nor the moon by night.

7 The LORD will keep you from all harm—*
    he will watch over your life;*ᵉ*
8 the LORD will watch over your coming and
      going
    both now and forevermore.*ᶠ*

---

a Ps 124:8; 146:6; Hos 13:9.—b Ps 66:9; 91:12; Dt 32:10; 1 Sa 2:9; Pr 3:23.—c Ps 1-6; 16:8; 73:23; Isa 25:4.—d Wis 18:3; Isa 49:10.—e Ps 9:9; 97:10.—f Ge 28:15; Dt 28:6; Job 5:17.

121:2 *Maker of heaven and earth:* the psalmist makes what amounts to a credal statement, which has been incorporated into the Apostles' Creed. It affirms the Lord's sovereignty over the whole universe—heaven and earth—and demolishes all claims of sovereignty made for the pagan gods. The source of help can come only from the Lord, whose power is unlimited (see Ps 115:3; 124:8; 134:3; 146:6; Jer 10:11f).

121:3 The pagan gods were said to sleep (as well as eat and drink), but the psalmist points out that the Lord never sleeps. Therefore, he can protect his devoted servants at all times and in all circumstances.

121:4 The Lord also watches over Israel without sleeping. He is a guard who never falls asleep at his post, never goes off duty. He is always watching over his people to protect them from their enemies.

121:5-6 The Lord maintains himself at his faithful's "right hand," the side of favor and trust, to "shade" them from the fierce heat of the sun and the malevolent influence of the moon. The ancients feared the evil spiritual effects of the moon (see Mt 17:15) as well as the bad physical effects of the sun (see Jud 8:3; Isa 49:10). The antiphon used with this psalm during the Easter Season in the Liturgy of the Hours, "The Lord watches over his people, and protects them as the apple of his eye," reminds us that because of Christ's Passion and Resurrection no physical or spiritual force can ever separate us from the love of God that is in Christ Jesus (see Ro 8:31-39).

121:7-8 The Lord is present to deliver his faithful both now and forever. *Your coming and going:* an idiom signifying all ordinary human activity (see Dt 28:6; 31:2; Jos 14:11; 2 Sa 3:25).

PSALM 122*

The Pilgrim's Greeting to the Holy City

A song of ascents. Of David.

1 I rejoiced with those who said to me,*
  "Let us go to the house of the LORD."g
2 Our feet are standing
  in your gates, O Jerusalem.

3 Jerusalem is built like a cityh
  that is closely compacted together.*
4 That is where the tribes go up,
  the tribes of the LORD,i
  to praise the name of the LORD
  according to the statute given to Israel.*

---

g Ps 42:4; 43:3-4; 84:1-4.—h Ps 48:12-13; Eph 2:19-22.—i Dt 16:16.

Ps 122 The pilgrims arrive where they can see Jerusalem, and their faces light up with joy, a joy that formed part of the Messianic Hope. They come to a halt to admire the holy city restored by Nehemiah, and their remembrances sing in their heart: those of the gathering of the tribes at the Tent of Meeting (see Nu 2:2) and of the happy era when David and Solomon ruled in their capital. The latter appeared to them as the symbol of unity and peace—"Shalom" signifies peace. In their desire for happiness, they already dream of the gathering together at some future time (see Isa 33:20; Zec 9:9ff).

One day Paul will speak of Christ present in his Church to reestablish the links of the human family (see Eph 2:19-22), and the visionary of Patmos will celebrate the definitively rediscovered unity in his marvelous description of a heavenly Jerusalem (see Rev 21:2—22:5). Hence, in praying this psalm, we as Christians must go beyond the original sense since we find ourselves drawn along by Christ in a spiritual pilgrimage that causes us to leave the world and enter ever further into the Church and ultimately leads us from earth to heaven, the heavenly Jerusalem.

122:1-2 The trials of an expatriate (see Ps 120) and the hazards of travel (see Ps 121) are overshadowed now by the joy that had drawn the pilgrim to his journey. The doxology in Jude 24 is the Christian equivalent of this progress and arrival: "To him who is able to keep you from falling [see Ps 121] and to present you before his glorious presence without fault and with great joy [see Ps 122]." *The house of the LORD:* the temple (see 2 Sa 7:5, 13; 1 Ki 5:3, 5).

122:3 *That is closely compacted together:* Jerusalem is the symbol of the unity of the chosen people and the figure of the unity of the Church (see Eph 2:20ff). The versions have translated this thusly: "where its community is one."

122:4 This verse presupposes the Deuteronomic law concerning unity of sanctuary (see Dt 12; 16:16; 1 Ki 12:27). *To praise:* for God's saving acts and blessings for his people.

⁵ There the thrones for judgment stand,
　　the thrones of the house of David.*

⁶ Pray for the peace* of Jerusalem:
　　"May those who love you be secure.
⁷ May there be peace within your walls
　　and security within your citadels."ʲ
⁸ For the sake of my brothers and friends,*
　　I will say, "Peace be within you."
⁹ For the sake of the house of the LORD our God,
　　I will seek your prosperity.

PSALM 123*

Prayer in Time of Spiritual Need

A song of ascents.

¹ I lift up my eyes to you, ᵏ
　　to you whose throne is in heaven.*

---

j Ps 128:5; SS 4:4.—k Ps 25:15; 119:82; 141:8; Isa 6:1.

122:5 Jerusalem was both the religious center, symbolized by the "house of the LORD" (v. 1), and the political center, symbolized by "the thrones for judgment." The kings of Judah ruled by God's will and upheld his kingship to the extent that they dispensed justice, which was a feature of the Messianic Age (see Isa 9:7; 11:3-5).

122:6ff *Peace:* the customary greeting in Hebrew, *shalom,* which also includes the idea of happiness and prosperity.

122:8-9 Jerusalem is transferred into an ideal, an eschatological expression of what God had planned for his people, and the psalmist prays for the fulfillment of God's plan. What Jerusalem was to the Israelite, the Church is to the Christian.

Ps 123 Upon returning from the Exile, Israel experienced prolonged and harsh humiliations: vexations from nearby nations and from the Persian administration and persecution later on. The pilgrims do not feel the need to recite at length the list of their misfortunes, for these are too well known. The prayer is expressed in a simple attitude: eyes humbly and perseveringly fixed toward the Lord await a sign of hope. Can people be more true before God?

This psalm can serve to show the right attitude we should have toward Christ. John (10:28f) amply indicates that the inner and outer life of the Church and Christians is sovereignly regulated by the risen Christ together with his Father. Our faith assures us that the almighty hand of Christ will save us when we call for help against our inner and outer enemies. We should keep our eyes fixed continuously on him in the never-ending battle we must wage in this world (see Heb 12:2).

123:1 The psalmist indicates the awesome power of God, the Ruler of the universe enthroned "in heaven," who "does whatever pleases him" (Ps 115:3), and whose love and wisdom are beyond our calculation (see Ps 36:5; Isa 55:9).

² As the eyes of slaves look to the hand of their
     master,
          as the eyes of a maid look to the hand of
          her mistress,
     so our eyes look to the LORD our God,
          till he shows us his mercy.*

³ Have mercy on us, O LORD, have mercy on
     us,*ⁱ*
          for we have endured much contempt.*
⁴ We have endured much ridicule from the
     proud,
          much contempt from the arrogant.*

ⁱ Ps 44:13-14; Ne 4:4; Job 12:4.

123:2 The fate of male or female slaves was entirely in the hands of their
masters or mistresses. Their welfare or their woe depended completely on the will
of their overseers, whose hands could bestow benefits or punishments. Hence,
the psalmist pictures the slaves as keeping their eyes fixed on their masters and
mistresses. In like manner, God's people fix their eyes on their Lord with utter dependence; like "slaves" and a "maid," they look to their Master—for acts of
kindness and mercy.

For the Lord rules sovereignly. He is on the throne (see Ps 2:4; 11:4; 102:12;
115:3) even when the arrogant assail his people. No matter how exalted this God
of Israel may be, he is still the Lord ("Yahweh"), the God who is faithful to the
covenant he has made with his people and is ever ready to help them in any adversity.

123:3 The psalmist prays for God's favor (see Ps 6:2; 57:1; 86:3) to right the
injustice done to God's children, who have unjustly endured great contempt (see
Ps 119:22) and ridicule (see Ps 44:13; Ne 2:19; 4:1). It is interesting to recall
that in the Sermon on the Mount contempt ("You fool") ranks as more grievous
than anger (see Mt 5:22). Yet, from the Christian point of view, to endure suffering (including contempt) for Christ is a necessity (see Lk 9:23; Col 1:24), as well
as an honor (see Ac 5:41), for all his followers as they make their way to glory
(see 1 Pe 4:13f).

123:4 As is the case in our day, the People of God are mocked by the proud
and the arrogant (see Ps 52:1; 73:2ff), who rely on and seek only themselves,
giving little thought to God. Although it is entirely permissible to pray to be
delivered from this ridicule, another approach is to accept it in union with the
suffering Christ. Even the Old Testament has passages recommending the
acceptance of such suffering: "Let him offer his cheek to one who would strike
him, and let him be filled with disgrace. For men are not cast off by the Lord forever. Though he brings grief, he will show compassion, so great is his unfailing
love. For he does not willingly bring affliction or grief to the children of men" (La
3:30-33).

PSALM 124*

Thanksgiving for the Lord's Help

A song of ascents. Of David.

¹ If the LORD had not been on our side—*
    let Israel say—* *m*
² if the LORD had not been on our side
    when men attacked* us,
³ when their anger flared against us,*
    they would have swallowed* us alive;*n*
⁴ the flood would have engulfed us,*
    the torrent would have swept over us,*o*

---

m Ps 118:25ff; 129:1.—n Pr 1:12.—o Ps 18:4; 69:2; 88:17.

Ps 124 This psalm is the thankful cry of the chosen people that God saves because he has made a covenant with them. It contains four classic images—the monster (v. 3: "swallowed"), the water (v. 4: "flood" and "torrent"; v. 5: "waters"), the bull (v. 6: "torn by their teeth"), and the trapped bird (v. 7: "out of the fowler's snare")—that evoke the trials undergone by Israel as well as the sudden and extreme danger in which each person can find himself.

Christians can pray this psalm with the sentiments suggested by Paul in a similar situation (see 2 Co 1:8-10). We can direct it to the Father and Christ, through whom God saves the Church. Without Christ, who will be with us till the consummation of the world (see Mt 28:20), the Church and her members could not hold out against the gates of Hades (see Mt 16:18). As the Good Shepherd, Christ gives his life to save his flock from the ravenous wolf who never ceases prowling around her, ready to devour her (see Jn 10:11-15; 1 Pe 5:8). Christ masters the storm that is on the verge of swallowing up the already sinking boat with his disciples (see Mk 4:35-41); he breaks the snare that holds his imprisoned apostles, among others Peter and Paul (see Ac 5:17-19; 12:1-11; 16:19-26). Truly, we can say with assurance: "Our help is in the name of the LORD, the Maker of heaven and earth" (v. 8).

124:1-2 Because the Lord has been with his people, they have not perished (see Ps 94:17; 119:92) and have hope instead (see Ne 4:20). The ancients had a grateful awareness of God's presence among them.

124:1 *Let Israel say:* the people are invited to repeat the first phrase like a refrain (see Ps 118:2; 129:1).

124:2 *Men attacked:* i.e., the arrogant (see Ps 123:4).

124:3-5 The trials undergone by Israel are described in traditional images (monsters, wild beasts, drowning, and snares) to indicate the totality of the disaster that loomed so near.

124:3 *Swallowed:* in addition to indicating death at the hands of some beast, it also functions as a metaphor for death itself, which is often portrayed by "Hades" that devours its victims (see Ps 55:15; Pr 1:12).

124:4-5 The metaphor of water as a destructive force is common in the Old Testament (see Ps 18:16 and note; 32:6; 42:7; 69:1f, 15; Isa 8:7f; La 3:54) because of the destructive torrential rains common to that part of the world (see Jdg 5:21; Mt 7:27).

5 the raging waters
would have swept us away.

6 Praise be to the LORD,
who has not let us be torn by their teeth.
7 We have escaped like a bird
out of the fowler's snare;
the snare has been broken,
and we have escaped.*
8 Our help is in the name of the LORD,[p]
the Maker of heaven and earth.*

PSALM 125*

God, Protector of His People

A song of ascents.

1 Those who trust in the LORD are like Mount Zion,[q]
which cannot be shaken but endures forever.*

---

p Ps 121:2; 134:3; 146:6.—q Pr 10:25; Isa 33:20.

124:7 A triumphant note underlies this verse: "we have escaped" by the Lord's doing; therefore, he is to be praised.

124:8 The psalm culminates in the great confession (see note on Ps 121:2).

Ps 125 In place of the grandeur and freedom to which it aspired during the Exile, Israel after the return experiences nothing but difficulties, miseries, and foreign oppressions. Under the weight of this cruel disillusionment, its courage fails and its faith in the Lord wavers. Fortunately, men of strong character like Zephaniah, Ezra, Nehemiah, and the aged prophet Haggai providentially appear to restore its confidence in the Lord's faithfulness.

The present psalm may date from this period of restoration. It sings of the perfect stability and security assured to his faithful by the Lord, who surrounds them as the mountains surround Jerusalem making it well-nigh impregnable. However, despite threats and against all appearances, God is the only certain power in human existence.

We can pray this psalm mindful of the help the Father granted to Israel of old but above all of the far superior aid he accords to the Church, to her Head as well as to each of her members. It is this same aid that we are to praise with Christ.

125:1 God's people ("those who trust in the Lord") are like Mount Zion, which symbolizes God's help (see Ps 121:1f; 124:8), his presence in helping and protecting his people (see Ps 76:6-9; 132:13-16), and the privileges of the covenantal relationship, and which cannot be shaken but endures forever (see Ps 16:8; 46:5; 112:6f; Isa 28:16; 54:10).

2 As the mountains surround Jerusalem,^r
  so the L<small>ORD</small> surrounds his people
  both now and forevermore.*

3 The scepter of the wicked will not remain
    over the land allotted to the righteous,
  for then the righteous might use
    their hands to do evil.*
4 Do good, O L<small>ORD</small>, to those who are good,*
  to those who are upright in heart.* ^s
5 But those who turn to crooked ways^t
  the L<small>ORD</small> will banish with the evildoers.*

Peace be upon Israel.^u

---

r Ps 32:10; Dt 32:11; Mt 28:20.—s Ps 18:25ff; 119:65.—t Ps 92:9; Pr 3:32.—u Ps 128:6.

125:2 In the mountain range around Jerusalem, Mount Zion is surrounded by higher peaks: to the east lies the Mount of Olives, to the north Mount Scopus, to the west and south other hills. So Mount Zion was regarded as secure because of its natural defensibility. God is around and present to his people (see Ps 34:7; Zec 2:7), both now and forevermore (see Ps 113:2; 115:18; 121:8).

125:3 Over the years the enemies of Israel have invaded and occupied the land of Canaan and even annexed all or part of Israel and Judah (see Ps 124:2-5). However, the psalmist declares that the Lord will never allow such a situation to endure. For foreign rulers often attempted to introduce the worship of their gods to the local population. Such foreign rule (symbolized by the term "scepter"—see Isa 14:5) imposed on Israel cannot coexist with the Lord's protecting presence. For it might be an occasion for some of the godly to be tempted, to lose heart, and to fall away. *Land allotted to the righteous:* i.e., the promised land (see Ps 78:55).

125:4-5 Though confident in the Lord's protection, the people pray for his help. For the Lord deals with everyone as that person is and does. In times of trouble, God gives his grace more abundantly; at the same time, he never permits his faithful to be tested above their strength. However, he wishes us to pray for that grace. The psalm therefore closes with a petition for grace and judgment. One's own weakness and the malice of the enemy conceal many dangers. May God not refuse his assistance to those who are of goodwill and try to walk the path of virtue, and at the same time may he banish those who follow the path of evil.

125:4 *Heart:* see note on Ps 4:7.

125:5 The "evildoers" are apostates who have turned to "crooked ways," i.e., paths that twist away from the main road (see Jdg 5:6). The psalmist invokes the law of talion against them (see Ps 18:26ff). *Peace be upon Israel:* perhaps a short form of the priestly blessing (see Nu 6:24-26), with Israel designating the group of the poor of the Lord (see Ps 73:1; 102:1; 128:6; 130:7f).

PSALM 126*

God, Our Joy and Our Hope

A song of ascents.

1 When the LORD brought back the captives to[d]
Zion,* [v]
we were like men who dreamed.* [e]
2 Our mouths were filled with laughter,
our tongues with songs of joy.[w]
Then it was said among the nations,
"The LORD has done great things for
them."*

---

d Or LORD *restored the fortunes of.*—e Or *men restored to health.*

v Ps 14:7; Ezr 1:1-3.—w Job 8:21; Lk 1:49.

Ps 126 The Jewish community takes pains to be reestablished. But joy fills the people's hearts. They still resound with the gladness and hope of the caravans returning from the Exile, and every pilgrimage unfolds like a new Exodus (vv. 1-3; see Isa 48:21), a return from the Exile. It is also faith in an even more wondrous future, the gathering together of all by the side of the Messiah. Such happiness is prepared for in the suffering of the present just as the harvest grows out of the grain sown into the earth where it dies (see Jn 12:24; Ro 8:8-25; 1 Co 15:35-49).

In praying this psalm, we can also be mindful of the wondrous spiritual salvation of sinners worked by Christ in accord with the will of the Father. This salvation constitutes a spiritual Exodus from the sinful world to the divine dwelling of the earthly Church and then of the heavenly Church, a transferral from satanic tyranny to the gentle yoke of Christ and then of the heavenly Father, a conversion from infidelity to fidelity toward Christ and his Father. Such are the wonders that God has worked radically for all in causing Christ to pass from the grave to heaven, from death to glorious life (see Eph 4:8), and that he works effectively for every believer who shares in this mystery through faith (see Jn 5:24).

126:1-3 The edict of the Persian King Cyrus the Great in 538 B.C. that permitted the exiles to return home was totally unexpected despite the oracles issued by Isaiah and Jeremiah. The long continuation of the captivity had caused many to give up hope. Hence, the joy of their deliverance was indescribable. The Gentiles, too, were impressed by this event; for many nations in the ancient Near East had vanished owing to conquest and exile, and the conventional wisdom was that little Israel would suffer the same fate. When this proved not to be the case, the People of God acknowledged that it was the Lord who had done great things for them.

126:1 The restoration of the captives to Zion took place in 538 B.C., in fulfillment of the prophetic word (see Isa 14:1f; 44:24—45:25; 48:20f; Jer 29:14; 30:3; 33:7, 10f; Am 9:14). However, when the actual moment came, it felt like a mirage. *Like men who dreamed:* can also be translated as "like men restored to health."

³ The LORD has done great things for us,
    and we are filled with joy.*

⁴ * Restore our fortunes,* ᶠ O LORD,
    like streams in the Negev.
⁵ Those who sow in tearsˣ
    will reap with songs of joy.*
⁶ He who goes out weeping,
    carrying seed to sow,
  will return with songs of joy,
    carrying sheaves with him.*

---

f Or *bring back our captives.*

---

x Isa 65:19; Bar 4:23; Rev 21:4.

126:3 The psalmist affirms that the Lord has done great things for the people, and they are filled with joy. We Christians can use this verse in our own right to declare the manifold blessings bestowed on us in Christ, especially his Resurrection, which turned the disciples' sorrow into joy and brought salvation to the world that had previously been in bondage to the devil.

126:4-6 The reality of life in Canaan soon tempered the joy of the repatriates, for they had to eke out an existence in the land that had remained untended for years. So the people cry out to God for a continuation of the restoration: restoration of their well-being in the land ("fortunes"; see Ps 14:7). And they are assured of God's continued fidelity to his promise.

126:4 The repatriates, disappointed by the limited fulfillment of the prophetic word, turn to the Lord. They beg him to grant them a complete restoration and give them a brighter future even if to do so he has to perform a miracle like creating streams in the Negev. *Restore our fortunes:* another possible translation is: "Bring back our people from captivity." No matter what the text, the prayer is one for a better future. *Streams in the Negev:* the wadis of southern Palestine, almost always dry, are suddenly filled with the winter rains and fertilize the earth (see 2 Ki 3:20; Isa 41:18), representing proverbially the sudden coming of God's blessing.

126:5 God will be true to his promise, but the people must also do their part—they must sow the seed in order to have a harvest. God will turn the people's "tears" into "songs of joy" by blessing them in their various endeavors and rewarding their laborious toil.

126:6 The psalm concludes on the expectation of another miracle to take place; the people will return singing songs of joy because of the plentiful harvest. The time of exile was like a sowing of tears; it was a time of penance. The time of the harvest has not yet come. But as certainly as in nature the harvest follows upon seeding, so certain is it that a time of joy will follow for God's people. Thus, the psalm attests to the certainty of the Lord's promise. *Seed to sow:* these words are a reminder of Haggai's word to sow whatever little one has: "Is there yet any seed left in the barn? Until now, the vine and the fig tree, the pomegranate and the olive tree have not borne fruit. 'From this day I will bless you' " (Hag 2:19).

PSALM 127*

Need of Divine Assistance

A song of ascents. Of Solomon.

¹ Unless the LORD builds the house,*
    its builders labor in vain.
  Unless the LORD watches over the city,
    the watchmen stand guard in vain.*
² In vain you rise early
    and stay up late,ʸ
  toiling for food to eat—
    for he grants sleep toᵍ those he loves.*

³ Sons are a heritage from the LORD,*
    children a reward from him.*ᶻ

---

g Or *eat— / for while they sleep he provides for.*

y Ecc 2:24-25; Mt 6:11.—z Ps 115:14; 128:3; Ge 1:28; Dt 28:11; Pr 17:6.

Ps 127 Without God, human undertakings are doomed to fail. It is God who is responsible for all of life's blessings (see Dt 28:1-14). There is no need for us to become overly anxious. His providence takes care of us (see Mt 6:25-34; Jn 15:5). This is the constant teaching of the Old and New Testament. Nowadays we know that natural laws follow a determined course that can be put to use in invention, technology, and the human sciences. But what do we expect to achieve? And if our endless affairs take away from us our time and taste for true joys, e.g., that of breaking bread together and of the fraternal home—what then?

We can and should recite this beautiful psalm in its original sense to praise the Lord who fills us with earthly goods and gifts. We can also transpose it to the spiritual plane to express our radical impotence in this sphere and to proclaim that all success and supernatural fecundity suppose the concurrence of Christ Jesus, acting in the name of the Father, in the holy Spirit (see Jn 15:4f).

127:1-2 The psalmist wishes to have the people become more God-centered in their everyday lives, for it is the Lord who provides shelter, security, and food.

127:1 The building of a "house" may refer to the construction of a house within the protective walls of the city or to the raising of a "family," for in the Old Testament it is usual to speak of a family as a house in much the same way as we speak of a prominent family as a dynasty (see Ge 16:2; 30:3; Ex 1:21; Ru 4:11; 1 Sa 2:35; 2 Sa 7:27). Even the best watchmen (see 2 Sa 13:34; 18:24-27; SS 3:3; 5:7) are not enough to protect the city against attack unless the Lord is guarding it (see Ps 121:4; 132).

127:2 The higher way of life is to trust the Lord in one's work. A good harvest results from God's blessing, not endless toil (see Pr 10:22; Mt 6:25-34; 1 Pe 5:7).

127:3-5 It is the Lord too who as a sign of his favor gives sons who provide protection for the family members.

127:3 The Lord gives children as an inheritance, thus ensuring the perpetuity of the family that is faithful to him.

⁴ Like arrows in the hands of a warrior
    are sons born in one's youth.*
⁵ Blessed is the man
    whose quiver is full of them.
They will not be put to shame
    when they contend with their enemies in
    the gate.*

PSALM 128*

Happy Home of the Righteous

A song of ascents.

¹ Blessed are all who fear the LORD,*ᵃ
    who walk in his ways.*

---

a Ps 37:3-5; 112:1.

127:4 Children, especially sons, also provide a sense of security and protection for the family—especially if they are born early in the parents' life (see Pr 17:6; La 3:13). As the arrows protect the warrior, so do sons guard the godly man.

127:5 A house full of children is a protection against loneliness and abandonment in society. They will speak on behalf of their aging parents, especially at the city gate, where court was held (see Ps 69:12; Dt 17:5; 21:19; 22:15, 24; Pr 31:23; Am 5:12).

Ps 128 A prosperous home, such is the happiness reserved by God for the righteous—so thought the sages of Israel (see Pr 3:33). Although the people soon realized that God's reward is more mysterious, the joy and intimacy of the hearth, delicately invoked in this psalm, and the gathering of all in a Jerusalem radiant with peace remain the most suggestive images of the happiness that God will bestow on the righteous. The psalmist is encouraging the individual to contribute to the building up of the kingdom of God by living a godly life. Through him his family will be established and God's blessing will be extended to all the People of God.

In praying this psalm, we can apply it above all to the spiritual goods that God reserves for Christian families. However, we know that the heavenly Father does not fail to add to his supernatural benefits such natural ones as the blessings and happiness promised by the psalmist: prosperity, professional success, fecundity, longevity, and peace.

128:1-4 The psalmist delineates the blessings of a God-fearing family: the right relationship with God, obedience to his words, fruitful labor, compatible loving parents, godly children, and domestic harmony.

128:1 The wise man was especially concerned with walking in the ways of the Lord (see Ps 1:1; 25:9f; Pr 14:2), ways of love, fidelity, and uprightness. *Blessed:* see note on Ps 1:1. *Fear the LORD:* see note on Ps 15:2-5. *His ways:* i.e., his commandments (see Ps 27:11; 86:11; 143:8).

2 You will eat the fruit of your labor;[b]
   blessings and prosperity will be yours.*
3 Your wife will be like a fruitful vine
   within your house;[c]
your sons will be like olive shoots
   around your table.*
4 Thus is the man blessed
   who fears the LORD.

5 May the LORD bless you from Zion*
   all the days of your life;[d]
may you see the prosperity of Jerusalem,
6   and may you live to see your children's
   children.*[e]

Peace be upon Israel.[f]

---

b Ps 58:11; 112:3.—c Ps 52:8; 144:12; Job 29:5.—d Ps 20:2; 122:9; 134:3.—e Ge 50:23; Job 42:16; Pr 17:6.—f Ps 125:5.

128:2 In godly living, the judgment of God on man (see Ge 3:17-19) is alleviated, for labor is truly blessed by God.

128:3 The imagery of vine and olive shoots recalls the times of David and Solomon (see 1 Ki 4:25) and the blessing associated with the Messianic Age (see Mic 4:4; Zec 3:10). To sit under one's vine and fig tree symbolized tranquility, peace, and prosperity. The metaphor of the vine indicates that the wife will not only be fruitful but also everything that a wife should be for the good of the family (see Pr 31:10-31). The children ("olive shoots") will be strong and later on continue the father's work (see Ps 52:8; Jer 11:16; Hos 14:6).

128:5-6 The psalmist further summarizes the blessedness of the righteous—unbroken prosperity, true relationship with God, secure national defense, and long life. In doing so, he implicitly calls upon and encourages each one of the faithful to contribute to the building up of the kingdom of God by leading an upright life in the presence of God.

128:5 The presence of God extends to his faithful servant wherever he may live. For the new People of God, it signifies the blessing of God on all who have the Spirit dwelling in them. *From Zion:* see Ps 9:11 and note; 20:2; 135:21.

128:6 *May you live to see your children's children:* this prayer for the righteous corresponds to the phrase found in v. 5: "all the days of your life." It calls down upon them God's blessing of longevity, which was one of the greatest favors to be sought in a time when an idea of the afterlife had not yet been fully attained. *Peace be upon Israel:* see note on Ps 125:5. By these words, the psalmist applies God's blessing on the individual to the whole People of God, requesting well-being and prosperity for all. Paul may be echoing this phrase in Gal 6:16: *"Peace and mercy to all who follow this rule, even to the Israel of God."* It sums up Paul's concern that God's people should show themselves true citizens of "the Jerusalem that is above" (Gal 4:26).

PSALM 129*

Prayer in Time of Persecution

A song of ascents.

1 * They have greatly oppressed me from my
      youth—*
   let Israel say—g
2 they have greatly oppressed me from my
      youth,
   but they have not gained the victory over
      me.h
3 Plowmen have plowed my back*
   and made their furrows long.i
4 But the LORD is righteous;
   he has cut me free from the cords of the
      wicked.

---

g Ps 88:15; 124:1.—h Ps 118:13; Mt 16:18; Jn 16:33.—i Isa 51:23.

Ps 129 The present psalm repeats the theme of Ps 124, concerning the past endurance of Israel, joining to it a prayer for the prompt defeat and eviction of its enemies. Recalling past oppressions and attacked on all sides, the pilgrims besought the Lord to overthrow the postexilic dominations. From the time of their Egyptian bondage, the chosen people have suffered oppression (vv. 1-2), but the Lord has always delivered them from their enemies. The poet expresses his theme by utilizing felicitous rural images. He leaves us a prayer of recourse to God—not of resignation—when we are haunted by the memory of fear or too much distress.

Christians can pray this psalm while evoking the continuous assaults that the Church has suffered from her birth and the future triumph that God will assure her over her enemies. The entire Book of Revelation illustrates the psalm in this sense.

129:1-4 The enemies of Israel, who are at the same time enemies of the Lord, have much stomped on, oppressed, and tried to snuff out the chosen people from their youth in Egypt and during the Exodus. But they have been unable to do so because the Lord has broken their yoke in time. The psalmist may be thinking of the nomads making incursions at the time of the Judges; the Philistines dangerously invading at the time of Saul and David; the Assyrians conquering and destroying Samaria; and the Babylonians conquering and destroying Jerusalem.

129:1 *From my youth:* from the sojourn in Egypt and the entrance into the promised land (see Ps 89:45; Eze 23:3; Hos 2:15).

129:3 *Plowmen have plowed my back:* in Ps 124 the enemies are likened to destructive floods and to a hunter; here they are likened to a farmer who plows the field with long furrows. The plowmen are the warriors, the long furrows are the wounds and adversities, and the field is the back of Israel—a metaphor of Israel's history of suffering (see Isa 21:10; 41:15; Jer 51:33; Am 1:3; Mic 4:13; Hab 3:12).

5 May all who hate Zion *
    be turned back in shame.*
6 May they be like grass on the roof,*
    which withers before it can grow;*j*
7 with it the reaper cannot fill his hands,
    nor the one who gathers fill his arms.
8 May those who pass by not say,
    "The blessing of the Lord be upon you;
    we bless you in the name of the Lord."*k*

PSALM 130*

Prayer for Pardon and Peace

A song of ascents.

1 Out of the depths I cry to you, O Lord;*
2   O Lord, hear my voice.*l*

---

j 2 Ki 19:26; Isa 37:27. —k Ps 118:26; Ru 2:4. —l Ps 5:1-2; 55:1-2; 86:6; 2 Ch 6:40; Ne 1:6; La 3:55-56; Jnh 2:2.

129:5-8 The psalmist prays that God may humiliate pagan powers to whom Israel remains subject after the Exile (see note on Ps 5:10 and introduction to Ps 35).

129:5 Those who hate Zion disregard God and include not only the wicked of the world but also the Israelites who do not fear the Lord (see Ps 125:5).

129:6-8 May God make the wicked suffer the same fate as the grass that sprouts in the protective coating of clay covering roofs (see 2 Ki 19:26; Isa 37:27), which the dry and burning desert wind brutally withers up or men hastily root out. Just as this grass is taken up neither by the reaper nor by the sower, so may God cause the enemies of Israel, once beaten, to find no one to gather them or lift them up, no ally or reaper to whom others would wish success in his task with the cry, "The blessing of the Lord be upon you," traditionally addressed by passers-by to the harvesters who in turn would respond in kind: "We bless you in the name of the Lord" (see Ru 2:4). May they thus be a wasted growth.

Ps 130 This is the sixth of the seven Penitential Psalms (see Ps 6) and perhaps the psalm that has been most often recited down the centuries since the time when it became an invocation on behalf of the dead. It is both a prayer of sorrow and a hymn of hope. No other psalm reveals in so marvelous a way the mystery of God who forgives, reconciles, and redeems even those who abandon him. While wonderfully suitable for the deceased, it also befits anyone in the depths of sadness (e.g., Israel), for it makes hope rise for them like the dawn.

Because of the lofty plane on which it moves, this psalm does not need a transformation but only a greater profundity to become a Christian prayer. The parable of the Prodigal Son illustrates this perfectly (Lk 15).

130:1 *Depths:* a metaphor of adversity (see Ps 69:1f, 14; Isa 51:10; Eze 27:34), connoting alienation from God (see Jnh 2:2, 5) and approaching death.

Let your ears be attentive
to my cry for mercy.*

3 If you, O LORD, kept a record of sins,*m*
O LORD, who could stand?*
4 But with you there is forgiveness;
therefore you are feared.*

5 I wait for the LORD, my soul waits,*n*
and in his word I put my hope.*
6 My soul waits for the LORD
more than watchmen wait for the morning,*o*
more than watchmen wait for the morning.*

m Job 9:2; Na 1:6.—n Ps 40:1; 119:81; Isa 8:17.—o 2 Sa 23:4; Isa 21:11;
26:9.

130:2 In his extremity, the psalmist appeals to the Lord, calling him by his
proper name and so obliging him to answer his prayers and intervene. Although
the reason for the distress is not indicated here, the petition "for mercy" implies
that it is related to sin, and the next verse makes this point explicit.
130:3 The unfortunate psalmist is well aware that the nature of his trouble is
different from the depression of illness, homesickness, or persecution seen in
some other psalms (e.g., Ps 6; 42; 69). It is guilt for sin, an evil that can cease
only if God puts an end to the sins that cause the evil. Unless God granted pardon, no one could "stand," i.e., pass through his judgment (see Ps 1:5) or enjoy
the benefits of his presence (see Ps 24:3).
130:4 But God is full of forgiveness (see Da 9:9; see also Ps 86:5; 103:3; Ex
34:7; 1 Jn 2:1f). And he is feared not only because of his great judgment and
chastisement but also because of his great love in forgiving. The righteous respond with love and holy fear (see Dt 5:29; 1 Pe 1:17) as well as the desire not to
offend him in the future (see Ro 2:4).
130:5 After noting that God liberally dispenses pardon, the psalmist expresses
in splendid phrases his desire (indeed his certitude) of seeing God come close to
him soon to grant him pardon. The words "I wait for the LORD" indicate that the
psalmist ardently desires God and seeks to draw near to him with all his might.
In patient waiting, faith looks up to the Lord to grant his grace (see La 3:25f). *My
soul:* see note on Ps 6:3. *His word:* especially his covenant promises (see Ps
119:25, 28, 37, 42, 49, 65, 74, 81, 107, 114, 147) and his word of pardon.
130:6 The psalmist waits for the Lord with much greater anticipation and certitude than watchmen wait for the dawn when they will be relieved of duty after
guarding the city from night attacks (see Ps 127:1). *More than watchmen . . . wait for the morning:* by this twofold repetition after a fourfold expression of "hope" in the Lord, the psalmist succeeds in inculcating a true a sense of
longing, dependence, and assurance.

7 O Israel, put your hope in the LORD,
    for with the LORD is unfailing love[p]
    and with him is full redemption.*
8 He himself will redeem Israel
    from all their sins.[q]

PSALM 131*

Childlike Trust in God

A song of ascents. Of David.

1 My heart is not proud, O LORD,
    my eyes are not haughty;[r]
I do not concern myself with great matters
    or things too wonderful for me.*

---

p Ps 71:14; 86:15; 100:5; 103:8; Isa 30:18.—q Ps 25:22; Mt 1:21; Lk 1:68; Tit 2:14.—r Ps 139:6; Mic 6:8; Ro 12:16.

130:7-8 Like the psalmist, crushed by miseries, Israel must also hope and wait for the Lord. Rich in grace (compassionate and saving love) and redemption (pardon), God will redeem Israel from all temporal and spiritual miseries; he will deliver the people from all their misfortunes and sins as he delivered them from Egypt once before. The word "redemption," at first applied to the deliverance from slavery in Egypt (see Ex 12:27), later designates every type of liberation, every form of salvation (see Ps 25:20; 31:5; 44:26; Isa 43:14); here it signifies the profound liberation effected by the forgiveness of sins. The New Testament uses the word in the same sense—the redemption wrought by Christ (see Lk 2:38; Ro 3:24; Eph 1:7; Col 1:14; Rev 5:9). *Unfailing love:* see note on Ps 6:4.

  Ps 131 Certainly the Prophets dared to state that God was like a mother for his people (see Isa 66:12f; Hos 11:4). But here is a man who has not fled from the experience of life; he lays bare the depth of his heart: the soul of a child before God. This psalm strikes us with great freshness and simplicity, and it is the most moving and evangelical of the psalms. A believer of the Old Testament has discovered the voice of spiritual childhood: "Unless you change and become like little children, you will never enter the kingdom of heaven" (Mt 18:3).

  We can pray this psalm with the awareness that after practicing abandonment to God's hands, Jesus offers it as an ideal for us also, for like him we are children of the heavenly Father: "Learn from me, for I am gentle and humble in heart" (Mt 11:29). We must flee from all desire to go beyond God and his help (see Mt 23:11; 1 Pe 5:5f; Jas 4:6f). The Father alone can make our labors fruitful through Christ (see Jn 15:1-17; 1 Co 3:5-8); without Christ we can do nothing (see Jn 15:5).

  131:1 The psalmist has completely submitted himself to God in all humility (see Mic 6:8). He is not like the proud who rely only on themselves (see note on Ps 31:23). He knows that true holiness begins in a heart bereft of pride (see Pr 18:12), with eyes that do not envy (see Ps 18:27; 101:5; Pr 16:5), and a manner of life that is not presumptuous, not preoccupied with great things (see Jer 45:5) and achievements that are "too wonderful," i.e., too difficult or arduous, beyond one's powers (see Dt 17:8; 30:11). *Heart:* see note on Ps 4:7.

² But I have stilled and quieted my soul;ˢ
　　like a weaned child with its mother,
　　like a weaned child is my soul within me.*

³ O Israel, put your hope in the LORD
　　both now and forevermore.*

PSALM 132*

The Divine Promises Made to David

A song of ascents.

¹ O LORD, remember David
　　and all the hardships he endured.*

---

s Isa 30:15; 66:12-13; Mt 18:3.

131:2 The psalmist keeps a guard over his desires. He is like a "weaned child," who no longer frets for what it used to find indispensable and walks trustingly by its mother or lies peacefully in its mother's arms. *Soul:* see note on Ps 6:3.

131:3 Likewise all Israel, all God's people, must hope only in the Lord. Weaned away from insubstantial ambitions, we must hanker for the sole solid fare: "My food . . . is to do the will of him who sent me and to finish his work" (Jn 4:34).

Ps 132 By means of this psalm, the pilgrims, assembled for the procession, sing the glory of Zion, the dwelling place of God and the residence of his anointed, i.e., the king descended from David and like him consecrated with holy oil. Doubtless, this is a celebration of the anniversary of the bringing of the ark of the covenant to Jerusalem at the time of King David (see 2 Sa 6; 1 Ch 13—16). This hymn provides a splendid occasion to remind God of the commitment he made in favor of his people: David had sworn to build a dwelling in which to house the ark, sign of the divine presence, and it was the Lord who promised him that he would ensure his lineage on the royal throne (see oracle of Nathan, 2 Sa 7 and 1 Ch 17) at Jerusalem, where the king had projected to build God's residence.

Each new reign gave birth to a new hope, for every one of David's descendants is "anointed," that is, "Messiah" in Hebrew and "Christ" in Greek. When the fallibility of the monarchy became flagrant, the hope subsisted with more intensity. All Israel awaits a last descendant of David, a true Messiah, who will permanently restore God's reign and his worship forever. It will be the time of God's glory and salvation; it will be the coming of Jesus Christ, son of David, whom Luke (1:69) presents to us by citing v. 17 of this psalm. Verses 8-10 and 16 are cited by the Chronicler at the end of the prayer of Solomon (see 2 Ch 6:41f).

Therefore, as we pray this psalm, we can remind God of the merits of David as well as those of Christ, asking him to fulfill the oaths made to David as supplementary motives for fulfilling those made to Christ. We can urge him to enthrone his Son fully in the heavenly Zion and establish therein his perfect kingship for the benefit of his faithful and the eternal confusion of his enemies.

132:1 *All the hardships he endured:* in the conquest of Jerusalem (see 2 Sa 5:6-12) and in bringing the ark to Jerusalem (2 Sa 6:1-23). Some translate: "And all his anxious care," i.e., to build the temple (see 2 Sa 7:1-17; 1 Ki 8:17).

² He swore an oath to the L<small>ORD</small>*
>   and made a vow to the Mighty One of
>   Jacob:
³ "I will not enter my house*t*
>   or go to my bed—
⁴ I will allow no sleep to my eyes,
>   no slumber to my eyelids,
⁵ till I find a place for the L<small>ORD</small>,
>   a dwelling for the Mighty One of Jacob."

⁶ We heard it in Ephrathah,
>   we came upon it* in the fields of Jaar**h·i**
⁷ "Let us go to his dwelling place;*
>   let us worship at his footstool—*u*
⁸ arise, O L<small>ORD</small>, and come to your resting place,*v*
>   you and the ark of your might.
⁹ May your priests be clothed with righteous-
>   ness;*
>   may your saints sing for joy."

---

h That is, Kiriath Jearim.—i Or *heard of it in Ephrathah. / we found it in the fields of Jaar.* (And no quotes around verses 7-9.)

t 2 Sa 7:1-2, 27; 1 Ch 28:2.—u Ps 99:5; 2 Sa 15:25.—v 8-10: Ps 2:2; 68:1; 89:20; 95:11; Nu 10:35; 2 Ch 6:41-42; Sir 24:7; Eph 6:14.

132:2-5 Although the oath and vow of David have not been recorded in the Bible, it is clear that when David heard that God had blessed Obed-Edom, the guardian of the ark (see 2 Sa 6:12), he immediately made efforts to bring the ark to Jerusalem. *Mighty One of Jacob:* a title used by Jacob in Ge 49:24 and by Isaiah (49:26; 60:16) that emphasizes God's action in saving and redeeming his people. *Jacob:* a synonym for Israel (see Ge 32:28).

132:6 *It . . . it:* often regarded as referring to the ark (see NIV textual note), but more likely it refers to the call to worship that follows. *Ephrathah:* David's home-town near Bethlehem (see Ru 4:11; Mic 5:2). *Fields of Jaar:* i.e., Kiriath Jearim, where the ark remained for a few generations (see 1 Sa 7:1f; 2 Sa 6:2; 1 Ch 13:5f).

132:7-8 Together with David and his men, the people wished to worship the Lord in Jerusalem. The ark had been transported by the priests until it was placed in the tabernacle at Shiloh (see 1 Sa 4:3). With the capture of the ark by the Philistines it was taken from city to city (see 1 Sa 4—6) until David brought it to Jerusalem and inaugurated a new era in God's rule over Israel: the Davidic era. The ark was the footstool of the Lord's throne (see Ps 99:5) and symbolized God's earthly rule (see Ps 99:1f; Nu 10:35f; 2 Ch 6:41f). *Arise, O Lord:* the invocation whenever the ark set out in the days of Moses (see Nu 10:35).

132:9 *Righteousness:* here synonymous with salvation (see 2 Ch 6:41), signifying victory, blessing, and deliverance (see Ps 4:1; 22:31; 24:5). *Saints:* the people of God who should be faithful to him (see note on Ps 34:9).

¹⁰ For the sake of David your servant,
     do not reject your anointed one.*

¹¹ The LORD swore an oath* to David,ʷ
     a sure oath that he will not revoke:ˣ
     "One of your own descendants
     I will place on your throne—
¹² if your sons keep my covenant
     and the statutes I teach them,
     then their sons will sit
     on your throne for ever and ever."*

¹³ For the LORD has chosen Zion,
     he has desired it for his dwelling:
¹⁴ "This is my resting place for ever and ever;
     here I will sit enthroned, for I have desired
     it—
¹⁵ I will bless her with abundant provisions;*
     her poor will I satisfy with food.
¹⁶ I will clothe her priests with salvation,
     and her saints will ever sing for joy.ʸ

¹⁷ "Here I will make a hornʲ grow for David*
     and set up a lamp for my anointed one.ᶻ

---

j *Horn* here symbolizes strong one, that is, king.

---

w Ps 110:4; 2 Sa 7:12; Mt 1:1.—x 11-14: Ps 68:16; 2 Sa 5:9f; 1 Ki 8:13; Sir 24:7.—y 2 Ch 6:41; Isa 61:10; Jer 31:14.—z Ps 92:10; 1 Ki 11:36; Isa 11:1; Jer 33:15; Eze 29:21; Zec 3:8; Lk 1:69.

132:10 The Messiah or Christ is the "anointed one" of the Lord (see Ps 2:2; 1 Sa 10:1), the descendant of David awaited by Israel.

132:11 *Swore an oath:* no oath is mentioned in 2 Sa 7. However, elsewhere God's promise to David is called a covenant (see Ps 89:3, 28, 34, 39; 2 Sa 23:5; Isa 55:3), and covenants were made with an oath.

132:12 God's sovereignty decrees that the dynasty of David will rule, but God's holiness and justice stipulate that such will hold only if David and his descendants are loyal to his covenant statutes.

132:15-16 The Lord will bless his people abundantly in his royal presence (see Dt 15:4-6); the poor and the priests will share in this new age.

132:17 *I will make a horn grow for David:* a line close to Eze 29:21; it has a Messianic sense (see Isa 11:1; Jer 33:15; Zec 3:8). The word "horn" here designates a powerful descendence (see Ps 75:5); God will strengthen the Davidic race from which the Messiah will arise (see Lk 1:69). *Set up a lamp for my anointed:* promise recorded in the Books of Kings (see 1 Ki 11:36; 15:4; 2 Ki 8:19). The house in which light no longer dawns is uninhabited (see Job 18:5; Jer 25:10). The Messiah will be the light of the Gentiles (see Isa 42:6; 49:6; Lk 2:32).

[18] I will clothe his enemies with shame,
    but the crown on his head will be resplen-
        dent."*

PSALM 133*

The Blessings of Brotherly Accord

A song of ascents. Of David.

[1] How good and pleasant it is
    when brothers live together in unity!*
[2] It is like precious oil poured on the head,
    running down on the beard,
        running down on Aaron's beard,[a]
    down upon the collar of his robes.*

---

a Ex 29:7; 30:25, 30.

132:18 This word of promise contains the Christian hope in the majesty, rule, and dominion of the Lord Jesus, who will put down all God's enemies (see 1 Co 15:25-28; Rev 19:17-21).

Ps 133 The fragrant oil of anointing and the beneficial dew—such images speak for themselves for a Palestinian; for the poet they evoke the charm of a living community gathered together around the priests and Levites in the holy city on the occasion of a pilgrimage. The holy city (v. 3), the priesthood (v. 2), and the communion of brothers—all is newness of grace at this moment.

This psalm easily finds an appropriate place on our lips to proclaim the advantages of concord among Christians in the bosom of the House of God, the Church. John the apostle reveals the evils of discord. The person who hates another is a murderer and remains in sin and death. Such a person is not loved by God and can receive no gift from him (see 1 Jn 3:15-17). Fraternal love constitutes the sign of true faith and with it the key to all the divine goods (see Mt 22:34-40; Jn 13:34f; 15:12-17). Only this love manifests that we are true children of God, born of him, and at the same time true disciples of Christ (see Jn 13:35; 1 Jn 4:7).

The words *Of David* in the superscription, omitted from some mss, refer to the reunion of the tribes of Israel at David's anointing in Hebron (see 2 Sa 5:1ff).

133:1 The psalmist pronounces a blessing on those who live together in unity, as, for example, those on pilgrimage who included people from many different walks of life, regions, and tribes, coming together for one purpose—to worship the Lord in Jerusalem.

133:2 Brotherly accord is compared with the copious oil running down the head, beard, and robes of the priests who were anointed. Just as the holy oil poured on the priests consecrated them to the Lord's service, so brotherly unity sanctifies God's people. Thus, the fellowship of God's people on earth is an expression of the priesthood of all believers (see Ex 19:6), promised to Israel and renewed for the Church in Christ (see 1 Pe 2:9f).

³ It is as if the dew of Hermon[b]
     were falling on Mount Zion.*
For there the LORD bestows his blessing,
     even life forevermore.[c]

PSALM 134*

Invitation to Night Prayer

A song of ascents.

¹ Praise the LORD, all you servants of the
     LORD[d]
     who minister by night in the house of the
     LORD.*
² Lift up your hands in the sanctuary[e]
     and praise the LORD.*

---

b Hos 14:5.—c Ps 36:9; Dt 28:8; 30:20.—d Ps 135:1-2; 1 Ch 9:33; Rev
19:5.—e Ps 28:2; 63:4; 141:2.

133:3 *Dew of Hermon . . . Mount Zion:* because of its height (nearly ten thousand feet above sea level) and the rain, snow, and dew that fell atop it, Mount
Hermon was famous for its rich foliage even during the dry summer months
(see Ps 89:12; Dt 33:28; SS 5:2; Hos 14:5). Thus, the dew of Mount Hermon would
make Mount Zion just as fruitful (see Ge 27:28; Hag 1:10; Zec 8:12). The
psalmist indicates that no matter how harsh the conditions of the pilgrimage
might be, the fellowship of God's people was refreshing. *For there . . . life forever*
more: the divine blessing almost personified (see Lev 25:21; Dt 28:8) will procure
happiness and salvation (see Ps 28:9; 36:10) in a definitive manner (see Ps 61:5;
73:26; Dt 30:16, 20).

Ps 134 As the pilgrims leave the temple and invite the priests to keep up their
praise during the night, the latter direct to them a blessing that brings to a close
the Songs of Ascents, the Pilgrim's Psalter, just as Ps 117 concludes the collection of Hallelujah or Alleluia psalms (Ps 111—117).

This psalm should remind us that Jesus spent whole nights in prayer (see Lk
6:12) and that he urged the disciples to pray always and not lose heart (see Lk
18:1), a point reiterated by Paul in his first Letter: "Pray continually; give thanks
in all circumstances" (1 Th 5:17f). Hence, this dialogued hymn can be exchanged
between Christians on earth: those who are often taken away from divine praise
by their earthly duties should ask those who are better prepared for this (priests
and religious) to assure in their name the work of praise that is so necessary.

134:1 The psalmist calls upon the priests and Levites to lead the people in
worship. These are the "servants of the LORD" who "minister" (literally, "stand")
in the house of the Lord. The priestly and Levitical ministry is often designated by
the verb "stand" (see Ps 135:2; Dt 10:8), and they offered up musical praise to
the Lord both day and night (see 1 Ch 9:33; 23:26, 30).

134:2 The priests and Levites also prayed with hands lifted up (see Ps 28:2; 1
Ti 2:8) "toward" the sanctuary (see 1 Ki 8:30).

³ May the LORD, the Maker of heaven and
    earth,*f*
    bless you from Zion.*

PSALM 135*

Praise of God, Benefactor of His People

¹ * Praise the LORD.ᵏ

Praise the name of the LORD;*g*
    praise him, you servants of the LORD,*
² you who minister in the house of the LORD,*h*
    in the courts of the house of our God.*

---

k Hebrew *Hallelu Yah*; also in verses 3 and 21.

f Ps 20:2; 118:26; 128:5; Nu 6:24.—g Ps 113:1; 134:1; Ne 7:73.—h Ps 134:1; Lk 2:37.

134:3 The words of this verse recall the words spoken by the priests when blessing (see Nu 6:24f). The blessing follows the people wherever they may go or live, because it comes from the Maker of heaven and earth, i.e., the Great King of the universe (see Ps 121:2). Yet, like God's commandments, the blessing is not "beyond reach," not "in heaven" nor "beyond the sea" but "very near" (see Dt 30:11-14; Ro 10:6ff)—"from Zion." And it is the true Mount Zion, the heavenly Jerusalem, where Jesus the "mediator of a new covenant" reigns in the midst of his people (see Heb 12:22-24).

Ps 135 Composed of fragments taken from other psalms (Ps 113; 115; 134; 136), this hymn sings the praises of the true God. The psalmist acclaims the one who holds the whole universe in his hands; he glorifies the one who chose the people of Israel and guided them to their destiny from the liberation from Egypt up to their establishment in Canaan. The entire people—priests, Levites, faithful, and God-fearers (vv. 19-20)—is convoked to this praise, which celebrates the Creator of the worlds and the Redeemer of Israel. In the face of such solid faith, all mention of false gods becomes a caricature. Are our hymns to God true enough to cast scorn on all the new idols that we ceaselessly create for ourselves?

We can use this psalm to praise the heavenly Father for his wonders in favor of Israel (with whom we are spiritually united) and in favor of his Son Jesus, King of Israel. We can also use it to praise the Lord Jesus, Master of nature for the service of the new Israel, Savior of his Church, the only true God in the unity of the Father and the Holy Spirit.

135:1-4 An exhortation to praise God, who is good and who has love for his own.

135:1 Taken from Ps 113:1; see Jud 4:14. The praise of God included a recitation of his wonders in creation (vv. 5-7) and in redemptive history (vv. 8-12). *Servants of the LORD*: although the identity of the "servants" is debated, the general consensus, based on the text itself, is that the word denotes the priests and Levites, who praised the Lord day and night (see 1 Ch 9:33; 23:26, 30).

135:2 Taken from Ps 134:1; see Ps 92:14.

³ Praise the LORD, for the LORD is good;
    sing praise to his name, for that is pleas-
        ant.*

⁴ For the LORD has chosen Jacob to be his own,ⁱ
    Israel to be his treasured possession.*

⁵ I know that the LORD is great,* ʲ
    that our LORD is greater than all gods.*
⁶ The LORD does whatever pleases him,ᵏ
    in the heavens and on the earth,
    in the seas and all their depths.*

⁷ He makes clouds rise from the ends of the
        earth;ˡ
    he sends lightning with the rain
    and brings out the wind from his store-
        houses.*

⁸ * He struck down the firstborn of Egypt,*
    the firstborn of men and animals.ᵐ
⁹ He sent his signs and wonders into your
        midst, O Egypt,*
    against Pharaoh and all his servants.

---

i Ps 33:12; 144:15; Ex 19:5; Dt 7:6; Mal 3:17.—j Ps 95:3; 145:3; Ex
18:11.—k Ps 115:3; Mt 6:10.—l Ps 148:8; Job 37:9; Isa 30:23; Jer 10:13;
51:16; Joel 2:23.—m 8-9: Ps 78:51; 105:27, 36; 136:10; Ex 4:23; 12:29.

135:3 Praise is due because the Lord himself is good and it is pleasant to
offer. The second part of the verse is close to Ps 147:1; see Ps 7:17. *That is
pleasant:* another possible translation is: "he is beautiful" (see Ps 27:4).

135:4 Although all the nations are the Lord's, he has chosen Israel as his own
in a special way. *Treasured possession:* this phrase is found in Ex 19:5; Dt 7:6;
14:2; 26:18; see also Ps 33:12.

135:5-7 The psalmist spells out the greatness of the Creator, who rules over
all creation and is above all gods.

135:5 *Our LORD is greater than all gods:* taken from Ex 18:11; see Ps 95:3.

135:6 The Lord does whatever pleases him (see Ps 115:3) in his acts in heaven,
on the earth, in the seas, and in subterranean waters ("all their depths").

135:7 The Lord's greatness extends to the elements and powers of nature: rain
(see Ps 29), lightning (see Ps 148:8), wind (see Ps 104:4), and the storehouses
from which any of the elements could be brought forth (see Ps 33:7; 65:9f).

135:8-14 The psalmist indicates the greatness of the Lord's redemption of Israel through the Exodus and the Conquest by using climactic strokes. Most of the
phrases in these verses reappear in Ps 136:10, 18-22.

135:8 *Struck . . . of Egypt:* the tenth plague (see Ps 78:51; 105:36; Ex 12:29).

135:9 *Into your midst, O Egypt:* similar in form to Ps 116:19, this phrase recalls Ps 136:11 (see Ps 78:43).

10 He struck down many nations[n]
    and killed mighty kings—
11 Sihon king of the Amorites,
    Og king of Bashan
    and all the kings of Canaan—*
12 and he gave their land as an inheritance,
    an inheritance to his people Israel.*

13 Your name, O LORD, endures forever,[o]
    your renown, O LORD, through all genera-
       tions.*
14 For the LORD will vindicate his people[p]
    and have compassion on his servants.*

15 The idols of the nations are silver and gold,*
    made by the hands of men.[q]
16 They have mouths, but cannot speak,
    eyes, but they cannot see;
17 they have ears, but cannot hear,
    nor is there breath in their mouths.
18 Those who make them will be like them,
    and so will all who trust in them.

19 O house of Israel, praise the LORD;*
    O house of Aaron, praise the LORD;[r]
20 O house of Levi, praise the LORD;
    you who fear him, praise the LORD.

---

n 10-12: Ps 44:2; 136:17-22; Nu 21:21-35; Dt 2:24—3:17; Jos 24:8-11.—
o Ps 102:12; Ex 3:15; Isa 63:12.—p Dt 32:36; Heb 10:30.—q 15-18: Ps
96:5; 115:4-6, 8.—r 19-20: Ps 115:9-11; 118:2-4.

135:11 *Sihon . . . Og . . . and all the kings of Canaan:* see Ps 136:19f; Nu
21:21-26, 33-35; Dt 2:30-33; 3:1-6; Jos 12:2-24).
135:12 Recalls Ps 136:17-22.
135:13 Extract from Ex 3:15; see Ps 102:12; Isa 63:12. The name God revealed
to Moses was to increase in significance as the Lord increased his activities in
redemptive history.
135:14 *Have compassion on his servants:* taken from Dt 32:36.
135:15-18 The psalmist reproduces Ps 115:4-6, 8 almost exactly. His point is
that idols, unlike the God of Israel, do not speak, reveal, promise, or utter any
spoken word. Ultimately divine revelation is the difference between the religions
made by humans and the true religion of the Lord (see Ps 115:4-8; Dt 4:16; Isa
44:9ff; Jer 10:1ff; Bar 6:7ff).
135:19-21 Employing the language of Ps 115:9-11 and 118:2-4 (with the addition of "O house of Levi"), the psalmist calls upon all to praise the Lord present
in Zion.

²¹ Praise be to the LORD from Zion,
    to him who dwells in Jerusalem.

Praise the LORD.*

PSALM 136*

Thanksgiving for the Creation
and Redemption

¹ Give thanks to the LORD, for he is good.*
            *His love endures forever.*ˢ
² Give thanks to the God of gods.
            His love endures forever.
³ Give thanks to the LORD of lords:
            His love endures forever.

⁴ to him who alone does great wonders,ᵗ
            His love endures forever.

---

s Ps 100:5; 105:1; 118:1.—t Ps 72:18; Ex 15:11.

135:21 *Praise the LORD:* some regard this line as belonging to the beginning of Ps 136.

Ps 136 This psalm was for Israel the last of the "Great Hallel" psalms or, according to some Jewish authorities, the only Hallel psalm, the supreme song of praise. Associated with the great annual feasts, especially with the Feast of Passover, it is made up of exclamations of gratitude to God (accompanying a list of his wonders) and of enthusiastic assents from the crowd. In this list there are three great wonders that are never separated in Israel. First the creation and life of the world (vv. 5-9). Next the deliverances worked by God for Israel: the Exodus from Egypt (vv. 10-12), the passage through the Red Sea (vv. 13-15), the sojourn and victories in the desert (vv. 16-20), and the Conquest of the promised land (vv. 21-24). Finally, God's solicitude for every living being, the grace of the bread for each day (v. 25). As it goes through this list of favors, Israel sings of God's merciful love.

Such a psalm could not fail to become a favorite of the Church for the Easter Vigil. By his Passion and Resurrection, Christ has given life to a new world; human beings are snatched from slavery to sin and advance in their earthly pilgrimage to become the people reunited around God in the new promised land, the kingdom of heaven. In the accents of the Great Hallel, Christians thus sing of the Passover of the world.

136:1-4 The words "give thanks" here mean "confess" or "acknowledge" (see Lev 5:5; Pr 28:13) and therefore call us to grateful worship indicating what we know of God's glory and his deeds. Since he is "the God of gods" and "the LORD of lords" (see Dt 10:17), he alone is to be thanked for all the acts in creation and redemption (see Ps 72:18; Ex 15:11).

5 who by his understanding made the heavens,*
>   *His love endures forever.*[u]

6 who spread out the earth upon the waters,*
>   *His love endures forever.*[v]

7 who made the great lights—
>   *His love endures forever.*

8 the sun to govern the day,
>   *His love endures forever.*

9 the moon and stars to govern the night;[w]
>   *His love endures forever.*

10 to him who struck down the firstborn of
    Egypt*
>   *His love endures forever.*[x]

11 and brought Israel out from among them
>   *His love endures forever.*

12 with a mighty hand and outstretched arm;[y]
>   *His love endures forever.*

13 to him who divided the Red Sea[1] asunder*
>   *His love endures forever.*

14 and brought Israel through the midst of it,
>   *His love endures forever.*

15 but swept Pharaoh and his army into the Red
    Sea;[z]
>   *His love endures forever.*

---

1 Hebrew *Yam Suph*; that is, Sea of Reeds; also in verse 15.

u Ge 1:9-19; Pr 3:19.—v Ps 24:2; Isa 42:5.—w Ge 1:16; Jer 31:35.—x
10-16: Ps 78:51-52; 105:43; 135:8; Ex 12:12, 29, 51; 14:22, 27; 15:22.—y
Ex 3:20; Dt 4:34.—z Ex 14:21f.

136:5-9 The psalmist here brings together two Old Testament treatments of
the creation theme: that of Proverbs, which speaks of the wisdom and "understanding" (v. 5) presupposed by creation (see Pr 3:19f; 8:1, 22-31; see also Ps
104:24; Jer 10:12), and that of Genesis, which gives the account of it (vv. 6-9:
see Ge 1:9f, 16-18).
136:6 *Upon the waters:* see Ps 24:2.
136:10-12 Of the many wonders during the Exodus from Egypt, the psalmist
mentions the tenth plague (see Ps 78:51; 105:36; 135:8) and the Lord's mighty
hand and outstretched arm, a metaphor for God's great and personal strength in
favor of his people (see Ex 6:1, 6; Dt 4:34).
136:13-15 At the Red Sea, the Lord discredited Pharaoh and his forces by
judging them (see Ex 14:27), while he rescued his people (see Ps 106:7; Ex 4:23).

¹⁶ to him who led his people through the
desert,*

> *His love endures forever.*[a]

¹⁷ who struck down great kings,[b]

> *His love endures forever.*

¹⁸ and killed mighty kings—

> *His love endures forever.*

¹⁹ Sihon king of the Amorites

> *His love endures forever.*

²⁰ and Og king of Bashan—

> *His love endures forever.*

²¹ and gave their land as an inheritance,*

> *His love endures forever.*

²² an inheritance to his servant Israel;

> *His love endures forever.*

²³ to the One who remembered us in our low es-
tate

> *His love endures forever.*

²⁴ and freed us from our enemies,

> *His love endures forever.*

²⁵ and who gives food to every creature.*

> *His love endures forever.*

²⁶ Give thanks to the God of heaven.

> *His love endures forever.*

---

a Ps 78:52.—b 17:22: Ps 135:10-12.

136:16-20 The Lord guided his people through the desert (see Dt 8:15; Jer 2:6; Am 2:10) and won victories for them. He struck down the great and mighty kings like Sihon and Og (see Ps 135:11; Dt 2:30ff; 3:1), who are representative of a long number of Canaanite kings. Verses 17-22 are practically identical with Ps 135:10-12.

136:21-24 God was with "his people Israel" during the Conquest of the promised land, which became their inheritance (see Ps 135:12), as well as from that time till the present. The Lord's remembrance is based on the covenant and is intended to effectively bring out the complete redemption of his afflicted people (see Ex 6:5).

136:25-26 Finally it is the Lord who provides daily bread for all his creatures; therefore, all should praise him. *God of heaven:* an expression current during the Persian epoch (see Ezr 1:2; 5:11; 6:9; Neh 1:5; 2:4) that became classic (see Jud 5:8; Da 2:18).

PSALM 137*

The Exiles' Remembrance of Zion

¹ By the rivers* of Babylon we sat and wept
   when we remembered Zion.ᶜ
² There on the poplars*
   we hung our harps,ᵈ
³ for there our captors asked us for songs,
   our tormentors demanded songs of joy;
   they said, "Sing us one of the songs of
   Zion!"ᵉ

---

c Ne 1:4; La 3:48; Eze 3:15.—d Isa 24:8; Jer 25:10; La 5:14.—e Ps 79:1-4; Jer 51:50.

Ps 137 Let us imagine the setting in which this psalm was sung for the first time. Some Levites, after returning from the Exile, have gathered for a penitential liturgy. They are unable to suppress the memory of the humiliations they suffered on the banks of the Euphrates, where, to heighten their sadness, they were compelled not to sing the songs they loved, since it would have been a profanation to make these known in a foreign land for the amusement of idolaters. Now their cry of attachment to Jerusalem becomes vehement and their song leads to an outburst of vengeful anger that, though in keeping with the custom of the time, seems to us cruel beyond description (see note on Ps 5:10 and introduction to Ps 35).

Events now in the distant past become symbols; the psalm speaks of Edom, but the singers think of all the forces united to destroy the People of God and the righteous; the psalm mentions Babylon, but this suggests the most hateful wickedness. This same wickedness the Book of Revelation will later image forth in the monstrous figure of "Babylon the great," mother of blasphemers (see Rev 17:5).

We can pray this psalm as citizens of heaven (see Php 3:20) living in exile on earth (see 2 Co 5:6f). Strangers to a world that does not acknowledge us as its own, we are hated and persecuted by it for this reason (see Jn 15:18f; 17:14-18). We are cognizant that our exile deprives us of our true home and our Father and dooms us to divers physical and moral miseries including death, and we "groan inwardly as we wait eagerly for . . . the redemption of our bodies" (Ro 8:23).

137:1 *Rivers:* the Euphrates and Tigris, as well as the numerous irrigation-canals that branched off from them (see Ezr 8:21; Eze 1:1; 3:15). *Sat:* the posture of mourning (see Job 2:8, 13; La 2:10); it could also refer to the idea of being settled in accord with the word of the prophet Jeremiah who urged the exiles to work for a living, to multiply, and to seek the peace and prosperity of the land (see Jer 29:4-9). *Wept:* see Isa 24:8; Jer 25:10; La 3:48; 5:14.

137:2-3 The exiles were tauntingly requested to "sing the songs of Zion" on their harps. The taunts were tantamount to the question "Where is your God?" (Ps 42:3, 10; 79:10; 115:2), and might have concerned the "songs of Zion" that celebrated the Lord's majesty and protection (see Ps 46; 48; 76; 84; 87; 122).

⁴ How can we sing the songs of the LORD
   while in a foreign land?*
⁵ If I forget you, O Jerusalem,*
   may my right hand forget [its skill].
⁶ May my tongue cling to the roof of my mouth
   if I do not remember you,
 if I do not consider Jerusalem
   my highest joy.

⁷ Remember, O LORD, what the Edomites did*
   on the day Jerusalem fell.*
 "Tear it down," they cried,
   "tear it down to its foundations!"ᶠ

⁸ O Daughter* of Babylon, doomed to destruction,
   happy is he who repays youᵍ
   for what you have done to us—
⁹ he who seizes your infantsʰ
   and dashes them against the rocks.*

---

f Jer 49:7; La 4:21-22; Eze 25:12-14; Ob 1:11.—g Isa 14:22; 47:1-3; Jer 50—51; Rev 18:6.—h Hos 14:1; Lk 19:44.

137:4 The exiles could not bring themselves to sing any of the holy songs while they rested on foreign, unclean soil; that would be a profanation (see Hos 9:3; Am 7:17).
137:5-6 The exiles could not forget Jerusalem and what it symbolized: cove- nant, temple, God's presence and kingship, atonement, forgiveness, and recon- ciliation. They vowed to wait for the redemption promised by God.
137:7-9 See note on Ps 5:10 and introduction to Ps 35.
137:7 *On the day Jerusalem fell:* literally, "the day of Jerusalem" or "that day at Jerusalem." The "day" in question is either the ninth day of the fourth month (June-July 587 B.C.) when the Chaldeans broke through the walls of Jerusalem (see Jer 39:2; 52:7) or the tenth day of the fifth month (July-August 587 B.C.) when the temple was set afire (see Jer 52:13; Zec 7:5; 8:19). The *Edomites* col- laborated with the besiegers and did everything they could to disgrace Judah and keep the people from escaping (see La 4:21f; Eze 25:12; 35:12; Ob 11), and their name became a symbol of Israel's enemies as well as an object of the Lord's judgments (see Isa 63:1-4; Jer 49:7-22; Eze 25:8, 12-14; 35; Ob 1-21).
137:8 *Daughter:* a personification of Babylon, on whom the Lord had passed judgment (see Isa 13; 21:1-10; 47; Jer 50—51; Hab 2:4-20).
137:9 *[Happy is] he who seizes . . . :* in accord with the ruthless practice of an- cient warfare, this scene was often played out during the sacking of a city after its fall (see 2 Ki 8:12; 15:16; Isa 13:16, 18; Hos 10:14; 13:16; Am 1:13; Na 3:10). A beatitude is here transformed into a terrible curse.

PSALM 138*

Thanksgiving for God's Favor

Of David.

¹ I will praise you, O LORD, with all my heart;[i]
  before the "gods" I will sing your praise.*
² I will bow down toward your holy temple
  and will praise your name*
  for your love and your faithfulness,
for you have exalted above all things
  your name and your word.
³ When I called, you answered me;
  you made me bold and stouthearted.

⁴ May all the kings of the earth praise you, O
  LORD,*
  when they hear the words of your mouth.
⁵ May they sing of the ways of the LORD,
  for the glory of the LORD is great.

---

i Ps 9:1; 95:3.

Ps 138 This psalm begins a collection of eight Davidic psalms (Ps 138—145). The believer, representing the people of Israel, knows from experience the God who saves the human race from its distress. He does not want to keep this conviction for himself but to share it with all peoples, all human beings. A deep faith in a universal plan of the Lord illumines this beautiful thanksgiving prayer.

We can pray this psalm keeping in mind the various victories that God empowers his Church to achieve against her material and spiritual enemies. These enable us to bless our Savior and to indicate the praise offered to him by earthly powers who witness and suffer under these victories.

138:1 The psalmist stresses that praise belongs to the Lord alone and not to the gods of the nations, whose kings will have to submit to the Lord. After the word "heart" the Greek adds another line: "for you have heard the words of my mouth," which is not in the Hebrew; it seems to have been a variant of v. 4b accidently inserted here. *Heart:* see note on Ps 4:7. *Gods:* the Hebrew is *"elohim,"* which is the word for "God," "gods," and sometimes "godlike beings," such as the angels. The Septuagint and Vulgate have "angels" (see Ps 8:5); other versions, "kings" or "judges."

138:2 *Name:* see note on Ps 5:11. *Love:* see note on Ps 6:4. *Your word:* i.e., God's promise. By his faithfulness to his promise, God has made his name renowned.

138:4-5 The psalmist prays that the nations together with their gods and kings will also pay homage to the Lord (see note on Ps 9:1). For the "words" and "ways" of the Lord reveal how great is his "glory" (see Ps 57:5; Isa 40:5; 60:1).

⁶ Though the LORD is on high, he looks upon
     the lowly,ʲ
  but the proud he knows from afar.*
⁷ Though I walk in the midst of trouble,
     you preserve my life;
  you stretch out your hand against the anger
     of my foes,
  with your right hand you save me.*
⁸ The LORD will fulfill [his purpose] for me;
     your love, O LORD, endures forever—
  do not abandon the works of your hands.*

PSALM 139*

God's Infinite Knowledge and
Universal Power

For the director of music. Of David. A psalm.

¹ O LORD, you have searched me*
     and you know me.

---

j Isa 57:15; Lk 1:51-52.

138:6 The Lord lifts up the lowly (see note on Ps 113:7-9; Lk 1:48, 52) and puts down the proud (see notes on Ps 31:23 and 131:1; see also Ps 101:5).

138:7 The psalmist describes the Lord extending his hand to offer help while passing judgment on those who cause his adversity (see Ps 144:7; Ex 3:20; 9:15), but in the psalmist it instills serenity and abandonment. *Right hand:* symbol of strength (see Ps 60:5; 139:10).

138:8 The Lord has loving concern for his people and creation (see Ps 90:16; 92:5; 143:5; Isa 60:21; 64:8) and has a purpose for them (see note on Ps 57:2).

Ps 139 This psalm is one of the pearls of the Psalter in its literary beauty and profound doctrine: the complete knowledge that God has about each person. The human heart is transparent to God's look; he knows the most secret and most unknown movements of our souls. Feeling the hand of God on himself provoked sadness and anxiety in Job (see Job 23:24; Jer 15:7), but in the psalmist it instills serenity and abandonment. He no longer asks God to turn away his face but to lead him on the path of fidelity. The psalmist awakens to God; the one that he thought he had to seek out is already there, present in him as his source of life, more present to him than he is to himself.

We can pray this psalm to remind ourselves of the complete knowledge that Jesus has of us (see Jn 10:14f). For he is our Creator and Savior (see Col 1:16f; Heb 1:1f), who restores the supernatural world and re-creates in this sphere each of his disciples, making new creatures of them to his own image (see Eph 2:10; Col 3:11).

The words *For the director of music* in the superscription are thought to be a musical or liturgical notation.

139:1-6 God is all-seeing and all-knowing. His knowledge is not sterile but personal and active, discriminating in favor of those who are faithful to the Lord.

2 You know when I sit and when I rise;*
  you perceive my thoughts from afar.*k*
3 You discern my going out and my lying down;
  you are familiar with all my ways.
4 Before a word is on my tongue
  you know it completely, O LORD.

5 You hem me in—behind and before;
  you have laid your hand upon me.*
6 Such knowledge is too wonderful for me,
  too lofty for me to attain.*l*

7 Where can I go from your Spirit?*
  Where can I flee from your presence?*
8 If I go up to the heavens, you are there;
  if I make my bed in the depths,**m** you are
    there.*m*
9 If I rise on the wings of the dawn,*
  if I settle on the far side of the sea,
10 even there your hand will guide me,
  your right hand will hold me fast.

11 If I say, "Surely the darkness will hide me*
  and the light become night around me,"
12 even the darkness will not be dark to you;
  the night will shine like the day,
  for darkness is as light to you.

---

m Hebrew *Sheol.*

k Ps 44:21; 2 Ki 19:27; Job 12:13; Heb 4:13.—l Ps 131:1; Ro 11:33.—m Job 23:8-9; Jer 23:23-24; Am 9:2-3.

139:2 *You know when I sit and when I rise:* a Hebrew idiom that, when combined with the parallel "go out and lie down" (or "go out and come in": see Isa 37:28), signifies: "in all that I do."
139:5 *Laid your hand upon me:* a gesture performed by the judge or the witness (see Job 9:33). It expresses God's absolute mastery over human beings (see Ex 33:22; Rev 1:17).
139:7-12 God is all-present; he is everywhere to protect his children. He perceives all things in all places and there is no escaping him.
139:7-8 The same images and teaching are found in Am 9:2f. See also Job 11:8; 23:8f; Pr 15:11; Isa 7:11; Jer 23:24; Jnh 1:3.
139:9 *Rise on the wings of the dawn:* go to the most distant extremities of the east. *Settle on the far side of the sea:* the uttermost bounds of the west.
139:11-12 There is only light with God, and his light brightens up the darkness. Some versions add here (after "hide me") a line that has been deemed to be a gloss: "Darkness and light are the same."

[13] For you created my inmost being;*[n]
  you knit me together in my mother's womb.[o]
[14] I praise you because I am fearfully and won-
    derfully made;
  your works are wonderful,
  I know that full well.
[15] My frame was not hidden from you
  when I was made in the secret place.
  When I was woven together in the depths of
    the earth,*
[16]   your eyes saw my unformed body.*
  All the days ordained for me
  were written in your book*
  before one of them came to be.[p]

[17] How precious to[n] me are your thoughts, O
    God!
  How vast is the sum of them!
[18] Were I to count them,
  they would outnumber the grains of sand.[q]
  When I awake,*
  I am still with you.

[19] If only you would slay the wicked, O God!*
  Away from me, you bloodthirsty men!*[r]

---

n Or *concerning.*

n Job 12:22; Da 2:22.—o Job 1:21; 10:8; Wis 7:1; Ecc 11:5; Jer 1:5.—p
Ps 69:28; Mal 3:16.—q Job 11:7; Ro 11:33.—r Ps 119:115; Job 21:14.

139:13-18 God not only sees all and penetrates the inaccessible, but he is
completely operative there, creating people and providing a purpose for all.
139:15 God knows all human beings intimately.
139:16-18 The text of these verses is obscure in several places.
139:16 *All the days . . . were written in your book:* an image familiar to the
Prophets (see Ne 13:14; Da 7:10; Mal 3:16) as well as the psalmists (see Ps
69:28; 109:13), which was reprised in the *Dies Irae* (the Sequence formerly used
at Masses for the Dead): *Liber scriptus proferetur, in quo totum continetur:* "Lo,
the book exactly worded, in which all has been recorded." See note on Ps 56:8.
139:18 *When I awake:* in this context, these words may express a glimpse of
the resurrection on the part of the psalmist, as in Ps 17:15 (see note there).
139:19-24 God is all-holy and offended by the wicked, whom he should punish
for their wrongdoing. He leads the psalmist and the righteous in the way of God
("the way everlasting": see Ps 1:6; 5:8; 73:18; 143:10; and note on Ps 16:9-11)
and not in the way of idolaters (the "offensive way": see Ps 16:4; Isa 48:5).
139:19-22 See note on Ps 5:10 and introduction to Ps 35.

20 They speak of you with evil intent;
   your adversaries misuse your name.
21 Do I not hate those who hate you, O LORD,
   and abhor those who rise up against you?[s]
22 I have nothing but hatred for them;
   I count them my enemies.

23 Search me, O God, and know my heart;*
   test me and know my anxious thoughts.[t]
24 See if there is any offensive way in me,
   and lead me in the way everlasting.

PSALM 140*

Prayer for Deliverance from the Snares of the Wicked

For the director of music. A psalm of David.

1 Rescue me, O LORD, from evil men;*
   protect me from men of violence,[u]
2 who devise evil plans in their hearts*
   and stir up war every day.

---

s Ps 119:158; 2 Ch 19:2.—t Ps 17:3; 26:2; Pr 17:3.—u Ps 17:13; 71:4.

139:23 *Heart:* see note on Ps 4:7.

Ps 140 More than once already we have heard the voice of a suffering righteous person; he is the persecuted victim of the wicked, thieves, and calumniators. He calls down the vengeance of God on his enemies, while retaining his trust in the Lord. The state of the righteous and the harshness of the wicked are expressed in images often used. The opposition that Biblical prayer places between poverty and violence, humility and arrogance, simplicity and falsehood is inescapable. To recite this psalm is to bear human misfortune, to become poor.

We can pray this psalm in the name of the Church who is continuously assailed by treacherous adversaries, both material and spiritual. Knowing the futility of earthly help, the Church takes her heavenly Spouse, Christ, as her sole refuge. He provides spiritual armor that is efficacious against the attacks of the enemy (see Eph 6:13-17; 1 Th 5:8).

The words *For the director of music* in the superscription are thought to be a musical or liturgical notation.

140:1-5 The psalmist prays for deliverance from evildoers who sow discord with their speech and devise evil schemes, leading to anarchy and continous agitation. Instead of following God's way, they have chosen the alternative way of the "father of lies" who was "a murderer from the beginning" (Jn 8:44).

140:2 *Hearts:* see note on Ps 4:7.

3 They make their tongues* as sharp as a ser-
    pent's;ᵛ
  the poison of vipers is on their lips.   *Selah*

4 Keep me, O LORD, from the hands of the
    wicked;
  protect me from men of violence
  who plan to trip my feet.ʷ
5 Proud men have hidden a snare for me;
  they have spread out the cords of their net
  and have set traps for me along my path.*
                                            Selah

6 O LORD, I say to you, "You are my God."*
  Hear, O LORD, my cry for mercy.ˣ
7 O Sovereign LORD, my strong deliverer,
  who shields my head in the day of battle—
8 do not grant the wicked their desires, O
    LORD;
  do not let their plans succeed,
  or they will become proud.   *Selah*

9 Let the heads of those who surround me*
  be covered with the trouble their lips have
    caused.
10 Let burning coals fall upon them;ʸ
  may they be thrown into the fire,
  into miry pits, never to rise.*

---

v Ps 64:3; Ro 3:13; Jas 3:8.—w Ps 56:6; 57:6; Sir 12:16; Jer 18:22.—x
Ps 16:2; 31:14.—y Ps 11:6; 120:4; Ge 19:24; Nu 16:31.

140:3 *Tongues:* see note on Ps 10:7.
140:5 The wicked seek to entrap the righteous as a fowler ensnares animals
with a snare, net, or trap (see Ps 31:4; 119:110; 141:9; 142:3; Mt 22:15; Lk
11:54). *Proud:* see note on Ps 31:23.
140:6-8 The psalmist seeks protection from the Lord of the covenant, for he
alone is God and the Master of the world.
140:9-11 The psalmist's plea now becomes an imprecatory prayer, which is an
expression for God's just rule. Using metaphors for the divine judgment (burning
coals, fire, and miry pits), he asks for redress (see note on Ps 5:10 and introduction to Ps 35).
140:10 Allusion to Sodom (see Ge 19) and Dathan (see Nu 16). See also Ps
11:6; 36:12; 55:23; 141:10.

¹¹ Let slanderers not be established in the
    land;
    may disaster hunt down men of violence.

¹² I know that the LORD secures justice for the
    poor*
    and upholds the cause of the needy.
¹³ Surely the righteous will praise your name
    and the upright will live before you.^z

PSALM 141*

Prayer for Protection against Evildoers

A psalm of David.

¹ O LORD, I call to you; come quickly to me.*
    Hear my voice when I call to you.
² May my prayer be set before you like in-
    cense;*
    may the lifting up of my hands be like the
    evening sacrifice.^a

---

z Ps 11:7; 16:11; 17:15; 138:2.—a Ps 134:2; Ex 30:8; Lev 2:2; Nu 28:4.

140:12-13 The psalmist is confident that the Lord, the just Judge (see Ps 7:8f; 9:4), will vindicate the righteous poor (see notes on Ps 22:26 and 34:6), who will then praise his name (see note on Ps 7:17) and live in his presence (see notes on Ps 23:5-6 and 27:4).

Ps 141 Surrounded by the wicked who persecute him in order to drag him with them into impiety, the psalmist offers up an evening prayer, matching the morning prayer referred to in Ps 5:3. The poet begs God to protect him against every defection, to help him refuse all connivance with the wicked, and to enable him ultimately to escape their plots against him.

This psalm is a reminder to us that, impelled by the devil, our greatest enemy, the world hates us because we are not of the world (see Jn 15:19; 17:14). By every available means, it strives to snatch us away from Christ to serve the devil. Aware of our weakness, we should "pray so that [we] will not fall into temptation" (Mk 14:38), reciting this psalm when necessary.

141:1-2 The psalmist is in a precarious position, so he hopes his prayer for help will be like a pleasing offering before the Lord.

141:2 *Incense:* literally, "smoke," i.e., the fragrant fumes that wafted from the altar at the daily burning of sacrificial animals or aromatic spices. *The lifting up of my hands:* a symbol of dependence on and praise of the Lord (see Ps 28:2; 63:4; 1 Ti 2:8).

³ Set a guard over my mouth, O Lord;*
    keep watch over the door of my lips.*b*
⁴ Let not my heart be drawn to what is evil,
    to take part in wicked deeds
  with men who are evildoers;
    let me not eat of their delicacies.

⁵ Let a righteous man*o* strike me—it is a kind-
        ness;*
    let him rebuke me—it is oil on my head.*c*
    My head will not refuse it.*

  Yet my prayer is ever against the deeds of
        evildoers;
⁶   their rulers will be thrown down from the
        cliffs,*
    and the wicked will learn that my words
        were well spoken.
⁷ [They will say,] "As one plows and breaks up
        the earth,
    so our bones have been scattered at the
        mouth of the grave."*p*

⁸ But my eyes are fixed on you, O Sovereign
        Lord;*
    in you I take refuge—do not give me over
        to death.*d*

---

o Or *Let the Righteous One.*—p Hebrew *Sheol.*

---

b Sir 22:27; Jas 1:26.—c Pr 9:8; 25:12; Ecc 7:5.—d Ps 2:12; 25:15;
123:1-2.

141:3-4 The psalmist, like the sages, carefully watches over his heart so as
not to give in to sins of speech or action, for he knows that the wicked use their
tongues for destruction (see Ps 140:3) while the righteous express love and fidelity (see Ps 15:2f). He begs the Lord to keep his heart from sin and temptation
so that he may do God's will (see Ps 119:10, 36, 133).
141:5-7 The psalmist delineates the fate of evil rulers at God's hands, and
hopes that the shock may bring their followers to their senses.
141:5 Oil was poured on the head in a gesture of welcome and hospitality (see
Lk 7:46).
141:6-7 The text of these verses is obscure and their meaning uncertain. As it
stands here, the meaning of v. 7 may be: As a farmer breaks up the soil and
brings up the rocks, so the bones of the wicked will be scattered without a decent
burial (see Ps 79:2-3).
141:8-10 The psalmist prays for deliverance and for vindication, for he remains with eyes of faith fixed on the Lord (see Ps 25:15).

⁹ Keep me from the snares they have laid for
     me,
     from the traps set by evildoers.*e*
¹⁰ Let the wicked fall into their own nets,
     while I pass by in safety.*

PSALM 142*

Prayer in Time of Abandonment

A *maskil* ⁹ of David. When he was in the cave. A prayer.

¹ I cry aloud to the LORD;*
     I lift up my voice to the LORD for mercy.
² I pour out my complaint before him;
     before him I tell my trouble.

³ When my spirit grows faint within me,*
     it is you who know my way.*f*

---

q Probably a literary or musical term.

e Ps 140:4; 142:3.—f Ps 6:2; 143:4.

141:10 God's vindication comes in the form of retribution; the schemes of the
wicked will recoil upon them (see note on Ps 5:10 and introduction to Ps 35).

Ps 142 The psalmist issues a prayer for deliverance from powerful enemies.
Whether he is King David (see 1 Sa 22:10) or someone unknown, he has been
trodden upon by everyone and is undergoing the agony and passion of so many
others. He is also an image of Christ, isolated and suffering without protest.

Often we too find ourselves exhausted on our journey through life, strewn as it
is with many snares. For some, it is social or political oppression that prevents us
from leading a fully human and Christian existence. For others, religious persecution itself intervenes to restrain or destroy our goods and freedom. Upon each
one, our spiritual enemies (the world and the devil) impose a continuous struggle, both fierce and treacherous, that each must wage practically without human
help. In these struggles, we can make use of this psalm to direct to God an ardent and confident appeal.

For the word *maskil* in the superscription, see introduction to Ps 32; for the
words *When he was in the cave,* see Ps 57:1; 1 Sa 22:10; 24:1f.

142:1-2 The psalmist uses the formal third person (customary when address-
ing kings) to pour out his troubles to God.

142:3-4 The psalmist is at the point of spiritual exhaustion (see Ps 76:12;
77:3; 143:4; Jnh 2:7), and only God can help for he knows the faithful's destiny,
his present and future life (see Ps 139:24). Yet the Lord is not present to help
him along this path of his enemies, which is filled with snares. *My right:* i.e., the
place where one's witness or legal counsel stood (see Ps 16:8; 109:31; 110:5;
121:5).

In the path where I walk^g
   men have hidden a snare for me.*^h
4 Look to my right and see;
   no one is concerned for me.
I have no refuge;ⁱ
   no one cares for my life.*

5 I cry to you, O LORD;*
   I say, "You are my refuge,^j
   my portion in the land of the living."* ^k
6 Listen to my cry,
   for I am in desperate need;
rescue me from those who pursue me,^l
   for they are too strong for me.*
7 Set me free from my prison,*
   that I may praise your name.

Then the righteous will gather about me
   because of your goodness to me.

---

g Ps 139:24.—h Ps 141:9.—i Ps 16:8; 73:23; 121:5; Jer 30:17.—j Ps
46:1; 91:2, 9.—k Ps 16:5; 27:13; 116:9; Isa 38:11.—l Ps 79:8; Jer 31:11.

142:3c *Path where I walk:* the present path on which the psalmist is walking,
i.e., the path of his opponents, which is covered with such snares as to fill him
with dread, in contrast to the path of the Lord, which leads to such salvation as
to fill him with hope (vv. 6-7).
   142:4 *No one cares for my life:* the psalmist is like an outcast for whom no one
cares and whom no one comes forward to protect. He is alone and extremely vul-
nerable.
   142:5-7 The psalmist reiterates his distress and his plea for deliverance, confessing that the Lord is his refuge (see Ps 91:2; Jer 17:17) and his hope ("my portion in the land of the living": see Ps 16:5; 73:26; 119:57; La 3:24). In turn, he
will give thanks for his deliverance (see note on Ps 7:17), and the righteous will
rejoice in the Lord with him (see Ps 22:25; 34:3; 64:10; 107:42).
   142:5 Hence, the psalmist cries out to the Lord for help. The Lord is his covenant God; he most of all should be solicitous for his servant. *In the land of the
living:* i.e., here below, during his earthly life (see Ps 27:13).
   142:6 The enemies of the psalmist are too strong for him. Unless the Lord
comes to his aid, the afflicted man is lost. There is no one else who can save him.
   142:7 *Prison:* a word that may denote actual imprisonment or may be a
metaphor for his desperate plight characterized by adversity and isolation (see
Ps 107:10; Isa 42:7). *Gather about me:* the Greek and Syriac translate this phrase
as "hope" (see Job 36:2). All the friends of God are united in praise and joy (see
Ps 22:25; 34:3; 64:10; 107:42).

PSALM 143*

Prayer of a Penitent in Distress

A psalm of David.

¹ O LORD, hear my prayer,*
     listen to my cry for mercy;
   in your faithfulness and righteousness
     come to my relief.
² Do not bring your servant into judgment,*m*
     for no one living is righteous before you.*

³ The enemy pursues me,*
     he crushes me to the ground;*n*
   he makes me dwell in darkness*o*
     like those long dead.*
⁴ So my spirit grows faint within me;
     my heart* within me is dismayed.*p*

---

m Ps 14:3; Job 4:17; Ecc 7:20; Ro 3:20.—n Ps 7:5.—o Ps 107:10; La 3:6.—p Ps 30:7; 142:3; Job 17:1.

Ps 143 This is the seventh and last of the Penitential Psalms (Ps 6; 32; 38; 51; 102; 130; 143), probably because of v. 2, with its admission of universal guilt, the only reference to sin and forgiveness in it. Throughout the Psalter, amid praise and joy, there is the lament of the poor person who is dependent on God for everything. Here is the last pressing supplication of the sufferer who cannot despair of God, of his love and his righteousness. The true Israel, the community of the poor of the Lord, understood it even unto suffering. As Paul indicates (Ro 3:20ff), no one merits to be delivered from evil, not even the person who observes the Law; one can only rely on the Lord's unfailing love for human beings. Those who truly pray will experience the Lord's deliverance.

There are many occasions on which we too can pray this simple and ardent psalm to implore divine aid. The demons and all those whom they incite never cease to threaten us, either in our material sustenance or in our physical and spiritual life.

143:1-2 The psalmist cries out to God to have mercy because of his faithfulness and righteousness, for he knows that God's judgment could find him guilty of sin and condemn him to remain afflicted (see Ps 130:3).

143:2 This text is used in Ro 3:20 (see Ps 51:5; 130:3; Job 9:2; 14:3f; 15:14; Ecc 7:20).

143:3-6 The psalmist sketches the distress he suffers and is encouraged by the memory of God's past acts of deliverance.

143:3 The same images are found in Ps 7:5; La 3:6; Mic 7:8. *Darkness:* see note on Ps 27:1.

143:4 *Heart:* see note on Ps 4:7.

⁵ I remember the days of long ago;
    I meditate on all your works*q*
    and consider what your hands have done.*
⁶ I spread out my hands* to you;
    my soul thirsts for you like a parched
        land.*r*   *Selah*

⁷ Answer me quickly, O LORD;*
    my spirit fails.*s*
  Do not hide your face from me
    or I will be like those who go down to the
        pit.*
⁸ Let the morning* bring me word of your un-
        failing love,
    for I have put my trust in you.
  Show me the way I should go,
    for to you I lift up my soul.*t*
⁹ Rescue me from my enemies, O LORD,
    for I hide myself in you.
¹⁰ Teach me to do your will,
    for you are my God;*
  may your good Spirit
    lead me on level ground.

¹¹ For your name's sake,* O LORD, preserve my
        life;
    in your righteousness, bring me out of
        trouble.

---

q Ps 77:5, 12; Ge 24:63.—r Ps 42:1; 63:1; Ex 9:29.—s Ps 27:9; 28:1;
30:3; 88:4; Pr 1:12.—t Ps 6:4; 17:15; 25:4; 27:11; 86:11; 119:12, 35.

143:5 See Ps 42:4; 77:5, 12.
143:6 *Spread out my hands:* in supplication (see Ps 44:20; 88:9; Ex 9:29).
Soul: see note on Ps 6:3. *Thirsts for you:* see Ps 63:2.
143:7-12 The psalmist here appends a mosaic of prayers for deliverance,
guidance, and commitment to the Lord.
143:7 See similar phrases in Ps 10:1; 28:1; 69:17; 84:2; 88:4; 102:2; 141:1.
143:8 *The morning:* see introduction to Ps 57 and note on Ps 57:8; see also Ps
17:15; 90:14; 101:8; 108:2. *Unfailing love:* see note on Ps 6:4. *I lift up my soul:*
see Ps 25:1; 27:8; 32:6; 33:22; 86:4.
143:10 *Teach me . . . my God:* see Ps 25:4f; 118:28. *Spirit:* the divine Spirit
was regarded as a force and not yet as a person (see Ps 51:11; Ne 9:20; Eze
36:27). *Lead . . . ground:* see note on Ps 26:12 (see also Ps 27:11; 139:24).
143:11 *For your name's sake:* see Ps 25:11. *Preserve my life:* see Ps 31:4; Ps
119:25, 88; 142:7.

¹² In your unfailing love, silence my enemies;ᵘ
    destroy all my foes,
  for I am your servant.*

PSALM 144*

Prayer for Victory and Peace

Of David.

¹ * Praise be to the LORD* my Rock,
    who trains my hands for war,
    my fingers for battle.
² He is my loving God and my fortress,
    my stronghold and my deliverer,
  my shield, in whom I take refuge,
    who subdues peoplesʳ under me.*

³ O LORD, what is man that you care for him,ᵛ
    the son of man that you think of him?*

---

r Many manuscripts of the Masoretic Text, Dead Sea Scrolls, Aquila, Jerome and Syriac; most manuscripts of the Masoretic Text *subdues my people.*

u Ps 54:5; 116:16. — v Ps 8:4; Job 7:17; Heb 2:6.

143:12 The psalmist calls upon the Lord to deal righteously with his adversaries, reflecting a hope that is expressed in the imprecatory psalms (see note on Ps 5:10 and introduction to Ps 35; see also Ps 54:5).

Ps 144 This psalm combines two compositions that are quite different in rhythm and tone. The first is suited to a royal liturgy and is drawn largely from Ps 18, a canticle of the king's victories. The second part was originally a kind of fine painting to illustrate a time of prosperity. By the time of the final redaction of the psalm, the monarchy had disappeared, and the two compositions were combined into a hymn of the Messianic Hope.

A new David will come, the true Messiah upon whom will rest the blessing of God for the benefit of the whole community. He will inaugurate an era of happiness and peace. The ancient images are nothing more than starting points, giving color and life to this prayer of expectation. The essential point is to preserve the hope of a humanity finally filled with the joy of God. It is in this vein that we can pray it with Christ in mind.

144:1-4 In jubilant language the psalmist praises God as the Redeemer-King who cares for him and watches over him, because he has the inherent weakness of all humans and is in need of help.

144:1 *Praise be to the LORD:* the psalm begins with the prayer of David in 1 Ch 29:10 and the prayers in Tob 3:11; 8:5, 15; 13:1 (see Da 3:28; Lk 1:68; Eph 1:3). *My Rock . . . for battle:* see Ps 18:46, 34.

144:2 This verse reflects Ps 18:2, 47. *My loving God:* literally, "my unfailing love" (see note on Ps 6:4).

144:3 This verse reflects Ps 8:4.

4 Man is like a breath;[w]
  his days are like a fleeting shadow.*

5 Part your heavens, O LORD, and come down;*
  touch the mountains, so that they smoke.*[x]

6 Send forth lightning and scatter [the ene-
  mies];
  shoot your arrows and rout them.*

7 Reach down your hand from on high;
  deliver me and rescue me
 from the mighty waters,
  from the hands of foreigners*

8 whose mouths are full of lies,*
  whose right hands are deceitful.

9 I will sing a new song to you, O God;*
  on the ten-stringed lyre I will make music
  to you,*[y]

10 to the One who gives victory to kings,[z]
  who delivers his servant David from the
  deadly sword.*

---

w Ps 39:5-6; 62:9; 90:9-10; Job 7:16; 14:2; Wis 2:5; Ecc 6:12.—x Ps 18:9; Isa 64:1.—y Ps 28:7; 33:2-3.—z Ps 18:50; 2 Sa 8:14.

144:4 This verse is close to Ps 39:4-6 (see also Job 14:2).
144:5-8 The psalmist calls upon God to become involved and deliver him, to come as the Divine Warrior as he did at Sinai. There he came accompanied by volcanic eruption, thunder, and lightning to save his people (see Ex 19:11, 18f).
144:5 This verse takes up Ps 18:9 and Ps 104:32. It also reveals the anxious expectation of Israel, the prey of persecutors and haunted by the hope of a divine intervention.
144:6 See Ps 18:14. *Arrows:* i.e., the Lord's lightning that serves to rout the enemies and take away their power.
144:7 See Ps 18:16, 45. *Hand:* symbolic of the Lord's power (see Ps 18:16), which is capable of rescuing the psalmist out of the "mighty waters" into which he is sinking, i.e., out of the clutches of foreigners. For the Lord, who has subdued the stormy seas (see Ps 65:7; Ge 1:2), can certainly overpower stormy "foreigners" (see Isa 56:6; 61:5).
144:8 The enemies are completely opposed to the law of God and filled with lies, deceit, and wickedness. *Mouths are full of lies:* see note on Ps 5:9. *Right hands are deceitful:* when they raise them to take an oath (see Ezr 10:19; see also Ps 106:26; Ex 6:8; Dt 32:40).
144:9-10 The psalmist makes a vow to praise the Lord for the expected victory.
144:9 This verse is close to Ps 33:2f (see Ps 40:3; 98:1; 149:1).
144:10 This verse takes up the conclusion of Ps 18. "My servant David" became a Messianic title (see Jer 33:21; Eze 34:23ff; 37:24); it is found again in Ps 78:70; 89:3, 20).

¹¹ Deliver me and rescue me
      from the hands of foreigners
   whose mouths are full of lies,
      whose right hands are deceitful.*

¹² Then our sons in their youth*
      will be like well-nurtured plants,ᵃ
   and our daughters will be like pillars
      carved to adorn a palace.*
¹³ Our barns will be filled
      with every kind of provision.
   Our sheep will increase by thousands,
      by tens of thousands in our fields;*
¹⁴   our oxen will draw heavy loads.*ˢ
   There will be no breaching of walls,
      no going into captivity,
      no cry of distress in our streets.ᵇ

¹⁵ Blessed   are   the   people   of   whom   this   is
         true;ᶜ
      blessed   are   the   people   whose   God   is   the
         LORD.*

---

s Or *our chieftains will be firmly established.*

a Ps 128:3; Job 42:14-15.—b Lev 26:6; Isa 65:19.—c Ps 29:11; 33:12.

144:11 The psalmist repeats the prayer in vv. 7-8, probably as an introduction to vv. 12-15.

144:12-15 The psalmist prays for the people, asking the Lord to bless their children, their lives, and their livelihoods. When the enemies are defeated, the rule of the Lord will reach its height and the Messianic blessings will pour in upon his people and upon the land. The blessings are described in terms that are understandable to a people whose main occupation was agriculture and cattle raising. Even the fortified cities will receive a Messianic blessing, that of invincibility.

144:12 The Hebrew text of this verse is obscure and its meaning uncertain. It may refer to the great strength of the sons and the physical beauty of the daughters.

144:13 Material abundance is a gift of God (see Lev 26:5; Dt 7:13).

144:14 *Our oxen will draw heavy loads:* other possible translations are: "our oxen will be heavy with flesh" or "our oxen will be heavy with young" or "our chieftains will be firmly established."

144:15 Blessed are the people who experience the Lord's ability to save, protect, and bless. *Blessed:* see note on Ps 1:1.

PSALM 145* t

Praise of the Divine Majesty

A psalm of praise. Of David.

1 I will exalt you, my God the King;*
    I will praise your name for ever and ever.*
2 Every day I will praise you[d]
    and extol your name for ever and ever.*

3 Great is the LORD and most worthy of praise;*
    his greatness no one can fathom.*[e]
4 One generation will commend your works to
        another;[f]
    they will tell of your mighty acts.*

---

t This psalm is an acrostic poem, the verses of which (including verse
13b) begin with the successive letters of the Hebrew alphabet.

d Ps 34:1; 68:19.—e Ps 48:1; 95:3; 96:4; 2 Sa 22:4; Job 36:26.—f Ps
22:30-31; 48:13-14; 71:18; 78:4; Ex 10:2; Dt 4:9; 11:19.

Ps 145 This psalm is a hymn to God the Great King. It is not original, for the
psalmist strings together his verses in the order of the alphabet and takes the
passages from several other psalms. The cantors of Israel were not reluctant to
dip into the common treasury of sacred chant to celebrate God's praise with the
same words and the same phrases. But the repetition or the acclamation of certain terms also enables one to express the ardor of a conviction, which is the
case here. By means of the words *kingdom, power, majesty, name, works, mighty
acts, righteousness, faithfulness, compassion, love,* and *truth,* the psalm exalts
above all the God of the covenant. It then proclaims his benevolence that is manifested in the help, subsistence, and salvation accorded in some manner to all
who invoke him. Thus, the cantor acknowledges God's presence in the world, in
history, and in life.

We can pray this psalm to bless, praise, and extol the heavenly Father in his
perfections and prodigious works. But we can also recite it in honor of Christ,
who shares fully in the perfections (see Col 1:15, 19; Heb 1:3) and works of his
Father (see Jn 5:19).

145:1-2 The psalmist calls for praise of God the Great King.

145:1 See Ps 30:1; 44:5; 71:14. *Praise your name:* see note on Ps 5:11.

145:2 See Ps 34:1; 68:19; 71:14; 146:2. This verse has been incorporated into
the *Te Deum,* the great prayer of Christian praise to the Trinity.

145:3-7 The psalmist specifies the reason for praising God: his mighty acts,
which reveal his greatness and goodness.

145:3 See Ps 48:1; 96:3f; Job 36:26.

145:4 See Ps 71:17; 78:4; Isa 38:19. Salvation history is transmitted from
generation to generation by the proclamation of God's mighty acts and wonderful
works (see Ps 22:30f). *Your works:* of creation, providence, and redemption.

⁵ They will speak of the glorious splendor of
     your majesty,ᵍ
    and I will meditate on your wonderful
     works.ᵘ
⁶ They will tell of the power of your awesome
     works,
    and I will proclaim your great deeds.ʰ
⁷ They will celebrate your abundant good-
     ness
    and joyfully sing of your righteousness.

⁸ The LORD is gracious and compassionate,*
    slow to anger and rich in love.*ⁱ
⁹ The LORD is good to all;
    he has compassion on all he has made.ʲ
¹⁰ All you have made will praise you,* O LORD;
    your saints will extol you.ᵏ
¹¹ They will tell of the glory of your kingdom
    and speak of your might,*
¹² so that all men may know of your mighty
     acts
    and the glorious splendor of your king-
     dom.ˡ
¹³ Your kingdom is an everlasting kingdom,
    and your dominion endures through all
     generations.*

---

u Dead Sea Scrolls and Syriac (see also Septuagint); Masoretic Text *On
the glorious splendor of your majesty / and on your wonderful works I will
meditate.*

g Ps 96:3; 105:2; 148:13.—h Ps 66:3; 78:4.—i Ps 86:5, 15; 103:8; Ex
34:6; Sir 2:11.—j Ps 103:13; Wis 1:13-14; 11:24; Mt 19:17.—k Ps 8:6; Da
3:57.—l Ps 10:16; 102:12; 146:10; Dt 7:9; La 5:19; Da 3:100; 1 Ti 1:17;
Rev 11:15.

145:8-13a Now the psalmist moves to praise God because of his divine attributes, e.g., compassion and love.
145:8 See Ps 86:15; 103:8, 13; Ex 34:6f; Nu 14:18; Wis 1:13f; Isa 63:7.
145:10 *All you have made will praise you:* see note on Ps 65:13. *Saints:* see
notes on Ps 4:3 and 34:9.
145:11 See Ps 93:1; 1 Ch 29:11.
145:13ab Text cited in Da 3:100; 4:31, and applied to Christ the King. See Ps
102:12; Tob 13:7; Da 7:14; 1 Ti 1:17; Rev 11:15.

The LORD is faithful to all his promises*
and loving* toward all he has made.[v]
14 The LORD upholds all those who fall[m]
and lifts up all who are bowed down.*
15 The eyes of all look to you,
and you give them their food at the proper time.[n]
16 You open your hand
and satisfy the desires of every living thing.*

17 The LORD is righteous in all his ways*
and loving toward all he has made.*[o]
18 The LORD is near to all who call on him,[p]
to all who call on him in truth.*
19 He fulfills the desires of those who fear him;[q]
he hears their cry and saves them.*
20 The LORD watches over all who love him,[r]
but all the wicked he will destroy.*

21 My mouth will speak in praise of the LORD.
Let every creature* praise his holy name
for ever and ever.[s]

---

v One manuscript of the Masoretic Text, Dead Sea Scrolls and Syriac (see also Septuagint); most manuscripts of the Masoretic Text do not have the last two lines of verse 13.

---

m Ps 37:17; 94:18; 146:8.—n Ps 104:27-28; 136:25; Ge 1:30; Mt 6:25-26.—o Dt 32:4; Ezr 9:15.—p Dt 4:7; Isa 55:6; 58:9; Jer 29:13.—q Ps 20:4; 34:18.—r Ps 1:6; Jdg 5:31.—s Ps 71:8; Sir 39:35.

145:13c-16 The psalmist calls for praise of God because of his faithfulness to the covenant.

145:13b *Loving:* see note on Ps 6:4.

145:14 See Ps 94:17; 146:7.

145:16 See Ps 104:27f; Mt 6:25.

145:17-21 The psalmist calls upon all creatures to praise God for his righteous acts—acts of restoration, redemption, and vindication.

145:17 See Dt 32:4.

145:18 See Dt 4:7; Isa 58:9; Jer 29:13.

145:19 See Ps 85:9.

145:20 See Ps 34:17; 91:14; 104:35; 139:19; Jud 5:31.

145:21 *Every creature:* literally, "all flesh."

THE CONCLUDING HALLEL—Ps 146–150*

PSALM 146*

Trust in God, Creator and Redeemer

[1] * Praise the LORD.w

Praise the LORD, O my soul.*
[2]   I will praise the LORD all my life;t
        I will sing praise to my God as long as I
        live.*

[3] Do not put your trust in princes,
        in mortal men, who cannot save.u
[4] When their spirit departs, they return to the
        ground;v
        on that very day their plans come to noth-
        ing.*

---

w Hebrew *Hallelu Yah*; also in verse 10.

---

t Ps 7:17; 63:4; 103:1; 104:33.—u Ps 118:8-9; Isa 2:22.—v Ps 90:3;
104:29; Ge 3:19; 1 Mac 2:63; Job 34:14-15; Ecc 3:20; Sir 40:11; 1 Co 2:6.

Ps 146—150 The Concluding Hallel (see introduction to Ps 113—118). After
all the prayers and praises of the Psalter, we are now at the end; all the instruments of creation and all the voices of human beings enter into a great chorus, a
symphony destined never to end. The Psalms are a foretaste of and prelude to the
acclamations of eternity.

Ps 146 The long procession of the unhappy and the persecuted has wound its
way through the Psalter, endlessly repeating their supplications. This time, their
prayer takes the form of a hymn of happiness and security. How uncertain is the
help of the mighty! God alone truly frees us of every anxiety.

Inaugurating the third Hallel and composed of reminiscences, this hymn sings
of what the Prophets promised (see Isa 29:18f; 49:9; 61:1), promises whose fulfillment Jesus proclaims (see Lk 4:16-21). "The blind receive sight, the lame
walk, those who have leprosy are cured, the deaf hear, the dead are raised, and
the good news is preached to the poor" (Mt 11:5)—such is the kingdom that
comes; it inaugurates a new time, that of peace. Accordingly, like the next four
psalms, it is framed with "Alleluia" or "Hallelujah" ("Praise the LORD").

We can pray this psalm in honor of the heavenly Father but also in honor of
Christ "[whom] God exalted . . . to his own right hand as Prince and Savior that
he might give repentance and forgiveness of sins to Israel" (Ac 5:31).

146:1-4 The psalmist calls upon his people to praise and trust the Lord, for
human beings are unable to provide salvation owing to their mortality.

146:1 The Septuagint and Vulgate attribute this psalm to the prophets Haggai
and Zechariah. *Soul:* see note on Ps 6:3.

146:2 Life is for the purpose of praising the Lord (see Ps 103:1; 104:33).

146:4 See Ps 90:3; 104:29; Ecc 9:5; 12:7; Isa 2:22.

⁵ Blessed is he whose help is the God of
      Jacob,*
    whose hope is in the LORD his God,*
⁶ the Maker of heaven and earth,ʷ
    the sea, and everything in them—
    the LORD, who remains faithful forever.*
⁷ He upholds the cause of the oppressed*ˣ
    and gives food to the hungry.ʸ
  The LORD sets prisoners free,
⁸   the LORD gives sight to the blind,*
  the LORD lifts up those who are bowed down,
    the LORD loves the righteous.ᶻ
⁹ The LORD watches over the alien
    and sustains the fatherless and the widow,*
    but he frustrates the ways of the wicked.ᵃ

¹⁰ The LORD reigns forever,*
     your God, O Zion, for all generations.

  Praise the LORD.ᵇ

---

w Ps 115:15; 121:2; 124:8; Ex 20:11; Dt 7:9; Ac 14:15; Rev 14:7.—x Ps
103:6.—y Ps 68:6; 107:9; Isa 49:9; 61:1.—z Ps 145:14; Pr 20:12.—a Ps
68:5; Ex 22:22; Dt 10:18.—b Ps 145:13; Ex 15:18; La 5:19; Rev 11:15.

146:5-10 The psalmist identifies this Lord as the "God of Jacob," the covenant
God who is Creator and Lord over all, Sustainer and Provider, the Righteous One
who dispenses justice to both the godly and the wicked, and the Great King who
reigns forever.
   146:5 See Ps 2:12; Dt 33:29; Jer 17:7. *God of Jacob:* the God of Zion (see v. 10
below), whose kingship is established (see Ps 47:8; 48:2), and who blesses those
who trust in him (see Ps 84:12).
   146:6 The Lord is faithful, using his power to control creation, including the
unruly sea, and to bless his creatures (see Ps 107:8f) with his unfailing love (see
note on Ps 6:4). *Maker of heaven and earth:* see Ps 121:2 and note; 124:8; Ex
20:11; Jer 32:17; Ac 14:15.
   146:7 *He upholds the cause of the oppressed:* see Ps 103:6; Dt 7:9. *The LORD
sets prisoners free:* see Ps 68:6; Isa 49:9; 61:1.
   146:8 *Sight to the blind:* see Bar 6:36; Isa 35:5; Mt 9:30; Jn 9:1ff; Ac 26:18.
Lifts up those . . . bowed down: see Ps 145:14; Lk 13:12.
   146:9 *Watches over the alien . . . the fatherless and the widow:* see Ps 68:5; Ex
22:21. *Frustrates the ways of the wicked:* see Ps 11:6; 147:6; Job 5:12.
   146:10 The Lord is the Great King who has promised to dwell with his people
and to deliver them (see Ps 29:10; 132:13-15; Ex 15:17). *The LORD reigns forever:*
see Ps 145:13; Ex 15:18.

PSALM 147*

Hymn to the City of God

¹ * Praise the LORD.ˣ

How good it is to sing praises to our God,ᶜ
how pleasant and fitting to praise him!*

² The LORD builds up Jerusalem;ᵈ
he gathers the exiles of Israel.*

³ He heals the brokenheartedᵉ
and binds up their wounds.*

⁴ He determines the number of the starsᶠ
and calls them each by name.*

---

x Hebrew *Hallelu Yah*; also in verse 20.

c Ps 33:1; 92:1; 135:3.—d Ps 51:18; Isa 11:12; 56:8; Jer 31:10.—e Ps 34:18; Job 5:18; Isa 30:26; 61:1; Jer 33:6; Eze 34:16.—f Ge 15:5; Isa 40:26.

Ps 147 Three times the psalmist sounds the invitation to praise, and three times he acclaims the almighty God. Immense is his power deployed throughout the universe, and without measure is his benevolence for his people. He rebuilds Jerusalem, leads captives back to freedom, and reveals his Law. Yet the author of wonders in nature and the liberator of his people is a God who takes pleasure in the lowly. "He will wipe every tear from their eyes" (Rev 21:4)—such will be the grace of the Almighty in the new Jerusalem (see Isa ch. 60 and 62).

In the Septuagint and Vulgate this psalm is divided into two (147:1-11 = Ps 146; 147:12-20 = Ps 147) and attributed to the prophets Haggai and Zechariah. It contains many reminiscences of Isaiah, Job, and Psalms.

We can pray this psalm while keeping in mind that the restoration of Jerusalem and Israel after the disaster of 587 and the Babylonian Captivity constitutes a wonderful work of God. However, it is only a pale image of a more beautiful work of restoration that the heavenly Father accomplishes through Christ in building his Church.

147:1-6 The psalmist enumerates the reasons why it is good to praise the Lord: the restoration that he has worked for his people in accord with his word by rebuilding Jerusalem and bringing back the exiles; his concern for all creation; and his redemption, i.e., the vindication of his people.

147:1 See Ps 92:1 and note on Ps 135:3.

147:2 See Dt 30:3f; Isa 11:12; 56:8; Jer 31:10; Da 9:25.

147:3 See Job 5:18; Isa 61:1; Jer 33:6. *Brokenhearted:* e.g., those in exile (see Ps 137) and those who returned from exile and attempted to rebuild the walls of Jerusalem (see Ne 2:17-20; 4:1-23).

147:4 See Isa 40:26; Bar 3:34f. In this connection, scholars cite the Wisdom of Ahiqar (VIII, 116): "Numerous are the stars of heaven, and no one knows their names."

5 Great is our Lord and mighty in power;[g]
    his understanding has no limit.*
6 The Lord sustains the humble[h]
    but casts the wicked to the ground.*

7 Sing to the Lord with thanksgiving;*
    make music to our God on the harp.[i]
8 He covers the sky with clouds;[j]
    he supplies the earth with rain
    and makes grass grow on the hills.*
9 He provides food for the cattle[k]
    and for the young ravens when they call.*

10 His pleasure is not in the strength of the
    horse,*
    nor his delight in the legs of a man;[l]
11 the Lord delights in those who fear him,
    who put their hope in his unfailing love.

12 Extol the Lord, O Jerusalem;*
    praise your God, O Zion,
13 for he strengthens the bars of your gates[m]
    and blesses your people within you.*
14 He grants peace to your borders[n]
    and satisfies you with the finest of wheat.*

---

g Ps 48:1; Jud 16:13; Isa 40:28; Jer 51:15.—h Ps 37:9-10; 146:9; 1 Sa 2:7-8.—i Ps 30:4; 71:22.—j Ps 104:13f; Dt 11:14; 2 Sa 1:21; Job 5:10; Jer 14:22; Joel 2:23.—k Ps 104:27-28; Job 38:41; Mt 6:26.—l Ps 20:7; 33:16-17.—m Ps 48:13; 128:5.—n Ps 81:16; Lev 26:6.

147:5 See Job 36:5; Isa 40:28.
147:6 See Ps 145:20; 146:9; 1 Sa 2:7f; Job 5:11; Lk 1:52.
147:7-11 God is owed praise because he is the Great King over his creation, sustaining all that he has made, both the creatures in the heavens and the creatures on earth. He wants the people to trust in him rather than in themselves.
147:8 See Ps 104:10-14, 27f; Jer 14:22; Joel 2:23.
147:9 See Job 38:41; Mt 6:26. *When they call:* the Lord feeds the birds, especially the ravens, whose cawing resembles a call for food (see Mt 6:26-30).
147:10-11 Arrogant reliance on one's own natural ability is both futile (see Am 2:14f) and displeasing to God, who comes to the aid of those who trust only in him (see Ps 20:7f; 33:16-18; Ecc 9:11; Mal 3:16).
147:12-18 The psalmist stresses that God is to be praised because he has brought about restoration, security, peace, and prosperity, for he alone commands the forces of nature.
147:13 See Ps 48:13; Isa 65:18f; Jer 33:10f.
147:14 See Ps 81:16 and note; Lev 26:6.

¹⁵ He sends his command to the earth;^o
      his word runs swiftly.
¹⁶ He spreads the snow like wool^p
      and scatters the frost like ashes.*
¹⁷ He hurls down his hail like pebbles.
      Who can withstand his icy blast?*
¹⁸ He sends his word and melts them;
      he stirs up his breezes, and the waters flow.

¹⁹ He has revealed his word to Jacob,*
      his laws and decrees to Israel.^q
²⁰ He has done this for no other nation;
      they do not know his laws.

Praise the LORD.

PSALM 148*

Song of the Universe

¹ * Praise the LORD.^y

Praise the LORD from the heavens,
      praise him in the heights above.

---

y Hebrew *Hallelu Yah*; also in verse 14.

o Ps 33:9; 107:20; Isa 55:10-11.—p Ps 148:8; Job 6:16; 37:10; 38:22.—q Ps 78:5; Dt 4:7-8; 33:3-4; Bar 3:37; Ro 3:2.

147:16 See Job 37:6.
147:17 See Job 6:16; 37:10; 38:22.
147:19-20 Finally, God is to be praised because he has given his people his word of revelation, making known his saving plan (see Ps 50:16f; Dt 33:3f; Ne 8; Eph 3:10f), which he has done for no other people (see Dt 4:7f; Ac 14:16).
Ps 148 The exiles have returned home, the temple has been rebuilt, and its precincts have been restored. God has reestablished the people he loves. What a testament to his glory (vv. 13-14). Joy invades all hearts and expands to world-wide dimensions. The whole universe and all earthly creatures are invited to praise the Lord, the Creator and Redeemer. This theme also permeates the next two psalms, forming the conclusion and the synthesis of the Psalter.
We can pray this psalm to exhort all creation, both animate and inanimate, to praise the Triune God not only as the Creator but also as the Savior and Sanctifier. For although all creation is presently subject to vanity, it is only with the hope of being freed from corruption so as to enter into the freedom of God's children, when God will transform the universe with a new heaven and a new earth (see Ro 8:19-22; Rev 21:1-5). May the angels and saints of heaven do likewise.
148:1-6 The psalmist calls upon all creatures in the heavens to praise the Lord because of his creative and redeeming acts.

2 Praise him, all his angels,[r]
    praise him, all his heavenly hosts.*
3 Praise him, sun and moon,
    praise him, all you shining stars.*
4 Praise him, you highest heavens
    and you waters above the skies.*
5 Let them praise the name* of the LORD,
    for he commanded and they were created.[s]
6 He set them in place for ever and ever;
        he gave a decree that will never pass
        away.*

7 Praise the LORD from the earth,*
        you great sea creatures and all ocean
        depths,[t]
8 lightning and hail, snow and clouds,
    stormy winds that do his bidding,*
9 you mountains and all hills,
    fruit trees and all cedars,[u]
10 wild animals and all cattle,[v]
    small creatures and flying birds,*
11 kings of the earth and all nations,
    you princes and all rulers on earth,
12 young men and maidens,
    old men and children.*

---

r Ps 103:20; Job 38:7; Da 3:58-63.—s Ps 33:9; Ge 1:3f; Jud 16:14; Jn
1:3, 10.—t Ps 33:2; 74:13-14; 135:6; Ge 1:21.—u Isa 44:23; 55:12.—v Ge
1:21, 24f; Isa 43:20.

148:2 See Ps 103:20f; Job 38:7.
148:3 See note on Ps 65:13.
148:4 See Ge 1:6f; 1 Ki 8:27; 2 Co 12:2; Eph 4:10. *Highest heavens:* literally,
"the heavens of the heavens," i.e., the space above the "expanse," which separated the "waters above" from the "waters below" (see Ps 104:3, 13; Ge 1:6f).
148:5 *Name:* see note on Ps 5:11.
148:6 See Jer 31:35f.
148:7-12 The psalmist now calls upon all creatures on earth to praise the
Lord: sea creatures, depths, the powers of nature, mountains and hills, fruit trees
and the cedars, animals and birds, and finally all peoples.
148:8 *His bidding:* literally, "his word" (see Ps 147:15).
148:10 See Isa 43:20; 44:23.
148:12 See Jer 31:13.

¹³ Let them praise the name of the LORD,*
   for his name alone is exalted;ʷ
   his splendor is above the earth and the
       heavens.*
¹⁴ He has raised up for his people a horn,* ᶻ
   the praise of all his saints,
   of Israel, the people close to his heart.

   Praise the LORD.

PSALM 149*

Glorification of God, Lord and Creator

¹ * Praise the LORD.ᵃ

   Sing to the LORD a new song,*
   his praise in the assembly of the saints.ˣ

---

z *Horn* here symbolizes strong one, that is, king.—a Hebrew *Hallelu Yah*;
also in verse 9.

w Ps 30:4; 113:2; Dt 4:7.—x Ps 22:22; 26:12; 35:18; 40:10; 103:1; Jud
16:1; Rev 5:9.

148:13-14 The psalmist gives the reasons behind the praise: God is the exalted Ruler, who is not subject to the limitations of earth or the heavens, and he
has unique concern for his people, i.e., those devoted to him, his saints.
   148:13 See Ps 108:5; 113:4.
   148:14 *Horn:* i.e., the Lord's anointed (see note on Ps 18:2; see also Ps 2:2); it
may also refer to the strength and power of God's people (see Ps 92:10; 1 Sa 2:1;
Jer 48:25; La 2:17).
   Ps 149 The spiritual elite of God's people rebuilt the walls of Jerusalem,
weapons at the ready (see Ne 4:11); they put up an unyielding resistance to the
persecution of Antiochus IV Epiphanes (see 1 Mac; 2 Mac). They were conscious
of defending the rights of God and the right to worship him. This was their glory:
Israel was the sword of God against the advance of blasphemous and wicked
forces (see Zec 9:13-16). But the images of war foretell victories, those of God's
elect over the forces of evil at the time of the Messiah. The seer of the Book of
Revelation will also describe great battles in heaven (see Rev 11:14).
   We can pray this psalm for the Church, the new People of God, enduring in this
world an ever-difficult existence, an ever-renascent war. She scores blows and
gains victories against her spiritual enemies, but never decisive ones. Happily, it
is Christ who leads her and animates her in battle in order to ensure victory for
her and renew her fervor (see Mt 16:18; 28:20).
   149:1-5 The psalmist calls on the people to sing a new song in view of the
restoration and the eschatological expectation of the Lord's complete victory over
evil (see Isa 61:2ff; Rev 14:3). The object of praise is the Maker and King of his
people, and the devout among them are the beneficiaries of his mighty acts.
   149:1 *New song:* see note on Ps 33:3. *Saints:* see notes on Ps 4:3 and 34:9.

² Let Israel rejoice in their Maker;
　　let the people of Zion be glad in their King.
³ Let them praise his name* with dancing
　　　　and make music to him with tambourine
　　　　and harp.ʸ
⁴ For the LORD takes delight in his people;
　　he crowns the humble with salvation.*
⁵ Let the saints rejoice in this honor
　　and sing for joy on their beds.*

⁶ May the praise of God be in their mouths*
　　and a double-edged sword in their hands,*ᶻ
⁷ to inflict vengeance* on the nations
　　and punishment on the peoples,ᵃ
⁸ to bind their kings with fetters,
　　their nobles with shackles of iron,
⁹ to carry out the sentence written against
　　　　them.*
　　This is the glory of all his saints.

Praise the LORD.

---

y Ps 68:25; 81:1-2; 87:7; 150:3-4; Ex 15:20.—z Ps 66:17; Ne 4:16-18; 2 Mac 15:27.—a Nu 31:3; Wis 3:8; Zec 9:13-16.

149:3 *Name:* see note on Ps 5:11. *Dancing:* which formed part of the liturgy (see Ps 87:7; 150:4; Ex 15:20; 2 Sa 6:14; Jer 31:4).
149:4 See Ps 73:1; 1 Sa 2:8; Isa 49:13; 61:9; 62:4f.
149:5 *Beds:* the beds, which had before been soaked with tears, share in the Lord's deliverance (see Ps 4:4; 6:6; 63:6; Hos 7:14).
149:6-9 The psalmist envisages the eschatological future (see Isa 61:2ff) and presents God's people as the instruments of the divine vindication (see Zec 9:13-16). The Lord will grant victory to his people, as he did to Nehemiah and his men (see Ne 4:9, 16-23), which will be their glory.
149:6 The godly will become the sword of the Lord (see Jud 3:16; Pr 5:4; Zec 9:13). Some interpret this verse as saying that the praise of God is a fearsome but peaceful weapon in the hands of the godly (see 2 Ch 20:17ff).
149:7 *Vengeance:* see note on Ps 5:10 and introduction to Ps 35. The new People of God depends on the "sword of the Spirit" to combat the powers of evil (see 2 Co 6:7; 10:4; Eph 6:12, 17; Heb 4:12) and will obtain complete victory only at the Last Judgment (see 1 Co 6:2f).
149:9 Allusion to the prophecies against the nations, announcing their final defeat by Israel (see Ps 139:16 and note; Eze 25:14; 39:10; Joel 3:7; Mic 4:13; Zec 10:5; 12:6; 14:3, 12ff).

PSALM 150*

Harmonious Praise of God

¹ Praise the LORD.ᵇ

Praise God in his sanctuary;*ᵇ*
   praise him in his mighty heavens.*
² Praise him for his acts of power;*ᶜ*
   praise him for his surpassing greatness.*
³ Praise him with the sounding of the trum-
      pet,*
   praise him with the harp and lyre,*ᵈ*

---

b Hebrew *Hallelu Yah*; also in verse 6.

b Ps 102:19; Da 3:53.—c Ex 15:7; Dt 3:24.—d 3ff: Ps 57:8; 81:2-3;
149:3; 2 Sa 6:5; 1 Ch 13:8; 16:5, 42; 2 Ch 5:12-13; 7:6.

Ps 150 In the same manner in which our "Glory to the Father" concludes the
recitation of our psalms, this doxological psalm concludes the Psalter on an urgent invitation to praise (see the conclusions to the first four books: Ps 41:13;
72:18f; 89:52; 106:48). May every living creature praise the Lord everywhere, on
the part of everyone, and by every means. The word "Hallelujah" or "Alleluia"
(translated as "Praise the LORD" or "Praise him") echoes thirteen times in this
psalm. The Psalter could not end on a richer or more powerful note. Everything
leads to the immensity of God's glory (see Rev 15:3-4; 19:4-8). "Then I heard every
creature in heaven and on earth and under the earth and on the sea, and all that
is in them, singing: 'To him who sits on the throne and to the Lamb be praise and
honor and glory and power, for ever and ever!'. . . Amen!" (Rev 5:13f).

We should heed this recommendation and carry it out, for we Christians are
more aware than the psalmist of the work of God and Christ in the world and in
us. Christ is enthroned in the highest heavens, his own sanctuary, but he is present and active in the heart of every creature, giving to each existence, motion,
and life, as the case may be. He is in the heart of the whole world, directing its
march in the material, living, human, and spiritual spheres and realizing his
greatest exploit in the last—the construction of the Church, his Body, his spiritual Spouse.

150:1 God is to be praised in his sanctuary on earth and his sanctuary in
heaven (see Ps 8:3). The Church of the New Covenant has the mission to glorify
God in the world, and her members must gather in the house of God in order to
carry out this mission. *Mighty heavens:* literally, "expanse [or firmament] of his
power," which ensures the well-being of those on earth.

150:2 God is to be praised because of his creating and redeeming "acts of
power" (see Ps 106:2; 145:4, 12), which reveal his greatness (see Ps 145:3;
147:5; 1 Ch 29:11).

150:3-5 God is to be praised with a full orchestra (with trumpet, harp, lyre,
and tambourine) and with dance in a liturgy of praise that will reach as high as
the heavens.

⁴ praise him with tambourine and dancing,
  praise him with the strings and flute,*e*
⁵ praise him with the clash of cymbals,
  praise him with resounding cymbals.

⁶ Let everything that has breath praise the
  LORD.*f*

  Praise the LORD.*

---

e Ps 68:25; Ex 15:20. —f Ps 103:22; Rev 5:13.

150:6 God is to be praised by everyone and everything endowed with life by the Creator (see Ps 103:22; 148:7-12; Rev 5:13). By doing so, Christians will be following the "way" of the Lord, with which the Psalter began (see Ps 1:2), a way that leads to eternal life.

APPENDIX

INDEX OF SUNDAY RESPONSORIAL PSALMS

Year A

Year B

Major Feasts of the Year

TABLE OF PSALMS IN FOUR-WEEK PSALTER
FOR MORNING AND EVENING PRAYER